Granville's New Key
to Stock Market
PROFITS

It is not the critic who counts, not the man who points out how the strong man stumbled or where the doer of deeds could have done them better. The credit belongs to the man who is actually in the arena; whose face is marred by dust and sweat and blood; who strives valiantly; who errs and comes up short again and again; who knows the great enthusiasms, the great devotions, and spends himself in a worthy cause; who at the best knows in the end the triumph of high achievement; and who at the worst, if he fails, at least fails while daring greatly; so that his place shall never be with those cold and timid souls who know neither defeat nor victory.

THEODORE ROOSEVELT

Granville's New Key
to Stock Market
PROFITS

Joseph E. Granville

PRENTICE-HALL, INC., ENGLEWOOD CLIFFS, N.J.

PRINTED IN THE UNITED STATES OF AMERICA
36340-B&P

To my wife, Polly, and our six
children who suffered in silence,
patiently awaiting the
end of the final revision.

Fabian Bachrach

JOSEPH E. GRANVILLE is well-known on Wall Street as the writer of a daily market letter for one of the largest and best-known brokerage firms. More recently, he has set up an investment advisory service which publishes the *Granville Market Letter*.

A graduate of Duke and Columbia Universities, Mr. Granville is the author of seven books, his most recent being Prentice-Hall's *A Strategy of Daily Stock Market Timing for Maximum Profits*.

Preface

In this work, my second on the stock market, the purpose is to go on from where *A Strategy of Daily Stock Market Timing For Maximum Profit* left off. *Strategy*, while being rather comprehensive in bending the reader toward the technical viewpoint, did brush over several areas which deserved a much fuller treatment.

The greatest portion of this new book will be devoted to the use of stock *volume* figures to illustrate the use of what this writer considers to be a rather revealing technical tool. No book exists at this writing devoted to a study of stock trading volume. This book is an attempt at filling a conspicuous void.

No discussion of the market is dry or uninteresting if it suggests possible improved methods toward realizing higher stock market profits and it is felt that, while some charts and tables are unavoidable, the reader will be able to grasp a simple and new concept and perhaps be able to translate it into higher profits. Sometimes the simplest things are the most profound and there is perhaps to be found here a key to improved performance which deserves a full and detailed discussion. The key is *volume*, but it is measured in a certain way. The book goes into all this in great detail and, the writer hopes, with great clarity. The reader should have no great difficulty in the practical application of the new principles expounded here.

But this is not enough. Life is too short to accept the prosaic, the safe and tested theories and methods which now exist as being an end to further investigations. A new trail is being blazed in technical analysis which may have profound effects on the future methods of correctly gauging the market. It is not enough to merely understand and use the things introduced in the *Strategy* book (Barron's Confidence Index, 200-day moving average price lines, disparity etc.) and say that anything near the ultimate has been approached. This, while certainly a major step in the right direction, merely whetted the appetite of the author to go deeper into new researches aimed at perhaps revealing further truths about the market. One of the more fascinating lines of inquiry was that devoted to new concepts relating to volume. There was a crying need to fill in some of the conspicuous voids within the famous Dow Theory, voids consisting of a lack of detailed discussion and use of stock volume figures. This book is an attempt to go beyond this and in the process find a discussion of the laws of nature, principles of physics and technical principles relating to music useful in shaping the newer concepts.

To some it may appear that technical analysis is a short cut to gauging future stock prices and is not very reliable. However, there has seldom been an important advance or decline in the stock market to which the technical indicators were completely blind. Here then is something tangible to work with and be developed.

Like the study of natural law, physics, mathematics, music, it will be found that technical market analysis knows no language barriers. It is a universal language. It speaks in terms of charts and numbers, pictures and numbers understood the world over without the necessity of translation. Perhaps this is why the *Strategy* book (discussing only the American stock market in the English language) quickly stirred up interest in more than a score of foreign countries without the need for translation. The answer is rather simple. The world is growing smaller every day and what affects one area in the world of finance more quickly reverberates on another area. Dollar stocks are being traded on foreign stock exchanges and there is an increasing trend toward the listing of more foreign securities on domestic exchanges. When one is less likely to be well informed on fundamental developments affecting these foreign based companies then technical analysis has an increasing role to play in helping to make up for this lack of information. Many other exchanges are far less efficient than the well-developed and advanced domestic exchanges but these foreign stock exchanges are quickly adopting the ways of the big domestic exchanges. The moving tape, the open, high, low and closing price, the daily volume for each stock and the far more complete financial section is eventually going to be quite common throughout the free world. In the wake of these fast moving developments is an increasing interest in technical analysis.

Success in the correct interpretation of technical market indicators is up to the individual. I looked upon the writing of these market books as I would look upon the writing of a piece of music. Everything is there in black and white and is capable of being read by anybody who will take the time to put the music on the piano rack and sit down and practice. The difference as to whether the pianist remains a hack or becomes a virtuoso is up to the individual, not up to the composer. Some composers are poor pianists or just average, not virtuosos. Tchaikovsky was a great composer but Anton Rubinstein played the initial performances of his great piano concerto and thus it is that some market technicians will lose money for their clients. This reflects not on the tools (not on the music) but on the interpretation of them. In the hands of a trained technician, one who knows what to look for and knows how to weigh one factor against another, the market may never contain too many surprises.

Successful stock trading largely depends upon *reversing* human nature. In order to best do this it is necessary to become *unemotional* about stocks. The language of the market is unemotional. Strictly listening to what the market is saying rather than to what others are saying should create a shield against the injection of emotional factors which only tend to mislead and confuse.

One can never be right all the time but this is the *human error,* seldom the error of the indicators when treated collectively. To put it another way, only the interpreter can err. Who can find fault with the music of Bach, Beethoven or Chopin? Not a day goes by, however, but that some pianist is being criticized for his *interpretation* of Bach, Beethoven or Chopin. If one always knew what was in his partner's hand then how dull the game of bridge would become. In fact, that would be the end of the game. In bridge one partner signals to the other and in the stock market the market signals to the buyers and sellers (technical indicators), but, like bridge signals, these can be misinterpreted and this is why we need to constantly study and look for new things to aid in arriving at correct interpretations.

Being human, it goes against the grain to reverse human nature but this is what we must try to do when it comes to stocks if better results are desired. American Motors back in 1958 and 1959 is a good example of the errors of human nature as opposed to the technical language of the stock.

The maximum technical attraction of American Motors common stock occurred when the stock was selling for $5 a share. Obviously the news at that time was poor. How else could it be? If the news was good the stock would not have been selling at $5 a share. The company had problems, plenty of them. Disbelief was at a maximum. Extremely few people expected that American Motors stock was headed sharply higher. While the news was the worst the stock was technically attractive.

What happened at the top? The exact opposite occurred as to what happened at the bottom. On November 4, 1959 the stock reached a closing peak of 95¼. It then reacted to 82¾ that same month, returned once more to the low 90's and then after November 25th proceeded to decline sharply, never to see the November 1959 high price again.

How was the news for American Motors during that momentous month of November 1959? Here are a few comments taken directly from the *Wall Street Journal* (italics are the author's):

November 3, 1959

"The two smaller auto makers, Studebaker-Packard and American Motors, again led trading activity and ran up smart gains. Studebaker-Packard gained 3 points and American shot up 8¼ to close at 88¼, a new high. Their steel inventories reportedly are in better shape than those of the big three of the auto industry."

November 5, 1959

"The smaller auto makers continued to attract attention. American Motors, Studebaker-Packard and Studebaker-Packard when issued all had *delayed openings* because of heavy buy orders. During the day American touched 96⅞ and closed at 95¼, up 7 points. It was the second most active stock. *American announced plans to increase auto body production 35%.*"

November 6, 1959

"After the close, the Stock Exchange ordered *cancellation of all "stop" orders in American Motors,* effective today, "in view of the conditions which exist in the market for the stock."

November 20, 1959

"American Motors predicted third place for the Rambler in 1959 car sales, but the stock lost 2⅞ as the fourth most active stock."

December 2, 1959

"The small motors were the day's most popular stocks. American, which *announced a three-for-one split, an extra, and an increased dividend* after Monday's close, opened up 5½ points and then fell back to close with a loss of 2. It was the most active issue on 152,900 shares."

In many ways the stock was suggesting it be sold. At the top here were the sell signals:

  (a) The news was never better.
  (b) Volume and price action was climactic.
  (c) Delayed openings because buy orders were so heavy.
  (d) "Stop" orders cancelled.
  (e) Stock began to turn a deaf ear on bullish news.

These sell signals tend to go against the grain of human nature. It is the cold, unemotional technical indicators talking to the emotional holder of the stock. Once one owns a stock it is more difficult to turn bearish on it than if it wasn't owned. Ownership creates bullish bias. That is human nature. Maximum market success demands that one turn inhuman when it comes to stocks, coldly unemotional. This takes practice and patience but, once sharpened on the grindstone of experience, the trader is capable of eventually blocking out that bothersome bias and when that is done the message of the market is more likely to come through louder and clearer.

The very fact that there is a far better dissemination of fundamental data concerning companies today *demands that investors and traders increase their knowledge of the technical side of the market.* The market usually *anticipates* and if everyone has a simultaneous knowledge of earnings, dividends, management changes, awarded contracts etc., then the future stock price may be more easily ascertainable by *technical* methods rather than by fundamentals alone.

These are fast moving times and to keep up with them one must necessarily at times dare to be different. Old methods of analysis oftentimes leave much to be desired in new markets. Experimentation is necessary at times to get at new truths. (e.g.—While lecturing at the New School of Social Research in New York on October 26, 1961, I wanted to demonstrate my theory that Bach was not only a great composer, but also a born stock market technician. To get the point across effectively it was necessary for me to break out singing *Jesu, Joy of Man's Desiring.* This was the first [and probably the last] vocal rendition at the New School but it managed to get across a point of technical analysis in a more vivid manner.)

There is still so much to be learned about the stock market that this writer has no qualms about revealing what some people might consider to be valuable information best left for only the few to know and use. There is no danger that the revelation of new techniques will so enlighten the masses to render them useless. The application of such things requires time and work, and human nature is such that most people will neither have the time, patience or desire to do the work necessary to achieve the results which might be had when these things are done. There is no easy road to stock market success. Here in the United States there are millions of pianos and each one is basically the same in that they all have 88 notes. Yet, how many piano virtuosos are there in the United States? It is the same with the stock market. The printed music can be distributed to everyone but many cannot play it at all, a large number can just manage to play it, another group plays well and a much smaller group is downright brilliant. So, there are no qualms about distributing the "music." It is up to the reader and his patience, desire to work and ability to interpret as to whether he plays at all, plays well, or plays like a virtuoso. Such analogy is worth considering when studying the market.

The reader, after being taken through some basic concepts and known avenues of technical theory, will be gradually shown the way into the lesser known avenues and introduced to the writer's newest methods and findings, not taking away from the concepts covered in the *Strategy* book, but going on from where they left off.

The heart of the book is *on-balance volume*. Like all technical market indicators, it must be interpreted. It is not perfect, no indicator being such. It is presented as an avenue opening up potential new areas of technical research.

Acknowledgements are in order for William Jiler of Commodity Research Publications, M. C. Horsey & Company and Frank Peluso for the preparation and use of various charts. A particular degree of thanks is extended to Joseph A. Sherwood for his close cooperation and advice throughout the preparation of this book.

JOSEPH E. GRANVILLE

New York, 1963

Publisher's Note

The nub of modern technical stock market analysis is in this new study by Joseph E. Granville. Here is the new technique of selection laid down by the man who was the first to systematize the technical indicators, a technique Granville calls "equity physics." Physics is the science of energy and in this book the author demonstrates how stock energies are measured in terms of his new volume technique. His concept reveals that stock price fluctuations tend to adhere to the laws of harmony, laws of the universe rather than a patternless jumble of hit or miss chances. We earnestly feel that this book, together with *A Strategy of Daily Stock Market Timing for Maximum Profits,* lays down the newest concept of the stock market since the Dow Theory was formulated over 60 years ago.

The Publisher

Contents

American Motors (Continued)

tive Total Volume Expressed as a Percentage of Capitalization · Initial Phase Shows Accumulation with Little or No Price Movement · The Base Line · Let's Apply these New Technical Tools to American Motors · Accumulation Must Be Smooth and Persistent · Second Phase Shows Sharp Velocity Gains · Characteristic of Smoothness Continues throughout Second Phase · Stock Now Ready for Third Phase Shakeout · Four Column Analysis Indicates Short-Term Sell Signal · End of Shakeout in American Motors Suggested by Gap Theory · End of American Motors Shakeout Also Suggested By Excessive Pessimism · New Concept of Overhead Supply Suggests End of Shakeout · Stock now Ready for Fourth Phase Leading to Price Maturity · The Well Defined Characteristics of the Top · The "Spring" Principle · Velocity Precedes Price · The Second Key Measurement of Price Maturity · Series of Price Gaps Most Reliable Indication of the Top · Tension —The "Snapback" Principle · The Summing up

What You Are about to Learn · A Possible New Path To Improved Profit Possibilities · Selection of Most Promising Chart Patterns (Step 1) · What You Can Do Now · Recording Of On-Balance Volume On The Stocks Selected (Step 2) · What You Can Do Now · Daily Surveillance Of The Most Active Stocks (Step 3) · What You Can Do Now · Purchase (Step 4) · What You Can Do Now · Concentration (Step 5) · What You Can Do Now · Patience (Step 6) · What You Can Do Now · Sell (Step 7) · What You Can Do Now · The Summing up

Granville's New Key

to Stock Market

PROFITS

Chapter One

A Review of Basic Concepts

How the technical precedes the fundamental in indicating price moves.

What You Are about to Learn

Your views about the stock market are expected to become somewhat reoriented after reading the following pages. This book leaves fundamental research, previous technical consideration, field research and other market approaches to other writers and books, this volume taking up from there and covering an exploration of the new possibilities in volume study techniques. This, by definition, is an extension of the technical approach. This approach has in the past rather faithfully acted as a sort of EARLY WARNING SYSTEM of impending stock price changes. It is not perfect and never will be. This writer feels that a detailed discussion of the volume factor should impressively add to the already existing store of technical market knowledge and help increase the reader's profit-making potential.

You will learn that sometimes disparities exist where earnings and dividends have not been a certain guide to what a stock may do (especially over short-term periods). Technical analysis has been an especially useful approach during such times. You will be shown that technical developments often precede fundamental changes but more importantly, it will be revealed to you that volume often has a distinct tendency to precede price. Most technical market theories, practices or systems are in some way linked to stock *prices* and the volume approach discussed in this book is presented as a departure, perhaps serving as a more efficient technical early warning system than an approach based purely on the analysis of price action. The volume technique is particularly helpful in recognizing accumulation before price advances and distribution before price declines, an area of study in which pure price analysis has lagged. In order to become fully conditioned to the volume techniques which will be covered throughout the book, you will first be introduced to some basic matter covering the movement of stock prices. Once you have mastered this section on prices, then you will be better prepared to move on to the early warning features based on volume, those features covered in later chapters.

Technical Precedes Fundamental

Perhaps the most important thing to get across in the introduction to the technical side of the market is the fact that we are dealing with the *language of the market itself.* Now, if you want to discuss business trends, what the economy is doing and what it may do, the outlook for corporate earnings, that is all well and good. You may be able to forecast the business trend accurately; you may know exactly what the economy is doing and what it may do; you may end up making an excellent estimate of future earnings for a particular company. *You may do all these things and more and yet not be any closer to finding out what the stock market may do.*

Technical analysis is particularly helpful at such times, such analysis strongly aiding in the detection of buying and selling pressures before there is a widely seen fundamental reason for buying or selling. Since the technical signs lead the fundamental factors, it follows that there must be some technical factors which have better leading tendencies than others and their use could provide competitive advantages to market technicians employing them in addition to already existing tools.

It is important to hear everything the market has to say because that message as it pertains to market traders has more to do with the short-term course of stock prices than anything else at the time. Anything in whole or in part which the market has to say is largely spoken in technical terms, the language of the market. These are things to do with volume, price, short interest, etc. Fundamental things such as earnings, dividends, corporate developments, management changes—all have their place but the basic concept here to be grasped first if you are truly interested in more profitable market trading is that *the technical precedes the fundamental.* To put it another way, fundamental changes only *confirm* what was first detected technically, what was first *told* to you by the market itself. This then is the basic concept—*the technical precedes the fundamental.*

Why Is this so?

Since market traders are primarily concerned with market timing, timing being essential for trading success, profits are determined by answering the WHENS rather than the WHYS. The technical approach attempts to answer the whens while the fundamental approach answers the whys. Nine times out of ten when you know why a stock is weak the peak price has been well passed and when you know why a stock is strong the low point has been well passed.

The correct interpretation of the market itself should enable you to sell closer to the peaks and buy closer to the valleys. Putting first things first, the primary preoccupation of the market technician is with *technical* things, and his buying and selling decisions are not closely linked with what a stock earns or is expected to earn. He is more interested in the whens rather than the whys. The technician feels that if he put too much stress on the whys then he would be less likely to be selling near peaks and buying near valleys inasmuch as so many stocks tend to peak out when the news is highly optimistic and bottom out when the news is highly pessimistic. In order to put more stress on the whens it would be helpful to revise the viewpoint concerning earnings and news developments.

Some Misconceptions about Earnings and News Developments

If you hold to the belief that there is necessarily a good correlation between stock prices and earnings then you are in for a shock. An examination of hundreds of stocks reveals that there is sometimes a confusing lack of correlation between what a stock does and the earnings per share. If what a stock earned was always a valid indication of where the stock price was headed then (by definition) the ratio of price to earnings would be a rather steady figure. On the contrary, price/earnings ratios are known to fluctuate quite widely and it is that very fluctuation which dilutes the widely held belief that good earnings are a necessary accompaniment to advancing stock prices. The validity is enhanced generally over longer term periods but often greatly distorted over the short run periods.

Now, as you can see in the following table, the stock showed a tendency to move rather independently, trending higher regardless of the erratic ups and downs in annual earnings. The table shows that a rise in earnings is a fundamental improvement and that a drop in earnings is noted as a downward fundamental change. Notice how the price of the stock reacted to these earnings changes. In the year 1945 the dividend was halved, earnings were slightly lower and the average annual price of the stock advanced from $52 to $62 a share. The next year (1946) saw earnings per share rise sharply from $1.62 to $9.19 and the dividend was doubled and yet the average annual price of the stock remained at $62. In 1947 the dividend payment was raised by 150%, earnings declined and the average price of the stock advanced to $68 a share. In 1948 record earnings of $12.59 per share were achieved and the dividend was more than doubled. This was one of the few times that the stock responded in tune with the fundamental improvement. The next year (1949) earnings declined sharply and the dividend payment also declined. This had no effect on the price of the stock. It rose to an average annual price of $91 a share. In 1950 the dividend payment and earnings fell again and the average price of the stock rallied to $103 a share. The rest of the table is self-explanatory.

CANNON MILLS

Year	Dividend	Earnings	P/E Ratio	Average Price	Fundamental Change
1944	$1.00	$1.65	31.5	$52	————
1945	.50	1.62	38.2	62	Down
1946	1.00	9.19	6.7	62	Up
1947	2.50	7.28	9.3	68	Down
1948	5.25	12.59	6.8	86	Up
1949	3.75	4.30	21.1	91	Down
1950	3.00	3.48	29.5	103	Down
1951	3.00	6.32	17.4	110	Up
1952	3.00	3.70	27.5	102	Down
1953	2.25	4.95	19.5	97	Up
1954	3.00	4.39	23.9	105	Down
1955	3.00	4.86	22.8	111	Up
1956	3.00	5.16	20.5	106	Up
1957	3.00	6.30	15.2	96	Up
1958	3.00	5.31	20.9	111	Down
1959	3.00	5.04	25.0	126	Down
1960	3.00	6.49	17.8	116	Up

In the above table it can be seen that there was often little correlation between earnings and the price of the stock. A dependable connection between earnings and the stock price would have been reflected by a price/earnings ratio showing little fluctuation. In this example the p/e ratio fluctuated wildly with no discernible relationship to any explainable pattern. Annual fundamental earnings changes were at complete odds with the price changes in twelve of the sixteen years shown.

It is often easy to misjudge a stock from a trading standpoint if one puts total stress on earnings and news developments. In the following cases a fundamental cause existed but the surface developments might have been misleading at the time when it came right down to making the correct trading decision.

Question: In 1955 earnings per share for New York Central climbed to $8.03, the highest in twelve years. In anticipation of this the price of the stock rose to 50, the highest level seen since 1937. Was the stock a buy or a sell?

Answer: The stock in retrospect was a sale. Over the next two years the stock declined from 50 to 13, a 74% decline.

Question: In early 1958 the United States was going through a recession. New

York Central was selling at 13, the lowest level in eight years. Earnings per share had fallen from the 1955 peak of $8.03 to $1.30 in 1957 and they were going to be down to only 62¢ a share in 1958. The $2 dividend of 1955 was cut to $1 in 1957 and was going to be omitted altogether in 1958. Was the stock a buy or a sale?

Answer: A buy. From that point the stock rose to 33 by late 1959, a percentage gain of over 150% from the trough of bad news.

Question: In late 1957 Underwood stock was selling for $12 a share. There was a deficit that year of $2.13 per share. Over the next three years there were deficits per share of $9.35, $9.34 and $10.29. Was the stock a buy or a sale in 1957?

Answer: A buy. Throughout those three years of tremendous deficits the stock rose from 12 to 57, a percentage gain of 375%. There was a fundamental cause for this rise which came to the surface later but the earnings figures alone kept many traders out of the stock while it was making that sharp price advance.

Question: U.S. Steel was selling at 103 in early January 1960. Earnings were expected to be the best since 1957. The steel strike had just been settled. Was the stock a buy or a sale?

Answer: A sale. Beginning with the good news of strike settlement, the longest steel strike on record (116 days), the stock declined from 103 to just under 70 that year, a decline of 33%.

Question: In August 1960 the price of Lockheed common stock was down to 21. If you had known then that the company was going to lose $42 million and show a deficit of $5.82 per share would you have bought the stock?

Answer: The stock more than doubled in the next ten months, the buying opportunity occurring in the trough of bad news.

Question: Boeing Airplane was selling at 23 in early 1960. There was bad news. The company was being pressed by the government on a $20 million tax judgement. Was the stock a buy or a sell?

Answer: A buy. It doubled over the next ten months.

Question: Capitol Airlines in 1960 declared bankruptcy. The stock was selling under $6 a share. Was it a buy or a sell?

Answer: A buy. It more than doubled over the next four months.

This type of quiz could go on and on. The fundamental causes behind each of the examples just given generally came to the surface later but the *technical* reasons for buying or selling were in strong evidence at the time when most people would not have taken action at those price levels. By adding the technical approach to your existing knowledge of the market what sometimes looks illogical suddenly becomes logical.

So then, Let's Look at the Technical Side

Technical does not mean difficult. It is only a term which refers to the language of the market. So there is no reason why much of what the market says cannot be presented in terms of apples and oranges.

The Dow Theory—Three Pitfalls

The Dow Theory is over 60 years old and it is time that something more effective and specific be applied to bring about better market timing. The new technical methods described in this book are expected to help overcome the three great deficiencies of the Dow Theory: (1) it is based on *price*, (2) the signals are late by definition and (3) it is not applicable to individual stocks.

Let us look at each of these deficiencies separately.

The theory is based on price. New research conducted by the writer convincingly suggests that, contrary to the widest beliefs, price movements in the stock market as indicators of future price movements are not nearly as important as are volume movements considered as indicators of future price movements. In other words, *volume has a strong tendency to precede price.* It is only natural that price would seem to be more important than volume since this is what we pay for a stock when we buy and receive for a stock when we sell. It is what most people look at. However, when it comes to determining future price changes it will be shown that volume presents revealing indications superior to oftentimes confusing price action.

Dow Theory follows the movements of the Dow-Jones Industrial Average and the Dow-Jones Rail Average through three types of market swings—the primary, secondary and day-to-day price movements. The primary swing is the basic trend of market prices and is capable of persisting for many months and even many years before changing direction. The secondary, or intermediate price movement is a deviation of market direction within a primary trend and is capable of lasting for several months. Dow theorists put most of the stress on these first two types of price movement and tend to pass quickly over the day-to-day movement as rather inconsequential.

It is not the purpose of this book to go into all the ramifications of Dow Theory other than to say that it is likened unto a study of the tides. When the tide is coming in the Dow-Jones Industrial and Rail averages both rise above previous high points and when the tide is going out these averages fall beneath previous low points. A price movement in one average through a previous high unconfirmed by a movement in the other average through a previous high does not provide a reliable signal for higher

prices. Conversely, unconfirmed downside penetrations are equally unreliable as signals for lower prices to come.

The Dow Theory is good as far as it goes but falls far short of modern day technical
methods for trying to pick the right stock at the right time. Since the Dow Theory
continuously follows the movements of two stock price averages it is therefore a
theory based on *price*. When it comes to price and volume it will be found that *price
is often the lagging indicator* and this is only one reason why legitimate Dow Theory
signals for a higher market to come occur long after a bottom has been reached and
legitimate signals for a lower market to come occur long after a top has been reached.

Stock prices fluctuate because of supply and demand. Here is cause and effect.
The supply and demand make up the cause and the stock price is the effect. Since
Dow Theory is based on price this writer contends that it is based on effect rather
than on cause. Doesn't it make far more sense to put greater stress on the cause? The
best technical analysis must therefore look to supply and demand and this is where
the study of volume comes in. Supply and demand are seen to be the *energies* which
move stock prices and the ENERGY OF A STOCK OR OF THE STOCK MARKET
AS A WHOLE IS SEEN TO BE BEST MEASURED IN TERMS OF STOCK
TRADING VOLUME. The Dow Theory has very little to say about volume and is
quite vague on the subject. This book is an attempt at filling that conspicuous gap.
Dow theory signals are late by definition. This is the second deficiency of Dow
Theory. Inasmuch as the theory states that two price averages must fall below a
previous important low in order to receive a sell signal, then it is obvious that one
will not be selling stocks at or near their highs according to this theory alone. Conversely, if two price averages must move above some previous important high point
in order for the theory to provide a buy signal, then it is obvious that one will not be
buying stocks at or near their lows according to this theory alone. Bearish signals
(indications of stock price declines to come) must be forthcoming while the Dow-
Jones Industrial Average is still rising and bullish signals (indications of stock price
advances to come) must be forthcoming while the Dow-Jones Industrial Average
is still falling. The Dow Theory taken alone is deficient in this respect.

In my previous market book, *A Strategy of Daily Stock Market Timing For Maximum Profit*, I discussed many of these technical indicators which have a strong tendency to precede movement in the averages. The *volume indicator* is based on new
research since the writing of that book and is thus receiving a detailed and separate
treatment.

The Dow Theory is not applicable to individual stocks. This is the third deficiency
of Dow Theory. That theory talks in terms of primary, intermediate and daily movements for the market as a whole. But we can only buy and sell specific stocks, and
without the specific buy and sell signals for individual issues we would be pretty
much groping in the dark. We must have specific indicators for applying to individual

stock issues and this writer will attempt to demonstrate that the correct measurement and interpretation of volume is one of them. This is not an attempt to completely dilute the value of Dow Theory but to constructively add to it with new theory more specifically applicable to maximizing trading profits in modern day stock markets.

Tides

The rhythmical inflow and outflow of the tidal movement of stock prices is well expressed in Dow's stock market theory and this does provide the *germ* upon which other market theories can be built. Dow's key observation over sixty years ago was actually an old law of physics: *a body in motion tends to remain in motion.* To put it another way, new highs beget new highs and new lows beget new lows. Here we see the importance of the penetration or breakout to new price highs and the subsequent advance which follows, and the penetration or breakout to new price lows and the subsequent decline which follows.

The Stock Price Chart—a Quick Review

The commonest and (up until now) the most essential device used by stock market technicians is the stock price chart. This is a running pictorial commentary on the price history of the stock. Every advance and decline is seen in this day-to-day diary of price change. Before you can graduate to the more important volume concepts to be presented later, it is first necessary to grasp the simple rudiments of price mechanics. After all, price is what most people are concerned with. It is what they pay for a stock when buying and what they receive when selling. Let us therefore see what there is in a price chart which prompts buying and selling by astute stock traders. Once you have mastered the art of interpreting a stock price chart you will then be introduced to the volume factors which preceded the price changes. So let us first look at what most stock market technicians observe daily.

The Breakout

This is the most important single technical phenomenon in the entire gamut of technical market literature. The price breakout is just what the term implies, a breaking away from a previously held pattern of price movement. The breakout is especially interesting to market traders because once it takes place the price of the stock generally continues to move in the direction of the breakout. An upside price breakout means that the price of a stock has moved above some previous range of price movement which it has not until then been able to better. Conversely, a downside breakout means that the price of a stock has moved below some previous range of price movement it has until then been fluctuating within.

The bullish and bearish implications of price breakouts vary according to whether the breakout is seen to be major, intermediate or minor.

As the Chinese say, a picture is worth ten thousand words, so let us examine some stock price charts so we can see what is being said.

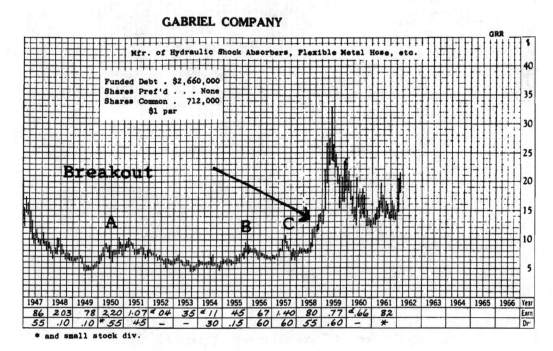

Chart 1

In Chart 1 we see the price of Gabriel stock move above points A, B and C in the summer of 1958. The bettering of these levels for the first time in many years comprised a very important upside breakout and a very profitable buying opportunity. The more previous tops the stock price moves through the more bullish the upside breakout becomes. Points A, B and C were all earlier promises of being important buy points which failed.

In Chart 2 several buy and sell points are indicated merely according to upside and downside breakouts, these breakouts best reflecting the physical principle of a body in motion remaining in motion. At point A the stock broke through the previous 1946 reaction low and fell rapidly until late in the year when it was able to partially rally back a bit. The rally was temporary and the stock fell back toward the 1946 low. At point B the 1946 low was penetrated on the downside, the second downside breakout. This created the first 1947 low which was followed by a very shortlived rise.

NATIONAL CASTINGS COMPANY

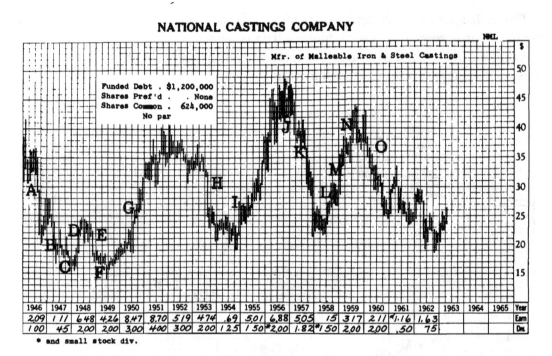

Chart 2

Following that rise the stock declined once again and made a third downside break-out by falling beneath the first 1947 low. This was at point C.

At point D the stock price scored a minor upside breakout by rising above the little price shelf traced out in the early months of 1948. This did not last long because late that year the price moved under the 1948 summer reaction lows at point E. This downside breakout produced some lower prices going into 1949. A little sideways movement in the first five months of 1949 was followed by another downside break-out in June 1949 at point F, the point of downside exhaustion. This was the fifth downside breakout recorded in four years. Note that the *first* downside breakout in 1946 (from a selling or shortselling standpoint) was the most important one, each succeeding one losing some downside momentum.

Once the stock has exhausted itself on the downside (shown by the five downside breakouts) the upside breakouts take on more significance. The first upside breakout at point D gave rise to only a temporary advance (preceded by three downside breakouts) while the upside breakout at point G was of major import. Here the upside breakout was preceded by five downside breakouts. It was a major confirmation of the developing bullish pattern (moving above the 1948 highs), and it was a tracing out of the bullish W-formation. The forming of the letter W in stock price charts usually develops into a good rise as long as the "right leg" of the letter betters the top level of the "middle leg".

When the advance following the upside breakout at point G exhausted itself and ran into a declining trend in 1952 and 1953, the major downside breakout from this upper trading range occurred at point H in the summer of 1953. This declining trend was not reversed until a move above the 1954 Spring recovery high occurred late that year at point I. Point I commenced an upswing which was constantly reinforced by upside breakouts all along the rising line. When the series of upside breakouts exhausted their effectiveness in 1956 the next important breakout was on the downside at point J. Being the *first* downside breakout on that swing, it turned out to be the most profitable from a shortselling viewpoint, again confirmed by a second downside breakout at point K. Point L repeated the series of upside breakouts similar to what started at point I. That swing topped out after point N was passed and the downside pattern again commenced at point O.

The Flatbase Breakout

The flatbase breakout when fully capitalized upon by astute stock traders constitutes one of the most profitable of all moves in the market. This pattern was described in the *Strategy* book with some examples. The profitability stems from the fact that the more extended the price base is, the sharper and more sustained is the price movement following an upside or downside breakout from that sideways price movement. Once noted, the pattern is never forgotten. Here are a few examples:

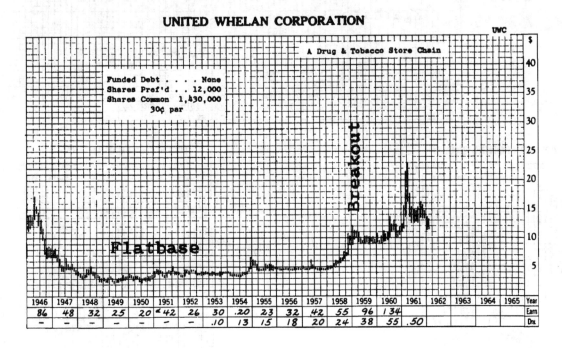

UNITED WHELAN CORPORATION

1946	1947	1948	1949	1950	1951	1952	1953	1954	1955	1956	1957	1958	1959	1960	1961	1962	1963	1964	1965	Year
86	48	32	25	20	42	26	30	.20	23	32	42	55	96	134						Earn
–	–	–	–	–	–	–	.10	13	15	18	20	24	38	55	.50					Div.

Chart 3

INTERNATIONAL BUSINESS MACHINES

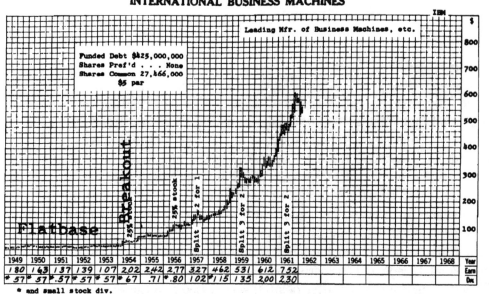

Leading Mfr. of Business Machines, etc.

Funded Debt $425,000,000
Shares Pref'd . . . None
Shares Common 27,466,000
$5 par

Flatbase   Breakout   25% stock   2 for 1 Split   Split 3 for 2   Split 3 for 2

Chart 4

Year	1949	1950	1951	1952	1953	1954	1955	1956	1957	1958	1959	1960	1961	1962	1963	1964	1965	1966	1967	1968
Earn	1.80	1.43	1.37	1.39	1.07	2.02	2.42	2.77	3.27	4.62	5.31	6.12	7.52							
Div.	*.57	*.57	*.57	*.57	*.57	*.67	.71	*.80	1.02	*1.15	1.35	2.00	2.30							

* and small stock div.

SHAHMOON INDUSTRIES, INC.

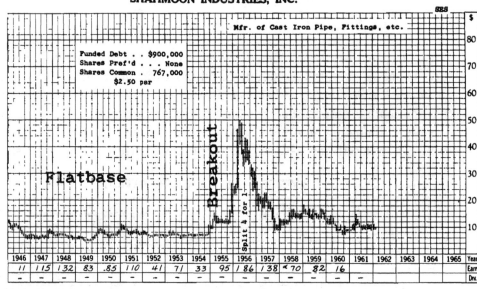

Mfr. of Cast Iron Pipe, Fittings, etc.

Funded Debt . . $900,000
Shares Pref'd . . . None
Shares Common . 767,000
$2.50 par

Chart 5

Flatbase   Breakout   Split 4 for 1

Year	1946	1947	1948	1949	1950	1951	1952	1953	1954	1955	1956	1957	1958	1959	1960	1961	1962	1963	1964	1965
Earn	.11	1.15	1.32	.83	.85	1.10	.41	.71	.33	.95	1.86	1.38	*.70	.82	.16					
Div.	–	–	–	–	–	–	–	–	–	–	–	–	–	–	–					

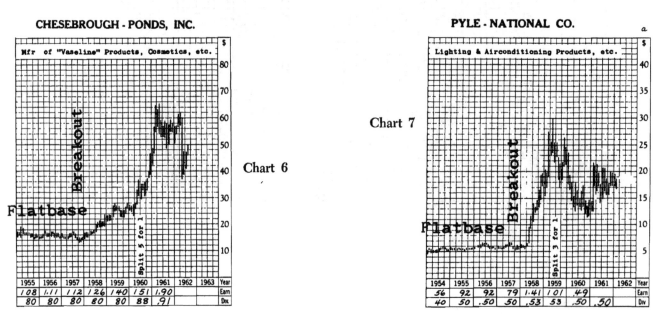

CHESEBROUGH - PONDS, INC.

Mfr of "Vaseline" Products, Cosmetics, etc.

Flatbase   Breakout   Split 5 for 1

Chart 6

Year	1955	1956	1957	1958	1959	1960	1961	1962	1963
Earn	1.08	1.11	1.12	1.26	1.40	1.51	1.90		
Div.	.80	.80	.80	.80	.80	.88	.91		

PYLE - NATIONAL CO.

Lighting & Airconditioning Products, etc.

Chart 7

Flatbase   Breakout   Split 3 for 1

Year	1954	1955	1956	1957	1958	1959	1960	1961	1962
Earn	.56	.92	.92	.79	1.41	1.01	.49		
Div.	.40	.50	.50	.50	.53	.53	.50	.50	

UNITED STATES PIPE & FOUNDRY CO.

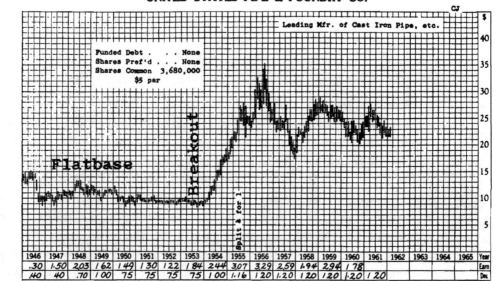

Leading Mfr. of Cast Iron Pipe, etc.

Funded Debt . . . . None
Shares Pref'd . . . None
Shares Common 3,680,000
$5 par

Flatbase

Breakout

Split ½ for 1

Chart 8

Year	1946	1947	1948	1949	1950	1951	1952	1953	1954	1955	1956	1957	1958	1959	1960	1961	1962	1963	1964	1965
Earn	.30	1.50	2.03	1.62	1.49	1.30	1.22	1.84	2.44	3.07	3.29	2.59	1.94	2.94	1.78					
Div.	.40	.40	.70	1.00	.75	.75	.75	.75	1.00	1.16	1.20	1.20	1.20	1.20	1.20	1.20				

NAFI CORPORATION

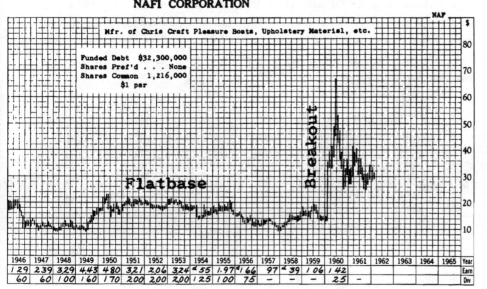

Mfr. of Chris Craft Pleasure Boats, Upholstery Material, etc.

Funded Debt $32,300,000
Shares Pref'd . . . None
Shares Common 1,216,000
$1 par

Flatbase

Breakout

Chart 9

Year	1946	1947	1948	1949	1950	1951	1952	1953	1954	1955	1956	1957	1958	1959	1960	1961	1962	1963	1964	1965
Earn	1.29	2.39	3.29	4.43	4.80	3.21	2.06	3.24	ᵈ.55	1.97	ᵈ.66	.97	ᵈ.39	1.06	1.42					
Div	.60	.60	1.00	1.60	1.70	2.00	2.00	2.00	1.25	1.00	.75	–	–	–	.25	–				

AMERICAN MOTORS CORPORATION

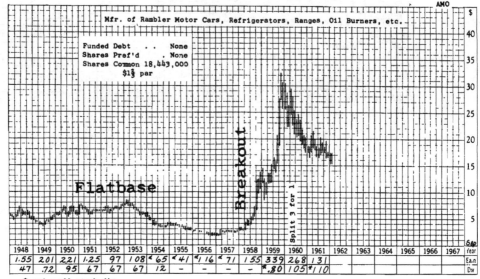

Mfr. of Rambler Motor Cars, Refrigerators, Ranges, Oil Burners, etc.

Funded Debt . . None
Shares Pref'd . . None
Shares Common 18,443,000
$1⅔ par

Flatbase

Breakout

Split 3 for 1

Chart 10

Year	1948	1949	1950	1951	1952	1953	1954	1955	1956	1957	1958	1959	1960	1961	1962	1963	1964	1965	1966	1967
Earn	1.55	2.01	2.21	1.25	.97	1.08	ᵈ.65	ᵈ.41	ᵈ1.16	ᵈ.71	1.55	3.39	2.68	1.31						
Div	.47	.72	.95	.67	.67	.67	.12	–	–	–	–	*.80	1.05	*1.10						

* and small stock div.

These are just a few of the upside breakout examples which have occurred from flatbase patterns, all quite profitable to those who took advantage of the bullish implications of this type of chart formation. Later in the book you will be shown how to recognize buying opportunities in such situations BEFORE THE UPSIDE PRICE BREAKOUT with helpful knowledge as to which direction the stock should break out. This is highly important because there have been flat bases which were followed by *downside* price breakouts. Those stocks presented the safest *shortsale* opportunities. If one bought into a flatbase pattern on the blind hope that the stock had to break out on the upside then that blind hope could prove to be highly expensive. If there was nothing else to go on, then the safest course would be to only buy or sell on such breakouts and not to anticipate them. Later on you will be shown how to *anticipate* the direction of price breakouts so you can be in a better position to buy or sell ahead of the majority. Here are a few examples of downside breakouts following flat bases. Like the rapidity of the advance following an upside flat base breakout, note the same rapidity on the downside when the flat base is broken by a decline in the price under that base.

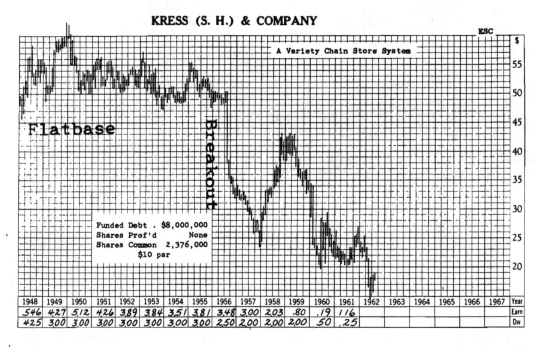

Chart 11

Support and Resistance

These are the two commonest words used in the practice of chart reading. The price *support* area in a stock chart refers to the level under which the price is not expected

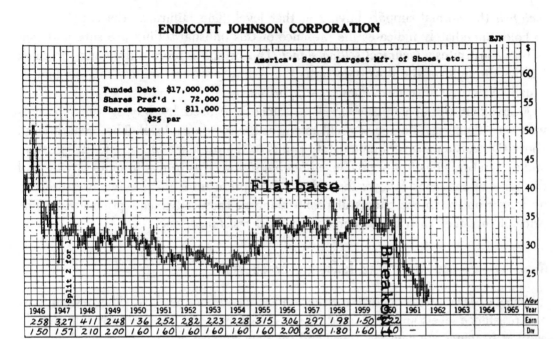

ENDICOTT JOHNSON CORPORATION

America's Second Largest Mfr. of Shoes, etc.

Funded Debt $17,000,000
Shares Pref'd . . 72,000
Shares Common . 811,000
$25 par

Flatbase

Split 2 for 1

Breakout

Year	1946	1947	1948	1949	1950	1951	1952	1953	1954	1955	1956	1957	1958	1959	1960	1961	1962	1963	1964	1965
Earn	2.58	3.27	4.11	2.48	1.36	2.52	2.82	2.23	2.28	3.15	3.06	2.97	1.98	1.50	2.22					
Div	1.50	1.57	2.10	2.00	1.60	1.60	1.60	1.60	1.60	1.60	2.00	2.00	1.80	1.60	.40	—				

Chart 12

to move. It denotes an opportunity to buy the stock on the assumption that the stock should rise from that level. Price *resistance* is the opposite of support. Resistance describes the area in a stock price chart where the price is expected to stop advancing. It denotes an opportunity to sell the stock at that level on the assumption that the next move will be a downward one.

Support and resistance levels are determined on a basis of past performance. If a stock price stopped declining at some previous level it is expected to stop declining the next time it comes down and approaches that level. The logical assumption is that chart readers observed that those earlier purchasers at that level benefitted from a subsequent price advance. If the stock was a good buy then it is a good buy now at that reaction low. That is the reasoning. As for resistance, that is a price level measured back to a previous similar level at which the stock stopped advancing. The reasoning of the chart reader is the same. If previous holders of the stock sold the stock at a certain advanced level, future holders would also be tempted to sell when the stock returned to those high levels.

Obviously, support and resistance levels are often broken. The stock price moves under the support level or above the resistance level. These moves are called *breakthroughs* (or *breakouts*). You have already seen the effects of breakouts. When a support level is violated by a downside breakout it usually results in a further price decline, the price of the stock reflecting the physical principle of a body in motion remaining in motion. The stock price then seeks *the next support level*. Why was the first support level violated? The answer lies in the fact that selling pressure *out-*

weighed the normal support buying at that level. The failure of the support level to hold immediately indicates the presence of this unusual selling pressure and that in turn constitutes a *technical selling signal.* This brings in more selling and the stock follows through on the downside until the selling pressure abates, this abatement usually occurring at or near *the next support level.*

A breakout through upside price resistance is caused by buying pressure outweighing the normal degree of profit-taking at the resistance level. The breakthrough above the resistance level immediately points to the presence of this buying pressure and that in turn constitutes a *technical buying signal.* This brings in more buying and the price of the stock follows through on the upside until the buying pressure can no longer outweigh the effects of profit-taking at those advanced price levels. The price of the stock then traces out its own *new resistance level.*

New Support and Resistance following Breakouts

Once a breakout has occurred, either on the upside or the downside, new support and resistance levels are designated. If the breakout occurs on the downside *the old support becomes the new resistance* and the new support is a level further down the price scale determined by the same observations of price past performance. If the breakout is on the upside then *the old resistance becomes the new support* and the new resistance is equivalent to some other previous price peak or is yet to be determined if the stock is moving in new high ground.

The longer that a stock fluctuates between a given support and resistance level without penetrating either level the more bullish is a future upside breakout and the more bearish is a future downside breakout. This was shown in Charts 1-12.

Chart 13 is now shown to illustrate the presence of price *support* levels in a stock price pattern:

Chart 13

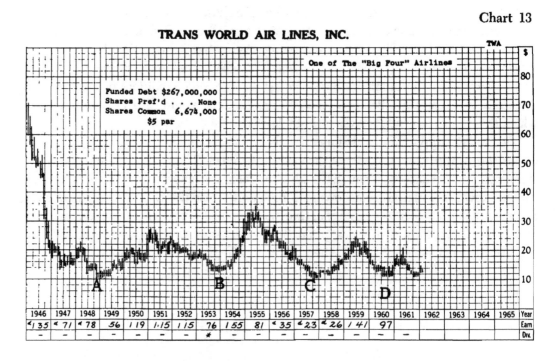

TRANS WORLD AIR LINES, INC.

1946	1947	1948	1949	1950	1951	1952	1953	1954	1955	1956	1957	1958	1959	1960	1961	1962	1963	1964	1965	Year
⁴/35	⁴71	⁴78	56	/19	1·15	115	76	155	81	⁴35	⁴23	⁴26	/41	97						Earn
–	–	–	–	–	–	*	–	–	–	–	–	–	~	–						Div.

Long-term support levels are indicated at points A, B, C and D in the above chart of Trans World Airlines. Each time the stock price declined to those levels or close to them an upturn followed. Note that in late 1953 the price came down to the 12 area instead of all the way down to around 10 where support at the A point was met. The whole idea of price support is better understood if it is thought of in terms of support *areas* rather than specific support levels at a certain exact price. If a trader was thinking of buying TWA common stock in late 1953 but insisted on buying at $10 a share because the stock turned up previously at that level in late 1948, then he would have missed the entire swing from $12 to almost $36 which occurred in the 1954-55 period. On the other hand, if the 10-12 price *area* was noted as being the support area then buying anywhere in that area would have been profitable and no markets would have been missed.

Now note that when the stock again returned to the support area in late 1957 (Point C) the stock price went under $10 a share. The upturn still followed even though points A and B were penetrated on the downside. The longer term support levels (where several years exist between each support price) do not have to be measured as closely as do those which exist closer together. Following the upturn after point C, the stock again declined to the support area at Point D. Note that the exact support levels were $10 at Point A, $12 at Point B, $9 at Point C and $11 at Point D. Considering the fact that the stock declined from over $70 a share in 1946, the very small differentials between the exact turning points at the lows were inconsequential as long as the support was thought of in terms of the *area* rather than an exact price. If the area was considered each time, then traders would have consistently bought TWA in the $9 to $12 range.

Viewing the TWA chart again with Points A, B, C and D in mind, the long-term *base line* is seen to exist and some day this is likely to be capitalized upon with an upside breakout of very bullish significance.

Chart 14

TEXTRON, INC.

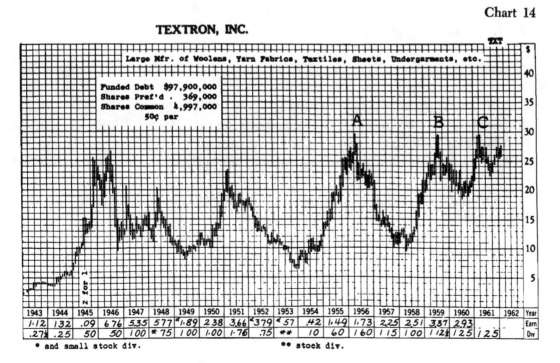

	1943	1944	1945	1946	1947	1948	1949	1950	1951	1952	1953	1954	1955	1956	1957	1958	1959	1960	1961	1962	Year
Earn	1.12	1.32	.09	6.76	5.35	5.77	*1.89	2.38	3.66	*3.79	*.57	.42	1.49	1.73	2.25	2.51	3.37	2.93			Earn
Div	.27½	.25	.50	.50	1.00	*.75	1.00	1.00	1.76	.75	**	.10	.60	1.60	1.15	1.00	1.12½	1.25	1.25		Div

* and small stock div.   ** stock div.

Chart 14 illustrates a perfect example of repetitive resistance levels. Each time the stock rallied to the $28 to the $30 area it was followed by a decline. Some day this stock may move above points A, B and C and then if it does the *new support* price would be the *old* resistance price.

Now look at Chart 15 where this principle is illustrated.

NEW YORK CENTRAL RAILROAD CO.

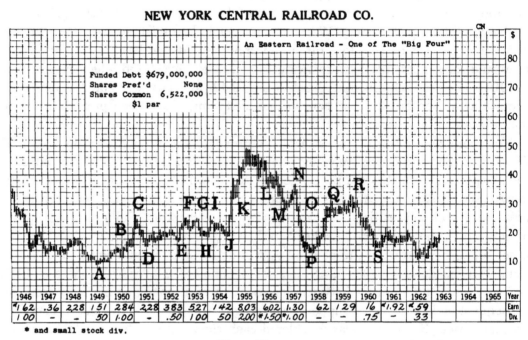

Chart 15

In Chart 15 all the basic points of reading a line chart are shown. These can be summarized as follows:

1. Long-term support areas at A, P and S.

2. Upside breakout at B.

3. First upside resistance at C, F, G and I.

4. First reaction from C carries down to support at the breakout point shown at B.

5. This new support area is shown by D, E, H and J.

6. Major upside breakout at K carrying above the C, F, G and I tops.

7. This leads to the major rise leading to the peak.

8. C, F, G and I resistance levels now become the support levels on reaction from the peak.

9. Downside penetration at L carries to M which is in line with C, F, G, I and K support levels.

10. Next advance stops at N because the L penetration designated that level as the resistance level.

11. Next decline sees a downside penetration of M support at point O. This decline breaks through the D, E, H and J supports and thus long-term support is met at point P in line with point A.

12. Upside resistance has been designated by the previous downside penetration at point O. This resistance is also in line with points C, F, G, I, K and M.

13. Stock tops out between Q and R which runs into the resistance area, an area set up at points M and N.

14. Resulting decline carries down to point S which is the long-term support area also seen by the stock at points A and P.

15. Hitting point S, the stock is again ready to move up and the entire process starts again.

Gaps

Now a quick review of gaps is in order. Gaps are just what the name implies. These are skips in the price pattern. Suppose a stock fluctuates one day between $28.50 and $30 a share, closing that day at 30, and the next morning opens at 32. There is a gap between 30 and 32. While the jump opening may have very short term bullish implications it nevertheless leaves a hole to be filled and almost invariably the stock will find its way back down to 31 and then to 30 to completely fill the gap. *It is safer to assume that all gaps will be filled.*

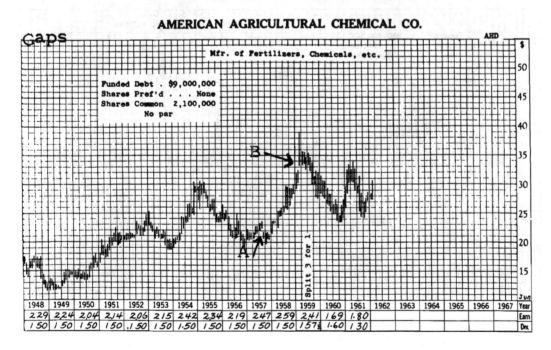

Chart 16

The theory behind the filling of gaps is simply that over-enthusiasm for a stock caused the upside gap and such enthusiasm always leads to *second* thoughts where the trader questions whether that quick an advance is justified. Conversely, downside price gaps are caused by over-pessimism and the move is questioned by many traders as to whether that much pessimism is justified. Second thoughts in that case lead to some buying and the downside gap is filled by a price advance.

Chart 16 shows a price gap at point A on the downside which was filled a few months later by an advance. At point B an upside gap occurred which was filled a few months later by a decline.

Climactic Moves

Any move which appears to be strictly out of character on the upside or the downside is likely to be a *climactic* move, the end of the line, either a great buying opportunity if it is on the downside or a great selling opportunity if it is on the upside. Usually such unusual moves are accompanied by heavy volume since a sharp and unusual downswing to new lows usually catches the majority bearish at the bottom and a very fast run-up to new highs in unusual fashion usually catches the majority most bullish on the stock at the top. In order that the appearance of climactic moves can become more familiar, study the following charts:

McCRORY CORPORATION (THE)

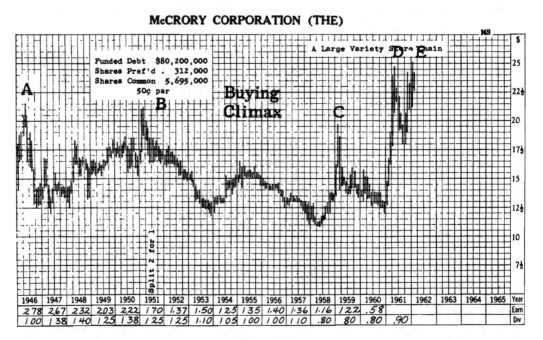

Chart 17

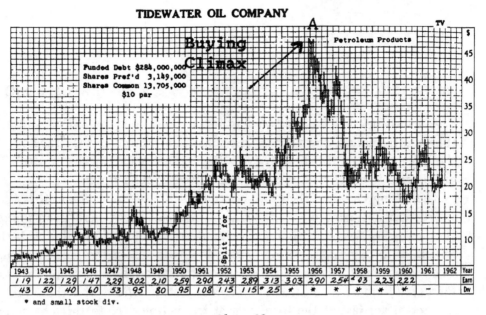

TIDEWATER OIL COMPANY

Buying Climax

Petroleum Products TV

Funded Debt $284,000,000
Shares Pref'd 3,149,000
Shares Common 13,705,000
$10 par

Split 2 for 1

Year	1943	1944	1945	1946	1947	1948	1949	1950	1951	1952	1953	1954	1955	1956	1957	1958	1959	1960	1961	1962
Earn	1.19	1.22	1.29	1.47	2.29	3.02	2.10	2.59	2.90	2.43	2.89	3.13	3.03	2.90	2.54	*.03	2.23	2.22		
Div	.43	.50	.40	.60	.53	.95	.80	.95	1.08	1.15	1.15	*.25	*	*	*	*	*	*	—	

* and small stock div.

Chart 18

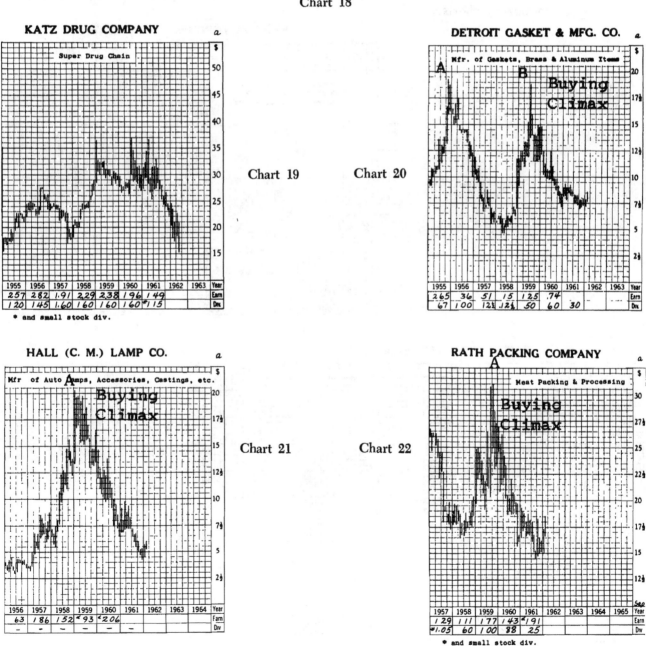

KATZ DRUG COMPANY

Super Drug Chain

Year	1955	1956	1957	1958	1959	1960	1961	1962	1963
Earn	2.57	2.82	1.91	2.29	2.38	1.96	1.49		
Div	1.20	1.45	1.60	1.60	1.60	1.60	*1.15		

* and small stock div.

Chart 19

Chart 20

DETROIT GASKET & MFG. CO.

Mfr. of Gaskets, Brass & Aluminum Items

A   B   Buying Climax

Year	1955	1956	1957	1958	1959	1960	1961	1962	1963
Earn	2.65	.36	.51	.15	1.25	.74			
Div	.67	1.00	.12½	.12½	.50	.60	.30	—	

HALL (C. M.) LAMP CO.

Mfr of Auto Lamps, Accessories, Castings, etc.

A   Buying Climax

Chart 21

Year	1956	1957	1958	1959	1960	1961	1962	1963	1964
Earn	.63	1.86	1.52	*.93	*.206				
Div	—	—	—	—	—	—			

Chart 22

RATH PACKING COMPANY

Meat Packing & Processing

A   Buying Climax

Year	1957	1958	1959	1960	1961	1962	1963	1964	1965
Earn	1.29	1.11	1.77	1.43	*1.91				
Div	*1.05	.60	1.00	.88	.25				

* and small stock div.

After a stock has been advancing for a rather long period after breaking out of the base formation, the vertical rise almost invariably is the "race to the summit," the buying climax. It is best to avoid buying into such "upside spears." The risk that a top price is being paid is greatly increased at such times.

The selling climax is the exact opposite of the buying climax. It is the last downward spear occurring on a climax of bearishness. Now, here is an important point: It is necessary to cover all short positions on a selling climax but *it is not nearly as important to buy into a selling climax as it is to sell in the face of a buying climax.* The reason for this is simply the *law of gravity* applied to technical stock analysis. *Prices fall from a peak faster than they rise from a bottom.* It is therefore far more important to act fast at the tops than at the bottoms. Note this characteristic in the following charts:

McINTYRE PORCUPINE MINES, LTD.

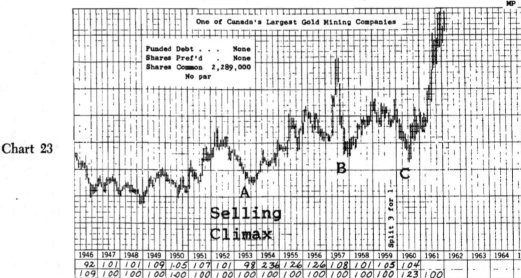

Chart 23

EASTERN STAINLESS STEEL CORP.

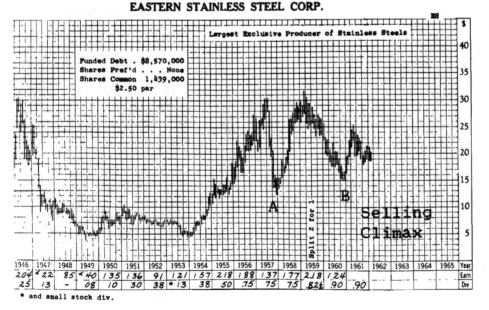

Chart 24

* and small stock div.

POOR & COMPANY

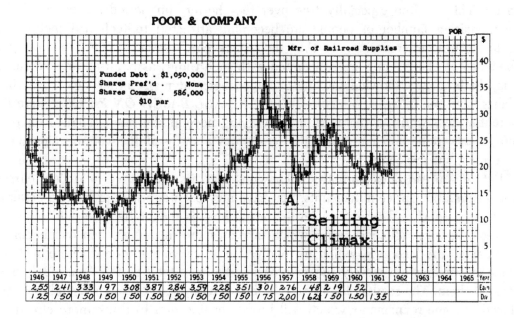

Chart 25

Year	1946	1947	1948	1949	1950	1951	1952	1953	1954	1955	1956	1957	1958	1959	1960	1961	1962	1963	1964	1965
Earn	2.55	2.41	3.33	1.97	3.08	3.87	2.84	3.59	2.28	3.51	3.01	2.76	1.48	2.19	1.52					
Div	1.25	1.50	1.50	1.50	1.50	1.50	1.50	1.50	1.50	1.50	1.75	2.00	1.62	1.50	1.50	1.35				

JEFFERSON LAKE SULPHUR

Chart 26

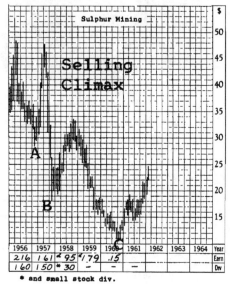

Year	1956	1957	1958	1959	1960	1961	1962	1963	1964
Earn	2.16	1.61	*.95	*1.79	.15				
Div	1.60	1.50	*.30	-	-	-			

* and small stock div.

The Summing up

You have now quickly run through some of the basic concepts of chart reading and have seen how the technical leads the fundamental in indicating price moves. A study of stock price charts tends to make one increasingly aware of the uncertain relationship between earnings and dividends and what a stock price is going to do. This is often especially true over the shorter run periods. Because of this, an increasing number of people are becoming attracted to technical methods so as to be in a better position to time their stock purchases and sales. In turning to the study of charts, they are confronted with such things as point-and-figure charts, line charts, charts showing moving average lines and many other types. All these charts have one thing in common—*THEY ARE ALL BASED ON PRICE.* There is a potential new world of technical analysis lying beyond the mere reliance on price movements alone and much of this stems from a study of the volume movements in a stock, but this comes later.

Before you can delve into the unknown it was first necessary to review current knowledge about price movements. You have now been apprised of what a breakout is, what support and resistance levels mean, what is meant by gaps and climactic moves. These are all chart terms which take on more meaning when one begins to think about the "energies" which are involved in the movement of a stock up or down. Price movements are merely the *reflection* of the sum-total of the "energies" which created them. The reader should now be better equipped to move on and be introduced to some refinements which will further enable him to think more effectively in terms of these stock "energies" and some of the laws which tend to guide their direction.

Chapter Two

The Rhythm of

Market Movements

How the market tends to break, back and fill in response to the same mathematical laws as those governing melody and music.

What You Are about to Learn

There are very few "accidents" in the stock market. When a stock advances or declines there is a "reason" behind the move. It is not the primary concern of a market technician to determine what the reason is, the assumption being that there is always a reason. The technician is primarily concerned with timing, *when* a stock moves rather than *why* it moves. Since there cannot be any motion without the presence of some kind of energy, a study of stock price movements prompts an investigation of some of the forces behind these movements and this leads us into a brief discussion of simple physics.

Stock price movements often show a tendency to adhere to some physical laws. You have been introduced to some basic concepts and now it is time to add some refinements, relating the *breakout*, the *flatbase breakout*, *support* and *resistance*, *gaps* and *climactic moves* to the laws of motion. It will be illustrated that stocks tend to develop their own "rhythm" and back and fill with a tendency to respond to some of the mathematics of melody and music. You will be shown that the effectiveness of great art is as much a matter of timing as it is construction. This short chapter should better prepare you for the later material, making you increasingly conscious of the presence of stock "energies" which create the stock prices which reflect them.

Bach, Beethoven and Kosma

There is a predictable order in the universe. All motion is governed by *laws* of motion. There are no accidents. All vacuums are filled. Bodies in motion tend to remain in motion. Bodies at rest tend to remain at rest. You have already seen some of these laws at work in reading a stock price chart. An advance follows an upside breakout. A decline follows a downside breakout. A failure to reach a previous peak leads to a decline. All gaps are filled. All these movements are based on universal laws of motion. They not only apply to the stock market but they equally apply to laws of physics, medicine and mathematics as well as to music.

Jesu, Joy of Man's Desiring

Johann Sebastian Bach, who was born in 1685 and died in 1760, could have been a great stock market technician if he were alive today. His great music *followed every technical principle of stock market analysis*. He might be today a stock price chart reader *par excellence*. Of course Bach was remotely removed in terms of time and temperament from the modern day stock market. However, his music consciously or unconsciously *follows the direction forecasted by the very notes themselves*. Bach was inspired and yet his music almost fits a *mathematical* formula.

Below is written the theme of Bach's *"Jesu, Joy of Man's Desiring"*.

Johann Sebastian Bach
Arranged by Bryceson Treharne

Since there are eight notes in the scale (12 in the chromatic scale) the figure 1 will be assigned to the lowest note in the above theme. Putting the notes of the theme in terms of numbers and letting the first note start with the number 4, they read as follows: 4, 5, 6, 8, 7, 7, 9, 8, 8, 11, 10, 11, 8, 6, 4, 5, 6, 7, 8, 9, 8, 7, 6, 5, 6, 4, 3, 4, 5, 1, 3, 5, 7, 6, 5, 6, 4, 5, 6, 8, 7, 7, 9, 8, 8, 11, 10, 11, 8, 6, 4, 5, 6, 2, 8, 7, 6, 5, 4, 1, 4, 3, 4. Now these numbers are plotted on the chart, on page 45.

Checking the numbers against the chart, pretend that each number represents the fluctuating price of a stock and see how the chart follows all the technical chart principles just reviewed.

The first four figures are 4, 5, 6, and 8. This sets up a *gap* and predicts that the gap will be filled. The next two figures are a pair of 7's, thus filling in the gap. The next figure is a 9 and this represents an *upside breakout* above the previous high of 8.

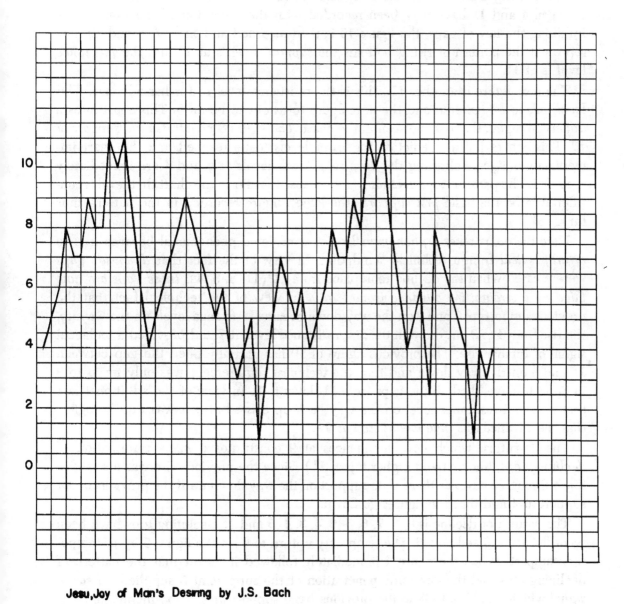

Jesu, Joy of Man's Desiring by J.S. Bach

Chart 27

The gap from 7 to 9 on that jump is immediately filled in with a pair of 8's. The pair of 8's and the previous pair of 7's represent *rising bottoms* and this, together with the upside breakout to 9, *constitutes a bullish prediction of new highs to come.*

The new highs are then immediately scored with a *climactic* jump to 11. All figures between 4 and 11 have now been recorded with the exception of the number 10. Fulfilling the law of gaps, the figure 10 is then recorded and since 7, 8 and 10 now represent the pattern of rising bottoms the *support* level is at 10 and the *resistance* level is at 11.

The next figure is another 11. This is the resistance level to further advance. *This level fails to be bettered* and the next figure turns out to be an 8. This constitutes a *downside signal,* the first one seen in the chart. *The figure 8 penetrates the support at 10.* This is a technical prediction for lower levels to be reached and the chart immediately obliges. Following the drop to 8, lower levels of 6 and 4 are immediately recorded. The pattern stops declining at 4 because thus far in the chart that level is considered to be the basic *first support* (the lowest figure recorded in the pattern thus far).

Here the chart takes a *phenomenal* twist, considered phenomenal because it is so *utterly logical* from a technical standpoint. In view of the fact that *downside gaps* were created when the decline took place from 11 (11, 8, 6, 4), *these gaps are now filled by a straightline advance from 4 to 9.* In view of the technical fact that the previous supports of 7 and 9 on the way down became resistance levels on the way up, the rise from 4 to 9 cut through the first resistance level at 7 and provided a technical signal of further rise. The previous figure of 10 has partially filled the gap between 11 and 8 on the way down and thus the technical requirement was only to go to 9 in order to have filled all the gaps from 11 down to 8. In view of the additional fact that a second resistance level on the way back up existed at 9 it was utterly logical that the advance this time *would stop at 9.*

The downturn which now commences at 9 constitutes a *bearish* formation of *declining tops* (the first and higher top at 11). Since the previous rise was a straightline 4 through 9 advance there is no support on the way down until the previous major support at 4 and thus the figures go down.

The pattern of decline is 9, 8, 7, 6, 5, 6, 4, 3, 4, 5 and 1. Declining tops have been recorded at 11, 9 and now 6. The temporary upturn to 6 set the figure 5 up as temporary support. When the figure 4 immediately followed it meant that the pattern of declining tops and the downside penetration of the support at 5 supplied a *bearish signal* which would not allow the previous basic support at 4 to be maintained this time. Sure enough, the support at 4 was immediately broken with the drop to 3 for the first time. The drop to 3 was another bearish signal for lower figures yet to come but first there was a temporary rise, the figures 4 and 5 following the drop to 3. *The rise had to be temporary for two strong technical reasons.* The drop to 3 had already given a bearish signal and the previous support at 5 on the way down *became the resistance level on the way up.* The pattern then completed itself with a *climactic* decline to 1 (as predicted by the bear signal at 3). Just as the jump from 8 to 11 in the early figures on the way up was climactic on the upside, so was the drop from 5 to 1 climactic on the downside.

Following an upside climax there is a fast retreat. Bach showed this when the initial jump from 8 to 11 was followed by the 8, 6, 4 retreat. *Following a downside climax there is fast advance.* Bach now showed this with the 3, 5, 7 advance after the drop to 1 was recorded. This advance pattern set up gaps at 2, 4, and 6. The gaps at 4 and 6 were then filled by the succeeding figures of 6, 5, 6, 4, 5, 6. The next figure is an 8 and this provides the bull signal for rise, penetrating the previous recovery high of 7. The entire pattern repeats with the remaining variation of filling in the last remaining gap at 2 and providing a balancing upside jump from 2 to 8 with the remaining figures filling in that gap, a masterful piece of music which follows all the directions implied by sound technical stock market analysis.

Beethoven and the Fifth

Ludwig van Beethoven (1770-1827) also subconsciously followed the "technical" line in his music and the opening bars of his immortal fifth symphony provide a good example:

Translating these notes into numbers we have the following sequence: 5, 5, 5, 3, 4, 4, 4, 2, 5, 5, 5, 3, 6, 6, 6, 5, 10, 10, 10, 8, 4, 4, 4, 2, 6, 6, 6, 5, 11, 11, 11, 9, 12, 12, 11, 10, 12, 12, 11, 10, 12, 12, 11, 10, 8, 12.

These numbers are now plotted on a chart:

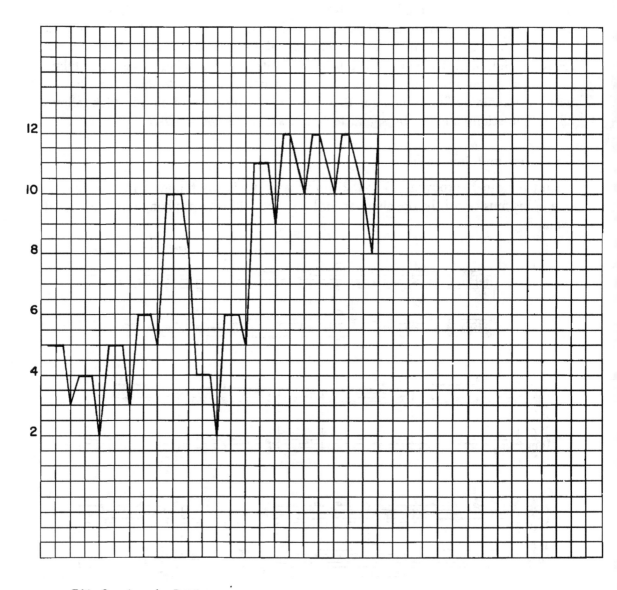

Fifth Symphony by Beethoven

Chart 28

The clear pattern of *rising bottoms* and *rising tops* followed by the *upside breakout* to a *climactic* top is seen followed by a *longer* term *double bottom* which supports the second ascent to a new series of tops. The first seventeen numbers trace out the very bullish pattern of a *rounding bottom* and the upside breakout (at 6) is a key buy signal. This is a pattern which many stock prices follow and it is well to recognize it immediately so as to capitalize on the very bullish upside breakout from this type of rounding bottom.

From Classics to the Popular Idiom

While classical music can be analyzed from a technical standpoint, so then can representative examples be found among twentieth century popular tunes. Look at the following piece of music. It is *Autumn Leaves* by Joseph Kosma:

Here we find some sharps as well as whole steps and so the scale will be numbered counting every half step letting the lowest note in the theme equal the number 1. AUTUMN LEAVES reduced to numbers then reads as follows:

6, 8, 9, 14, 4, 6, 8, 13, 13, 2, 4, 6, 11, 1, 3, 5, 9,

6, 8, 9, 14, 4, 6, 8, 13, 13, 2, 4, 6, 11, 8, 11, 9, 6,

5, 6, 8, 1, 8, 8, 6, 8, 9, 9, 8, 9, 11, 4, 16, 14, 13,

12, 13, 14, 14, 11, 11, 8, 14, 13, 13, 6, 11, 9, 8,

9, 1, 6

These numbers are now charted:

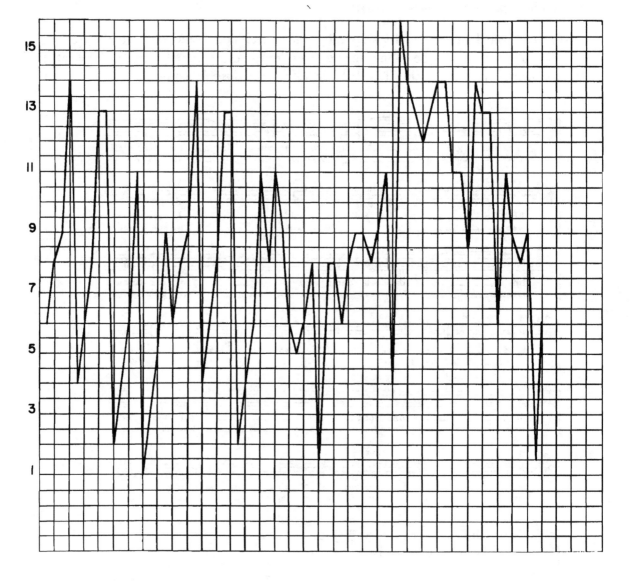

Autumn Leaves by Kosma

Chart 29

A close look at the sequence of these numbers first reveals the pattern of descending tops and bottoms which carries the descending trend from a peak of 14 to a low of 1. The three descending tops are marked by the numbers 14, 13 and 11. The three descending bottoms are marked by the numbers 6, 4 and 2.

The first change in trend to the upside is shown by the upside penetration above 9 the second time the theme is repeated. Following the second peak at 14 the declining trend repeats (declining tops and bottoms). A more lasting turn to the upside is shown when a longer range double bottom is recorded at 1 and the first 9 is recorded following the 8, 1, 8, 8, 6, 8 sequence. This is very bullish in stock price charts, the upside breakout following a double bottom. In this case it led to a new and final peak of 16 and thereafter a declining trend of descending tops and bottoms carried the numbers right back down to 1 and the piece comes to a close, a very orderly and logical piece of work. It wasn't necessarily planned that way but man has a sub-conscious tendency to follow the order and logic of higher vibrations.

The Stock Market Reflects a Mixture of Truths

Technical analysis of the stock market is largely based on many repetitive observations and the truths revealed often can be shown to have parallels in such things as music, medicine, physics, etc. In other words, here and there some natural laws seem to be involved. You have already seen many technical similarities between stock price movements and a piece of music. There is some logic and order in both. There is a strong hint of something which goes beyond just pure chance. Though it is presumptious to say that there is a predictable design, there is enough evidence to more than justify further investigation.

In medicine a disease has certain symptoms which enables the doctor to diagnose correctly. Some diseases have similar symptoms and a less experienced physician may make the wrong diagnosis simply because he overlooks the one symptom which differentiates that disease from many others. There is always a specific set of symptoms which singles out and labels a particular disease correctly. It is the same in the stock market with technical analysis. Each situation in the market has a specific set of technical indicators (symptoms) which correctly labels (diagnoses) the situation for what it is. A less experienced market technician may misread the market simply because he is overlooking perhaps the one indicator which is calling the situation correctly. One cannot expect to become a good market diagnostician overnight anymore than one could become a good doctor without the necessary years of practice and training.

A study of the stock market reveals the workings of many laws of physics and laws of nature. Some of these are:

1. A body in motion tends to remain in motion.
2. A body at rest tends to remain at rest.

   3. What goes up must come down (gravity).
   4. It takes more energy to go up than down (gravity).
   5. There are no vacuums in nature.

Let us examine these verities and apply them to the market:

1.   *A Body in Motion Tends to Remain in Motion.* In the market we would call this *price momentum*. If a stock repeatedly failed to move above a price of 30 for a number of years and ultimately did better the 30 level it obviously had a price momentum it did not have in the past. The move above 30 would obviously carry the price still higher. Upside price breakouts through previous price resistance levels have *momentum* and the physical laws of motion can be profitably capitalized upon. This would equally apply when a stock declines below a previous low point. The downside momentum would carry through and a series of new lows would be expected to ensue.

2.   *A Body at Rest Tends to Remain at Rest.* Right away the *base formation* comes to mind. The stock is doing nothing and the base line may be adhered to for a number of years. Later on in the book you will discover how to differentiate between those stocks in base formations which may sit on their base for a number of additional years and those stocks in base formations just ready to break out of them on the upside. A stock which is literally doing nothing will tend to continue doing nothing until either accumulation or distribution starts. These two terms will be explained in detail a little later on.

3.   *What Goes up Must Come Down (Gravity).* There are many refinements of this generalization. If a stock price advances too rapidly then the dangers of retracement on the downside are enhanced. The speed of advance greatly depends on the level it started from. Obviously, if the rapid advance started from a *base formation* then the first physical law has precedence and the price momentum will not be quickly diluted. If the rapid advance occurs after the stock has been advancing in price for some time then this physical law takes precedence and the danger of decline is increased.

   It is easier to understand this when it is realized that the price of a stock tends to move in *three phases:* (1) the base formation, (2) the advance from the base formation at about a 30 degree angle and (3) the third phase of maturity where the price is advancing at almost a vertical or 90 degree slant. It is in this latter phase where the danger of sharp decline is the greatest. This is the phase in which the above physical law is most commonly applied.

4.   *It Takes More Energy to Go up Than Down (Gravity).* It may take a stock one or two years to rise from 20 to 50 but it could lose half that advance in a period of weeks.

   The gravity principle shows the downward pull the greatest next to the earth and as we rise above the earth the pull gradually lessens until we gain an easier upside momentum. When enough energy has been expended on the upside then exhaustion wins out and the body returns to earth. It is this way with stocks. This is why a stock will stay in a base area (Phase One) for awhile until enough upside energy (volume buildup) has been generated to overcome the pull of gravity or price inertia. When this takes place the stock moves into the second phase of advance. Upside energy keeps building up until it accelerates the price into the rapid Third Phase and here the *balance* of the upside energy is *expended* and then the stock has nothing left to *fuel* the rise any further and then the laws of gravity once again *predominate*. In other words, it takes energy to overcome gravity. Of course there is nothing new here but these things should be thought of when it comes to stocks.

A stock can fall more quickly than it rises by merely the turning off of the faucet of upside energy leaving nothing left except the natural law of gravity to predominate. It was there all the time but it took constant upside energy exerted to overcome it. Remove it and the price would have to fall of its own accord.

5. *There Are No Vacuums in Nature.* Nothing happens without a reason. In nature there is reason and nature wasteth not. Therefore, vacuums are waste and thus there are no vacuums in nature. Being UN-natural, they are thus *filled.* All natural phenomena can be reduced to ENERGY and nature fills vacuums with energy. We have seen the gaps filled between notes in the music of Bach, Beethoven and Kosma and in technical stock analysis we can also say that the *natural* laws of vacuum-filling are fulfilled.

The Summing up

You have undoubtedly by now become more aware that stock prices often show a tendency to adhere to some physical laws. You have been introduced to the theory that most gaps are usually filled, that a body in motion tends to remain in motion (the momentum of a stock price movement), that a body at rest tends to remain at rest (no price movement of import unless there is strong evidence of accumulation or distribution), and many other points of orthodox technical phenomena. The more you see of these things the more convinced you may become that the technical approach can be a great aid to those who have previously relied on fundamentals alone and that the fundamental is seen to be a confirmation of the technical development which has preceded it.

You have also seen that if there were no fundamental confirmation immediately forthcoming that the technical was still a decisive stock market factor, stock prices being quite real regardless of what made them. Underwood was a good example of this, the stock rising 375% in the face of tremendous deficits. In short, you have seen that the technical usually precedes the fundamental.

But now, you are being told that something has a strong tendency to *precede* the movement of stock prices. This implies that the opportunities to buy a stock BEFORE it makes an upside breakout are enhanced. You should have better knowledge in advance as to whether a stock is going to stop declining around a previous price support level or whether a stock has the technical ability to rise above a previous price resistance level. It would be very helpful to know whether an advance had the ability to continue or whether a decline was important or a slight buying opportunity dip.

If there was such a thing it would greatly improve chart reading. Is there such a thing? This writer believes there is and that it is *volume*. At this point you may be still unimpressed. After all, there are many stock price charts with accompanying bar charts showing the volume of trading in the stock. You will soon learn, however, that this is a less than satisfactory way to express the true technical meaning of volume movements.

The new "early warning" theory you are about to read about tends to improve upon all the orthodox chart buy and sell signals you could derive from existing ordinary price charts. It is highly important to point out that the ability to buy into a base formation with the improved knowledge that the stock was more likely to break out on the upside means that by the time the stock does break out the early buyer is much closer to capital gains. It would mean that you could accumulate stock on the base line without fighting the crowd, acquiring the stock at your price, not theirs. The majority of traders tend to follow prices. By following volume signals there appears to be a better chance of completing accumulations before price run-ups.

You could not do this without first becoming acquainted with the way stock prices tend to move. Now that you have a better idea of this, you are in a better position to capitalize on this latest technical concept, volume preceding price. This is the "early warning" theory which helps you to detect accumulation and take a position, thus enhancing your chances for *earlier* capital gains.

Suppose you were still following old methods. A stock breaks out at 30 and runs up to 40 in three weeks. Since you are following old technical methods you are attracted to price and you buy the stock at 30 on the price breakout. You congratulate yourself on your ability to pick a stock which runs up a paper profit of 33⅓% in three weeks. You sell out and take your 10-point profit, a short-term gain. You pay the full tax. The higher your tax bracket was the less attractive was the short term gain. You may have had a net profit after taxes of 1, 2, 3 or 4 points, depending on your bracket. Now, suppose that you could detect beforehand that this particular stock was *under accumulation* as it backed and filled for months between a price of 27 and 29⅞. The new technical "early warning" theory would probably detect this accumulation and you would have had the opportunity to buy the stock between 27 and 29⅞ or lower and then, after sitting on the stock for five months, sold it a month later for 40, thus keeping a profit of 7 or more points *after taxes*.

You are now ready to be introduced to on-balance volume, a new key to stock market profits.

Chapter Three

The Early Warning

Technique Itself

On-balance volume (OBV) explained as a new key to stock market profits.

What You Are about to Learn

You are about to be introduced to *on-balance volume,* a term which will continue to crop up from here on out. You will learn about the theory of volume movements preceding price movements. You will be shown how to measure volume more effectively and to use these measurements to detect the presence of accumulation and distribution patterns. You will also be shown that the current usefulness of stock price charts can be greatly enhanced by the addition of the on-balance volume measurements. The new volume technique can also be related to the Dow-Jones Industrial Average and the market as a whole as well as to any individual stock. You will be shown that on-balance volume can be a particularly effective "early warning" of future price movements, more effective than relying wholly on the price movement itself. The first discussion of on-balance volume in this chapter will stress the importance to the short term market trader, later chapters going into long-term implications.

From the material to be covered here, the reader may learn something which might enable him to sell into certain types of rallies and buy into certain types of declines with greater confidence as to the outcome of his actions. Nobody is going to catch every turn in the market but the use of the new volume theory is expected to help the stock trader reduce the number of surprises which so often catch many traders off guard.

Volume Has a Tendency to Precede Price

We now turn to a most interesting application of everything which has come before, the application of stock trading volume to all the charting principles previously applied to price. On the theory (which is about to be discussed) that volume has a tendency to precede price we can therefore put more stress on the on-balance volume line, a *volume* breakout, *volume* support levels, *volume* resistance levels, *volume* gaps and *volume* base formations knowing that these things have a strong tendency to precede the same things in terms of price.

How to Measure Volume Correctly

Sometimes the simplest things are the most profound. Many market technicians put a great deal of stress on volume as an important indicator but generally fail to measure it in the most effective and meaningful manner. *It is proposed that an on-balance volume line be constructed to serve as a technical indicator of future price.*

Here is how it would function: Suppose on a Monday a stock rises from 8 to 8⅛ on a total daily trading volume of 10,000 shares. Since the stock advanced in price ALL THE VOLUME IS ASSIGNED TO THE BUY SIDE. *This is the new departure*, assigning all the volume in the direction taken by the price of the stock on a closing basis. As long as you are consistent in doing this, there is no distortion in the volume indicator.

Now let us start to construct a revealing table of figures. In the first column we will record all the volume on the upside. In this case it is 10,000 shares. In the second column we will record all the volume on the down side. Since we have thus far only discussed one trading day (and the stock rose in price) there is no recorded volume in the downside column. In a third column we will subtract the downside volume from the upside volume and this will give us a volume *net differential* reading and these readings will always be called the *on-balance volume*. It is in this third column where the indication of *technical strength* lies. Below is the first line of our table:

Date	Buy Volume	Sell Volume	On-Balance Volume	Price
Monday	10,000	0	10,000	8.13*

*Fractional stock prices are written out in decimal form since it simplifies the make-up of such a table. Throughout the book an eighth will be written as .13 and succeeding fractional values will be written as .25, .38, .50, .63, .75 and .88.

Technical strength or weakness can only be seen by comparisons and so we are ready to construct the second line of our hypothetical table. Suppose on Tuesday our sample stock declined an eighth of a point on a total volume of 5,000 shares.

Here is how the table would look on the second day:

Date	Buy Volume	Sell Volume	On-Balance Volume	Price
Monday	10,000	0	10,000	8.13
Tuesday	10,000	5,000	5,000	8.00

The table shows that the stock advanced on Monday on 10,000 shares of "upside energy" and fell an equivalent amount in price on Tuesday on 5,000 shares of "downside energy". You will note that the price of the stock is the same on Tuesday as it was the previous Friday. The casual observer who may only look at stock *prices* sees that the stock at the close of Tuesday trading has made no "progress" since the Friday close. This observation is right in terms of the price but is WRONG IN TERMS OF VOLUME. Something has changed between Friday and Tuesday. The price is the same *but there is a net 5,000 shares left on the buy side*. This residual is the on-balance volume, the *technical strength* the stock has added between the Friday closing and the Tuesday closing. In other words, the stock is technically stronger at a price of $8 on Tuesday than it was at $8 on Friday. Or, to put it still another way, the stock is a better buy at $8 on Tuesday than it was at the same price on Friday.

You will note that the 10,000 share figure recorded on Monday in the BUY column was carried down unchanged on Tuesday. Each column will be *cumulative* inasmuch as *technical strength or weakness is also cumulative.*

Now let us turn to the third day in our hypothetical case and see what happens. Since the stock picked up technical strength on Tuesday, a price advance the next day would not be surprising. Let us say that the stock advanced an eighth of a point on 7,000 shares of volume. Our table now looks like this:

Date	Buy Volume	Sell Volume	On-Balance Volume	Price
Monday	10,000	0	10,000	8.13
Tuesday	10,000	5,000	5,000	8.00
Wednesday	17,000	5,000	12,000 UP	8.13

With the addition of 7,000 shares on the buy side the on-balance volume has climbed above the previous high reached on Monday. The price is the same on Wednesday as it was on Monday but *the stock has reached an apparent new degree of technical strength on a volume upside breakout.* Note the word UP on the 12,000 share on-balance volume figure. THIS DENOTES AN UPSIDE VOLUME BREAKOUT. It implies that the price of the stock seems likely to go higher later on because on-balance volume is "energy" and the energy of the stock is increasing. This is the concept of *volume having a tendency to precede price.*

Light Volume on the Upside not Necessarily Unfavorable

Most technicians consider that light volume advances have unfavorable indications. This is generally so because it indicates that the stock is *losing upside energy*. However, if the light volume price advance pushes the on-balance volume through a previous high for an upside breakout then that lighter volume has done a bullish job and should not be construed to have unfavorable connotations.

Note what took place on the third day of our hypothetical table. The stock rose an eighth of a point on 7,000 shares. On Monday, however, the stock rose an eighth of a point on 10,000 shares. Would not one ordinarily say that the advance on Wednesday was less bullish than the advance on Monday? Yes, ordinarily. However, this is not an ordinary case. The 7,000 shares on the buy side on Wednesday raised the on-balance volume through for an *upside breakout* and any volume upside breakout in the early stage should be treated bullishly. The stock should still be considered to be a buy at 8⅛ on Wednesday because of the addition of technical strength shown by a breakout by the on-balance volume.

In our hypothetical table the fourth day turns out to be a big one. The stock rallies a whole point on 48,000 shares of volume. The table now looks like this:

Date	Buy Volume	Sell Volume	On-Balance Volume	Price
Monday	10,000	0	10,000	8.13
Tuesday	10,000	5,000	5,000	8.00
Wednesday	17,000	5,000	12,000 UP	8.13
Thursday	65,000	5,000	60,000 UP	9.13

The on-balance volume shows another new high and this rates another UP designation. The stock is indicated to be in a bullish trend as shown by the rapid rise in the on-balance volume. It must be noted that at this point, however, *two gaps have been created*. There is a volume gap between the OBV figures of 12,000 and 60,000 and a price gap between 8.13 and 9.13. Most gaps are generally filled and it is logical to now expect this process to get underway. On the fifth day the stock declines a quarter of a point on volume of 25,000 shares. The table now looks like this:

Date	Buy Volume	Sell Volume	On-Balance Volume	Price
Monday	10,000	0	10,000	8.13
Tuesday	10,000	5,000	5,000	8.00
Wednesday	17,000	5,000	12,000 UP	8.13
Thursday	65,000	5,000	60,000 UP	9.13
Friday	65,000	30,000	35,000	8.88

No downside signal has been forthcoming because on-balance volume has not gone under any previous low point (support level) and thus the stock remains in a bullish trend. For the next few days the stock backs and fills within the volume and price gaps. The thorough filling of these cavities (gaps) greatly strengthens the technical position of the stock. Here is how the table looks three weeks later:

Date	Buy Volume	Sell Volume	On-Balance Volume	Price
Monday	10,000	0	10,000	8.13
Tuesday	10,000	5,000	5,000	8.00
Wednesday	17,000	5,000	12,000 UP	8.13
Thursday	65,000	5,000	60,000 UP	9.13
Friday	65,000	30,000	35,000	8.88
Monday	65,000	38,000	27,000	8.75
Tuesday	65,000	46,000	19,000	8.50
Wednesday	65.000	51,000	14,000	8.25
Thursday	77,000	51,000	26,000	8 38
Friday	77,000	61,000	16,000	8.13
Monday	90,000	61,000	29,000 UP	8.25
Tuesday	110,000	61,000	49,000 UP	8.63
Wednesday	120,000	61,000	59,000 UP	9.13
Thursday	120,000	66,000	54,000	9.00
Friday	120,000	70,000	50,000	8.88
Monday	145,000	70,000	75,000 UP	9.13
Tuesday	195,000	70,000	125,000 UP	10.00
Wednesday	195,000	100,000	95,000	9.75
Thursday	295,000	100,000	195,000 UP	11.00
Friday	295,000	100,000	195,000 UP	11.00

The above table now represents a broad cross section of the key points of technical analysis. Let's review each of these points:

1. The first buy signal was given when on-balance volume reached 12,000 (upside volume breakout).

2. The stock would have been purchased at 8⅛ on the first Wednesday because of this bullish volume confirmation. It could have been purchased at 8 on the first Tuesday but in this case the on-balance volume breakthrough was waited for.

3. The stock price ran up too fast on the first Thursday and created a volume gap between 12,000 and 60,000 and a price gap between 8.13 and 9.13.

4. The volume gap was filled when on-balance volume fell to a subsequent reaction low of 14,000 on the second Wednesday, holding above the 12,000 level. The price gap was filled when the stock price fell to 8.13 on the second Friday.

5. With both gaps adequately filled, the stock seemed technically ready to move up again in price and test the earlier high.

6. On the price reaction from the first recorded 9.13, note that on-balance volume gave the signal for the next upturn which followed the price reaction back to 8.13. On-balance volume hit a reaction low of 14,000 *while the price of the stock was still working lower*. When the price of the stock fell to the support level of 8.13 the on-

balance volume was already back up to 16,000. This indicated that the stock was stronger technically at 8.13 on the second Friday than it was the previous Wednesday at 8.25 when the on-balance volume was down to 14,000.

7. Following the on-balance volume signal for an upturn, a pattern of rising tops and bottoms was traced out in the on-balance volume figures. This upward zig-zag is indicated as bullish. Note the rising pattern after the 14,000 OBV reading. The upward zig-zag occurred when on-balance volume reached 29,000, bettering the recent 26,000 minor OBV peak. This again rated an UP designation, such designations always assigned to every on-balance volume upside breakout, whether it is major or minor.

8. As the on-balance volume rose, not the rise in the price of the stock back to the earlier high of 9.13 and observe why the stock price failed to break through to a new high at that point. Checking back to the first Thursday, you will see that on-balance volume was at a high point of 60,000 when the price of the stock first reached 9.13. The second time the stock price reached 9.13 on-balance volume *failed to make a new high above 60,000*. It was likely that the price would react once more very temporarily in order for the stock to build up more upside energy.

9. There is another reason why the stock price probably would have reacted once more. Note that up to the time of the second recorded 9.13 price the stock had "done some work" at every eighth of a point level between 8.13 and 9.13 with the one exception of the 9.00 price level. With the on-balance volume at 59,000 on the second 9.13 price level together with a missing 9.00 closing, the slight second reaction was technically indicated.

10. The stock price filled in the "missing" 9.00 quotation on the third Thursday and reacted to 8.88 with the on-balance volume only falling back to 50,000. Here is an example of where light volume on the downside proved to be very bullish.

11. On the fourth Monday the stock price moved back up to 9.13 for the third time and traced out a "triple top". This triple top seemed to carry no unfavorable indications because the on-balance volume figure stood at a new high of 75,000 and this served as a strong technical indication that this time the stock was ready to break through to a new price high. The on-balance volume figure of 75,000 constituted an upside breakthrough. The first 9.13 price carried with it an on-balance volume of 60,000. The second 9.13 showed 59,000 and the third 9.13 showed a new on-balance volume high of 75,000. Aware of this new degree of technical strength, stock traders would be encouraged to buy the following day and this is what the table showed.

12. The following day (the fourth Tuesday) the stock price broke out of a triple top and moved up to 10 on 50,000 shares which carried the on-balance volume to a new cumulative high of 125,000 shares. The breakout brought in minor profit-

taking the next day and then on the last Thursday shown a heavy wave of buying on volume of 100,000 shares created two climactic gaps, one in the on-balance volume between 95,000 and 195,000 and one in the price between 9.75 and 11.00. From a day-to-day trading standpoint, the stock looked vulnerable for some kind of profit-taking. On the last Friday in the table the price of the stock closed unchanged at 11.00. Whenever the price of the stock remained unchanged the on-balance volume remained at the level recorded the day before. The following table now covers what happened next, illustrating the first demonstration of the DOWN signal:

Date	Buy Volume	Sell Volume	On-Balance Volume		Price
Friday*	295,000	100,000	195,000	UP	11.00
Monday	295,000	140,000	155,000		10.38
Tuesday	310,000	140,000	170,000		10.50
Wednesday	310,000	165,000	145,000	DOWN	10 38
Thursday	310,000	195,000	115,000	DOWN	10.00
Friday	320,000	195,000	125,000		10.13
Monday	320,000	220,000	100,000	DOWN	9.13
Tuesday	350,000	220,000	130,000	UP	9.50
Wednesday	385,000	220,000	165,000	UP	9.88
Thursday	385,000	235,000	150,000		9.75
Friday	405,000	235,000	170,000	UP	10.13
Monday	435,000	235,000	200,000	UP	10.63
Tuesday	510,000	235,000	275,000	UP	11.63

* Carryover from first table

On-balance volume declined to 155,000 on the first Monday in the new table, rose to 170,000 on Tuesday and then fell under the 155,000 level on Wednesday. This move was under a previous low point and thus is marked with a DOWN designation. A further decline took place on Thursday, on-balance volume falling to 115,000. Since this was under the previous low point, it also is marked with a DOWN designation. A slight rise to 125,000 occurred on Friday and then the following Monday the on-balance volume falls to a new low of 100,000. This downside penetration of the previous low of 115,000 receives another DOWN designation.

These DOWN designations are all of only *short-term* significance, only of interest mainly to day-to-day traders. The on-balance volume was still holding above the reaction lows of 50,000 and 95,000 shown in the first table. It will also be noted that the price of the stock on this minor reaction came down to 9.13 and that is the level which marked the top of the earlier price range. When the stock broke out above the 9.13 level it meant that technically the 9.13 level was no longer the resistance level but was now the support level. Now look at the last table and you will see that on-balance volume of 100,000 at the 9.13 price level is much stronger than it was the last time the stock was selling at 9.13. This implied that the stock is ready to rise again as the next reading on the table shows. The next on-balance volume reading of 130,000 goes above the minor high of 125,000 and this then is a minor upside break-out requiring an UP designation. This UP designation is followed by a major on-balance volume breakout at the 200,000 level (above the old 195,000 high). Note that at this point the price of the stock is still under the old high of 11.00. However, the new on-balance volume high again implies a higher price coming and the last reading in the table shows the price breakout to 11.63.

As these tables show, the day-to-day trader will be attempting to buy a stock on the *last* DOWN designation or the *first* UP designation and sell a stock on the last UP designation or the *first* DOWN designation. In the beginning a trader will not recognize a DOWN designation as the last until he sees the first UP designation following it and will not recognize an UP designation as the last until he sees the first DOWN designation following it. Later on he should be able to sharpen his timing to hit closer to the first signals by the recognition of climactic characteristics and previous on-balance volume support and resistance levels.

On-balance volume has a far more important role to play than merely signalling brief one or two-day advances or declines in the price of a stock. It is also capable of signalling when to buy and sell a stock on a long-term basis. This more important function will be described later on in Chapter IV. Now it is important to become increasingly familiar with the early warning aspects of on-balance volume.

Accumulation and Distribution

Probably the most important thing to learn in the technical approach to stocks is how to tell the difference between accumulation and distribution. Accumulation is the buying which does not immediately reflect in a price advance, the greatest price advance occurring *after* accumulation has taken place. Distribution is the selling which takes place without visible signs of price weakness, the price weakness seen *after* distribution has taken place.

This writer is trying to point out that before a stock has the ability to go up importantly in price on any kind of *sustained* upswing, it must first evidence some kind of accumulation. The new volume theory claims that accumulation (or distribution) can best be detected by way of on-balance volume on the theory that volume has a good tendency to precede price movements.

A few years ago, a leading point-and-figure chart service published a chart of Ampex in its newspaper advertisements. The chart showed the price base line and the upside breakout point and the ultimate advance. That service went to great length to explain how attractive the stock looked as the price crossed above the breakout point from the base line. However, it also went on to explain that the stock should not have been bought on the base line because there was no way of telling which way the stock price would move or when.

The use of on-balance volume measurements would have helped indicate at that time that Ampex *could have been purchased right on the base line prior to the upside price breakout* with greater expectations that such a breakout was likely to occur. Stocks under accumulation on their base lines more often than not break out on the upside and stocks under distribution on their base lines more often than not break out on the downside. Many traders have not been in position to profit from this kind of knowledge because they have not known how best to detect accumulation and distribution.

Effectiveness of Current Charts about to Be Changed

A breakthrough in charting technique is at hand which may change the effectiveness of existing charting techniques. Current charts trace out price changes and volume changes but accumulation and distribution cannot be quickly detected by looking at these orthodox charts.

Look at the chart of Stock A on page 64.

Here is a sideways price movement. Note the standard bar chart recording of volume changes at the bottom of the chart. Question: IS THE STOCK UNDER ACCUMULATION OR DISTRIBUTION? In other words, which way is the stock most likely to break out? In a standard book of stock price charts that is all you are going to see. On the basis of what most technicians know, they would say WAIT AND SEE. They would probably say to buy the stock on an upside breakout and sell the stock or go short on it on a downside breakthrough.

But suppose you had means of knowing in advance which way the stock would most likely move. That would mean that you could buy the stock if you were pretty sure that it was under accumulation. If you were pretty sure that the stock was under distribution you could sell it short without waiting for a downside breakthrough. You could do these things without competing with the majority which begins to take notice when the price of the stock does something worthy of attention.

Let us now apply the new theory. If volume tends to precede price then the on-balance volume should point in the direction of the ultimate breakout. The bar chart of volume on the chart as just shown tells us nothing. If it did, you would have an answer already as to which direction the stock was likely to move in and it would not be necessary to look further. But can you do this? No, you cannot. Therefore, current charting of stocks can be improved importantly.

Now, the price chart will be left untouched on Stock A, but the bar chart of volume for a few of the previous months will now be translated in terms of on-balance volume, as shown on page 65.

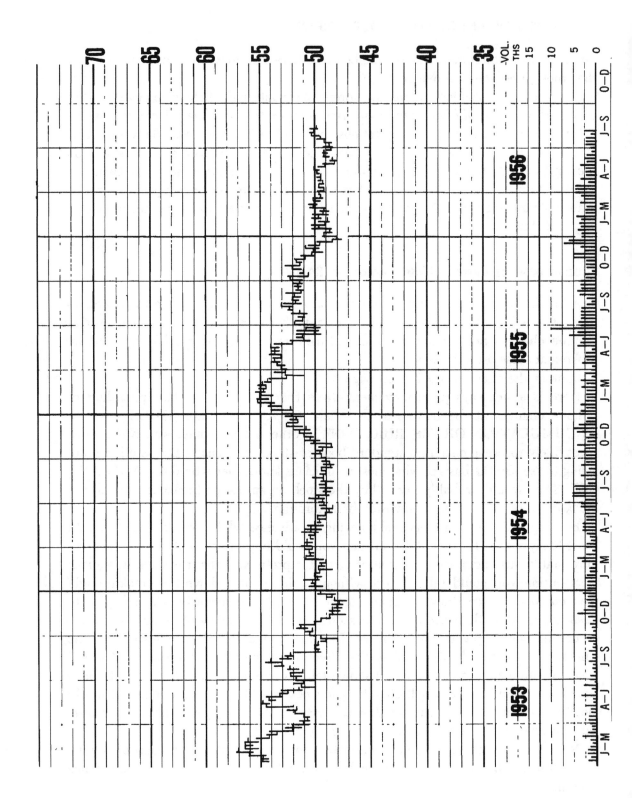

Chart 30

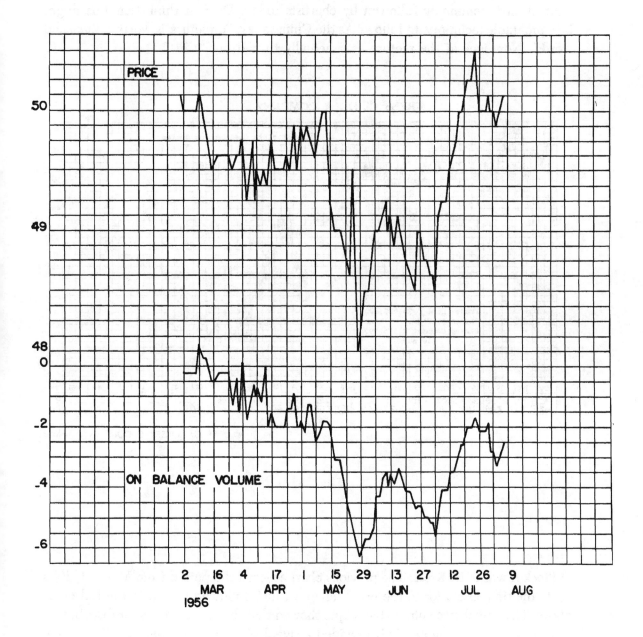

PRICE

ON BALANCE VOLUME

50

49

48
0

-2

-4

-6

2   16   4   17   1   15   29   13   27   12   26   9
MAR   APR   MAY   JUN   JUL   AUG
1956

Chart 31

Now the correct answer is easier to make. The stock is shown by the OBV line to be UNDER DISTRIBUTION. It is likely to break out on the downside and you could take a short position without waiting for the downside price breakout, the orthodox method most commonly followed by chartists today. Do you think that this might be a profitable technique to follow? As the Chinese say, "a picture is worth a thousand words". Now look at the picture as it actually turned out:

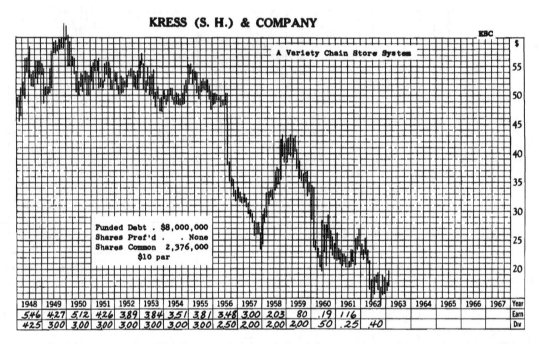

KRESS (S. H.) & COMPANY

A Variety Chain Store System

Funded Debt . $8,000,000
Shares Pref'd . . None
Shares Common 2,376,000
$10 par

© M. C. HORSEY & COMPANY, Publishers,

Year	1948	1949	1950	1951	1952	1953	1954	1955	1956	1957	1958	1959	1960	1961	1962	1963	1964	1965	1966	1967
Earn	5.46	4.27	5.12	4.26	3.89	3.84	3.51	3.81	3.48	3.00	2.03	.80	.19	1.16						
Div	4.25	3.00	3.00	3.00	3.00	3.00	3.00	3.00	2.50	2.00	2.00	2.00	.50	.25	.40					

Chart 32

Stock A was S. H. Kress. The previous chart covered the period from March 1, 1956 up to the time just prior to the price collapse which followed shown in the full chart above. The on-balance volume technique showed that the stock was under distribution prior to the price collapse. This provided a signal of things to come at a time when all *orthodox* charting methods would have called for a "wait and see" attitude.

This is not an isolated example. Let us go on with the accumulation-distribution quiz and look at Stock B, on page 67.

Again it is difficult to determine whether the stock is about to do anything truly

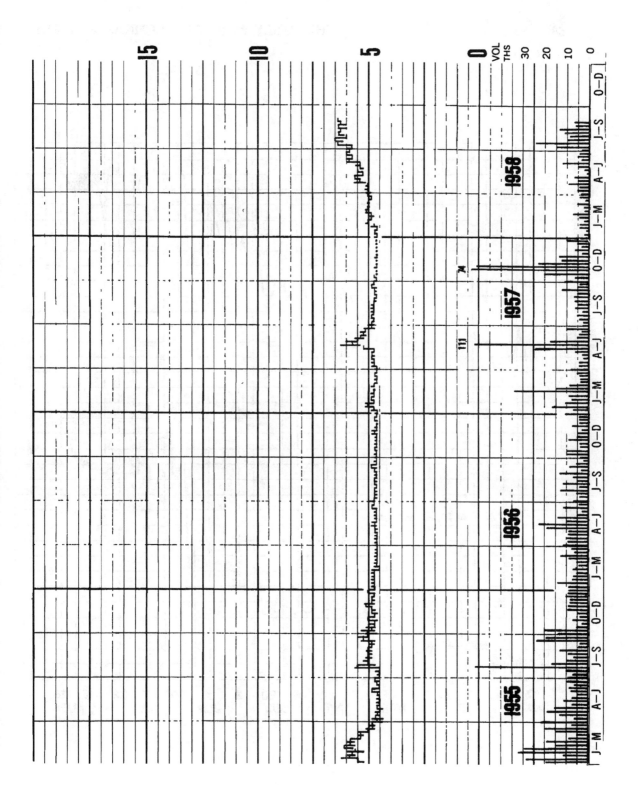

Chart 33

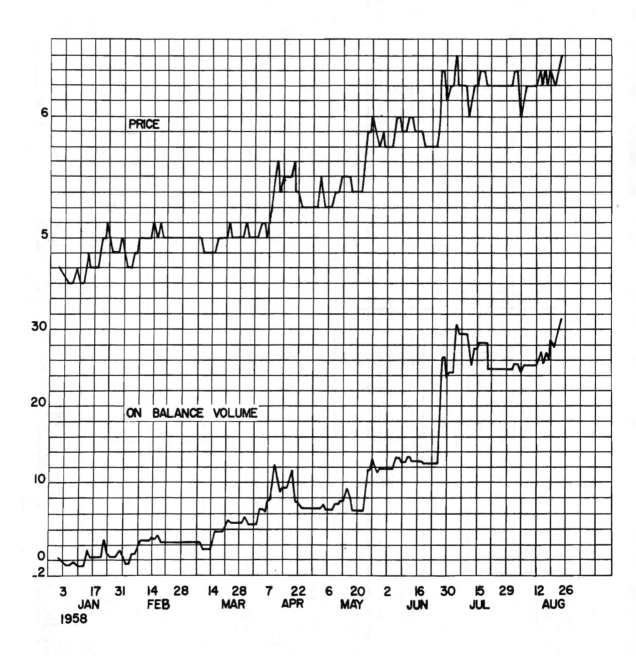

Chart 34

important. There is no measurement of "energy", a term aptly used to describe a rising on-balance volume line. Now translate the volume bar chart into on-balance volume. (See page 68).

Now we have the proper technical evidence to show us that the stock is under important accumulation and can be bought. Was it profitable? Look below.

UNITED WHELAN CORPORATION

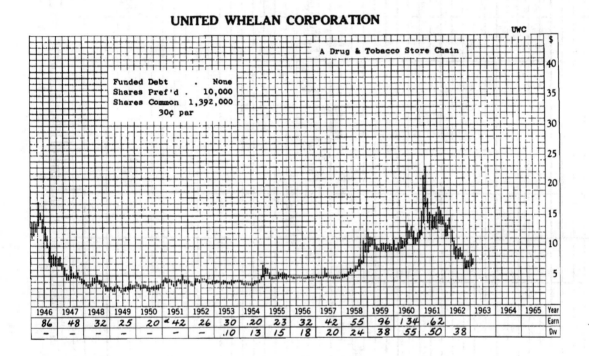

Year	1946	1947	1948	1949	1950	1951	1952	1953	1954	1955	1956	1957	1958	1959	1960	1961	1962	1963	1964	1965
Earn	86	48	32	25	20	⁓42	26	30	.20	23	32	42	55	96	134	.62				
Div	–	–	–	–	–	–	–	.10	13	15	18	20	24	38	55	.50	38			

Chart 35

Stock B was United Whelan. The stock scored an important upside price breakout in the middle of 1958 and went on to ultimately reach a price of 23 in early 1961. Prior to 1958 the stock had been *moving on a flat base line for twelve years*. Just watching the price and holding the stock through such a long period of inactivity would make little sense. The stock price pattern was one of the most bullish BUT THIS IS NO GOOD UNTIL THE STOCK SHOWS EVIDENCE OF ACCUMULATION. Such evidence did not show up until early 1958, thanks again to the on-balance volume line.

Now look at the chart of Stock C on page 70.

Here is another potentially bullish chart pattern, the long flat base. How can one tell from the above chart when the stock is going to break out from that long flat base? Orthodox technical methods again say do nothing until the stock price moves up and breaks out. The on-balance volume, however, gives an "early warning". The chart on page 71 covers the last six months of the first chart.

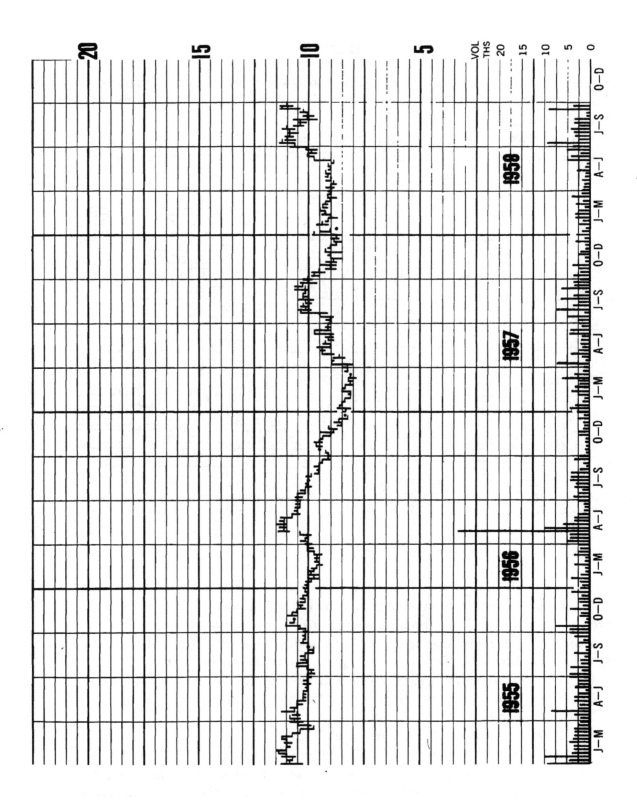

Chart 36

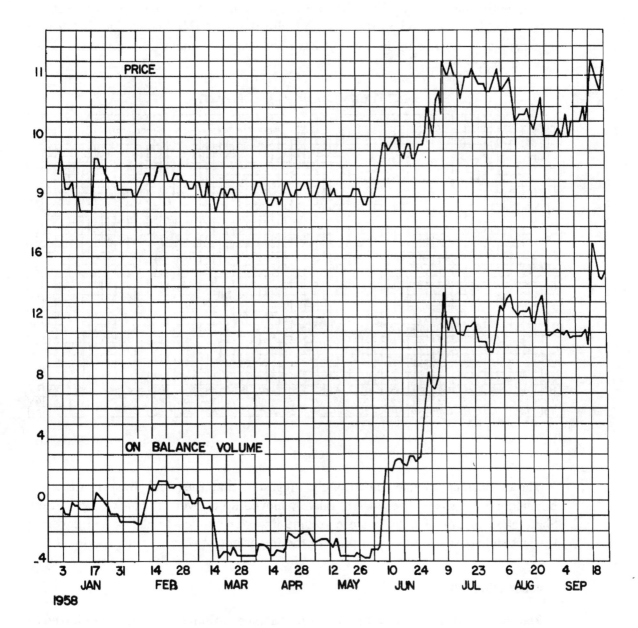

Chart 37

The on-balance volume line shows accumulation to be underway and thus the stock could be purchased on the base line with the profitable knowledge that it now appears ready to move up in a way it has been unable to move in many years. Look at what happened next:

SHATTUCK (FRANK G.) COMPANY

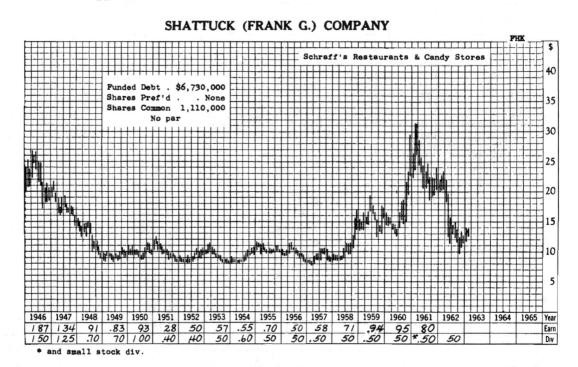

Chart 38

The on-balance volume line strongly suggested that the stock was an attractive buy under $10 a share. The stock ultimately moved up to over 31. Stock C was Frank Shattuck Company. The on-balance volume line was applied to the period covering the first six months of 1958, just prior to the important price breakout.

The Summing up

You have now been introduced to on-balance volume. You have followed a hypothetical illustration revealing the construction of an on-balance volume line and have seen this line in action in three charted instances. You have seen a demonstration of the tendency this line has to detect accumulation and distribution. This chapter has accented the technique of on-balance volume more than interpretation. Thus far you have seen the simplified concept of upside and downside penetrations in on-balance volume and have been introduced to the very short-term aspects these signals convey to a market trader but only the surface has been scratched. You are now ready to move on and discover more about the application of on-balance volume to the Dow-Jones Industrial Average, the market as a whole and specific stocks.

Chapter Four

Allied Chemical, 1961-1962

A typical example of the use of on-balance volume and the related "field" theory in predicting possible longer-term price changes.

What You Are about to Learn

Here you will see some of the longer-term implications of on-balance volume by the application of the "field" theory. Allied Chemical is chosen to demonstrate the theory in action during the critical market period bridging the May 1962 market break. Here you will see a demonstration of the major buy and sell signals given by on-balance volume as well as the day-to-day trading signals. You will also be shown how to apply on-balance volume to the Dow-Jones Industrial Average in order to quickly determine whether this important average is in an advancing, doubtful or declining phase. You will see all the familiar price movements of breakouts, supports and resistances, gaps and climactic moves reflected in on-balance volume first, on-balance volume shaping up as a more effective early warning of impending price changes.

Applying the New Volume Technique to the Dow-Jones Industrials

You now have been introduced to the technique of setting up an on-balance volume line. Inasmuch as stress is being placed on the concept that volume has a tendency to precede price, an improved indication of where the Dow-Jones Industrial Average is headed should therefore be obtainable by setting up an on-balance volume line for that important stock average. The only way that this is possible is first to construct an on-balance volume line for each of the thirty stocks in the average. Once this

73

is done you should have a better indication of where each of these stocks seems headed. It is then a matter of combining these thirty on-balance volume totals into one figure. Such a figure can be distorted, inasmuch as two or three Dow-Jones issues trading on very heavy volume, would weight the final figure. The maximum technical intelligence will come from analyzing each individual issue while using the advanced techniques of the "field" theory and the "climax indicator", two terms we will be working with shortly.

The first step in the new departure is to apply the basic concept of on-balance volume in the simplest form to a few of the Dow-Jones stocks and then gradually work into the advanced concepts as you begin to understand the evolution of the theory from its crudest form through to a refined and practical finished product.

For those who wish later on to construct on-balance volume figures for all the Dow-Jones issues, the list of these 30 stocks going to make up the industrial average is given below:

1. Allied Chemical
2. Aluminum Company of America (Alcoa)
3. American Can
4. American Telephone
5. American Tobacco
6. Anaconda
7. Bethlehem Steel
8. Chrysler
9. DuPont
10. Eastman Kodak
11. General Electric
12. General Foods
13. General Motors
14. Goodyear
15. International Harvester
16. International Nickel
17. International Paper
18. Johns-Manville
19. Owens Illinois Glass
20. Procter & Gamble
21. Sears Roebuck
22. Standard Oil of California
23. Standard Oil of New Jersey
24. Swift
25. Texaco
26. Union Carbide

27. United Aircraft
28. U. S. Steel
29. Westinghouse Electric
30. Woolworth

We will now examine a few of these stocks separately and as an average for the period covering June 1961 through December 1961 and again in the later period from December 1961 through to August 1962. These periods are interesting because they cover a transition from a strong market to a weak market and then back again to a strong market. The study will commence with a look at Allied Chemical, the first Dow-Jones stock.

Before getting into the Allied Chemical table, it is important to quickly review the setting up of such a table. Every time the on-balance volume make an upside breakout above a previous daily high an *UP* designation is placed alongside the figure. Every time the on-balance volume falls under a previous daily low point the word *DOWN* is placed beside it.

The same basic technique regarding volume is followed here. Every time the stock moves up in price *all the volume for the day is assigned to the buy column* and every time the stock moves down in price *all the volume for the day is assigned to the sell column*. The daily difference between the cumulative volume in the buy column and the cumulative volume in the sell column is the on-balance volume, a cumulative daily reading. If the stock closes unchanged then on-balance volume stands still and there is no change.

In order that this be made perfectly clear, a few of the complete figures are shown for Allied Chemical:

ALLIED CHEMICAL

Date	Upside Volume (Buy Column)	Downside Volume (Sell Column)	On-Balance Volume	Closing Price of Stock
June 20, 1961	2,000	0	2,000	61.63
June 21, 1961	2,000	3,600	−1,600	60.75
June 22, 1961	5,900	3,600	2,300 UP	61.75
June 23, 1961	5,900	7,800	−1,900 DOWN	61.38
June 26, 1961	5,900	11,600	−5,700 DOWN	60.00
June 27, 1961	5,900	15,300	−9,400 DOWN	59.00

This is the important volume picture on a stock and the suggested way it should be set up and recorded by technicians. Later on in the other tables only the on-balance volume figures will be given together with the closing prices but it is important at this juncture that the reader know how these figures are derived.

In the above example the table shows that Allied Chemical rose in price on June 20th on a daily volume of 2,000 shares. The figure 2,000 is placed in the upside volume column and the figure zero is placed in the downside volume column and the on-balance volume is a *plus 2,000*. That becomes the *first* reading in the column of on-balance volume readings. (Note: On-balance volume is an advance-decline line using volume figures and, like the orthodox price advance-decline line, can be started at any point. Obviously, the longer the line becomes the more it reveals).

The table shows that on the next day, June 21st, the price of the stock declined ⅞ points on a total volume of 3,600 shares. The figure 2,000 is carried down unchanged in the upside volume column (since it is cumulative) and the 3,600 figure is placed in the downside column. The difference between the upside volume column and the downside volume column now becomes a *minus 1,600*. That is the *second* reading in the on-balance volume column.

On June 22nd the stock advances a whole point from 60¾ to 61¾ on 3,900 shares volume. The upside volume column jumps from 2,000 to 5,900 and the downside column remains the same at 3,600. This means that the differential between the two columns becomes a *plus 2,300*. *That on-balance volume figure rates an UP designation because it moved above the June 20th on-balance volume of 2,000, an upside breakout.*

On June 23rd the stock declines by ⅜ points from 61¾ to 61⅜ on a volume of 4,200 shares. The upside volume column remains unchanged at 5,900 while the downside volume column jumps from 3,600 to 7,800. The on-balance volume then becomes *minus 1,900*. Here is a minor illustration of the tendency that volume movements have in preceding price movements. The *minus 1,900* is lower than the *minus 1,600* recorded on June 21st. This suggests that the stock is weaker technically at 61⅜ on June 23rd than it was at 60¾ on June 21st. *The downside penetration of the previous on-balance volume low point rates a DOWN designation and this is placed next to the low on-balance volume figure*. The stock would be likely to decline a bit further.

The price of Allied Chemical stock at this point declined a bit further. The *minus 1,900* provided a volume signal. On June 26th the stock declined 1⅜ points on 3,800 shares volume. The upside volume column remained unchanged at 5,900 and the downside volume column rose from 7,800 to 11,600. The on-balance volume declined from a *minus 1,900* to a *minus 5,700*. A lower low rated another DOWN designation.

On June 27th Allied Chemical declined another point on 3,700 shares volume. The upside column remained unchanged at 5,900 while the downside volume column rose again from 11,600 to 15,300. This dropped the on-balance volume figure from a *minus 5,700* to a *minus 9,400*. This latter OBV reading, being lower than the previous one, also rated a DOWN designation.

Now that you have seen details of the calculations of on-balance volume, it should not be necessary to show the upside and downside volume columns in all the tables to follow, only the on-balance volume figures alone together with the stock prices.

We are now up to a point where we can get into discussing the heart of the volume theory—the *tables, charts,* the *"field" theory* and the *"climax indicator"* which, when

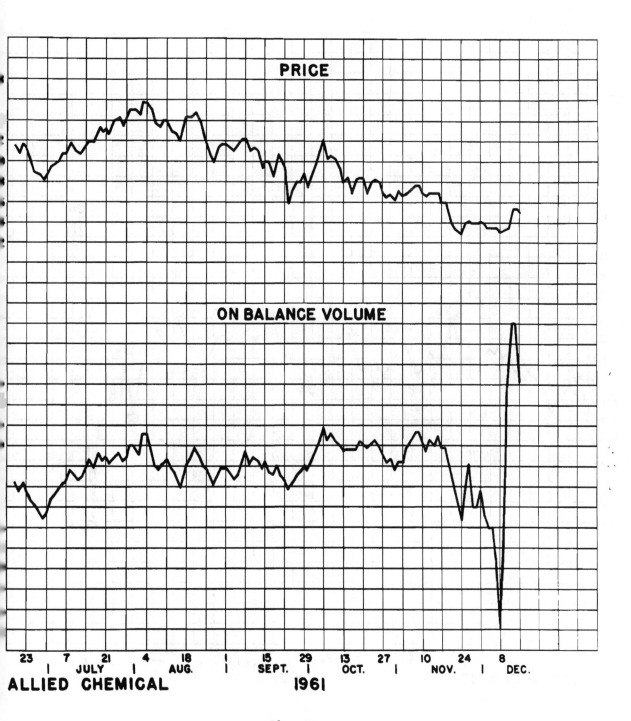

PRICE

ON BALANCE VOLUME

23   7   21   4   18 | 15   29   13   27   10   24   8
| JULY | AUG. | SEPT. | OCT. | NOV. | DEC.

ALLIED CHEMICAL   1961

Chart 39

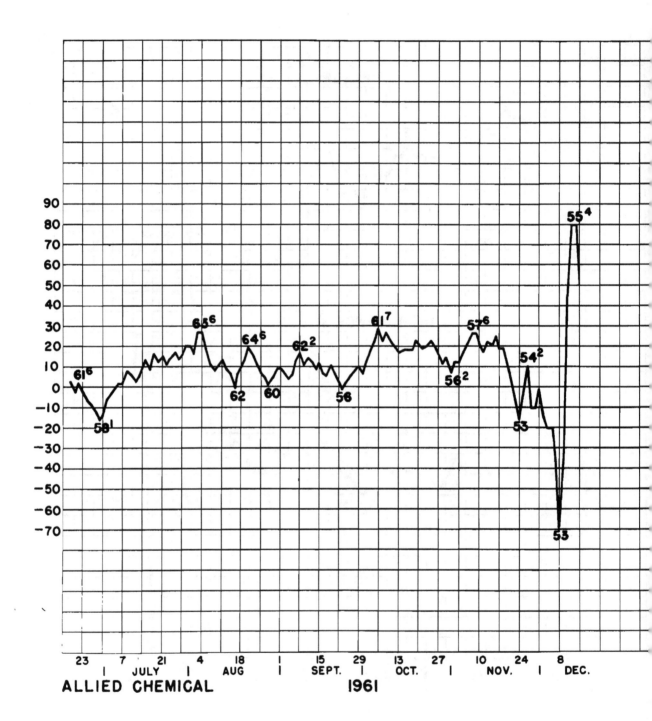

ALLIED CHEMICAL   1961

Chart 39 (cont.)

properly interpreted, portrays a better picture of the day-to-day trend as well as the more important longer-term trends for both individual stocks as well as the market taken as a whole. The 30-Dow-Jones stocks offer a logical starting point in the demonstration of how the theory works.

The presentation is as follows: A few Dow-Jones stocks will be discussed in terms of what the volume table and charts show. The time period runs from June 20, 1961 through August 1, 1962. This will enable the reader to see the theory in action in the months *prior* to the December 1961 market peak as well as in the months *after* this top was recorded. The figures also run through the panic market of May 28th and 29th in the year 1962 as well as part of the recovery which followed. The "field" theory will be discussed in its application to several Dow-Jones issues throughout the next few chapters and then the "climax indicator" will be covered, the latter being based on the 30 Dow-Jones stocks taken as a whole. The entire theory is a study of volume as a new aid in determining which stocks to buy and sell and when to take such action.

ALLIED CHEMICAL

(June to December 1961)

Date	On-Balance Volume		Price	Date	On-Balance Volume		Price
June 20	2,000		61.63	July 20	13,100		63.00
June 21	−1,600		60.75	July 21	14,700		63.25
June 22	2,300	UP	61.75	July 24	10,800	DOWN	62.75
June 23	−1,900	DOWN	61.38	July 25	13,700		64.00
June 26	−5,700	DOWN	60.00	July 26	16,700	UP	64.25
June 27	−9,400	DOWN	59.00	July 27	12,500		63.63
June 28	−11,800	DOWN	58.75	July 28	15,100		64.00
June 29	−15,000	DOWN	58.13	July 31	19,900	UP	65.00
June 30	−13,000		58.75	Aug. 1	19,900	UP	65.00
July 3	−6,200		59.50	Aug. 2	16,100		64.50
July 5	−1,400		60.00	Aug. 3	25,800	UP	65.75
July 6	2,400	UP	60.63	Aug. 4	25,800	UP	65.75
July 7	2,400	UP	60.63	Aug. 7	18,700		64.88
July 10	7,900	UP	61.75	Aug. 8	10,500	DOWN	63.75
July 11	5,900		61.00	Aug. 9	7,500	DOWN	63.50
July 12	3,000		60.75	Aug. 10	11,200		63.88
July 13	5,200		61.13	Aug. 11	12,700		64.00
July 14	9,500	UP	61.63	Aug. 14	9,000		63.00
July 17	13,200	UP	62.13	Aug. 15	6,700	DOWN	62.75
July 18	9,400		62.00	Aug. 16	−400	DOWN	62.00
July 19	16,400	UP	63.25	Aug. 17	7,000		63.00

Date	On-Balance Volume		Price	Date	On-Balance Volume		Price
Aug. 18	10,600		64.50	Oct. 18	18,400	UP	58.25
Aug. 21	14,000	UP	64.63	Oct. 19	22,500	UP	58.63
Aug. 22	18,800	UP	64.75	Oct. 20	20,700		58.50
Aug. 23	14,800		64.00	Oct. 23	18,900		57.00
Aug. 24	10,300		62.50	Oct. 24	20,400		57.88
Aug. 25	7,500		62.25	Oct. 25	23,000	UP	58.25
Aug. 28	4,700		60.75	Oct. 26	20,000		58.00
Aug. 29	1,300		60.00	Oct. 27	16,000	DOWN	57.00
Aug. 30	5,400		61.38	Oct. 30	12,400	DOWN	56.50
Aug. 31	9,300		61.75	Oct. 31	13,800		56.75
Sept. 1	9,300		61.75	Nov. 1	8,000	DOWN	56.25
Sept. 5	3,500		61.00	Nov. 2	11,600		57.25
Sept. 6	5,700		61.50	Nov. 3	11,600		56.75 ex.
Sept. 7	13,200	UP	62.00	Nov. 6	17,700	UP	57.00
Sept. 8	16,000	UP	62.25	Nov. 8	26,100	UP	57.75
Sept. 11	11,400		61.13	Nov. 9	26,100	UP	57.75
Sept. 12	15,400		61.25	Nov. 10	22,200		57.00
Sept. 13	13,000		61.13	Nov. 13	16,700		56.75
Sept. 14	8,800	DOWN	59.25	Nov. 14	22,500		57.00
Sept. 15	11,600		60.00	Nov. 15	19,500		56.88
Sept. 18	7,400	DOWN	59.88	Nov. 16	24,800	UP	57.00
Sept. 19	5,600	DOWN	58.63	Nov. 17	18,600	DOWN	56.00
Sept. 20	10,300		60.38	Nov. 20	18,600	DOWN	56.00
Sept. 21	6,100		59.75	Nov. 21	8,100	DOWN	54.00
Sept. 22	4,400	DOWN	59.38	Nov. 22	−3,000	DOWN	53.50
Sept. 25	−1,100	DOWN	56.00	Nov. 24	−16,100	DOWN	53.00
Sept. 26	2,000		57.25	Nov. 27	−1,500		54.13
Sept. 27	5,500		58.00	Nov. 28	10,200		54.25
Sept. 28	7,300		58.13	Nov. 29	−9,500		54.00
Sept. 29	10,200		58.75	Nov. 30	−9,500		54.00
Oct. 2	7,600		57.50	Dec. 1	−3,200		54.25
Oct. 3	12,600	UP	58.75	Dec. 4	−14,200	DOWN	54.00
Oct. 4	18,500	UP	60.13	Dec. 5	−19,800	DOWN	53.63
Oct. 5	22,500	UP	61.25	Dec. 6	−19,800	DOWN	53.63
Oct. 6	28,800	UP	61.88	Dec. 7	−34,700	DOWN	53.50
Oct. 9	22,800		60.25	Dec. 8	−69,100	DOWN	53.00
Oct. 10	25,600		60.50	Dec. 11	−35,600		53.25
Oct. 11	22,100	DOWN	60.25	Dec. 12	45,300	UP	53.38
Oct. 12	19,800	DOWN	59.25	Dec. 13	80,300	UP	55.50
Oct. 13	16,700	DOWN	58.00	Dec. 14	80,300	UP	55.50
Oct. 16	18,200		58.50	Dec. 15	51,900		55.25
Oct. 17	16,000	DOWN	57.00				

Introduction to the "Field" Theory

When something new about the market is discussed it requires some past performance to serve as a platform of demonstration. One cannot take a one-day position of the Dow-Jones Industrial Average, the Dow-Jones Rail Average, the on-balance volume line, the high-low ratio or any other single market statistic and draw a conclusion as to what the market might do next. One must look at some kind of past record in order to make some kind of intelligent guess as to what the market might do next. The Allied Chemical on-balance volume table and charts of the 1961 period indicate important volume clues having a bearing on the 1962 market action.

Let us first examine the table of on-balance volume. Here we see only the on-balance volume figures which were computed by subtracting the cumulative volume on the downside from the cumulative volume on the upside. This line of on-balance volume denotes the "energy" of the stock in a given direction, a volume force. When the volume breaks out on the upside an UP designation is placed next to it and when the breakout is on the downside a DOWN designation is affixed. Each succeeding high or low gets an UP or DOWN designation and thus it develops that every now and then a *series* of UPS or DOWNS is seen throughout the Allied Chemical on-balance volume table. These series of UPS and DOWNS are called "fields". If an UP or DOWN designation is rather isolated it is also called a "field". There was a DOWN "field", for example, from June 23rd to June 29th, 1961 between the on-balance volume readings of *minus* 1,900 and *minus* 15,000. There was an UP "field" from July 6th through August 4th, 1961 between the on-balance volume readings of 2,400 and 25,800.

Now Determine the Trend

The first major step in looking at the table of on-balance volume is to try to determine the *major volume trend*. This is done by recording the various "fields", taking the *highest* number of an UP field and the *lowest* number of a DOWN field. Putting these figures in order of their time occurrence, *a major volume trend may be determined*. It is that trend which has the *tendency to precede price* and this should largely determine whether the stock should be bought or sold in *long-term accounts*. A still more intriguing and finer interpretation will be necessary for successful short-term trading, this discussion to follow shortly.

As long as each UP field is above the last and each DOWN field is above the last the stock is said to have a *rising field pattern*. When the pattern of the rising field is broken by an UP field *below* the previous one and a DOWN field below the previous one (a downside zig-zag in the fields) then the stock is considered to be *WEAK*. When each UP field is below the last and each DOWN field is below the last then the stock is said to have a *declining field pattern*. In order for the stock to turn *STRONG* a DOWN field must occur above the previous one followed by an UP field above the previous one.

Applying the Field Theory to Allied Chemical for the June to December 1961 period, a table is presented below giving the sequence of rising and falling "fields". Here we can talk once again in terms of technical support and resistance levels, using *on-balance volume figures rather than prices*. For instance, the *last* DOWN designation on June 29th at *minus 15,000* becomes an on-balance volume *support* level and the highest UP designation on August 4th at 25,800 becomes an on-balance volume *resistance* level. The next DOWN field was on August 15th and 16th. Taking the *last* DOWN figure in the field we find it is a *minus 400*. That is *above* the *minus 15,000* DOWN field recorded on June 29th and it is thus far seen that Allied Chemical still had a *long term favorable trend* up to August 16th, 1961. Below is a table showing the field trend from June to December 1961:

Allied Chemical

June to December 1961

"The Field Theory"

Interpretation of Field	Field Maximum On-Balance Volume	Type of Field	Price	Date
————	−15,000	DOWN	58.13	June 29, 1961
————	16,400	UP	63.25	July 19, 1961
————	10,800	DOWN	62.75	July 24, 1961
Rising	25,800	UP	65.75	Aug. 4, 1961
Doubtful	−400	DOWN	62.00	Aug. 16, 1961
Doubtful	16,000	UP	62.25	Sept. 8, 1961
Falling	−1,100	DOWN	56.00	Sept. 25, 1961
Doubtful	28,800	UP	61.88	Oct. 6, 1961
Doubtful	16,000	DOWN	57.00	Oct. 17, 1961
Doubtful	23,000	UP	58.25	Oct. 25, 1961
Falling	8,000	DOWN	56.25	Nov. 1, 1961
Doubtful	24,800	UP	57.00	Nov. 16, 1961
Doubtful	−69,100	DOWN	53.00	Dec. 8, 1961
Doubtful	80,300	UP	55.50	Dec. 14, 1961

Now look at the interpretation of each field. By August 4th it was possible to denote the rising field trend. This did not last long. The August 16th field was below that of July 24th and thus the field trend turned doubtful, this one downleg breaking the pattern of the upward zig-zag. Since no downward zig-zag had yet developed, the in-between description of doubtful is used. The UP field of September 8th failed to reach the August 4th on-balance volume high and the doubtful description is continued. The next DOWN field carried the on-balance volume to minus 1,100 on September 25th. This created a downward zig-zag in the fields and the interpretation changed from doubtful to falling. However, since the minus 1,100 was not as much weakness as the minus 15,000 on-balance volume of June 29th, the interpretation of weakness shown by the falling field trend was not yet a long-term signal of weakness, just one of the earlier technical warnings.

With on-balance volume rising to 28,800 on October 6th the field trend turned from falling to doubtful. The reason why the new higher on-balance volume figure of 28,800 did not change the falling field trend to a rising one is because *it did not trace out a rising zig-zag in the fields*. The previous field maximum on-balance volume of minus 1,100 broke that pattern. The next DOWN field at 16,000 was well above the minus 1,100 and the field trend remains doubtful. The higher field occurred on October 25th at 23,000 and, inasmuch as this on-balance volume breakout was on a *lower key* than the October 6th upside volume breakout, the field trend again remains doubtful. The next down field on November 1st at 8,000 created a *downward zig-zag* from the October 6th volume peak and the interpretation of the field trend showed it to once again be a falling one. The next up field of 24,800 on November 16th turned the interpretation from falling to doubtful, the 24,800 reading being less than the 28,800 reading of October 6th but greater than the 23,000 reading of October 25th. This was not an upward zig-zag inasmuch as the down field of 8,000 was weaker than the previous down field of 16,000.

The earlier weak field warnings then blossomed into a MAJOR down field of minus 69,100 on December 8, 1961. An earlier warning of this development was recorded on November 24th when the on-balance volume first slipped under the long-term support level of June 29th. In terms of the field theory, this move under the on-balance volume *support level* of minus 15,000 recorded a few months before in June technically broke the back of the stock and *completely eliminated the significance of the next up field of 80,300 recorded on December 14, 1961.*

Eliminating the Significance of Some High Fields

The high field of 80,300 for Allied Chemical reached on December 14, 1961 was diluted in significance for two important reasons:

1. *The previous field reading had broken a long-term on-balance volume support* and this negated any bullishness which might have been attached to the next *immediate* up field.

2. The 80,300 on-balance volume of December 14th was 149,400 above the December 8th field, *completely out of line with all the other on-balance volume differentials between each field*, the widest previous differentials being 40,800 on the

upside between June 29th and August 4th and 93,900 on the downside between November 16th and December 8th. The upward leap in on-balance volume of December 14th shows up as an upside GAP (See Allied Chemical chart of on-balance volume) and here the *interpretation of gaps applies*. The move created nothing more than a large vacuum which was likely to be filled with a resumption of the declining field trend. The field interpretation of 80,300 on the upside under these circumstances was therefore considered to be unfavorable.

The Paradox of Trading

Now look again at the Field Theory as applied to Allied Chemical in the last table, noting the alternating up and down field designations. The DOWN designation at the top of the table was at a price of 58.13, the UP designation was at 65.75, the next DOWN designation was at 62.00, the next UP was at 62.25, the next DOWN was at 56.00 and so on. As you will recall, these field designations were recorded at the levels of *maximum volume pressure*. If a trader bought a stock on maximum volume pressure on the upside and sold a stock on maximum volume pressure on the downside he would eventually dissipate his entire trading capital. By waiting until volume pressures are at a maximum before acting, the trader tends to *play into the hands of mass psychology* and *THIS HE MUST AVOID DOING* if he wants to increase his success. One of the principles of successful trading is that the trader must try to do things in an *OPPOSITE MANNER*, going diametrically opposite to the natural emotions of greed and fear. These emotions show up in terms of stock trading volume. Now look at the next table, it being assumed here that the trader moves in the OPPOSITE direction of the short-term field designations:

He buys in the DOWN field at 58.13 and sells in the UP field at 65.75
Profit   7.63 points
He buys in the DOWN field at 62.00 and sells in the UP field at 62.25
Profit   .25 points
He buys in the DOWN field at 56.00 and sells in the UP field at 61.88
Profit   5.88 points
He buys in the DOWN field at 57.00 and sells in the UP field at 58.25
Profit   1.25 points
He buys in the DOWN field at 56.25 and sells in the UP field at 57.00
Profit   .75 points
He buys in the DOWN field at 53.00 and sells in the UP field at 55.50
Profit   2.50 points
Total points less commission: 18.25 points

The reason WHY the trader should act in the opposite direction to maximum on-balance volume readings and buy into the face of a DOWN designation is that he is attempting to catch the *last* DOWN in a DOWN field, a groups of DOWN designations. Obviously, the *last* DOWN would be a BUY point. Conversely, the *last* UP designation in an UP field would be a SELL point.

The Field theory of volume is a study of the undulating pressures on a stock in terms of volume waves. The trader tries to sell his stock into the face of buying pressure and to buy his stock in the face of selling pressure. His risk is that he may estimate his sell point short of the maximum buying pressure (the last UP in a series or field of UPS) and may estimate his buy point prior to the maximum selling pressure (the last DOWN in a series or field of DOWNS). In such errors of judgment the trader would sell a stock and it would still rise for awhile or we would buy a stock and it would still decline for awhile. This is where the knowledge and use of *on-balance volume support and resistance levels* as well as *on-balance volume gaps* can aid the trader in estimating the levels of maximum buying and selling pressures in terms of on-balance volume levels.

The value of the field theory is that a trader is in a position to move with greater confidence in the stocks having a healthy long-term rising on-balance volume *trend* and can be more careful in those stocks showing unfavorable falling field trends.

How to Give a Stock the On-Balance Volume Test

After recording on-balance volume figures on a stock long enough to present a reasonable amount of past performance, several tests can be performed. These tests are ennumerated as follows:
  1. Check out OBV at each price level.
  2. Determine whether the stock is under accumulation or distribution
  3. The one-day reversal
  4. Does the OBV support the price on price breakouts?
  5. Signs of longer term strength or weakness.
  6. Record longer term support and resistance levels.
  7. Check out OBV against price "lines".
  8. The zig-zag test.
Additional tests might include:
  9. Checking on-balance volume moving average
  10. On-balance volume "angles".
The latter two tests are unnecessary but might prove interesting to market theoreticians. These tests are described as follows:

1. *Check out OBV at each price level.* Usually a stock provides some technical signal when it is ready to decline from a high level. It is useful to check out OBV readings at each *price* support level. Going back now to the Allied Chemical figures we can note that as the price of the stock approached the high of 65.75 reached on August 3rd it had several one-day retreats. These little price retreats serve as very

minor support levels which could be compared with on-balance volume. On July 24th the price of the stock retreated for one day to 62.75 and the OBV reading stood at 10,800. The stock then went on to reach 65.75 and thereafter fell back to 62.75 on August 15th. On August 15th the OBV stood at 6,700, well under the 10,800 of July 24th while the price of the stock was the same at 62.75. This was a sign that the stock was weakening.

The lowest closing price for Allied Chemical between June 20th and the time of the 65.75 high on August 3rd was 58.13 on June 29th. That 58.13 price became an important support. That price was broken on September 25th when the stock declined to 56.00. However, in comparing the OBV levels with the June 29th reading of minus 15,000, we find that the break on September 25th only carried OBV down to minus 1,100. This is what a trader would be looking for, *a chance to move in the opposite direction of the crowd.* The stock breaks through to a new price low but OBV is *higher* than on the last price low and the trader suspects that this is the last reading in a DOWN field. He *buys the stock* while the obvious appearance to the majority is one of weakness, the stock breaking price support. The stock advanced almost 6 points over the next nine trading sessions.

It is important then to compare OBV readings with various similar price levels as this indicates whether the stock is weaker or stronger technically at those repeating price levels.

2. *Determine whether the stock is under accumulation or distribution.* If a stock is under *accumulation* you will find that on-balance volume figures usually continue to *trend* higher over a good period of time. You will note the span of on-balance volume readings in the case of Allied Chemical between June and November 1961. The OBV remained in a narrow span between *minus* 15,000 and plus 28,800. That is too small a span for a relatively active stock over a period of five months to suggest any kind of accumulation. When the stock on-balance volume fell under minus 15,000 on November 24th then something distinctly was different. Everything that went before could be considered to be *distribution.*

3. *The one-day reversal.* Looking over the Allied Chemical table, you can note several instances where the UP and DOWN designations are right next to each other. This is called a *one-day reversal* and is a useful thing for the day-to-day trader to know about. Usually a stock will go for a few days in the direction of the reversal. If an UP is immediately followed by a DOWN designation the trader might consider selling his stock and buying it back when the on-balance volume reaches a support level. If a DOWN is immediately followed by an UP designation then this is a day-to-day buying opportunity. This is only a day-to-day trading indication.

In the Allied Chemical table a DOWN designation immediately followed an UP on June 23rd and this proved to be a short-term SELL signal. On October 18th an UP immediately followed a DOWN designation and the stock rose the next day.

In that instance the trade would not have been profitable but the trader would have had ample opportunity to cut his small loss short. On November 17th a DOWN immediately followed an UP designation and that proved to be an excellent selling opportunity. All of these one-day reversals do not work out but the *majority* of them do for the day-to-day trader and this gives the informed trader the benefit of the odds.

4. *Does the OBV support the price on price breakouts?* Study the relationship of OBV to price and see where one gets "out of gear" with the other. Bullish looking on-balance volume figures are those which tend to move slowly but *persistently* higher. Note in the Allied Chemical table the fact that it took twenty four market sessions to move from a low on-balance volume of minus 15,000 to a high of 25,800 between June and August. However, in late September on-balance volume turned at the minus 1,100 level and moved up to a new high of 28,800 by October 6th. This move took place in only *nine sessions.* This energy was expended *too rapidly* and the price of the stock was *sluggish* on that rally, only reaching 61.88. That was another sign of technical weakness, the fact that OBV and price could not get back "into gear". You will note that the differential between minus 15,000 and plus 25,800 is 43,800 shares of total upside OBV. The total upside OBV on the later move from minus 1,100 to 28,800 was 29,900 shares, so this was another way of showing the loss of upside energy in the stock.

5. *Signs of longer term strength or weakness.* The first important thing to determine in looking at a table of on-balance volume figures is whether the stock is moving above long-term support levels and whether it is moving above important previous OBV resistance levels. When Allied Chemical on-balance volume moved under minus 15,000 the long-term trend had definitely moved down. The consistent inability to move above 28,800 after October 6th, 1961 was a forerunner to that weakness.

6. *Record longer term support and resistance levels.* It is important to record and fix firmly in your mind what the long-term on-balance volume support level in a stock is. As long as on-balance volume is moving above that level the trader who might have mistimed a trade might still be extricated from his position profitably. Now look at the previous high point reached by on-balance volume. If the stock persists in recording lower OBV levels than this for a good period of time then there is a danger that the stock may sometime with little warning move down to the critical support levels, perhaps without holding there.

7. *Check out OBV against price "lines."* A "line" is formed when a stock price tends to move in a very narrow range for a period of time. This may be a "base" or it may be a "top". It is up to on-balance volume to detect which. *This is when OBV is most effective.* Ascending OBV would point to the "line" being a base and the trader and investor would be most interested in these situations. Descending OBV would point to the "line" being a top and this would prompt some selling.

8. *The Zig-Zag test*. It is important to count the swings on the zig-zagging changes in on-balance volume readings. Below are listed various combinations of zig-zags and how they should be interpreted:

The Simple Zig-Zag

It takes a minimum of *three* swings or legs to create a simple zig-zag. This would be defined as an advance-decline-advance, where the last advance ends up higher than the first. A simple downward zig-zag would simply be a decline-advance-decline, where the last decline ends at a level lower than the first. In the case of the simple 3-day upward zig-zag on on-balance volume, an ability for the stock to continue moving upward is very healthy. If the reverse is mostly happening, then the stock is acting in a *weak manner*. Allied Chemical showed a record of mostly *reversing the direction* immediately following upward 3-day OBV zig-zags.

If the stock reverses after a simple 3-day downward zig-zag it means the stock is still healthy. You will note that Allied Chemical rose after the 3-day downward zig-zag which ended on July 24th, 1961. This meant that the stock was still technically healthy at that time. The next 3-day simple downward zig-zag in OBV occurred on October 11th, 1961. You will note that this time a further decline ensued. This showed that the stock was *weakening*.

The simple three-swing zig-zag also takes the form of lasting several days. Here again the test can be given the stock. If the stock continues to move upward after an upward zig-zag in OBV it may be construed showing technical strength. If a stock continues to move downward after a downward OBV zig-zag it is showing technical weakness.

The Compound Zig-Zag

The compound zig-zag consists of five swings, an upward compound being an advance-decline-advance-decline-advance, where each advance is higher than the previous one and each decline level is higher than the previous one. Such a combination is a very bullish one when the last advance penetrates a long-term OBV resistance level. A declining compound zig-zag is a serious warning of weakness when OBV falls under a major support.

The Trend

Anything in *excess* of five swings creates a *trend*.

Field Zig-Zags

One is less likely to be whipsawed by putting greater stress on the fields, the clusters of UP and DOWN designations. Here the zig-zags have greater meaning.

(a) *Simple*—   Easily capable of being reversed. Such reversals suggest important approaching weakness. Note the change in Allied

Chemical in the table after the simple upside field zig-zag
was completed on August 4th, 1961.

(b) *Compound*— A rising compound zig-zag in fields is bullish only if OBV
goes through long-term resistance level, otherwise it offers
a selling opportunity. A declining compound zig-zag is only
bearish at that point if it goes through long-term OBV
support level, otherwise it offers a buying opportunity.

(c) *Trend*— This means that OBV fields have zig-zagged higher or lower
by more than five swings. These have gone as far as nine
swings but there is a very strong tendency for MAJOR RE-
VERSAL OF TREND AFTER A NINTH SWING.

Additional Tests

9. *Checking on-balance volume moving average.* These tests are not entirely necessary, being rather time consuming to prepare, but they are included here for the
benefit of market theoreticians. You will recall the long-term selling signal in Allied
Chemical when OBV moved under minus 15,000 in November. Most people are
curious to see whether a moving average adds to the effectiveness of a new market
tool. Below is the Allied Chemical table showing just the OBV figures with a 10-day
moving average.

ALLIED CHEMICAL

(June to December 1961)

10-Day Moving Average
of On-Balance
Volume

Date	Average OBV		Date	Average OBV	
July 3	−6,300		July 24	10,120	UP
July 5	−6,370		July 25	10,900	UP
July 6	−5,970		July 26	12,270	UP
July 7	−5,960		July 27	13,000	UP
July 10	−4,980		July 28	13,560	UP
July 11	−3,820		July 31	14,230	UP
July 12	−2,580		Aug. 1	15,280	UP
July 13	−880		Aug. 2	15,250	
July 14	1,570	UP	Aug. 3	16,520	UP
July 17	4,190	UP	Aug. 4	17,630	UP
July 18	5,750	UP	Aug. 7	18,420	UP
July 19	7,530	UP	Aug. 8	18,100	
July 20	8,600	UP	Aug. 9	17,180	
July 21	9,830	UP	Aug. 10	17,050	

Date	Average OBV		Date	Average OBV	
Aug. 11	16,810		Oct. 13	20,180	UP
Aug. 14	16,200		Oct. 16	21,240	UP
Aug. 15	14,880	DOWN	Oct. 17	21,580	UP
Aug. 16	13,230	DOWN	Oct. 18	21,570	
Aug. 17	11,350	DOWN	Oct. 19	21,570	
Aug. 18	9,830	DOWN	Oct. 20	20,760	
Aug. 21	9,360	DOWN	Oct. 23	20,370	
Aug. 22	10,190		Oct. 24	19,850	
Aug. 23	10,920		Oct. 25	19,940	
Aug. 24	10,830		Oct. 26	19,960	
Aug. 25	10,310		Oct. 27	19,890	
Aug. 28	9,880		Oct. 30	19,310	DOWN
Aug. 29	9,340	DOWN	Oct. 31	19,090	DOWN
Aug. 30	9,920		Nov. 1	18,050	DOWN
Aug. 31	10,150		Nov. 2	16,960	DOWN
Sept. 1	10,020		Nov. 3	16,050	DOWN
Sept. 5	8,970	DOWN	Nov. 6	15,930	DOWN
Sept. 6	7,660	DOWN	Nov. 8	16,500	
Sept. 7	7,500	DOWN	Nov. 9	16,810	
Sept. 8	8,070		Nov. 10	17,030	
Sept. 11	8,460		Nov. 13	17,100	
Sept. 12	9,530		Nov. 14	18,110	
Sept. 13	10,700	UP	Nov. 15	18,680	
Sept. 14	11,040	UP	Nov. 16	20,360	UP
Sept. 15	11,270	UP	Nov. 17	21,060	UP
Sept. 18	11,080		Nov. 20	21,760	UP
Sept. 19	11,290	UP	Nov. 21	20,800	
Sept. 20	11,750	UP	Nov. 22	17,890	
Sept. 21	11,040	DOWN	Nov. 24	13,670	DOWN
Sept. 22	9,880	DOWN	Nov. 27	11,300	DOWN
Sept. 25	8,630	DOWN	Nov. 28	10,650	DOWN
Sept. 26	7,290	DOWN	Nov. 29	7,450	DOWN
Sept. 27	6,540	DOWN	Nov. 30	4,550	DOWN
Sept. 28	6,390	DOWN	Dec. 1	1,750	DOWN
Sept. 29	6,250	DOWN	Dec. 4	−1,530	DOWN
Oct. 2	6,270		Dec. 5	−5,370	DOWN
Oct. 3	6,970		Dec. 6	−8,160	DOWN
Oct. 4	7,790		Dec. 7	−11,330	DOWN
Oct. 5	9,430		Dec. 8	−16,630	DOWN
Oct. 6	11,870	UP	Dec. 11	−20,040	DOWN
Oct. 9	14,260	UP	Dec. 12	−16,530	
Oct. 10	16,620	UP	Dec. 13	−7,550	
Oct. 11	18,280	UP	Dec. 14	1,430	
Oct. 12	19,530	UP	Dec. 15	6,940	

Here the long-term OBV support of minus 6,370 was not penetrated on the downside until December 6th, 1961. The conclusion in this case warrants discarding the necessity of using an on-balance volume moving average. The raw OBV figures are usually enough.

10. *On-Balance volume "angles."* As long as a consistent chart scale is employed one can compare the angles of ascent and descent in OBV readings. An angle is a function of motion and one will find a definite relationship between an angle of ascent and the angle of retreat which follows as well as between the angle of descent and the angle of rebound which follows.

Completing the Picture on Allied Chemical

The OBV analysis showed Allied Chemical falling under long-term supports in late 1961. The following charts and tables show what followed in 1962.

ALLIED CHEMICAL

(December 1961 to August 1962)

Date	On-Balance Volume		Price	Date	On-Balance Volume		Price
Dec. 18	62,400		55.50	Jan. 19	68,400		53.25
Dec. 19	57,500		54.88	Jan. 22	60,800	DOWN	52.63
Dec. 20	50,600	DOWN	54.50	Jan. 23	60,800	DOWN	52.63
Dec. 21	42,700	DOWN	54.25	Jan. 24	53,500	DOWN	52.13
Dec. 22	49,300		54.50	Jan. 25	47,300	DOWN	52.00
Dec. 26	49,300		54.50	Jan. 26	39,100	DOWN	51.50
Dec. 27	49,300		54.50	Jan. 29	43,900		51.63
Dec. 28	57,200		54.63	Jan. 30	49,100		52.37
Dec. 29	66,800	UP	55.63	Jan. 31	58,200		53.13
Jan. 2	60,700		55.50	Feb. 1	58,200		53.13
Jan. 3,	73,200	UP	56.13	Feb. 2	63,700		53.25
Jan. 4	84,400	UP	56.50	Feb. 5	71,200	UP	53.75
Jan. 5	78,000		55.37	Feb. 6	77,000	UP	53.63 ex.
Jan. 8	91,600	UP	56.63	Feb. 7	85,600	UP	54.25
Jan. 9	82,200		56.50	Feb. 8	96,300	UP	54.37
Jan. 10	76,400	DOWN	55.37	Feb. 9	91,000		54.13
Jan. 11	76,400	DOWN	55.37	Feb. 12	91,000		54.13
Jan. 12	71,900	DOWN	54.88	Feb. 13	83,800		53.75
Jan. 15	66,400	DOWN	53.88	Feb. 14	77,800		52.63
Jan. 16	62,500	DOWN	53.13	Feb. 15	86,000		52.75
Jan. 17	68,400		53.25	Feb. 16	71,900	DOWN	52.37
Jan. 18	68,400		53.25	Feb. 19	81,900		52.63

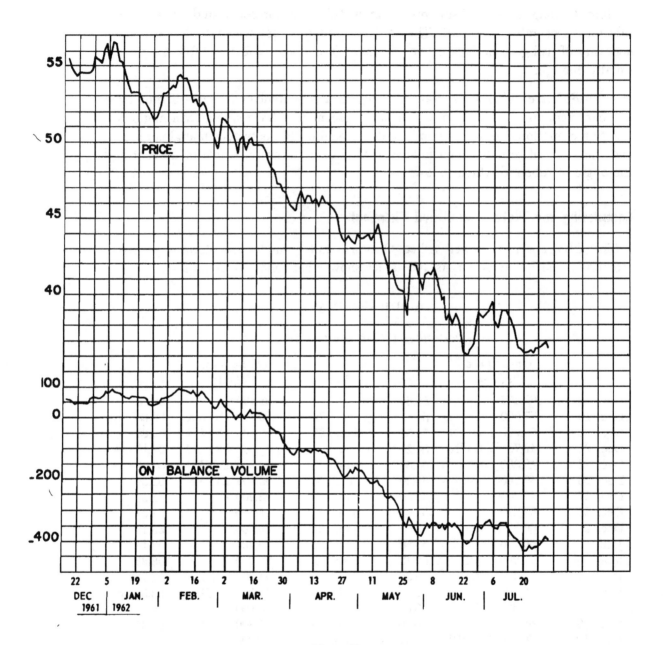

Chart 40

Date	On-Balance Volume		Price	Date	On-Balance Volume		Price
Feb. 20	73,300		52.37	Apr. 27	−195,100 DOWN		43.50
Feb. 21	60,800	DOWN	51.37	Apr. 30	−184,900		43.88
Feb. 23	44,800	DOWN	50.50	May 1	−170,000		44.50
Feb. 26	27,900	DOWN	49.63	May 2	−181,100		44.37
Feb. 27	42,300		50.50	May 3	−165,000	UP	45.00
Feb. 28	57,800		51.63	May 4	−170,800		44.63
Mar. 1	43,500		51.50	May 7	−170,800		44.63
Mar. 2	33,300		51.25	May 8	−189,000 DOWN		43.88
Mar. 5	21,200	DOWN	50.75	May 9	−202,300 DOWN		43.00
Mar. 6	8,600	DOWN	50.00	May 10	−218,200 DOWN		42.50
Mar. 7	− 6,500	DOWN	49.25	May 11	−218,200 DOWN		42.50
Mar. 8	900		50.13	May 14	−204,500		44.63
Mar. 9	10,000		50.37	May 15	−221,500 DOWN		43.88
Mar. 12	− 300		49.50	May 16	−237,600 DOWN		42.88
Mar. 13	10,500	UP	50.13	May 17	−255,400 DOWN		42.25
Mar. 14	27,900	UP	50.25	May 18	−269,300 DOWN		41.25
Mar. 15	13,800		49.88	May 21	−257,300		41.63
Mar. 16	13,800		49.88	May 22	−267,900		40.88
Mar. 19	13,800		49.88	May 23	−288,400 DOWN		40.37
Mar. 20	13,800		49.88	May 24	−310,600 DOWN		40.25
Mar. 21	1,900		49.25	May 25	−330,600 DOWN		40.13
Mar. 22	− 8,600	DOWN	48.75	May 28	−355,200 DOWN		38.63
Mar. 23	− 27,600	DOWN	48.37	May 29	−324,200		42.00
Mar. 26	− 35,900	DOWN	48.00	May 31	−352,300		41.88
Mar. 27	− 48,000	DOWN	47.37	June 1	−379,500 DOWN		41.25
Mar. 28	− 48,000	DOWN	47.37	June 4	−386,800 DOWN		40.25
Mar. 29	− 73,500	DOWN	46.88	June 5	−367,200		41.25
Mar. 30	− 81,900	DOWN	46.75	June 6	−345,300		41.37
Apr. 2	−100,200	DOWN	46.00	June 7	−360,000		41.25
Apr. 3	−114,300	DOWN	45.75	June 8	−341,900	UP	41.75
Apr. 4	−123,100	DOWN	45.50	June 11	−347,700		40.50
Apr. 5	−109,700		46.37	June 12	−365,400 DOWN		39.63
Apr. 6	−100,000		46.75	June 13	−349,500		39.88
Apr. 9	−108,300		46.00	June 14	−366,300 DOWN		38.25
Apr. 10	−100,500		46.50	June 15	−342,400	UP	38.75
Apr. 11	−100,500		46.50	June 18	−352,800		38.00
Apr. 12	−108,300		46.00	June 19	−344,700		38.75
Apr. 13	−102,700		46.37	June 20	−352,600		38.37
Apr. 16	−112,300	DOWN	45.75	June 21	−365,900 DOWN		37.50
Apr. 17	−104,700		46.50	June 22	−394,300 DOWN		36.25
Apr. 18	−116,600	DOWN	46.00	June 25	−412,900 DOWN		36.00
Apr. 19	−116,600	DOWN	46.00	June 26	−401,700		36.37
Apr. 23	−127,300	DOWN	45.63	June 27	−389,900		36.75
Apr. 24	−141,200	DOWN	45.37	June 28	−359,800		38.00
Apr. 25	−162,800	DOWN	44.13	June 29	−348,700		38.88
Apr. 26	−175,900	DOWN	43.75	July 2	−360,400		38.50

Date	On-Balance Volume		Price	Date	On-Balance Volume		Price
July 3	−349,000		39.00	July 19	−415,600	DOWN	36.50
July 5	−338,600	UP	39.50	July 20	−434,800	DOWN	36.25
July 6	−352,200		38.25	July 23	−434,800	DOWN	36.25
July 9	−364,000	DOWN	37.88	July 24	−417,200		36.37
July 10	−344,800		39.00	July 25	−432,200		36.13
July 11	−344,800		39.00	July 26	−421,800		36.50
July 12	−344,800		39.00	July 27	−421,800		36.50
July 13	−356,900		38.88	July 30	−403,700	UP	36.75
July 16	−370,900	DOWN	38.00	July 31	−380,500	UP	37.00
July 17	−386,800	DOWN	37.50	Aug. 1	−397,600		36.50
July 18	−399,200	DOWN	36.63				

Allied Chemical in 1962

The first few months of 1962 for Allied Chemical were prefaced by a *major long-term sell signal* when OBV moved under the June 1961 lows in November of that year. The very fact that OBV has given a long-term signal *colors the actions of the short term trader as well*. He is more careful about being tempted to buy into the DOWN designations since the field trend is unfavorable. The trader finds it profitable on the short side and this is accentuated in the figures when OBV fell under the December 8, 1961 low on March 29, 1962. That was the second recorded long-term downside penetration of OBV support, a very significant sign of weakness. Below is shown the field trend for Allied Chemical in the 1962 market:

ALLIED CHEMICAL

December 1961 to August 1962

"The Field Theory"

Interpretation of Field	Field Maximum On-Balance Volume	Type of Field	Price	Date
Doubtful	42,700	DOWN	54.25	Dec. 21, 1961
Rising	91,600	UP	56.63	Jan. 8, 1962
Doubtful	39,100	DOWN	51.50	Jan. 26, 1962
Doubtful	96,300	UP	54.37	Feb. 8, 1962
Doubtful	− 6,500	DOWN	49.25	Mar. 7, 1962
Doubtful	27,900	UP	50.25	Mar. 14, 1962
Falling	−195,100	DOWN	43.50	Apr. 27, 1962
Falling	−165,000	UP	45.00	May 3, 1962
Falling	−386,800	DOWN	40.25	June 4, 1962
Falling	−341,900	UP	41.75	June 8, 1962
Doubtful	−366,300	DOWN	38.25	June 14, 1962
Doubtful	−342,400	UP	38.75	June 15, 1962
Falling	−412,900	DOWN	36.00	June 25, 1962
Doubtful	−338,600	UP	39.50	July 5, 1962
Doubtful	−434,800	DOWN	36.25	July 23, 1962
Doubtful	−380,500	UP	37.00	July 31, 1962

Note the large number of doubtful field trend interpretations after the one rising designation. When a large number of doubtfuls follows a rising interpretation it usually implies that the next change from doubtful will be a falling designation. Conversely, when a large number of doubtfuls follow falling interpretations then the stock may be actually turning up and a rising interpretation could be expected to follow. The signals described here of coming change requires *three or more consecutive doubtfuls*. On this basis it was apparent that Allied Chemical had signalled a long-term change for the better by July 31, 1962, three doubtful interpretations following a falling trend interpretation. This signal occurred only one point off the June 25th price low of 36.

When to Buy and Sell Using On-Balance Volume Signals

A trader can either try to go in and out of a stock on very short term trades using OBV signals or can (usually more profitably) play for the wider swings on a trend basis using the OBV field theory. Investors and longer term traders will not be interested in the very minor day-to-day OBV signals but will restrict their use of OBV to the field theory. Below is a compilation of the volume signals both traders and investors will find the most useful.

The buying and selling signals based on on-balance volume listed below are *graded* in order of their *effectiveness*.

Nine OBV Buying Signals for the Day-to-Day Trader

1. Buy into DOWN designations when the field trend is rising.
2. Buy when price of stock sharply outpaces OBV on the downside.
3. Buy when OBV records unusual day-to-day decline.
4. Buy on first UP in a rising field trend.
5. Buy into the first DOWN designation following three intermittent clusters of DOWN designations. (A cluster is defined as three or more consecutive similar designations)
6. Buy when UP designation immediately follows a DOWN designation (only when field trend is favorable)
7. Buy when UP designation follows an UP designation with several undesignated sessions in between.
8. Buy after several days of DOWNS if the OBV is still above an important support level.
9. Buy when OBV breaks through long-term resistance level providing there have only been one or two UPS.

Nine OBV Selling Signals for the Day-to-Day Trader

1. Sell into UP designations when the field trend is falling.
2. Sell when price of stock sharply outpaces OBV on the upside.
3. Sell when OBV records unusual day-to-day advance.

4. Sell on first DOWN in a falling field trend.
5. Sell into the first UP designation following three intermittent clusters of UP designations. (A cluster is defined as three or more consecutive similar designations).
6. Sell when DOWN designation immediately follows an UP designation (only when field trend is unfavorable)
7. Sell when DOWN designation follows a DOWN designation with several undesignated sessions in between.
8. Sell after several days of UPS if the OBV is still below an important resistance level.
9. Sell when OBV breaks under a long-term support level, providing there have been only one or two DOWNS.

Memorize these trading signals as you would a set of bridge rules. Pretty soon, with a little practice, the recognition of them will tend to come automatically. From your own experience you will increasingly note which ones are the most helpful.

Applying all *18 signals*, let us see how they would have worked out on Allied Chemical between June 1961 and August 1962:

THE TRADING RECORD

Date and Action	Signal	Profit	Loss	Cumulative
BUY June 30, 1961 at 58.75	B-3			
BUY July 17, 1961 at 62.13	B-7			
BUY July 27, 1961 at 63.63	B-4			
SELL Aug. 4, 1961 at 65.75	S-3	7.00	- 0 -	7.00
BUY Aug. 9, 1961 at 63.50	B-3			
SELL Aug. 16, 1961 at 62.00	S-7		1.50	5.50
BUY Aug. 17, 1961 at 63.00	B-3			
BUY Aug. 29, 1961 at 60.00	B-2			
BUY Sep. 8, 1961 at 62.25	B-7			
SELL Sep. 11, 1961 at 61.13	S-8		1.88	3.63
BUY Sep. 26, 1961 at 57.25	B-2, B-8 (These cancel.			
SELL Sep. 26, 1961 at 57.25	S-4 NO action)			
BUY Oct. 3, 1961 at 58.75	B-2			
SELL Oct. 6, 1961 at 61.88	S-1	3.13		6.75
SELL Oct. 20, 1961 at 58.50	S-8			
BUY Oct. 26, 1961 at 58.00	B-7			
SELL Oct. 31, 1961 at 56.75	S-4		1.25	5.50
BUY Nov. 2, 1961 at 57.25	B-8			
SELL Nov. 9, 1961 at 57.75	S-3	.50		6.00
SELL Nov. 10, 1961 at 57.00	S-1			
BUY Nov. 17, 1961 at 56.00	B-7 (These cancel.			
SELL Nov. 17, 1961 at 56.00	S-8 NO action)			
SELL Nov. 20, 1961 at 56.00	S-6			
BUY Nov. 22, 1961 at 53.50	B-8			

Date and Action	Signal	Profit	Loss	Cumulative
SELL Nov. 24, 1961 at 53.00	S-4		.50	5.50
BUY Nov. 27, 1961 at 54.13	B-3			
BUY Nov. 30, 1961 at 54.00	B-3			
SELL Dec. 5, 1961 at 53.63	S-7		.38	5.13
SELL Dec. 6, 1961 at 53.63	S-9			
BUY Dec. 11, 1961 at 53.25	B-3			
SELL Dec. 13, 1961 at 55.50	S-3 (These cancel.			
BUY Dec. 13, 1961 at 55.50	B-9 NO action)			
SELL Dec. 14, 1961 at 55.50	S-3	2.25		7.38
SELL Dec. 15, 1961 at 55.25	S-1			
BUY Jan. 5, 1962 at 55.37	B-4, B-9			
SELL Jan. 9, 1962 at 56.50	S-3	1.13		8.50
SELL Jan. 23, 1962 at 52.63	S-7			
BUY Jan. 26, 1962 at 51.50	B-1, B-8			
BUY Feb. 26, 1962 at 49.63	B-8			
BUY Feb. 27, 1962 at 50.50	B-3			
SELL Mar. 1, 1962 at 51.50	S-3	- - -		8.50
SELL Mar. 6, 1962 at 50.00	S-7			
SELL Mar. 15, 1962 at 49.88	S-3, S-8			
SELL Mar. 30, 1962 at 46.75	S-4, S-9 (These cancel.			
BUY Mar. 30, 1962 at 46.75	B-3 NO action.)			
SELL Apr. 17, 1962 at 46.50	S-7			
SELL Apr. 24, 1962 at 45.37	S-9			
SELL May 4, 1962 at 44.63	S-1			
SELL May 10, 1962 at 42.50	S-9			
SELL May 15, 1962 at 43.88	S-9			
SELL May 24, 1962 at 40.25	S-9			
BUY May 29, 1962 at 42.00	B-3			
SELL May 31, 1962 at 41.88	S-2, S-3		.13	8.38
BUY June 4, 1962 at 40.25	B-5 (These cancel.			
SELL June 4, 1962 at 40.25	S-9 NO action)			
SELL June 11, 1962 at 40.50	S-1			
SELL June 18, 1962 at 38.00	S-3			
SELL June 25, 1962 at 36.00	S-4, S-9			
SELL June 29, 1962 at 38.88	S-3			
SELL July 6, 1962 at 38.25	S-1			
SELL July 17, 1962 at 37.50	S-7			
BUY July 19, 1962 at 36.50	B-8			
SELL July 20, 1962 at 36.25	S-9		.25	8.13

Footnotes on trading record: Action is taken the next day since the signal is not seen until the closing of the day before. Considering the fact that Allied Chemical is not a particularly good trading stock, it is interesting to note the results (considering the fact that the trader is theoretically only trading the long side of the market) turned out to be positive using the daily OBV signals. This was a stock getting ready to make a major decline and the fact that the daily OBV signals kept the trader out of the major downswing is encouraging evidence of the value of these volume signals. The trader would have been restricting losses to very minor proportions. Now, if the trader executed a short sale position on the sell signals, he would have done considerably better. Note how the buy signals of March 20th and June 4th were cancelled. This would have kept a trader on the short side from March 1st through May 29th when the stock declined from 51.50 to 42.00. The rather acid test of the effectiveness of day-to-day trading OBV signals is the fact that here was a stock in the throes of making a major decline and yet OBV signals being followed by a trader following the *long* position resulted in a gain. Recognizing the field trend as being a weak one, the trader would be leaning more in the direction of short selling. By following the above OBV signals and going short on each SELL signal the potential profit would have been 30.50 points (less commissions), a considerable difference from the 8.13 points on the long side.

What Does the Longer Term Trader Do?

Longer term traders skip over some of the signals which only have day-to-day significance and act upon the more important ones such as the B-1's and S-1's. From this longer term standpoint the B-9 and S-9 signals become more important. The *trend* of the stock now becoms the most important thing the longer term trader and investor thinks about and that trend is best expressed from the OBV standpoint in terms of the *field* trend. The longer term trader could have sold Allied Chemical short on the October 6th S-1 signal at 61.88 and covered the short sale on the Jan. 26th B-1 signal at 51.50. The investor, on the other hand, would *restrict his decision to buy or to sell to the long-term OBV signals,* buying when OBV moves above long-term resistance levels at a depressed price level and selling when OBV moves under a long-term support level at advanced price levels.

Long Term Trader

Signals

He follows day-to-day OBV signals but only acts on signals #1, #4, #8 and #9.

The Investor

Signals

Only BUYS when OBV moves above long-term resistance at a depressed price level
Only SELLS when OBV moves under long-term support at an advanced price level

Example of How to Handle the Long-Term Signals

Allied Chemical OBV moved under the June 29, 1961 support of minus 15,000 on November 24th of that year, OBV moving down to minus 16,100. *That was the*

OBV long-term sell signal. Additional confirmations occurred on December 5th at Minus 19,800, March 29th at minus 73,500 and April 23rd at minus 127,300.

The July 5th, 1962 UP reading of minus 338,600 became the upside OBV resistance level and a move above that on a rising field after August 1962 *became the OBV long-term buy signal.* The investor should look for the rising field trend and think in terms of the importance of the simple compound and trend field zig-zags as previously discussed. Obviously a rising field trend of long duration at advanced price levels becomes increasingly suspicious and susceptible to change while a long-term falling field trend which has carried the price to depressed levels is close to a change for the better. The use of OBV tends to put the finger on those changes. The longer-term handling of OBV also involves a closer association of such indicators as short interest, 200-day line position etc., this discussed again later on in the book.

The Summing up

Here you have seen the complete OBV analysis to the first of the Dow-Jones stocks during a critical period. You are now in position to set up a table of on-balance volume readings with the UP and DOWN designations. You can go beyond this now and apply the "field" theory to determine whether a stock is in a rising, doubtful or falling phase. You have seen the importance of buying into "surface" weakness when the field trend is healthy and selling into "surface" strength when the field trend is weak. You should have gained a new insight into the differences which exist when one is taking the day-to-day trading viewpoint as against the long-term viewpoint. You now may realize where previous personal trading failures have stemmed from, most of those being the natural inclination to buy into strength and sell into weakness. The use of OBV now should give you a new insight into the potentials for more successful trading.

You are now familiar with how to give a stock the OBV test, checking out OBV at each price level, determining whether the stock is under accumulation or distribution, acting on one-day reversals, recognizing signs of long-term strength or weakness, recording longer term support and resistance levels, checking out OBV against price "lines", counting the "zig-zags" as well as checking OBV moving averages and volume "angles."

All these things have been specifically expressed previously in terms of BUY and SELL signals for the day-to-day trader, the longer term trader and the investor, a trading record presented to show the effectiveness of these OBV signals. The next chapter shows the practical application of OBV theory to another Dow-Jones stock, Aluminum Company of America (Alcoa).

Chapter Five

Aluminum Company of America

Another example of on-balance volume used to indicate possible price movements

What You Are about to Learn

No two stocks are alike in their price movements but the use of on-balance volume signals can help to reduce vastly the number of surprises to both the trader and investor, providing earlier warnings of strong and weak price patterns. We now move on to Alcoa, the second stock in the Dow-Jones Industrial Average. In the presentation the same order will be followed. First comes the OBV Table covering the June to December 1961 period, the table showing the "field" trend, the second OBV table covering the period from December 1961 through to August 1962, the second "field" trend table and finally the application of the specific BUY and SELL OBV signals in the form of a trading record. Charts covering these periods are again included.

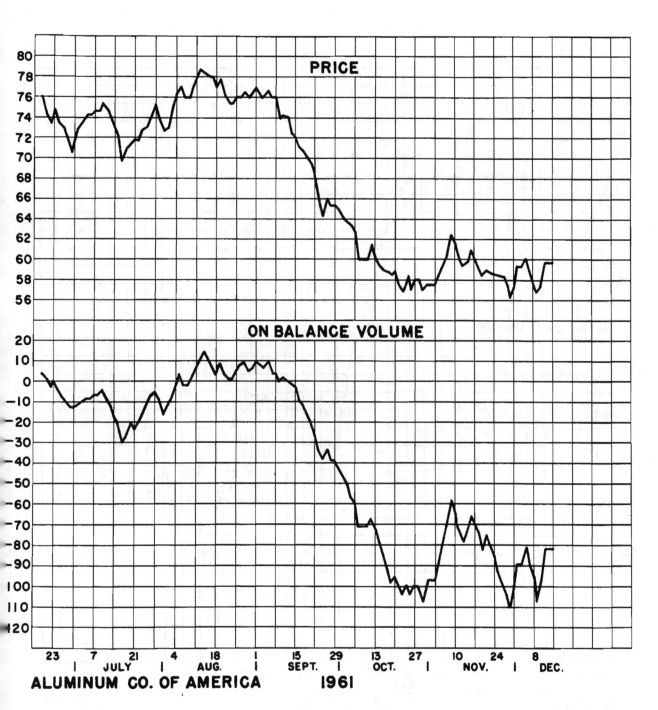

PRICE

ON BALANCE VOLUME

ALUMINUM CO. OF AMERICA   1961

Chart 41

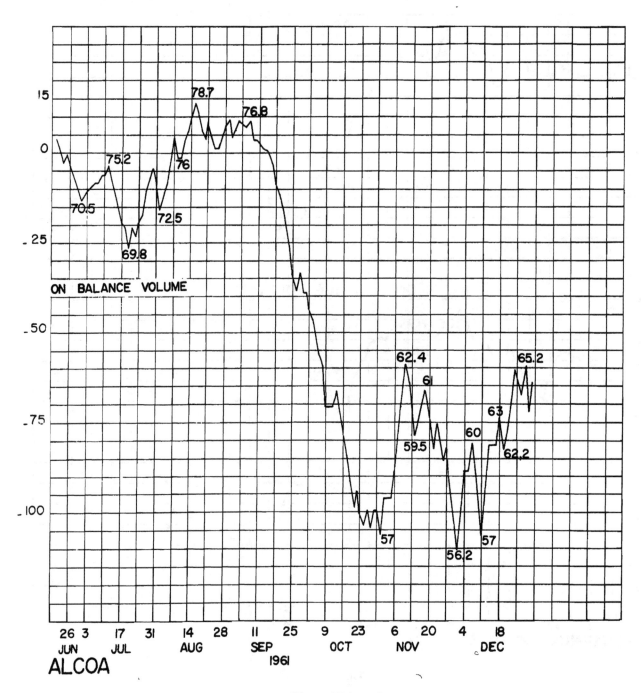

ON BALANCE VOLUME

ALCOA

Chart 41 (cont.)

Alcoa and OBV

Here is stock which went into sharp decline long before the general market break of 1962. A glance at the above charts shows the swift breaking of supports by the OBV line. A recording of those on-balance volume figures would have enabled investors to sell out at high figures. Below is the OBV table.

ALUMINUM COMPANY OF AMERICA
(June to December 1961)

Date	On-Balance Volume		Price	Date	On-Balance Volume		Price
June 20	4,300		76.00	Aug. 7	4,300	UP	77.13
June 21	1,600		74.25	Aug. 8	− 1,800		76.00
June 22	− 2,900		73.50	Aug. 9	− 1,800		76.00
June 23	− 300		74.75	Aug. 10	3,400		76.88
June 26	− 3,400	DOWN	73.50	Aug. 11	5,800	UP	78.00
June 27	− 6,600	DOWN	73.00	Aug. 14	10,000	UP	78.75
June 28	− 9,900	DOWN	71.75	Aug. 15	13,600	UP	78.50 ex.
June 29	− 12,900	DOWN	70.50	Aug. 16	11,000		78.13
June 30	− 12,500		71.50	Aug. 17	6,200		78.00
July 3	− 10,900		73.00	Aug. 18	4,400		77.13
July 5	− 8,300		74.25	Aug. 21	8,600		77.75
July 6	− 8,300		74.25	Aug. 22	4,300	DOWN	76.25
July 7	− 6,100		74.63	Aug. 23	1,200	DOWN	75.50
July 10	− 6,100		74.63	Aug. 24	1,200	DOWN	75.50
July 11	− 3,700		75.25	Aug. 25	5,000		76.00
July 12	− 8,600		74.50	Aug. 28	7,500		76.13
July 13	− 12,500		73.75	Aug. 29	9,000	UP	76.63
July 14	− 16,600	DOWN	73.13	Aug. 30	4,600		76.13
July 17	− 19,900	DOWN	72.25	Aug. 31	6,300		76.38
July 18	− 29,200	DOWN	69.75	Sep. 1	9,300	UP	76.88
July 19	− 26,500		71.00	Sep. 5	7,400		76.00
July 20	− 20,900		71.25	Sep. 6	9,100		76.75
July 21	− 23,200		70.75	Sep. 7	3,500	DOWN	76.00
July 24	− 19,800	UP	71.75	Sep. 8	3,500	DOWN	76.00
July 25	− 17,300	UP	72.75	Sep. 11	- 0 -	DOWN	74.00
July 26	− 10,400	UP	73.00	Sep. 12	1,900		74.25
July 27	− 7,400	UP	74.25	Sep. 13	500		74.00
July 28	− 4,700	UP	75.25	Sep. 14	− 1,100	DOWN	72.50
July 31	− 8,300		74.00	Sep. 15	− 3,400	DOWN	72.25
Aug. 1	− 15,900		72.75	Sep. 18	− 8,700	DOWN	71.25
Aug. 2	− 11,800		72.88	Sep. 19	− 11,900	DOWN	70.75
Aug. 3	− 8,000		75.13	Sep. 20	− 15,600	DOWN	70.13
Aug. 4	− 900	UP	76.50	Sep. 21	− 20,100	DOWN	69.38

Date	On-Balance Volume		Price	Date	On-Balance Volume		Price
Sep. 22	− 25,600	DOWN	68.13	Nov. 3	− 96,500		57.38
Sep. 25	− 34,000	DOWN	65.75	Nov. 6	− 88,800	UP	58.50
Sep. 26	− 38,100	DOWN	64.25	Nov. 8	− 70,600	UP	60.63
Sep. 27	− 33,700		66.00	Nov. 9	− 58,300	UP	62.38
Sep. 28	− 39,000	DOWN	65.25	Nov. 10	− 64,500		61.75
Sep. 29	− 39,000	DOWN	65.25	Nov. 13	− 70,500		60.13
Oct. 2	− 43,200	DOWN	65.00	Nov. 14	− 78,400		59.50 ex.
Oct. 3	− 46,400	DOWN	63.88	Nov. 15	− 73,200		59.75
Oct. 4	− 50,400	DOWN	63.75	Nov. 16	− 66,300		61.00
Oct. 5	− 55,600	DOWN	63.63	Nov. 17	− 69,500		60.00
Oct. 6	− 59,300	DOWN	62.75	Nov. 20	− 73,700		59.25
Oct. 9	− 70,600	DOWN	60.00	Nov. 21	− 82,200	DOWN	58.38
Oct. 10	− 70,600	DOWN	60.00	Nov. 22	− 75,100		58.88
Oct. 11	− 70,600	DOWN	60.00	Nov. 24	− 85,300	DOWN	58.75
Oct. 12	− 67,000		61.50	Nov. 27	− 92,400	DOWN	58.38
Oct. 13	− 73,100	DOWN	60.00	Nov. 28	− 98,200	DOWN	58.25
Oct. 16	− 78,000	DOWN	59.63	Nov. 29	−104,200	DOWN	57.50
Oct. 17	− 84,400	DOWN	59.13	Nov. 30	−110,500	DOWN	56.25
Oct. 18	− 91,700	DOWN	58.75	Dec. 1	−100,900		57.38
Oct. 19	− 98,300	DOWN	58.50	Dec. 4	− 88,600		59.50
Oct. 20	− 94,700		58.75	Dec. 5	− 88,600		59.50
Oct. 23	−100,300	DOWN	57.75	Dec. 6	− 80,800		60.00
Oct. 24	−103,900	DOWN	57.00	Dec. 7	− 89,400		59.00
Oct. 25	− 99,700		58.38	Dec. 8	− 94,500		57.50
Oct. 26	−104,700	DOWN	57.25	Dec. 11	−106,300		57.00
Oct. 27	− 99,100		58.00	Dec. 12	− 97,200		57.38
Oct. 30	− 99,100		58.00	Dec. 13	− 81,600		59.75
Oct. 31	−106,900	DOWN	57.00	Dec. 14	− 81,600		59.75
Nov. 1	− 96,500		57.38	Dec. 15	− 81,600		59.75
Nov. 2	− 96,500		57.38				

OBV Quickly Detects Line of Weakness

By checking out OBV at various similar price levels the stock showed several signs of weakness at the $76 level. Just before the worst of the decline got underway after September 8th the stock showed a loss of OBV. On September 5th the OBV was 7,400 and the price was at $76. Two days later the price was at $76 again but OBV had fallen to 3,500. Many signs similar to this pointed up the growing weakness in Alcoa stock. In setting up a record of the "field" trend, further guide lines are laid down.

OBV went under the July 18th low of minus 29,200 on September 25th when it reached minus 34,000. This was the long-term signal for selling. Note, however, that the field trend turned down when OBV went under 1,200 on September 11th when the price of the stock was still $74 a share and had already turned doubtful after September 1st when the price of the stock was $76.88.

The back of the price structure was thoroughly broken before the year 1961 was out. Now look at the charts covering the December 1961 to August 1962 period below and you will see the evidence of weak rallies at constantly descending levels of OBV.

ALUMINUM COMPANY OF AMERICA

June 1961 to December 1961
"The Field Theory"

Interpretation of Field	Field Maximum On-Balance Volume	Type of Field	Price	Date
	−29,200	DOWN	69.75	July 18, 1961
	13,600	UP	78.50	Aug. 15, 1961
	1,200	DOWN	75.50	Aug. 24, 1961
Doubtful	9,300	UP	76.88	Sept. 1, 1961
Falling	−106,900	DOWN	57.00	Oct. 31, 1961
Falling	−58,300	UP	62.38	Nov. 9, 1961
Falling	−110,500	DOWN	56.25	Nov. 30, 1961

ALUMINUM COMPANY OF AMERICA

(December 1961 to August 1962)

Date	On-Balance Volume		Price	Date	On-Balance Volume		Price
Dec. 18	− 73,800	UP	63.00	Jan. 16	− 85,400	DOWN	60.00
Dec. 19	− 82,600		62.25	Jan. 17	− 85,400	DOWN	60.00
Dec. 20	− 76,800		62.50	Jan. 18	− 85,400	DOWN	60.00
Dec. 21	− 66,200	UP	63.37	Jan. 19	− 75,300		60.25
Dec. 22	− 60,100	UP	64.50	Jan. 22	− 68,300	UP	60.50
Dec. 26	− 67,700		64.25	Jan. 23	− 71,800		60.13
Dec. 27	− 59,900	UP	65.37	Jan. 24	− 76,400		59.75
Dec. 28	− 72,800	DOWN	64.88	Jan. 25	− 80,200		59.13
Dec. 29	− 64,200		65.25	Jan. 26	− 76,400		59.37
Jan. 2	− 58,600	UP	65.37	Jan. 29	− 80,700	DOWN	59.25
Jan. 3	− 51,100	UP	66.37	Jan. 30	− 77,600		59.88
Jan. 4	− 51,100	UP	66.37	Jan. 31	− 83,200	DOWN	59.75
Jan. 5	− 58,200		66.25	Feb. 1	− 90,000	DOWN	59.37
Jan. 8	− 67,600		64.00	Feb. 2	− 93,100	DOWN	59.13
Jan. 9	− 74,100	DOWN	63.75	Feb. 5	− 85,800		59.50
Jan. 10	− 70,600		63.88	Feb. 6	− 89,900		58.75 ex.
Jan. 11	− 73,400		63.50	Feb. 7	− 84,500		59.13
Jan. 12	− 76,100	DOWN	62.00	Feb. 8	− 89,700		58.88
Jan. 15	− 82,600	DOWN	60.75	Feb. 9	− 93,100		58.25

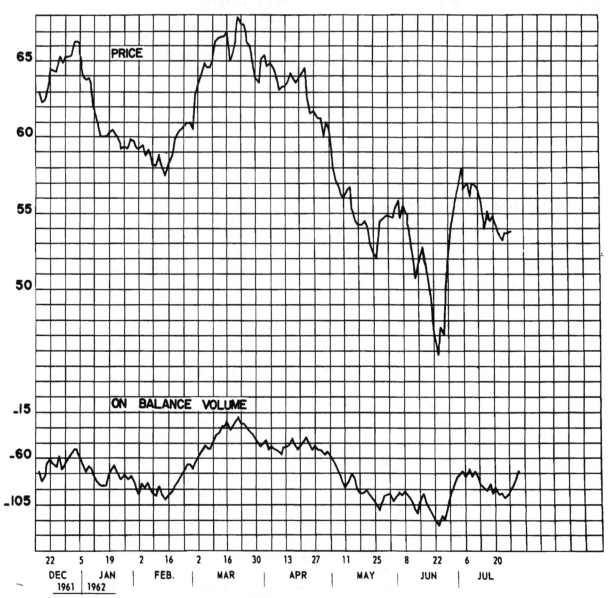

PRICE

ON BALANCE VOLUME

65

60

55

50

-15

-60

-105

| 22 | 5 | 19 | 2 | 16 | 2 | 16 | 30 | 13 | 27 | 11 | 25 | 8 | 22 | 6 | 20 |

DEC
1961 | JAN
1962 | FEB. | MAR | APR | MAY | JUN | JUL

ALUMINUM CO. OF AMERICA

Chart 42

Date	On-Balance Volume		Price	Date	On-Balance Volume		Price
Feb. 12	− 94,800	DOWN	58.13	Apr. 18	−46,700		63.75
Feb. 13	− 88,500		58.88	Apr. 19	−52,300		63.63
Feb. 14	− 94,200		58.00	Apr. 23	−44,400		64.25
Feb. 15	−100,500	DOWN	57.50	Apr. 24	−39,700	UP	64.50
Feb. 16	− 94,900		58.37	Apr. 25	−44,900		62.50
Feb. 19	− 91,900		58.88	Apr. 26	−51,500		61.63
Feb. 20	− 87,800	UP	59.88	Apr. 27	−47,100		61.75
Feb. 21	− 82,100	UP	60.37	Apr. 30	−52,100	DOWN	61.37
Feb. 23	− 74,800	UP	60.75	May 1	−52,100	DOWN	61.37
Feb. 26	− 66,500	UP	61.00	May 2	−56,400	DOWN	60.00
Feb. 27	− 66,500	UP	61.00	May 3	−54,000		61.00
Feb. 28	− 71,300		60.50	May 4	−57,000	DOWN	59.75
Mar. 1	− 63,800	UP	62.75	May 7	−63,700	DOWN	58.13
Mar. 2	− 59,600	UP	63.37	May 8	−70,700	DOWN	57.37
Mar. 5	− 53,900	UP	64.25	May 9	−77,300	DOWN	56.88
Mar. 6	− 46,300	UP	64.88	May 10	−85,600	DOWN	56.25
Mar. 7	− 51,400		64.63	May 11	−88,800	DOWN	56.00
Mar. 8	− 51,400		64.63	May 14	−83,600		56.50
Mar. 9	− 44,100	UP	64.88	May 15	−75,300		56.75 ex.
Mar. 12	− 38,600	UP	66.37	May 16	−83,700		55.25
Mar. 13	− 34,900	UP	66.50	May 17	−90,000	DOWN	54.50
Mar. 14	− 29,300	UP	66.63	May 18	−93,600	DOWN	54.25
Mar. 15	− 29,300	UP	66.63	May 21	−93,600	DOWN	54.25
Mar. 16	− 24,200	UP	67.00	May 22	−90,900		54.50
Mar. 19	− 31,800		65.00	May 23	−94,700	DOWN	54.13
Mar. 20	− 29,200		65.25	May 24	−99,300	DOWN	53.00
Mar. 21	−24,900		66.25	May 25	−104,100	DOWN	52.50
Mar. 22	−19,100	UP	67.88	May 28	−112,600	DOWN	52.00
Mar. 23	−25,700		67.50	May 29	−100,500		54.50
Mar. 26	−25,700		67.50	May 31	−95,100		54.88
Mar. 27	−30,100		66.25	June 1	−95,100		54.88
Mar. 28	−33,800	DOWN	66.00	June 4	−103,100		54.75
Mar. 29	−37,100	DOWN	64.75	June 5	−97,200		55.13
Mar. 30	−43,500	DOWN	63.88	June 6	−93,600	UP	55.88
Apr. 2	−47,400	DOWN	63.63	June 7	−96,000		54.75
Apr. 3	−45,100		65.25	June 8	−91,900	UP	55.50
Apr. 4	−43,600		65.37	June 11	−97,800	DOWN	54.88
Apr. 5	−52,200	DOWN	64.75	June 12	−103,400	DOWN	53.25
Apr. 6	−47,800		64.88	June 13	−108,400	DOWN	52.25
Apr. 9	−51,400		64.50	June 14	−113,000	DOWN	50.75
Apr. 10	−52,300	DOWN	64.00	June 15	−103,300		52.00
Apr. 11	−56,200	DOWN	63.13	June 18	−96,500		52.75
Apr. 12	−50,900		63.37	June 19	−102,100		52.00
Apr. 13	−50,900		63.37	June 20	−107,500		51.00
Apr. 16	−47,100	UP	63.63	June 21	−114,200	DOWN	49.63
Apr. 17	−42,500	UP	64.13	June 22	−118,500	DOWN	47.37

ALUMINUM COMPANY OF AMERICA

Date	On-Balance Volume		Price	Date	On-Balance Volume		Price
June 25	−128,200	DOWN	45.75	July 16	−88,000	DOWN	55.88
June 26	−116,600		47.50	July 17	−90,500	DOWN	54.00
June 27	−120,000		47.00	July 18	−86,600		55.13
June 28	−106,900	UP	50.00	July 19	−92,300	DOWN	54.50
June 29	−98,300	UP	52.00	July 20	−89,700		54.88
July 2	−89,800	UP	54.25	July 23	−92,600	DOWN	54.25
July 3	−80,500	UP	55.75	July 24	−95,200	DOWN	53.75
July 5	−74,300	UP	58.00	July 25	−101,300	DOWN	53.25
July 6	−80,800		56.63	July 26	−95,900		53.75
July 9	−72,100	UP	57.00	July 27	−91,500		56.00
July 10	−78,200		56.13	July 30	−88,400	UP	56.88
July 11	−74,700		57.00	July 31	−79,500	UP	58.25
July 12	−81,800	DOWN	56.88	Aug. 1	−72,900	UP	59.00
July 13	−85,400	DOWN	56.75				

Completing the raw material for the Alcoa analysis, the field trend figures are given below:

ALUMINUM COMPANY OF AMERICA

(December 1961 to August 1962)
"The Field Theory"

Interpretation of Field	Field Maximum On-Balance Volume	Type of Field	Price	Date
Falling	−59,900	UP	65.37	Dec. 27, 1961
Doubtful	−72,800	DOWN	64.88	Dec. 28, 1961
Rising	−51,100	UP	66.37	Jan. 4, 1962
Doubtful	−85,400	DOWN	60.00	Jan. 18, 1962
Doubtful	−68,300	UP	60.50	Jan. 22, 1962
Falling	−100,500	DOWN	57.50	Feb. 15, 1962
Doubtful	−19,100	UP	67.88	Mar. 22, 1962
Doubtful	−56,200	DOWN	63.13	Apr. 11, 1962
Doubtful	−39,700	UP	64.50	Apr. 24, 1962
Falling	−112,600	DOWN	52.00	May 28, 1962
Falling	−91,900	UP	55.50	June 8, 1962
Falling	−128,200	DOWN	45.75	June 25, 1962
Doubtful	−72,100	UP	57.00	July 9, 1962
Doubtful	−101,300	DOWN	53.25	July 25, 1962

Application of the 18 Trading Signals

Trading Record

Date and Action	Signal	Profit	Loss	Cumulative
BUY June 30, 1961 at 71.50	B-2			
SELL July 12, 1961 at 74.50	S-2	3.00		3.00
SELL July 17, 1961 at 72.25	S-7			

Date and Action	Signal	Profit	Loss	Cumulative
BUY July 19, 1961 at 71.00	B-3			
BUY Aug. 7, 1961 at 77.13	B-7, B-9			
BUY Aug. 14, 1961 at 78.75	B-7			
SELL Aug. 15, 1961 at 78.50	S-3	7.50		10.50
BUY Aug. 25, 1961 at 76.00	B-8			
BUY Sept. 5, 1961 at 76.00	B-7			
SELL Sept. 12, 1961 at 74.25	S-4			
SELL Sept. 15, 1961 at 72.25	S-7		1.75	8.75

Note that at this point the sell designation is in force until October 16th. During this period the OBV drops under the long-term support level on September 25th. The trader now shifts his strategy to the short side of the market, selling short on the sells and covering those shorts on the buys. The first step is going short at 64.25 on September 26th.

Date and Action	Signal	Profit	Loss	Cumulative
BUY Oct. 16, 1961 at 69.63	B-5	4.63		13.38
SELL Nov. 9, 1961 at 62.38	S-1, S-3			
SELL Nov. 10, 1961 at 61.75	S-8			
SELL Nov. 22, 1961 at 58.88	S-4			
BUY Nov. 30, 1961 at 56.25	B-8	6.13		19.50
SELL Dec. 22, 1961 at 64.50	S-1	(These cancel.		
BUY Dec. 22, 1961 at 64.50	B-7	NO action.)		
SELL Dec. 28, 1961 at 64.88	S-8			
SELL Dec. 29, 1961 at 65.25	S-6			
BUY Jan. 3, 1962 at 66.37	B-4		1.50	18.00
SELL Jan. 15, 1962 at 60.75	S-7			
BUY Jan. 16, 1962 at 60.00	B-2	.75		18.75
SELL Feb. 2, 1962 at 59.13	S-4			
SELL Feb. 13, 1962 at 58.88	S-7			
BUY Feb. 16, 1962 at 58.37	B-8	.75		19.50
SELL Feb. 23, 1962 at 60.75	S-1			
SELL Feb. 26, 1962 at 61.00	S-8			
BUY Mar. 12, 1962 at 66.37	B-7		5.63	13.88
SELL Mar. 23, 1962 at 67.50	S-5	(These cancel.		
BUY Mar. 23, 1962 at 67.50	B-7	NO action.)		
SELL Apr. 6, 1962 at 64.88	S-7			
SELL Apr. 11, 1962 at 63.13	S-7			
SELL Apr. 25, 1962 at 62.50	S-8	(These cancel.		
BUY Apr. 25, 1962 at 62.50	B-7	NO action.)		
SELL May 3, 1962 at 61.00	S-4			
SELL May 7, 1962 at 58.13	S-7			
SELL May 18, 1962 at 54.25	S-7			
BUY May 24, 1962 at 53.00	B-5	11.88		25.75
BUY May 28, 1962 at 52.00	B-8			
BUY June 11, 1962 at 54.88	B-7	(These cancel.		
SELL June 11, 1962 at 54.88	S-8, S-1	NO action.)		
SELL June 12, 1962 at 53.25	S-6, S-7			
BUY June 15, 1962 at 52.00	B-2	1.25		27.00

Date and Action	Signal	Profit	Loss	Cumulative
SELL June 22, 1962 at 47.37	S-4, S-7, S-9 (These cancel.			
BUY June 22, 1962 at 47.37	B-2	NO action.)		
BUY June 26, 1962 at 47.50	B-3			
BUY June 28, 1962 at 50.00	B-8			
SELL July 2, 1962 at 54.25	S-1			
SELL July 6, 1962 at 56.63	S-2			
BUY July 10, 1962 at 56.13	B-7		1.88	25.13
SELL July 20, 1962 at 54.88	S-7			
BUY July 26, 1962 at 53.75	B-8	1.13		26.25

Short Selling Advisable Only When OBV Breaks Major Supports

Alcoa provided short sale trading profit possibilities after OBV moved under the June lows in late September 1961. Note that here and there a loss occurs in the trading record. This is as it should be. The use of on-balance volume buy and sell signals never guarantees total success but the odds over a period of time are very much in the trader's favor and that is what counts, the batting average over a period of time, and this is one of the more comforting aspects of using on-balance volume buy and sell signals.

Other Aspects of the Trading Record

The day-to-day trader buys on the *first* BUY signal and sells on the *first* SELL signal. Sometimes you will see many buy signals occurring after the first one. Obviously the stock is held through that period until the first sell signal shows up. If the trader is selling short he maintains that position through all the sell signals until the first buy signal shows up at which point he covers his short sale (buys in). When two opposing signals occur on the same day they cancel each other out and the trader maintains his position.

Ploughing Back the Trading Gains

Dow-Jones stocks do not normally lend themselves to strong day-to-day trading gains and it was felt that if OBV signals resulted in a good record on a Dow-Jones stock the record would be as good or better on other issues. The acid test is to try a theory such as this on conservative blue chip issues. Working well under these conditions, the trader can gradually branch out into more speculative and faster moving trading stocks.

Trading capital would of course grow faster by ploughing back all the trading gains into an additional number of shares. In the Alcoa trading example just given, let us assume that the trader started with $7,150, enough to purchase 100 shares of Alcoa at 71.50 on June 30, 1961. By ploughing back the trading gains this modest capital might have grown to $10,119 by July 1962 by the automatic following of the OBV buy and sell signals. That was a gain of better than 41% in trading Alcoa for thirteen months. It will also be noticed that out of 13 trades in that period, *nine* were profitable and *four* showed a loss. This once again accents the point that one can lose over a very short run period in using the OBV buy and sell signals but the use of the trading technique over a reasonable period of time can yield promising results. This was pointed out in the Allied Chemical example where twelve potential trades yielded five at a profit and seven at a loss *and yet a gain for the entire trading period*. The explanation lies in the way OBV signals allow trading profits to run and losses to be generally cut short. The examples did not include the brokerage commissions and thus the actual gains are smaller. However, the theory of OBV signal trading stands up rather well under study and actual adaptation to specific cases.

The Summing up

Here it was shown that the day-to-day trader continues to trade on the long side of the market as long as the on-balance volume figures remain above an important long-term support level. Once those OBV levels are penetrated on the downside, the trader shifts his trading strategy and sells the stock short on all OBV sell signals and covers his short sales on the OBV buy signals. We now move on to American Tobacco to test the OBV theory further.

Chapter Six

American Tobacco

*On-Balance volume and related price moves traced
through the bull and bear cycles of 1961-1962*

What You Are about to Learn

Using the same technique of presentation, we now come to American Tobacco, showing the sharp transition from a strong position in 1961 to a weak position in 1962. Here is an example of a stock which rose to an all-time high of $111.38 a share on November 29, 1961, thus posing the problem of when to sell a stock when it rises to an all-time high. The on-balance volume signals gave the clearest indication, enabling the trader to detect profit-taking indications at $108 a share. You will again see a trading record based solely on the mechanics of OBV signals, the trading strategy again shifting to the short side of the market when long-term on-balance volume supports are penetrated. You will see how the following of these volume signals would have resulted in total trading gains of over 53 points in the period covered.

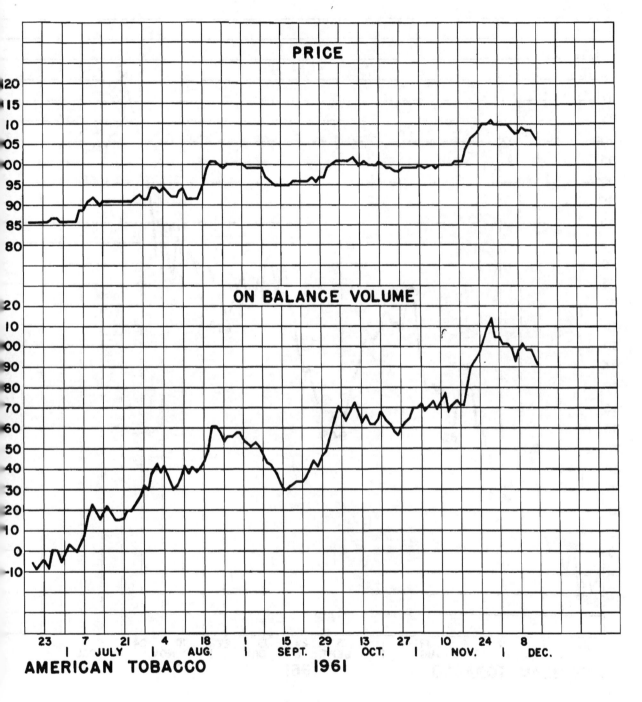

PRICE

ON BALANCE VOLUME

23   7   21   4   18   1   15   29   13   27   10   24   8
    JULY   AUG.   SEPT.   OCT.   NOV.   DEC.

AMERICAN TOBACCO   1961

Chart 43

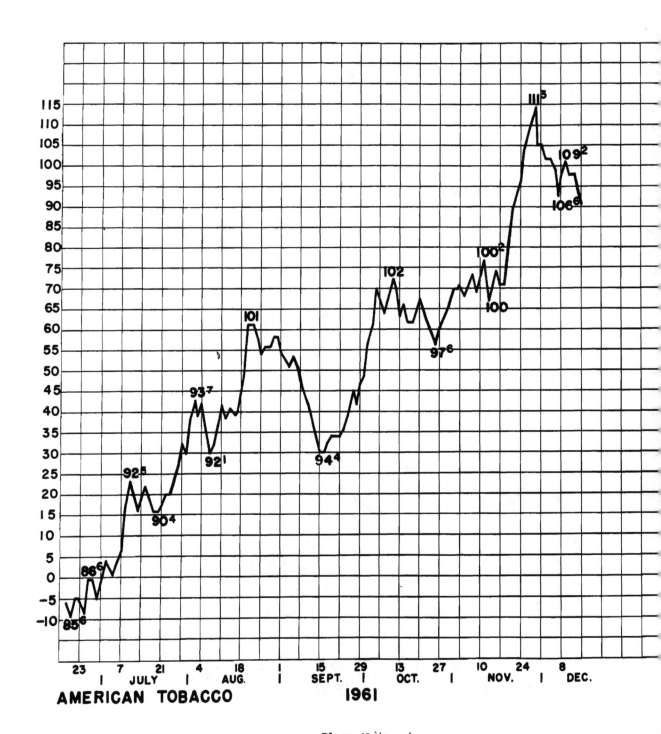

AMERICAN TOBACCO   **1961**

Chart 43 (cont.)

American Tobacco and OBV

Here is a picture of a true climactic top being recorded in 1961. Note the much swifter acceleration in the OBV line right at the peak. Note also how the OBV line drops while the stock price still hangs high almost two weeks after the top is recorded. The actual record of on-balance volume for this period is now shown in detail.

AMERICAN TOBACCO

(June to December 1961)

Date	On-Balance Volume		Price	Date	On-Balance Volume		Price
June 20	−5,800		86.00	Aug. 7	35,500	DOWN	92.50
June 21	−9,100		85.75	Aug. 8	29,600	DOWN	92.13
June 22	−4,500		86.25	Aug. 9	32,000		92.38
June 23	−4,500		86.25	Aug. 10	36,300		92.75
June 26	−7,500		85.75	Aug. 11	41,800		94.00
June 27	−500	UP	86.75	Aug. 14	37,900		92.00
June 28	−500	UP	86.75	Aug. 15	40,800		92.25
June 29	−5,400		85.75	Aug. 16	38,600		92.00
June 30	−1,000		85.88	Aug. 17	39,900		92.75
July 3	3,900	UP	86.25	Aug. 18	45,400	UP	94.63
July 5	300		85.75	Aug. 21	49,400	UP	98.75
July 6	4,000	UP	87.50	Aug. 22	61,100	UP	101.00
July 7	6,900	UP	87.75	Aug. 23	61,100	UP	101.00
July 10	16,900	UP	91.50	Aug. 24	57,800		99.50
July 11	23,400	UP	92.63	Aug. 25	53,800		99.38
July 12	19,100		90.50	Aug. 28	55,500		99.50
July 13	16,100		89.75	Aug. 29	55,500		99.50
July 14	19,500		91.00	Aug. 30	57,800		100.00
July 17	22,000		91.25	Aug. 31	57,800		100.00
July 18	18,600		90.63	Sept. 1	53,600	DOWN	99.50
July 19	16,300		90.50	Sept. 5	51,000	DOWN	99.25
July 20	16,300		90.50	Sept. 6	53,100		100.00
July 21	17,300		90.88	Sept. 7	50,700	DOWN	99.63
July 24	19,800		91.13	Sept. 8	46,800	DOWN	99.00
July 25	19,800		91.13	Sept. 11	44,000	DOWN	96.50
July 26	23,400		91.63	Sept. 12	41,600	DOWN	95.75
July 27	27,000	UP	92.63	Sept. 13	38,400	DOWN	95.25
July 28	32,400	UP	93.00	Sept. 14	34,200	DOWN	95.00
July 31	29,900		92.00	Sept. 15	29,500	DOWN	94.50
Aug. 1	37,500	UP	93.50	Sept. 18	29,500	DOWN	94.50
Aug. 2	43,000	UP	93.88	Sept. 19	32,300		95.13
Aug. 3	39,100		93.25	Sept. 20	33,600		95.50
Aug. 4	42,300		93.88	Sept. 21	33,600		95.50

Date	On-Balance Volume		Price	Date	On-Balance Volume		Price
Sept. 22	33,600		95.50	Nov. 3	71,300		100.25
Sept. 25	36,000		95.88	Nov. 6	68,100		99.13
Sept. 26	38,600		96.25	Nov. 8	72,700	UP	99.50
Sept. 27	44,700		96.50	Nov. 9	69,000		99.25
Sept. 28	41,500		96.13	Nov. 10	72,900	UP	99.75
Sept. 29	46,700	UP	96.50	Nov. 13	76,600	UP	100.25
Oct. 2	48,800	UP	97.00	Nov. 14	67,300	DOWN	100.00
Oct. 3	57,000	UP	99.13	Nov. 15	71,200		100.25
Oct. 4	62,100	UP	100.25	Nov. 16	73,600		100.63
Oct. 5	69,600	UP	101.13	Nov. 17	71,100		100.50
Oct. 9	64,200		100.50	Nov. 20	71,100		100.50
Oct. 10	68,300		100.75	Nov. 21	80,500	UP	104.00
Oct. 11	72,600	UP	102.00	Nov. 22	90,400	UP	106.75
Oct. 12	70,400		101.00	Nov. 24	96,900	UP	108.38
Oct. 13	62,900	DOWN	100.13	Nov. 27	104,100	UP	109.75
Oct. 16	66,100		100.63	Nov. 28	109,000	UP	109.88
Oct. 17	62,300	DOWN	100.00	Nov. 29	114,100	UP	111.38
Oct. 18	62,300	DOWN	100.00	Nov. 30	105,400		110.00
Oct. 19	64,500		100.13	Dec. 1	105,400		110.00
Oct. 20	67,000		100.50	Dec. 4	102,400		109.75
Oct. 23	64,100		99.75	Dec. 5	102,400		109.75
Oct. 24	62,300		99.25	Dec. 6	98,500		108.50
Oct. 25	58,200	DOWN	98.75	Dec. 7	93,400		106.75
Oct. 26	56,000	DOWN	97.75	Dec. 8	97,500		107.25
Oct. 27	59,700		98.00	Dec. 11	100,500		109.25
Oct. 30	62,900		98.63	Dec. 12	98,000		108.00
Oct. 31	65,300		98.75	Dec. 13	98,000		108.00
Nov. 1	69,600		99.25	Dec. 14	93,700		105.50
Nov. 2	69,600		99.25	Dec. 15	90,700	DOWN	103.75

The Mechanics of the Top

Significant stock price peaks are usually accompanied by unusual volume and an acceleration in the rate of price advance. American Tobacco had these characteristics as it ran up quickly to the all-time high of $111.38 a share on November 29, 1961. Note the characteristics of on-balance volume and price as that top is approached. Note that the on-balance volume rose from minus 9,100 to 27,000 between June 21st and July 27th, *a net gain of 36,100 in 25 trading sessions.* Between July 27th and November 20th the on-balance volume rose from 27,000 to 71,100, *a net gain of 44,100 in 79 trading sessions.* Between November 20th and 29th the on-balance volume rose from 71,100 to 114,100, *a net gain of 43,000 in 6 trading sessions.* In those last six sessions leading to the top the price of the stock rose almost 11 points. Dividing those 11 points into the 43,000 rise in OBV during those brief final sessions, we arrive at an average of 3,909 OBV upward force behind each of those final rising points. Average OBV per point on the previous 11 point advance between 89.75 on July 13th and 100.50 on November 20th was 5,000. This means that while the stock was climbing from 100.50 to 111.38 *fifteen times faster* than it did from 89.75 to 100.50, *average OBV per point on the final advance was almost 22% lower.* Price was therefore outrunning the on-balance volume on the last ascent, a rather typical characteristic of finality. To put it another way, the stock was running out of upside energy at a very rapid pace.

It is useful to translate on-balance volume figures into terms of *OBV per point.* In this way it can quickly be determined as to whether a stock is gaining or losing upside energy as it continues to advance, a particularly useful thing to know when a stock advances into all-time new high ground and there are no previous resistance levels for guidance.

Note the pullback in the price of the stock to 109.25 on December 11th with OBV only coming up to 100,500. The last time the stock was between 109 and 110 on December 5th the OBV stood at 102,400. These are additional telltale signs of the formation of a top.

AMERICAN TOBACCO

June to December 1961
"The Field Theory"

Interpretation of Field	Field Maximum On-Balance Volume	Type of Field	Price	Date
	43,000	UP	93.88	Aug. 2, 1961
	29,600	DOWN	92.13	Aug. 8, 1961
Rising	61,100	UP	101.00	Aug. 23, 1961
Doubtful	29,500	DOWN	94.50	Sept. 18, 1961
Doubtful	72,600	UP	102.00	Oct. 11, 1961
Doubtful	56,000	DOWN	97.75	Oct. 26, 1961
Rising	76,600	UP	100.25	Nov. 13, 1961
Rising	67,300	DOWN	100.00	Nov. 14, 1961
Rising	114,100	UP	111.38	Nov. 29, 1961

Looking at the field trend above, note the *smoothness* of the ascent in the OBV levels until late November. In late November the characteristics of the advance changed. Watch for such shifts in pattern. They usually precede an important shift in the price trend. Now look at the following charts on American Tobacco covering the December 1961 to August 1962 period, the followthrough of the late 1961 signals:

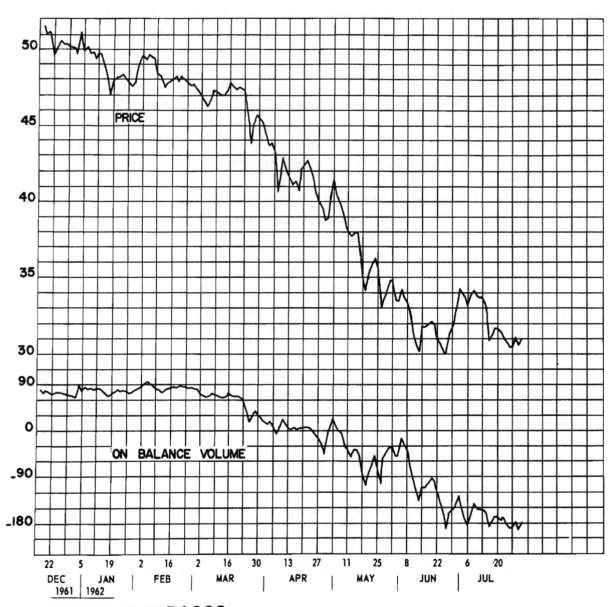

50

45   PRICE

40

35

30

90

0

        ON BALANCE VOLUME

-90

-180

22   5   19   2   16   2   16   30   13   27   11   25   8   22   6   '20
DEC | JAN | FEB | MAR | APR | MAY | JUN | JUL
1961 1962

AMERICAN TOBACCO

Chart 44

American Tobacco

(December 1961 to August 1962)

Date	On-Balance Volume		Price	Date	On-Balance Volume		Price
Dec. 18	80,200	DOWN	103.00	Feb. 15	81,000		95.75
Dec. 19	75,100	DOWN	102.00	Feb. 16	83,800		96.00
Dec. 20	77,600		102.25	Feb. 19	87,700		96.25
Dec. 21	76,400		102.00	Feb. 20	85,500		95.75
Dec. 22	72,100	DOWN	99.00	Feb. 21	88,700	UP	96.25
Dec. 26	75,800		101.25	Feb. 23	86,100		95.75
Dec. 27	73,300		100.75	Feb. 26	83,600		95.25
Dec. 28	73,300		100.75	Feb. 27	85,300		95.37
Dec. 29	71,400	DOWN	100.50	Feb. 28	82,600	DOWN	94.75
Jan. 2	67,700	DOWN	100.25	Mar. 1	79,900	DOWN	94.50
Jan. 3	65,600	DOWN	99.25	Mar. 2	74,900	DOWN	94.00
Jan. 4	89,800	UP	102.37	Mar. 5	69,700	DOWN	93.00
Jan. 5	79,100		99.75	Mar. 6	67,000	DOWN	92.50
Jan. 8	87,800		100.25	Mar. 7	69,700		93.25
Jan. 9	79,200		99.50	Mar. 8	73,600		94.63
Jan. 10	84,200		99.63	Mar. 9	70,400		94.50
Jan. 11	78,800	DOWN	98.75	Mar. 12	68,200		94.25
Jan. 12	83,600		99.50	Mar. 13	65,000	DOWN	94.00
Jan. 15	83,600		99.50	Mar. 14	65,000	DOWN	94.00
Jan. 16	77,700	DOWN	97.50	Mar. 15	66,500		94.50
Jan. 17	73,200	DOWN	96.00	Mar. 16	74,500	UP	95.50
Jan. 18	65,300	DOWN	94.00	Mar. 19	69,600		95.00
Jan. 19	68,400		95.88	Mar. 20	67,400		94.75
Jan. 22	73,900		96.13	Mar. 21	69,400		95.00
Jan. 23	77,100		96.25	Mar. 22	65,300		94.88
Jan. 24	74,200		95.50	Mar. 23	60,900	DOWN	94.63
Jan. 25	76,900		96.00	Mar. 26	42,400	DOWN	91.00
Jan. 26	74,500		95.88	Mar. 27	17,000	DOWN	87.75
Jan. 29	72,900	DOWN	95.00	Mar. 28	31,500		90.13
Jan. 30	74,800		95.50	Mar. 29	38,900		91.13
Jan. 31	78,900	UP	97.88	Mar. 30	30,500		91.00
Feb. 1	81,600	UP	98.50	Apr. 2	24,400		90.37
Feb. 2	85,300	UP	99.00	Apr. 3	19,300		88.50
Feb. 5	90,100	UP	98.50 ex.	Apr. 4	14,300	DOWN	87.13
Feb. 6	93,900	UP	99.25	Apr. 5	19,800		87.63
Feb. 7	91,500		99.00	Apr. 6	12,100	DOWN	86.75
Feb. 8	87,400		98.75	Apr. 9	−6,800	DOWN	81.25
Feb. 9	79,600		96.75	Apr. 10	11,800		84.00
Feb. 12	78,000		96.50	Apr. 11	22,500	UP	85.63
Feb. 13	73,600		95.00	Apr. 12	15,400		84.13
Feb. 14	76,400		95.50	Apr. 13	10,300		83.37

Date	On-Balance Volume		Price	Date	On-Balance Volume		Price
Apr. 16	4,100		82.37	June 11	−67,300	DOWN	32.13
Apr. 17	10,600		82.50	June 12	−93,700	DOWN	31.13
Apr. 18	3,000	DOWN	81.50	June 13	−117,900	DOWN	30.50
Apr. 19	7,900		84.13	June 14	−137,300	DOWN	30.25
Apr. 23	12,900		85.25	June 15	−114,100		31.88
Apr. 24	9,900		84.25	June 18	−114,100		31.88
Apr. 25	1,900	DOWN	82.50	June 19	−104,400		32.00
Apr. 26	−6,400	DOWN	81.13	June 20	−92,300		32.13
Apr. 27	−13,300	DOWN	80.00	June 21	−98,400		32.00
Apr. 30	−25,000	DOWN	79.25	June 22	−108,300		31.00
May 1	−47,900	DOWN	38.75*	June 25	−139,200	DOWN	30.63
May 2	−2,300		39.00	June 26	−158,400	DOWN	30.13
May 3	9,800		40.37	June 27	−189,200	DOWN	30.00
May 4	23,100	UP	41.37	June 28	−173,500		31.37
May 7	10,000		40.37	June 29	−158,300		31.63
May 8	200		39.75	July 2	−149,100		32.88
May 9	−1,700		39.25	July 3	−129,500		34.25
May 10	−21,000		38.63	July 5	−167,100		33.88
May 11	−32,500		38.00	July 6	−180,800		33.13
May 14	−51,400	DOWN	37.75	July 9	−164,200		34.00
May 15	−36,500		38.00	July 10	−142,200		34.13
May 16	−36,500		38.00	July 11	−152,600		33.75
May 17	−45,700		37.00	July 12	−152,600		33.75
May 18	−77,800	DOWN	35.25	July 13	−152,600		33.75
May 21	−108,000	DOWN	34.13	July 16	−160,900		33.13
May 22	−89,200		35.13	July 17	−187,100	DOWN	30.88
May 23	−64,700		36.00	July 18	−177,800		31.25
May 24	−49,800		36.37	July 19	−168,300		31.75
May 25	−69,300		35.75	July 20	−168,300		31.75
May 28	−106,500		33.00	July 23	−175,500		31.50
May 29	−58,400		33.63	July 24	−168,400		31.00
May 31	−31,000	UP	34.88	July 25	−180,200	DOWN	30.75
June 1	−31,000	UP	34.88	July 26	−188,800	DOWN	30.50
June 4	−49,100		33.50	July 27	−188,800	DOWN	30.50
June 5	−49,100		33.50	July 30	−179,100		31.13
June 6	−15,300	UP	34.13	July 31	−195,700	DOWN	30.63
June 7	−28,300		33.63	Aug. 1	−179,700		31.00
June 8	−38,600		32.37				

* 2-1 Split

Before any trading signals can be applied, it is necessary to complete the raw material for good OBV analysis with the field trend for the period covered. These figures are shown below:

AMERICAN TOBACCO

December 1961 to August 1962
"The Field Theory"

Interpretation of Field	Field Maximum On-Balance Volume	Type of Field	Price	Date
Doubtful	65,600	DOWN	99.25	Jan. 3, 1962
Doubtful	89,800	UP	102.37	Jan. 4, 1962
Doubtful	72,900	DOWN	95.00	Jan. 29, 1962
Doubtful	88,700	UP	96.25	Feb. 21, 1962
Falling	65,000	DOWN	94.00	Mar. 14, 1962
Falling	74,500	UP	95.50	Mar. 16, 1962
Falling	−6,800	DOWN	81.25	Apr. 9, 1962
Falling	22,500	UP	85.63	Apr. 11, 1962
Falling	−47,900	DOWN	38.75*	May 1, 1962
Doubtful	23,100	UP	41.37	May 4, 1962
Falling	−108,000	DOWN	34.13	May 21, 1962
Falling	−15,300	UP	34.13	June 6, 1962
Falling	−195,700	DOWN	30.63	July 31, 1962

* 2-1 Split

American Tobacco in 1962—Applying the Tests

A great deal about where this stock was headed could have been learned by the application of a few of the OBV tests previously outlined:

Checking out OBV at each price level. As an arbitrary starting point, examine the OBV readings every time the stock closed around $95:

Date	On-Balance Volume	Price	Field Trend
Jan. 19, 1962	68,400	95.88	Doubtful
Jan. 24, 1962	74,200	95.50	Doubtful
Jan. 26, 1962	74,500	95.88	Doubtful
Jan. 29, 1962	72,900	95.00	Doubtful
Jan. 30, 1962	74,800	95.50	Doubtful
Feb. 13, 1962	73,600	95.00	Doubtful
Feb. 14, 1962	76,400	95.50	Doubtful
Feb. 15, 1962	81,000	95.75	Doubtful
Feb. 20, 1962	85,500	95.75	Doubtful
Feb. 23, 1962	86,100	95.75	Doubtful

Date	On-Balance Volume	Price	Field Trend
Feb. 26, 1962	83,600	95.25	Doubtful
Feb. 27, 1962	85,300	95.37	Doubtful
Mar. 16, 1962	74,500	95.50	Falling
Mar. 19, 1962	69,600	95.00	Falling
Mar. 21, 1962	69,400	95.00	Falling

Fifteen times the price of American Tobacco closed between $95 and $96 a share between January 19th and March 21st, 1962. The on-balance volume figures showed an upward tendency for the first two months but fell back by March. However, the OBV reading on March 21st was above that of January 19th. This points up the importance of knowing what the field trend is when a stock gives a surface impression of stability. Note that the field trend changed from *doubtful* to *falling* when the stock was selling around $95 a share in March 1962, the same price it was selling at in January and February. The conclusion is that when the trend changes then similar OBV readings at similar price levels have no significance. In other words, *the trend is the thing*.

Determining accumulation and distribution. It was rather obvious that the accumulation phase of American Tobacco had ended in 1961. On-balance volume figures were no longer making new highs. There is an in-between period when a stock reflects neither accumulation or distribution. This is shown when on-balance figures move in a "line," a rather restricted range over a period of time. Between December 1961 and March 22, 1962 the stock was NEUTRAL. In this period the OBV figures fluctuated between a high of 93,900 and a low of 65,000, a rather narrow range for three months. On March 23rd that "line" of OBV was broken and then *distribution was clearly indicated as underway*. Look for these "lines" in OBV figures over a period of time, the neutral zones which occur between accumulation and distribution.

Note that when the on-balance volume broke the "line" on March 23rd by moving down to 60,900 that the price of the stock was 94.63. If one was following the price alone it would appear that the stock was still above the support price level of 92.50 reached on March 6th, still not showing serious weakness.

Long-term strength or weakness. Going back to the 1961 OBV figures on American Tobacco, it is determined that 29,500 recorded on September 15th and 18th is regarded as the *long-term OBV support level*. On-balance volume moved under that figure on March 27, 1962 when it reached 17,000. That was the definitive long-term selling signal, a signal upon which *investors* would sell American Tobacco shares.

Summing up the Tests

	Weakness Signalled With Key Date of Change
Checking OBV at Each Price Level	March 16, 1962
Distribution	March 23, 1962
Long-term Weakness	March 27, 1962

The Day-to-Day Trader Also Notes These Changes

The day-to-day trader in American Tobacco also notes the key changes taking place in the trend of American Tobacco because these changes will determine whether his strategy will remain on the long side of the market or shift to the short side. When he sees the definitive signal of long-term weakness recorded on March 27, 1962 his entire strategy changes accordingly. He sells out any long position he has in the stock on March 28, 1962 and proceeds to go short on the sell signals and cover on the buy signals. Now let us look at the entire trading record on American Tobacco covering the period from June 1961 to August 1962, employing the 18 signals for buying and selling based on on-balance volume.

Application of the 18 Trading Signals

AMERICAN TOBACCO

Trading Record

Date and Action	*Signal*	*Profit*	*Loss*	*Cumulative*
BUY July 5, 1961 at 85.75	B-7			
SELL July 11, 1961 at 92.63	S-2, S-3	6.88		6.88
BUY July 13, 1961 at 89.75	B-2			
BUY July 28, 1961 at 93.00	B-7			
BUY Aug. 8, 1961 at 92.13	B-1, B-3			
BUY Aug. 15, 1961 at 92.25	B-2			
BUY Aug. 21, 1961 at 98.75	B-4, B-9			
SELL Aug. 22, 1961 at 101.00	S-2	11.25		18.13
SELL Aug. 23, 1961 at 101.00	S-3			
BUY Sept. 12, 1961 at 95.75	B-2			
BUY Sept. 14, 1961 at 95.00	B-1			
BUY Sept. 15, 1961 at 94.50	B-8			
BUY Oct. 12, 1961 at 101.00	B-7			
BUY Oct. 16, 1961 at 100.63	B-3			
SELL Oct. 26, 1961 at 97.75	S-7	2.00		20.13
BUY Nov. 9, 1961 at 99.25	B-4, B-9			

Date and Action	Signal	Profit	Loss	Cumulative
BUY Nov. 15, 1961 at 100.25	B-1, B-3, B-8			
BUY Nov. 22, 1961 at 106.75	B-4, B-9	(These cancel.		
SELL Nov. 22, 1961 at 106.75	S-2	NO action)		
BUY Dec. 1, 1961 at 110.00	B-3			
BUY Dec. 8, 1961 at 107.25	B-2			
SELL Dec. 12, 1961 at 108.00	S-2	8.75		28.88
BUY Dec. 15, 1961 at 103.75	B-2			
BUY Dec. 18, 1961 at 103.00	B-1			
BUY Dec. 19, 1961 at 102.00	B-3			
BUY Dec. 26, 1961 at 101.25	B-2			
SELL Dec. 27, 1961 at 100.75	S-2		3.00	25.88
SELL Jan. 2, 1962 at 100.25	S-7			
BUY Jan. 3, 1962 at 99.25	B-8			
SELL Jan. 5, 1962 at 99.75	S-2, S-3	.50		26.38
SELL Jan. 17, 1962 at 96.00	S-7			
BUY Jan. 30, 1962 at 95.50	B-8			
SELL Feb. 1, 1962 at 98.50	S-2	3.00		29.38
BUY Feb. 23, 1962 at 95.75	B-7			
SELL Mar. 14, 1962 at 94.00	S-4, S-7		1.75	27.63
SELL Mar. 19, 1962 at 95.00	S-1			
SELL Mar. 26, 1962 at 91.00	S-4			
BUY Mar. 27, 1962 at 87.75	B-2, B-3			
SELL Mar. 28, 1962 at 90.13	*	2.38		30.00
SELL Mar. 29, 1962 at 91.13	S-3			
SELL Apr. 5, 1962 at 87.63	S-7			
BUY Apr. 10, 1962 at 84.00	B-3	7.13		37.13
SELL Apr. 11, 1962 at 85.63	S-3			
SELL Apr. 12, 1962 at 84.13	S-1			
SELL Apr. 19, 1962 at 84.13	S-4			
SELL Apr. 23, 1962 at 85.25	S-2			
SELL Apr. 26, 1962 at 81.13	S-7			
BUY May 1, 1962 at 38.75*	B-3	8.13		45.25
SELL May 3, 1962 at 40.37	S-3			
SELL May 7, 1962 at 40.37	S-1			
BUY May 11, 1962 at 38.00	B-3	2.37		47.62
SELL May 14, 1962 at 37.75	S-4			
SELL May 16, 1962 at 38.00	S-3			
SELL May 21, 1962 at 34.13	S-7	(These cancel.		
BUY May 21, 1962 at 34.13	B-2, B-3	NO action)		
SELL May 23, 1962 at 36.00	S-3			
SELL May 25, 1962 at 35.75	S-3			
BUY May 29, 1962 at 33.63	B-2, B-3	4.13		51.75
SELL May 31, 1962 at 34.88	S-3			

*Stock sold on March 28, 1962 since it broke long-term OBV support the day before. Here the trading strategy shifts to the short side. The next transaction is a short sale on the March 29th sell signal.

SELL	June	1,	1962	at	34.88	S-1	
SELL	June	7,	1962	at	33.63	S-3	(These cancel.
BUY	June	7,	1962	at	33.63	B-7	NO action)
SELL	June	12,	1962	at	31.13	S-4	(These cancel.
BUY	June	12,	1962	at	31.13	B-3	NO action)
SELL	June	18,	1962	at	31.88	S-3	
SELL	June	26,	1962	at	30.13	S-7	(These cancel.
BUY	June	26,	1962	at	30.13	B-3	NO action)
BUY	July	6,	1962	at	33.13	B-3	1.75 53.50
SELL	July	11,	1962	at	33.75	S-3	
SELL	July	18,	1962	at	31.25	S-7	(These cancel.
BUY	July	18,	1962	at	31.25	B-3	NO action)
SELL	July	26,	1962	at	30.50	S-7	

* 2-1 Split

It might be said that this is a superb example of on-balance volume signals in action. *Out of fourteen complete transaction opportunities, only two showed a loss.* Note that when the stock might have been sold with no gain because of commissions, that the stock tended to go lower thereafter, the sell signals preventing a greater loss. This cutting of losses short of potential is an additional feature of the on-balance volume selling signals. The above record is based on an *automatic* following of mechanical signals, no emotions or personal interpretation entering into the decisions.

The Summing up

On-balance volume buying and selling signals applied to American Tobacco for the period from June 1961 to August 1962 produced theoretical net gains of 53½ points exclusive of commissions, rather convincing proof that what a stock is going to do pricewise is often best detected by what it is doing volumewise. Note that at the end of the trading record on American Tobacco the trader is left short at 33.75, another trading profit yet potentially to be recorded.

Chapter Seven

Chrysler 1961-1962

A volatile stock often responds most dramatically to the suggested OBV forecasting device

What You Are about to Learn

Chrysler is a part of the Dow-Jones Industrial Average. The average reached a peak of 734.91 on December 13, 1961 but Chrysler kept rising for another two months. You will learn that it is important to treat each stock individually regardless of the averages. On-balance volume is a great aid in determining which stocks are showing the best independent action. If a stock shows good evidence of accumulation by way of the on-balance volume figures, this should be believed and acted upon. In 1963 Chrysler made a sensational advance starting from the June 14, 1962 low of 38.88. You will see that in the 1962 market break *Chrysler never recorded a long-term on-balance volume sell signal*, OBV consistently staying above the minus 48,800 recorded on November 29th and 30th, 1961 when the stock was down to 45.50. The market break of 1962 carried the stock down to 38.88 *but OBV never confirmed that weakness*. Very seldom will you see a stock selling almost 7 points under a previous low point without an OBV confirmation. This signalled excessive upside momentum. True, the stock dropped from a price of 62.13 on February 20, 1961 to 38.88 on June 14th of that year, the Dow-Jones Industrial Average falling in the whole bear market period over 200 points and yet CHRYSLER DID NOT RECORD A LONG TERM SELL SIGNAL. This points up the *independence* of stock action, the importance of relying more on volume figures rather than price figures.

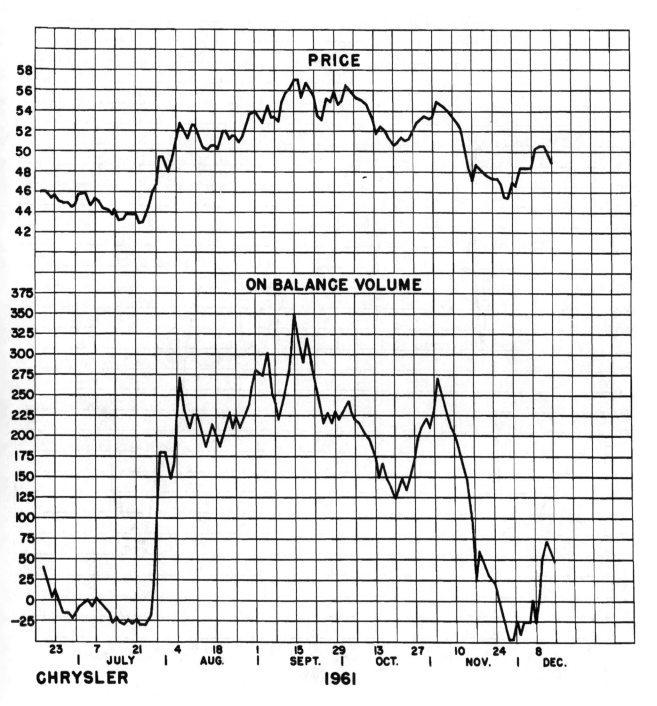

PRICE

ON BALANCE VOLUME

CHRYSLER   **1961**

Chart 45

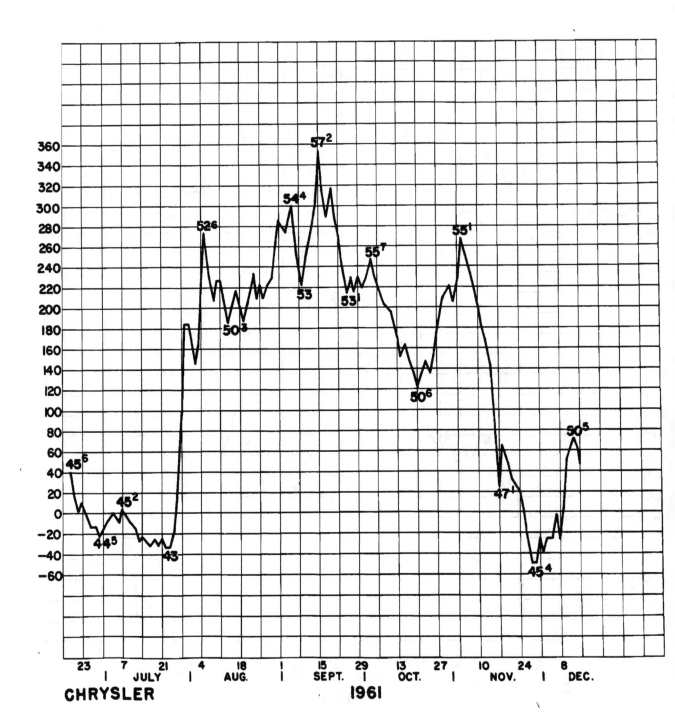

CHRYSLER 1961

Chart 45 (cont.)

Chrysler and OBV 1961-62

Here you can visually see the *lack of price confirmation* on the downside when Chrysler showed OBV going under the late July levels in December, reaching a minus 48,800 with the price holding up at 45.50, above the July low of 43.00. This showed the minus 48,800 on-balance volume as being the long-term major volume support level, a level which was not broken in 1962 when the price of Chrysler stock plummeted to 38.88 in the May-June market plunge. The *lack of volume confirmation* at that time was also important, *out of gear movements between OBV and price at critical extremes tending to coincide with significant turning points.*

The following figures provide the day-to-day account of Chrysler and OBV from June to December 1961:

CHRYSLER

(June 1961 to December 1961)

Date	On-Balance Volume		Price	Date	On-Balance Volume		Price
June 20	39,900		46.13	July 27	14,200	UP	46.00
June 21	15,700		46.00	July 28	89,200	UP	46.63
June 22	2,700		45.50	July 31	183,100	UP	49.50
June 23	14,100		45.75	Aug. 1	183,100	UP	49.50
June 26	−1,400	DOWN	45.25	Aug. 2	147,600		48.00
June 27	−13,700	DOWN	45.00	Aug. 3	164,400		49.13
June 28	−13,700	DOWN	45.00	Aug. 4	225,800	UP	51.38
June 29	−22,800	DOWN	44.63	Aug. 7	272,300	UP	52.75
June 30	−15,400		44.75	Aug. 8	232,400		52.38
July 3	−8,900		45.75	Aug. 9	208,500		51.38
July 5	−100		45.88	Aug. 10	227,000		52.75
July 6	−10,600		44.63	Aug. 11	227,000		52.75
July 7	2,800	UP	45.25	Aug. 14	208,300		51.50
July 10	−4,000		45.13	Aug. 15	184,800	DOWN	50.38
July 11	−10,400		44.63	Aug. 16	204,900		50.25 ex.
July 12	−17,200		44.25	Aug. 17	217,300		50.75
July 13	−27,000	DOWN	43.88	Aug. 18	201,200		50.50
July 14	−22,600		44.25	Aug. 21	187,600		50.25
July 17	−26,900		43.88	Aug. 22	206,500		52.00
July 18	−32,000	DOWN	43.25	Aug. 23	233,200	UP	52.13
July 19	−24,200		43.88	Aug. 24	211,300		51.38
July 20	−30,900		43.75	Aug. 25	223,100		51.50
July 21	−25,300		43.88	Aug. 28	212,300		50.88
July 24	−32,500	DOWN	43.00	Aug. 29	222,700		51.50
July 25	−32,500	DOWN	43.00	Aug. 30	238,500	UP	52.63
July 26	−17,900		44.50	Aug. 31	263,400	UP	53.75

Date	On-Balance Volume		Price	Date	On-Balance Volume		Price
Sept. 1	284,200	UP	54.00	Oct. 25	136,600		51.38
Sept. 5	274,000		52.63	Oct. 26	154,500	UP	51.75
Sept. 6	300,000	UP	54.50	Oct. 27	175,200	UP	52.00
Sept. 7	252,700	DOWN	53.88	Oct. 30	193,400	UP	52.75
Sept. 8	239,400	DOWN	53.13	Oct. 31	209,000	UP	53.13
Sept. 11	221,700	DOWN	53.00	Nov. 1	219,800	UP	53.63
Sept. 12	247,400		55.13	Nov. 2	206,800		53.25
Sept. 13	283,600		55.88	Nov. 3	228,100	UP	53.50
Sept. 14	311,700	UP	56.25	Nov. 6	268,700	UP	55.13
Sept. 15	353,000	UP	57.25	Nov. 8	233,100		54.50
Sept. 18	316,100		57.13	Nov. 9	213,600		54.00
Sept. 19	291,000		55.50	Nov. 10	201,100	DOWN	53.50
Sept. 20	318,100		56.88	Nov. 13	183,300	DOWN	52.75
Sept. 21	290,500	DOWN	56.00	Nov. 14	168,900	DOWN	52.38
Sept. 22	271,800	DOWN	55.50	Nov. 15	142,600	DOWN	50.63
Sept. 25	239,200	DOWN	53.63	Nov. 16	68,400	DOWN	48.38
Sept. 26	214,200	DOWN	53.13	Nov. 17	23,700	DOWN	47.13
Sept. 27	231,200		55.25	Nov. 20	62,800		48.50
Sept. 28	216,900		55.00	Nov. 21	47,600		48.25
Sept. 29	229,400		55.88	Nov. 22	33,400		47.75
Oct. 2	219,400		54.63	Nov. 24	19,600	DOWN	47.63
Oct. 3	229,900	UP	55.00	Nov. 27	1,900	DOWN	47.50
Oct. 4	244,700	UP	56.50	Nov. 28	−21,600	DOWN	46.75
Oct. 5	232,500		55.88	Nov. 29	−48,800	DOWN	45.50
Oct. 6	221,800		55.75	Nov. 30	−48,800	DOWN	45.50
Oct. 9	213,000	DOWN	55.25	Dec. 1	−24,000		46.88
Oct. 10	202,400	DOWN	55.13	Dec. 4	−39,100		46.75
Oct. 11	194,600	DOWN	54.63	Dec. 5	−23,800		48.25
Oct. 12	185,700	DOWN	53.75	Dec. 6	−23,800		48.25
Oct. 13	173,000	DOWN	53.38	Dec. 7	−3,600		49.25
Oct. 16	151,700	DOWN	51.75	Dec. 8	−24,800		48.38
Oct. 17	164,200		52.50	Dec. 11	5,000	UP	50.25
Oct. 18	147,800	DOWN	52.00	Dec. 12	51,500	UP	50.50
Oct. 19	138,000	DOWN	51.38	Dec. 13	72,800	UP	50.63
Oct. 20	125,000	DOWN	50.75	Dec. 14	61,500		49.88
Oct. 23	135,300		51.00	Dec. 15	48,200		49.00
Oct. 24	148,300		51.50				

Always after the basic table is prepared it is best to immediately set up the fields, inasmuch as the field trend has a great deal to do with the trading strategy as well as what the investor plans to do. Below is the application of field theory to Chrysler for the June to December 1961 period:

CHRYSLER

June to December 1961
"The Field Theory"

Interpretation of Field	Field Maximum On-Balance Volume	Type of Field	Price	Date
	−22,800	DOWN	44.63	June 29, 1961
	2,800	UP	45.26	July 7, 1961
Doubtful	−32,500	DOWN	43.00	July 25, 1961
Doubtful	272,300	UP	52.75	Aug. 7, 1961
Doubtful	184,800	DOWN	50.38	Aug. 15, 1961
Rising	300,000	UP	54.50	Sept. 6, 1961
Rising	221,700	DOWN	53.00	Sept. 11, 1961
Rising	353,000	UP	57.25	Sept. 15, 1961
Doubtful	214,200	DOWN	53.13	Sept. 26, 1961
Doubtful	244,700	UP	56.50	Oct. 4, 1961
Falling	125,000	DOWN	50.75	Oct. 20, 1961
Doubtful	268,700	UP	55.13	Nov. 6, 1961
Doubtful	−48,800	DOWN	45.50	Nov. 30, 1961
Doubtful	72,800	UP	50.63	Dec. 13, 1961

A Few Simple Tests

Assume that the investor and trader did not know what is coming in 1962 and only had the preceding figures to go by. He would then proceed with the few simple tests previously described, namely (1) checking OBV at each price level, (2) checking for accumulation or distribution and (3) checking for signs of long-term strength or weakness. He will now add the *non-confirmations* to his storehouse of quick tests.

Checking out OBV at each price level. Since 43.00 is the low and 57.25 is the high in the table, let us choose the *average price* as the arbitrary testing level for checking out the on-balance volume. In this case we will check the OBV everytime the price of Chrysler stock closes around the $50 level:

Date	On-Balance Volume	Price	Field Trend
Aug. 15, 1961	184,800	50.38	Doubtful
Aug. 16, 1961	204,900	50.25 ex.	Doubtful
Aug. 17, 1961	217,300	50.75	Doubtful
Aug. 18, 1961	201,200	50.50	Doubtful
Aug. 21, 1961	187,600	50.25	Doubtful
Aug. 28, 1961	212,300	50.88	Doubtful
Oct. 20, 1961	125,000	50.75	Falling

Date	On-Balance Volume	Price	Field Trend
Nov. 15, 1961	142,600	50.63	Doubtful
Dec. 11, 1961	5,000	50.25	Doubtful
Dec. 12, 1961	51,500	50.50	Doubtful
Dec. 13, 1961	72,800	50.63	Doubtful

The outcome of this first test shows the *lack of serious weakness*, only *one* falling field trend designation failing to be followed through by *another* falling designation. On-balance volume figures were smaller after August 28th but the field trend had quickly changed back to doubtful, again *the trend being the thing to watch.*

Checking for accumulation and distribution. From July 25, 1961 to September 15, 1961 the stock evidenced accumulation, OBV figures *trending* higher. This was not a long time for important accumulation, being only some seven weeks. The stock then made an OBV "line" between 353,000 and 214,200, this three-week movement separating the stock between accumulation and distribution. When OBV broke 214,200 on October 9th distribution was underway which ended in a *non-confirmation,* OBV making a new low of minus 48,800 but the price holding above the 43.00 low of late July. Between November 30th and December 15th it could only be said that Chrysler was again "neutral," neither under accumulation or distribution, the neutral zones or "lines" or OBV occurring in between. You will see later that Chrysler was about to be accumulated again but this accumulation could not be determined until the stock broke out of an on-balance volume "line", or neutral zone.

Checking for signs of long-term strength or weakness. Chrysler gave no sign of long-term weakness, *having recorded an important non-confirmation* on the downside in late November 1961. The very fact that the price of the stock was in a depressed zone also militated against a sign of long-term weakness occurring at those levels. It would then be determined that minus 48,800 was the long-term volume support level.

Non-confirmations. Non-confirmations between OBV and price at the point of extremes *should always be judged to be significant,* usually associated with important turning points in the trend of the stock. The greater the spread between OBV and price at the point of non-confirmation, the greater the significance of the resulting action. This naturally leads into a brief discussion of OBV and price confirmations.

Confirmations. Significant confirmations of OBV and price are those which tend to take place simultaneously. When OBV and price are "in gear" the movement tends to continue moving in the *same* direction. A non-confirmation suggests a *reversal.* Simultaneous OBV and price breakouts are more powerful than those occurring separately. You have seen these movements expressed in terms of the more important trading buy and sell signals. Price and OBV breakouts "in trend" (in the same direction with the field) tend to propel the movement further in the same direction while such breakouts "out of trend" suggest *reversal*. Note that the new low in on-balance volume for Chrysler in late November 1961 took place in a *doubtful* field trend and NOT a falling field trend.

An example of a simultaneous breakout on the upside, a strong confirmation of immediate strong upside action, is the confirmation of July 28, 1961. For over five weeks the price of Chrysler was forming a "line" between 43.00 and 46.13, a very narrow price range. OBV was moving between a minus 32,500 and a plus 39,900. On July 28th the price moved up to 46.63 and OBV shot ahead to 89,200, a simultaneous upside breakout from a double "line". The immediate effect was a sharp advance the next day of almost 3 points, moving almost as much in one day as in the previous five weeks. The stock went on to rise to 57.25 over the next six weeks. Breakouts from OBV "lines" and price "lines" are important and when they are *simultaneous* a great deal of "energy" is often released in the form of a sharp price advance or decline, depending on the direction of the breakout.

Summing Up the Tests

	Strength Signalled With Key Date of Change
Checking OBV At Each Price Level	Dec. 11, 1961
Stock judged to be "neutral"	Nov. 30 to Dec. 15, 1961
Long-term strength assumed	Nov. 30, 1961
Non-confirmation on the downside	Nov. 30, 1961

Conclusion: Chrysler was an "investment" buy between Nov. 30th and Dec. 15, 1961 at prices ranging from 45.50 to 50.63 despite the "top" being recorded in the general market. New lows in OBV had neither field confirmation or price confirmation. The neutral phase *followed* distribution and not accumulation and the non-confirmation on the downside signalled a strong reversal.

Now let us look at the charts covering the December 1961 to August 1962 period for Chrysler:

The most dramatic occurrence in these charts is the new low of 38.88 recorded on June 14, 1962 together with the *wide lack of downside confirmation in terms of on-balance volume*. It is now known that such glaring non-confirmations tend to coincide with *dramatic swings in the opposite direction*, Chrysler launched on an upward path which was not to end for many months later at considerably higher prices. The short interest apparently had an important role to play in the long Chrysler advance which followed the June 1962 low. Later on you will see just how

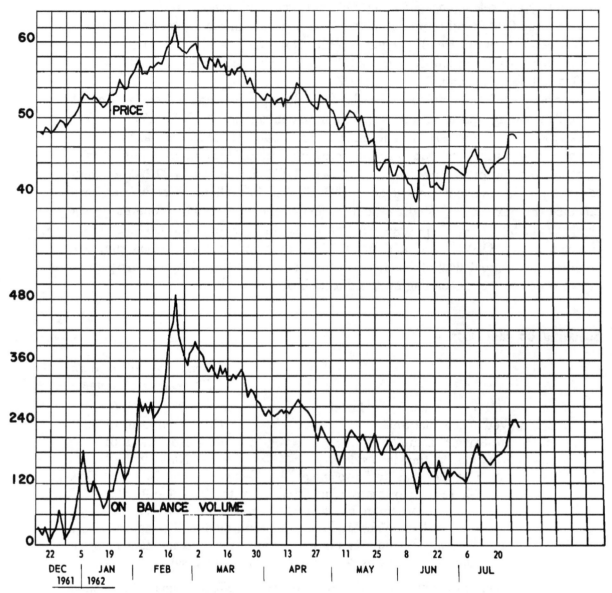

PRICE

ON BALANCE VOLUME

| 60 |
| 50 |
| 40 |

| 480 |
| 360 |
| 240 |
| 120 |
| 0 |

22   5   19   2   16   2   16   30   13   27   11   25   8   22   6   20

DEC   JAN   FEB   MAR   APR   MAY   JUN   JUL
1961 1962

CHRYSLER

Chart 46

important it is when a rising short interest goes hand in hand with a strong advancing on-balance volume trend.

Now here are the day-to-day Chrysler OBV and price figures for the December 1961 to August 1962 period:

CHRYSLER

(December 1961 to August 1962)

Date	On-Balance Volume		Price	Date	On-Balance Volume		Price
Dec. 18	32,100		48.00	Feb. 8	278,000	UP	56.88
Dec. 19	20,000		47.75	Feb. 9	246,300	DOWN	56.75
Dec. 20	32,800		48.63	Feb. 12	257,300		57.00
Dec. 21	19,900	DOWN	48.37	Feb. 13	269,900		57.13
Dec. 22	5,600	DOWN	47.88	Feb. 14	281,500	UP	57.00 ex.
Dec. 26	31,400		49.00	Feb. 15	399,400	UP	59.37
Dec. 27	69,600	UP	49.75	Feb. 16	411,000	UP	59.63
Dec. 28	39,600		49.50	Feb. 19	433,600	UP	60.00
Dec. 29	12,600		48.50	Feb. 20	489,800	UP	62.13
Jan. 2	31,200		50.00	Feb. 21	415,800		59.13
Jan. 3	50,000		50.37	Feb. 23	371,300		58.75
Jan. 4	80,100	UP	51.13	Feb. 26	352,700		58.63
Jan. 5	126,300	UP	52.25	Feb. 27	377,100		59.37
Jan. 8	181,100	UP	53.13	Feb. 28	386,700		59.63
Jan. 9	137,700		53.00	Mar. 1	397,100		59.88
Jan. 10	103,200		52.50	Mar. 2	385,200		58.50
Jan. 11	103,200		52.50	Mar. 5	373,500		57.63
Jan. 12	122,200		52.75	Mar. 6	351,400	DOWN	56.50
Jan. 15	111,200		52.25	Mar. 7	337,600	DOWN	56.25
Jan. 16	94,100	DOWN	51.75	Mar. 8	351,800		57.88
Jan. 17	73,400	DOWN	51.37	Mar. 9	334,000	DOWN	57.63
Jan. 18	86,400		51.88	Mar. 12	328,500	DOWN	56.63
Jan. 19	107,000		53.00	Mar. 13	350,700		57.75
Jan. 22	107,000		53.00	Mar. 14	335,500		56.63
Jan. 23	125,000	UP	53.13	Mar. 15	347,100		57.00
Jan. 24	167,300	UP	55.00	Mar. 16	324,600	DOWN	55.75
Jan. 25	142,700		54.37	Mar. 19	324,600	DOWN	55.75
Jan. 26	124,300		53.88	Mar. 20	331,900		56.13
Jan. 29	138,600		54.00	Mar. 21	325,000		55.75
Jan. 30	162,400		55.25	Mar. 22	331,600		56.25
Jan. 31	196,100	UP	56.00	Mar. 23	342,200	UP	56.50
Feb. 1	239,500	UP	57.00	Mar. 26	328,900		55.88
Feb. 2	286,100	UP	57.63	Mar. 27	300,900	DOWN	54.37
Feb. 5	259,600		55.75	Mar. 28	314,600		55.13
Feb. 6	275,600		55.88	Mar. 29	307,200		54.13
Feb. 7	262,800		55.75	Mar. 30	285,400	DOWN	53.63

Date	On-Balance Volume		Price	Date	On-Balance Volume		Price
Apr. 2	276,100	DOWN	53.25	June 4	185,200		42.25
Apr. 3	263,500	DOWN	52.75	June 5	185,200		42.25
Apr. 4	254,500	DOWN	52.25	June 6	196,300		43.75
Apr. 5	264,200		53.25	June 7	188,000		43.25
Apr. 6	255,000		52.88	June 8	182,000	DOWN	43.00
Apr. 9	247,300	DOWN	51.88	June 11	168,600	DOWN	41.50
Apr. 10	255,700		52.13	June 12	153,400	DOWN	41.13
Apr. 11	267,100	UP	52.50	June 13	133,300	DOWN	40.13
Apr. 12	257,200		51.37	June 14	99,200	DOWN	38.88
Apr. 13	266,300		52.37	June 15	134,400		43.00
Apr. 16	257,900		52.13	June 18	157,000		43.25
Apr. 17	265,500		52.37	June 19	160,800		43.50
Apr. 18	276,900	UP	53.50	June 20	150,300		42.75
Apr. 19	284,600	UP	54.50	June 21	134,400		40.75
Apr. 23	268,800		53.88	June 22	134,400		40.75
Apr. 24	263,500		53.75	June 25	162,600	UP	41.13
Apr. 25	255,300	DOWN	52.50	June 26	147,000		40.50
Apr. 26	243,600	DOWN	51.88	June 27	125,300	DOWN	40.37
Apr. 27	223,300	DOWN	51.50	June 28	148,600		43.88
Apr. 30	206,600	DOWN	51.37	June 29	134,200		43.25
May 1	229,000		53.00	July 2	145,900		43.50
May 2	218,600		52.50	July 3	136,400		43.37
May 3	207,700		52.37	July 5	129,100	DOWN	42.75
May 4	198,200	DOWN	51.13	July 6	123,500	DOWN	42.25
May 7	190,500	DOWN	50.88	July 9	136,400		44.13
May 8	175,300	DOWN	49.50	July 10	167,100	UP	44.75
May 9	155,500	DOWN	48.25	July 11	180,200	UP	45.50
May 10	173,400		48.63	July 12	197,900	UP	45.63
May 11	187,800		49.13	July 13	175,100		44.37
May 14	211,600		50.13	July 16	175,100		44.37
May 15	224,000		50.88	July 17	166,600		43.25
May 16	216,600		50.75	July 18	154,100		42.50
May 17	209,800		50.00	July 19	162,700		43.37
May 18	206,100		49.50	July 20	167,500		43.63
May 21	215,500		50.13	July 23	174,100		44.00
May 22	202,400	DOWN	48.13	July 24	179,800		44.13
May 23	180,000	DOWN	46.37	July 25	187,800		44.50
May 24	201,200		46.50	July 26	202,900	UP	45.25
May 25	217,500	UP	46.88	July 27	225,100	UP	47.38
May 28	186,700		43.25	July 30	241,000	UP	47.75
May 29	178,300	DOWN	43.00	July 31	241,000	UP	47.75
May 31	203,000		44.25	Aug. 1	231,300		47.00 ex.
June 1	203,000		44.25				

Now is added the field trend covering this period:

CHRYSLER

(December 1961 to August 1962)
"The Field Theory"

Interpretation of Field	Field Maximum On-Balance Volume	Type of Field	Price	Date
Doubtful	5,600	DOWN	47.88	Dec. 22, 1961
Rising	181,100	UP	53.13	Jan. 8, 1962
Rising	73,400	DOWN	51.37	Jan. 17, 1962
Rising	278,000	UP	56.88	Feb. 8, 1962
Rising	246,300	DOWN	56.75	Feb. 9, 1962
Rising	489,800	UP	62.13	Feb. 20, 1962
Rising	324,600	DOWN	55.75	Mar. 19, 1962
Doubtful	342,200	UP	56.50	Mar. 23, 1962
Falling	247,300	DOWN	51.88	Apr. 9, 1962
Falling	284,600	UP	54.50	Apr. 19, 1962
Falling	180,000	DOWN	46.37	May 23, 1962
Falling	217,500	UP	46.88	May 25, 1962
Falling	99,200	DOWN	38.88	June 14, 1962
Falling	162,600	UP	41.13	June 25, 1962
Doubtful	123,500	DOWN	42.25	July 6, 1962

Having the raw material for setting up the trading record, these figures now follow:

CHRYSLER

Trading Record

Date and Action	Signal	Profit	Loss	Cumulative
BUY July 31, 1961 at 49.50	B-9			
BUY Aug. 7, 1961 at 52.75	B-7			
BUY Aug. 31, 1961 at 53.75	B-7			
SELL Sept. 1, 1961 at 54.00	S-8	4.50		4.50
BUY Sept. 5, 1961 at 52.63	B-4			
BUY Sept. 8, 1961 at 53.13	B-3			
BUY Sept. 11, 1961 at 53.00	B-1			
BUY Sept. 12, 1961 at 55.13	B-8			
BUY Sept. 15, 1961 at 57.25 B-4,	B-9			
SELL Sept. 18, 1961 at 57.13	S-3	4.50		9.00
BUY Sept. 19, 1961 at 55.50	B-3			
BUY Sept. 25, 1961 at 53.63	B-1			
BUY Sept. 26, 1961 at 53.13 B-3,	B-8			
SELL Oct. 5, 1961 at 55.88	S-8	.38		9.38
SELL Oct. 10, 1961 at 55.13 S-4,	S-9			
SELL Oct. 30, 1961 at 52.75	S-1			

Date and Action	Signal	Profit	Loss	Cumulative
SELL Nov. 6, 1961 at 55.13	S-8			
SELL Nov. 8, 1961 at 54.50	S-3			
BUY Nov. 16, 1961 at 48.38	B-8			
BUY Nov. 17, 1961 at 47.13	B-3			
SELL Nov. 21, 1961 at 48.25	S-3		.13	9.25
BUY Nov. 24, 1961 at 47.63	B-8			
SELL Nov. 27, 1961 at 47.50	S-7		.13	9.13
SELL Dec. 13, 1961 at 50.63	S-3			
BUY Dec. 26, 1961 at 49.00	B-8			
BUY Jan. 5, 1962 at 52.25	B-4, B-7			
SELL Jan. 8, 1962 at 53.13	S-3	4.13		13.25
SELL Jan. 9, 1962 at 53.00	S-8			
BUY Jan. 10, 1962 at 52.50	B-3			
BUY Jan. 18, 1962 at 51.88	B-1, B-8			
BUY Jan. 24, 1962 at 55.00	B-4			
SELL Jan. 25, 1962 at 54.37	S-3, S-8	1.88		15.13
BUY Feb. 1, 1962 at 57.00	B-7			
SELL Feb. 2, 1962 at 57.63	S-3	.63		15.75
BUY Feb. 6, 1962 at 55.88	B-2			
BUY Feb. 9, 1962 at 56.75	B-7			
BUY Feb. 12, 1962 at 57.00	B-1			
BUY Feb. 15, 1962 at 59.37	B-4			
SELL Feb. 16, 1962 at 59.63	S-3	3.75		19.50
SELL Feb. 21, 1962 at 59.13	S-3			
BUY Feb. 23, 1962 at 58.75	B-3			
BUY Mar. 8, 1962 at 57.88	B-1			
SELL Mar. 19, 1962 at 55.75	S-7		3.00	16.50
BUY Mar. 20, 1962 at 56.13	B-8			
BUY Mar. 26, 1962 at 55.88	B-4			
SELL Mar. 28, 1962 at 55.13	S-4		1.00	15.50
SELL Apr. 2, 1962 at 53.25	S-7			
SELL Apr. 19, 1962 at 54.50	S-1	(These cancel.		
BUY Apr. 19, 1962 at 54.50	B-7	NO action)		
SELL Apr. 26, 1962 at 51.88	S-4			
BUY Apr. 27, 1962 at 51.50	B-8	(These cancel.		
SELL Apr. 27, 1962 at 51.50	S-9	NO action)		
SELL May 2, 1962 at 52.50	S-1			
BUY May 4, 1962 at 51.13	B-8			
SELL May 7, 1962 at 50.88	S-7		.25	15.25
SELL May 23, 1962 at 46.37	S-7			
BUY May 24, 1962 at 46.50	B-8			
SELL May 28, 1962 at 43.25	S-1		3.25	12.00
BUY May 29, 1962 at 43.00	B-2			
SELL May 31, 1962 at 44.25	S-4	1.25		13.25
BUY June 5, 1962 at 42.25	B-2			
SELL June 11, 1962 at 41.50	S-7		.75	12.50
BUY June 12, 1962 at 41.13	B-8			

Date and Action	Signal	Profit	Loss	Cumulative
SELL June 13, 1962 at 40.13	S-9		1.00	11.50
BUY June 15, 1962 at 43.00	B-3			
SELL June 18, 1962 at 43.25	S-2, S-3	.25		11.75
BUY June 22, 1962 at 40.75	B-2			
SELL June 26, 1962 at 40.50	S-1		.25	11.50
SELL June 28, 1962 at 43.88	S-4, S-7			
SELL June 29, 1962 at 43.25	S-2			
SELL July 6, 1962 at 42.25	S-7			
BUY July 9, 1962 at 44.13	B-8			
SELL July 19, 1962 at 43.88	S-7		.25	11.25
BUY July 27, 1962 at 47.38	B-7			

The trading record above showed moderate gains during the difficult period from June 1961 through the break of 1962. The day-to-day trader was left in a long position on July 27, 1962 at 47.38. Note that in many instances when the stock was sold at a minor loss that the loss would have been greater if the first sell signal had been ignored.

The Summing up

Here you can see how important the interplay between volume and price is at various extremes. When on-balance volume and price are "out of gear" at critical extremes, this lack of confirmation tends to coincide with significant turning points. You shall now look for important confirmations and non-confirmations between on-balance volume and price. Non-confirmation implies a coming *reversal* and confirmation implies a continuation in the same direction.

In order to get a "feel" of the stock before trading it, simple tests such as the following can be applied: (a) checking out OBV at various price levels, (b) checking for accumulation and distribution, (c) checking for signs of long-term strength or weakness and (d) looking for important confirmations and non-confirmations between OBV and price.

Chapter Eight

American Telephone

*Even this blue chip responds to the same OBV measures
and related field theories*

What You Are about to Learn

The examples thus far shown in this book of stocks responding to on-balance volume buy and sell signals are stocks which are part of the Dow-Jones Industrial Average. The purpose of these selections will be seen in later chapters, the relationship of on-balance volume to the Dow-Jones Industrial Average being a necessary follow-through to these initial discussions. All the stocks going to make up this average are well known companies and their stocks have quality. They are *not* necessarily the best stocks from a *trading* standpoint and for this reason their trading records, using the 18 OBV signals, are not meant to be thought of as particularly outstanding. The nub of the matter is simply that these blue chip issues *can* be successfully traded using the 18 OBV signals. It was felt that this was a far better test of the value of OBV rather than selecting sensational examples which most certainly do exist. In this section you will see OBV applied to American Telephone, a stock not particularly suited for day-to-day trading. You will see some important exceptions to some of the things previously pointed out. Like a bridge hand, no stock is going to work out exactly the same way. Each one is a little different. The exceptions are not difficult to see when they occur, there being a good reason for each exception. American Telephone is chosen now for presentation because it points up one of these important exceptions, an exception which can be easily understood and acted upon when it occurs again.

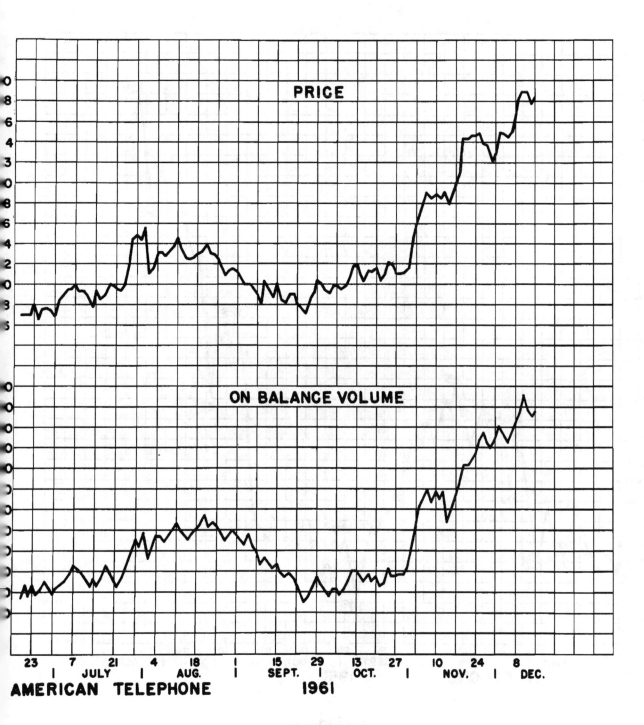

PRICE

ON BALANCE VOLUME

| 23 | 7 | 21 | 4 | 18 | 1 | 15 | 29 | 13 | 27 | 10 | 24 | 8 |

JULY | AUG. | SEPT. | OCT. | NOV. | DEC.

AMERICAN TELEPHONE   1961

Chart 47

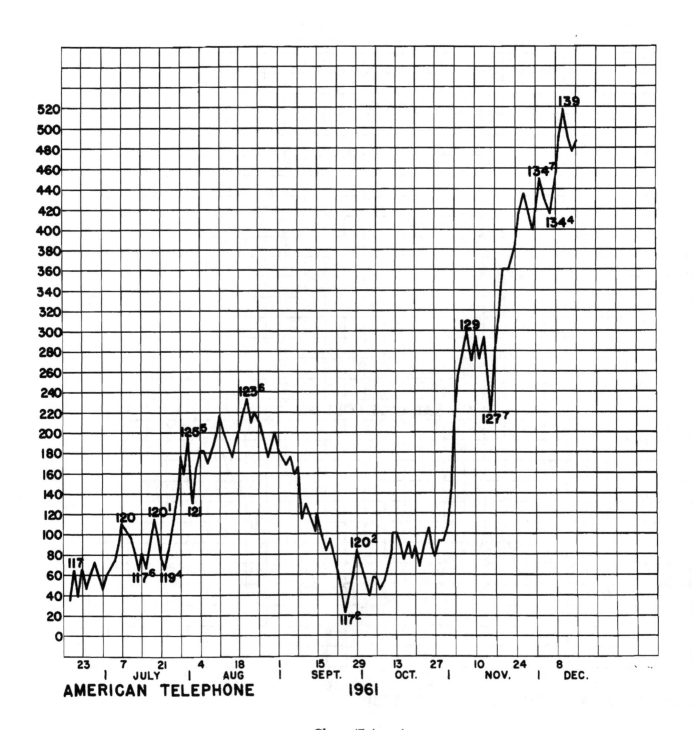

AMERICAN TELEPHONE   1961

Chart 47 (cont.)

American Telephone and OBV

The support level in the OBV line shows up well here as being recorded on September 26, 1961, on-balance volume standing at 22,800. Later on, when the 1962 period is discussed, you will see that that support level was broken together with a price confirmation on the downside, *that move practically corresponding with the bottom of the decline.* This could have been interpreted as a long-term sell signal BUT IT WAS NOT, the *characteristics* of the decline to a new low being entirely different from those recorded when other stocks gave valid long-term sell signals. Below are the day-to-day OBV and price figures covering the June to December 1961 period:

AMERICAN TELEPHONE

(June to December 1961)

Date	On-Balance Volume		Price	Date	On-Balance Volume		Price
June 20	36,900		116.75	July 27	147,600	UP	124.25
June 21	63,500		117.00	July 28	174,000	UP	124.75
June 22	39,900		116.88	July 31	159,500		124.38
June 23	64,500	UP	118.13	Aug. 1	193,600	UP	125.63
June 26	46,200		116.50	Aug. 2	130,000		121.00
June 27	61,900		117.25	Aug. 3	166,000		121.63
June 28	73,400	UP	117.50	Aug. 4	182,400		123.00
June 29	59,400		117.25	Aug. 7	182,400		123.00
June 30	43,400	DOWN	116.88	Aug. 8	168,100		122.63
July 3	58,600		118.25	Aug. 9	184,100	UP	123.25
July 5	73,600	UP	119.38	Aug. 10	199,600	UP	123.75
July 6	92,800	UP	119.63	Aug. 11	217,400	UP	124.50
July 7	109,900	UP	120.00	Aug. 14	201,600		123.50
July 10	96,900		119.25	Aug. 15	188,000		122.50
July 11	96,900		119.25	Aug. 16	175,600		122.38
July 12	81,800		118.88	Aug. 17	191,200		122.50
July 13	65,900		117.75	Aug. 18	201,100		122.88
July 14	81,400		119.13	Aug. 21	213,500		123.13
July 17	65,100	DOWN	118.50	Aug. 22	233,400	UP	123.75
July 18	86,600		118.75	Aug. 23	210,500		122.75
July 19	116,000	UP	120.13	Aug. 24	221,800		122.88
July 20	92,800		119.88	Aug. 25	209,500	DOWN	122.38
July 21	77,100		119.75	Aug. 28	193,200	DOWN	121.88
July 24	65,000	DOWN	119.50	Aug. 29	176,800	DOWN	120.75
July 25	84,600		120.13	Aug. 30	187,700		121.25
July 26	114,200		122.00	Aug. 31	199,300		121.50

Date	On-Balance Volume		Price	Date	On-Balance Volume		Price
Sept. 1	183,500		121.38	Oct. 25	104,200	UP	122.00
Sept. 5	167,900	DOWN	120.00	Oct. 26	87,100		121.75
Sept. 6	176,100		120.13	Oct. 27	78,000		120.88
Sept. 7	160,500	DOWN	119.75	Oct. 30	93,200		121.13
Sept. 8	144,100	DOWN	119.13	Oct. 31	93,200		121.13
Sept. 11	114,900	DOWN	118.00	Nov. 1	108,400	UP	121.63
Sept. 12	131,600		120.38	Nov. 2	150,700	UP	124.75
Sept. 13	115,500		119.50	Nov. 3	204,200	UP	125.88
Sept. 14	103,500	DOWN	118.75	Nov. 6	254,500	UP	127.88
Sept. 15	119,300		120.00	Nov. 8	299,700	UP	129.00
Sept. 18	97,800	DOWN	118.38	Nov. 9	267,900		128.50
Sept. 19	82,800	DOWN	118.13	Nov. 10	296,400		129.00
Sept. 20	93,600		119.00	Nov. 13	273,100		128.50
Sept. 21	79,900	DOWN	118.88	Nov. 14	293,400		129.13
Sept. 22	64,600	DOWN	118.13	Nov. 15	221,900	DOWN	127.88
Sept. 25	44,500	DOWN	117.63	Nov. 16	250,900		128.88
Sept. 26	22,800	DOWN	117.25	Nov. 17	280,300		130.13
Sept. 27	40,700		118.50	Nov. 20	313,000	UP	131.13
Sept. 28	61,000		119.25	Nov. 21	359,400	UP	134.25
Sept. 29	86,400		120.25	Nov. 22	359,400	UP	134.25
Oct. 2	69,000		119.88	Nov. 24	385,400	UP	134.50
Oct. 3	57,900		119.50	Nov. 27	416,300	UP	134.75
Oct. 4	40,700		119.13	Nov. 28	434,800	UP	133.88 ex.
Oct. 5	55,400		119.88	Nov. 29	417,100		133.75
Oct. 6	55,400		119.88	Nov. 30	399,900		131.88
Oct. 9	45,900		119.63	Dec. 1	420,000		133.13
Oct. 10	56,700	UP	119.88	Dec. 4	449,300	UP	134.88
Oct. 11	81,200	UP	120.75	Dec. 5	433,300		134.75
Oct. 12	101,900	UP	121.75	Dec. 6	415,300		134.50
Oct. 13	101,900	UP	121.75	Dec. 7	430,500		135.00
Oct. 16	88,000		120.88	Dec. 8	457,500	UP	136.50
Oct. 17	74,400		120.25	Dec. 11	488,900	UP	138.25
Oct. 18	93,100		121.38	Dec. 12	518,600	UP	139.00
Oct. 19	75,000		121.25	Dec. 13	490,500		138.88
Oct. 20	87,100		121.50	Dec. 14	477,000		137.88
Oct. 23	68,200	DOWN	120.38	Dec. 15	488,400		138.38
Oct. 24	83,900		120.88				

The next step again is to immediately set up the figures for the various fields:

AMERICAN TELEPHONE

June to December 1961

"The Field Theory"

Interpretation of Field	Field Maximum On-Balance Volume	Type of Field	Price	Date
	73,400	UP	117.50	June 28, 1961
	43,400	DOWN	116.88	June 30, 1961
Rising	109,900	UP	120.00	July 7, 1961
Rising	65,100	DOWN	118.50	July 17, 1961
Rising	116,000	UP	120.13	July 19, 1961
Doubtful	65,000	DOWN	119.50	July 24, 1961
Doubtful	233,400	UP	123.75	Aug. 22, 1961
Doubtful	22,800	DOWN	117.25	Sept. 26, 1961
Doubtful	101,900	UP	121.75	Oct. 13, 1961
Doubtful	68,200	DOWN	120.38	Oct. 23, 1961
Rising	299,700	UP	129.00	Nov. 8, 1961
Rising	221,900	DOWN	127.88	Nov. 15, 1961
Rising	518,600	UP	139.00	Dec. 12, 1961

Running a Few Tests Again

Checking OBV at various price levels. Arbitrarily choosing the 120 level, we can make up the following little table:

Date	On-Balance Volume	Price	Field Trend
July 7, 1961	109,900	120.00	Rising
July 19, 1961	116,000	120.13	Rising
July 25, 1961	84,600	120.13	Doubtful
Aug. 29, 1961	176,800	120.75	Doubtful
Sept. 5, 1961	167,900	120.00	Doubtful
Sept. 6, 1961	176,100	120.13	Doubtful
Sept. 12, 1961	131,600	120.38	Doubtful
Sept. 15. 1961	119,300	120.00	Doubtful
Sept. 29, 1961	86,400	120.25	Doubtful
Oct. 11, 1961	81,200	120.75	Doubtful
Oct. 16. 1961	88,000	120.88	Doubtful
Oct. 17, 1961	74,400	120.25	Doubtful
Oct. 23, 1961	68,200	120.38	Doubtful
Oct. 24, 1961	83,900	120.88	Doubtful
Oct. 27, 1961	78,000	120.88	Rising

The October 27th sign was encouraging, OBV holding above the October 23rd level on a pullback and the field trend changing from doubtful to rising. After a long series of doubtful designations the stock had reasserted its position and was ready for a more important advance.

Checking for accumulation and distribution. Accumulation showed up here in many forms. The most obvious form was the general rising curve of on-balance volume *where the setbacks lacked price confirmation.* Another sign is the price "line" between 116.50 and 120.13 which was recorded between June 20th and July 25th, the stock breaking out from this on July 26th carrying an OBV confirmation the next day. This carried the stock quickly to 125.63 on August 1st but left price gaps at 121 and 123. These gaps were filled soon thereafter and in the process OBV rose from 193,600 to 233,400 *with no price confirmation,* the stock remaining under the August 1st level of 125.63. This signalled short-term weakness, the stock then backtracking all the way down to 117.25 with OBV falling to a low of 22,800. The fact that the stock broke the June OBV low signalled nothing further on the downside, *the price of the stock holding above the June low.* Here was *lack of confirmation on the downside,* the stock ready for a new advance after September 26th, this being the final accumulation phase leading up to the December 12th high of 139.00.

The characteristics of that final accumulation centered on the rapidity of the climb in OBV, the *acceleration being a symptom of finality.* It took on-balance volume 26 days to rise from 22,800 to 108,400 between September 26th and November 1st *but in the next 28 trading sessions OBV rose from 108,400 to 518,600.* On the final upswing from 117.25 to 139.00 the stock left *price gaps* at 123, 126, 132 and 137, judged to be too many skips in a 12-point advance. The best work on the upside was then behind the stock, the mechanics of a top so often pointing up acceleration and gaps.

Long-term strength or weakness. When OBV fell to 22,800 on September 26th, 1961 and the price held up at 117.25 this was a bull sign calling for a *reversal.* The OBV figure of 22,800 became the long-term support. The later acceleration in OBV on the upside discouraged long-term buying but at the same time a long-term sell signal would only be forthcoming by a confirmed move under 22,800. The stock was vulnerable by December from a trading standpoint but no long-term sell signal had been given.

Now look at the followthrough from the December 1961 acceleration in the OBV advance:

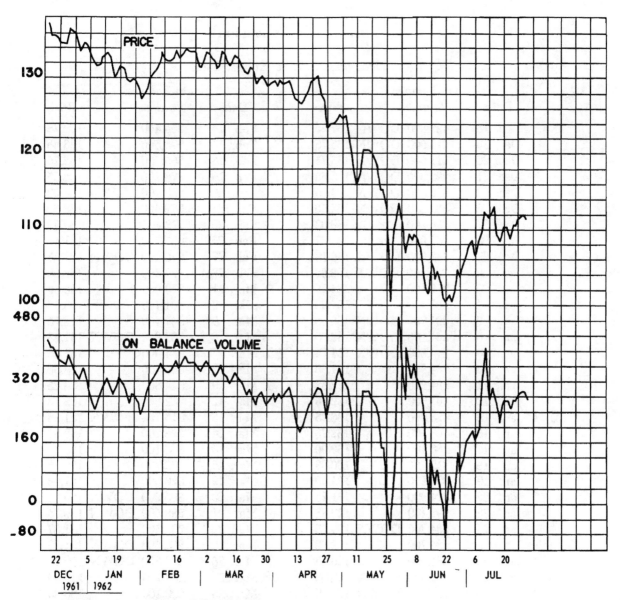

PRICE

130

120

110

100
480

ON BALANCE VOLUME

320

160

0

-80

22   5   19   2   16   2   16   30   13   27   11   25   8   22   6   20
DEC | JAN | FEB | MAR | APR | MAY | JUN | JUL
1961 1962

AMERICAN TELEPHONE

Chart 48

American Telephone

December 1961 to August 1962

Date	On-Balance Volume		Price	Date	On-Balance Volume		Price
Dec. 18	428,800	DOWN	137.25	Feb. 14	354,400		132.75
Dec. 19	411,600	DOWN	135.75	Feb. 15	375,500	UP	133.88
Dec. 20	411,600	DOWN	135.75	Feb. 16	355,700		132.75
Dec. 21	395,300	DOWN	135.63	Feb. 19	373,200		133.25
Dec. 22	375,200	DOWN	134.75	Feb. 20	385,900	UP	134.00
Dec. 26	363,200	DOWN	134.50	Feb. 21	372,400		133.50
Dec. 27	386,200		136.63	Feb. 23	372,400		133.50
Dec. 28	369,000		136.37	Feb. 26	357,700		131.88 ex.
Dec. 29	348,800	DOWN	136.13	Feb. 27	346,200	DOWN	131.75
Jan. 2	324,200	DOWN	133.63	Feb. 28	360,500		132.88
Jan. 3	352,100		134.75	Mar. 1	373,000		133.50
Jan. 4	331,400		134.63	Mar. 2	361,700		133.37
Jan. 5	301,700	DOWN	133.50	Mar. 5	347,400		132.75
Jan. 8	264,100	DOWN	132.00	Mar. 6	332,300	DOWN	131.13
Jan. 9	244,800	DOWN	131.75	Mar. 7	344,000		131.50
Jan. 10	264,800		131.88	Mar. 8	360,500		133.50
Jan. 11	284,200		132.63	Mar. 9	344,800		133.25
Jan. 12	304,600		132.88	Mar. 12	332,800		132.13
Jan. 15	323,200		133.25	Mar. 13	315,700	DOWN	131.88
Jan. 16	308,100		132.75	Mar. 14	328,200		132.37
Jan. 17	283,100		130.00	Mar. 15	343,100		133.00
Jan. 18	312,700	UP	130.88	Mar. 16	332,700		132.75
Jan. 19	330,200	UP	131.50	Mar. 19	320,000		131.88
Jan. 22	314,900		131.25	Mar. 20	305,200	DOWN	130.88
Jan. 23	297,400		129.88	Mar. 21	283,500	DOWN	130.75
Jan. 24	264,300	DOWN	129.75	Mar. 22	295,500		131.37
Jan. 25	284,700		129.88	Mar. 23	282,500	DOWN	131.13
Jan. 26	284,700		129.88	Mar. 26	260,600	DOWN	129.25
Jan. 29	262,500	DOWN	128.88	Mar. 27	280,700		130.00
Jan. 30	235,500	DOWN	127.25	Mar. 28	290,100		130.25
Jan. 31	259,800		128.00	Mar. 29	278,100		129.88
Feb. 1	285,600	UP	128.75	Mar. 30	257,500	DOWN	129.00
Feb. 2	302,800	UP	130.00	Apr. 2	270,100		129.37
Feb. 5	324,400	UP	130.75	Apr. 3	282,500		129.75
Feb. 6	336,800	UP	131.00	Apr. 4	266,300		129.00
Feb. 7	349,000	UP	132.00	Apr. 5	285,300	UP	129.88
Feb. 8	364,300	UP	133.37	Apr. 6	272,800		129.25
Feb. 9	352,100		132.63	Apr. 9	285,700	UP	129.37
Feb. 12	342,000		132.37	Apr. 10	302,300	UP	129.63
Feb. 13	342,000		132.37	Apr. 11	281,900		128.63

Date	On-Balance Volume		Price	Date	On-Balance Volume		Price
Apr. 12	246,800	DOWN	127.50	June 8	337,600		109.00
Apr. 13	210,100	DOWN	127.25	June 11	304,800	DOWN	107.37
Apr. 16	186,900	DOWN	126.88	June 12	242,300	DOWN	105.13
Apr. 17	205,800		127.50	June 13	135,400	DOWN	102.25
Apr. 18	234,100		128.50	June 14	−16,700	DOWN	101.50
Apr. 19	255,400		129.38	June 15	116,400		105.88
Apr. 23	283,600		130.00	June 18	52,600		103.50
Apr. 24	303,200	UP	130.13	June 19	84,300		104.25
Apr. 25	295,800		128.00	June 20	39,600	DOWN	103.00
Apr. 26	279,200		127.13	June 21	4,300	DOWN	101.00
Apr. 27	222,100		123.75	June 22	−89,500	DOWN	100.37
Apr. 30	285,500		124.00	June 25	69,800		101.25
May 1	285,500		124.00	June 26	4,000		100.37
May 2	331,000	UP	124.37	June 27	63,300		102.00
May 3	352,900	UP	125.13	June 28	134,600	UP	104.63
May 4	333,100		124.75	June 29	82,600		103.75
May 7	317,300		124.50	July 2	116,700		106.00
May 8	297,100		122.13	July 3	161,100	UP	107.63
May 9	236,000		119.50	July 5	190,700	UP	108.37
May 10	122,300	DOWN	117.50	July 6	163,600		106.63
May 11	53,100	DOWN	116.00	July 9	190,800	UP	108.50
May 14	219,400		117.50	July 10	302,100	UP	109.75
May 15	294,100		120.50	July 11	407,900	UP	113.25
May 16	294,100		120.50	July 12	305,200		113.00
May 17	294,100		120.50	July 13	269,600		112.75
May 18	279,000		120.00	July 16	301,800		113.00
May 21	259,300		119.00	July 17	265,800	DOWN	109.37
May 22	230,500		116.88	July 18	215,400	DOWN	108.37
May 23	148,300		115.13	July 19	253,100		109.13
May 24	148,300		115.13	July 20	269,800		110.25
May 25	17,000	DOWN	112.63	July 23	269,800		110.25
May 28	−265,800	DOWN	100.63	July 24	252,000		108.75
May 29	76,100		108.50	July 25	270,400	UP	110.50
May 31	490,900	UP	113.25	July 26	270,400	UP	110.50
June 1	390,200		111.75	July 27	285,400	UP	111.13
June 4	270,300		106.88	July 30	288,300	UP	112.00
June 5	412,300		109.37	July 31	288,300	UP	112.00
June 6	331,200		108.75	Aug. 1	272,900		111.13
June 7	365,100		109.25				

Translating the various ups and downs into the respective fields, we arrive at the following figures:

AMERICAN TELEPHONE

December 1961 to August 1962
"The Field Theory"

Interpretation of Field	Field Maximum On-Balance Volume	Type of Field	Price	Date
Rising	244,800	DOWN	131.75	Jan. 9, 1962
Doubtful	330,200	UP	131.50	Jan. 19, 1962
Falling	235,500	DOWN	127.25	Jan. 30, 1962
Doubtful	385,900	UP	134.00	Feb. 20, 1962
Doubtful	257,500	DOWN	129.00	Mar. 30, 1962
Doubtful	302,300	UP	129.63	Apr. 10, 1962
Falling	186,900	DOWN	126.88	Apr. 16, 1962
Doubtful	352,900	UP	125.13	May 3, 1962
Falling	−265,800	DOWN	100.63	May 28, 1962
Doubtful	490,900	UP	113.25	May 31, 1962
Doubtful	−89,500	DOWN	100.37	June 22, 1962
Doubtful	407,900	UP	113.25	July 11, 1962
Doubtful	215,400	DOWN	108.37	July 18, 1962

Stock Breaks Long-Term OBV Support but Is not a Sale

When OBV on American Telephone moved down to 22,800 on September 26, 1961 that level was considered to be the long-term on-balance volume support level. In the table above showing the 1962 performance you will note that the 22,800 OBV level was violated on May 25, 1962 when OBV fell to 17,000. This was both a volume and price confirmation on the downside. However, if that signal had been followed with long-term selling done the following day the seller would have been selling at just about the bottom. The reason that the downside penetration under the September 26, 1961 support level was not a valid long-term sell signal was because *the stock reached those depths too rapidly*. If the stock had shown a more gradual descent under the 22,800 OBV level then the long-term sell signal would have been valid. Instead, the OBV plummeted from 148,300 to 17,000 in one day and the severe decline to minus 265,800 the following day proved to be climactic on the downside. If OBV has to descend that rapidly in order to move under a long-term support then an important exception to the long-term selling rule is being recorded. The stock is seemingly "exhausted" in its descent by the time it cracks the support level.

Check OBV on the "Pullbacks"

An important "bottom" is usually recorded when a stock comes off a low and then "pulls back" to record a double bottom with OBV much stronger on the *second* low. This is what happened to American Telephone after it recorded the first low on May 28, 1962 at 100.63. Note that OBV was a minus 265,800 on that first bottom. On June 22, 1962 the price of the stock fell to 100.37 *but this time OBV was only minus 89,500.* The stock was considerably stronger at the second bottom from the OBV standpoint. The example became even more impressive when the stock reached 100.37 again on June 26, 1962 with OBV improving to 4,000. This serves as an excellent example of how a study of on-balance volume aids in the determination of important bottoming formations. Now look at the field trend of American Telephone at those designated low points. The field trend was *falling* on the first low and was *doubtful* on the second low, another indication that the stock had seen the worst. The double bottom formation with OBV considerably higher on the second bottom *is one of the most appealing buying opportunities a stock offers.* Note the rapidity of the advance in American Telephone following that OBV signal, some 13 points in twelve trading sessions.

AMERICAN TELEPHONE

Trading Record

Date and Action	Signal	Profit	Loss	Cumulative
BUY June 27, 1961 at 117.25	B-2			
BUY June 29, 1961 at 117.25	B-7			
BUY July 20, 1961 at 119.88	B-4			
BUY Aug. 3, 1961 at 121.63	B-2, B-3			
BUY Aug. 10, 1961 at 123.75	B-7			
SELL Sept. 6, 1961 at 120.13	S-7	2.88		2.88
SELL Sept. 13, 1961 at 119.50	S-2			
SELL Sept. 18, 1961 at 118.38	S-2			
BUY Sept. 22, 1961 at 118.13	B-8			
BUY Oct. 26, 1961 at 121.75	B-4			
BUY Nov. 2, 1961 at 124.75	B-7			
SELL Nov. 3, 1961 at 125.88	S-3	7.75		10.63
SELL Nov. 6, 1961 at 127.88	S-3, S-8			
SELL Nov. 8, 1961 at 129.00	S-3			
SELL Nov. 9, 1961 at 128.50	S-3			
BUY Nov. 16, 1961 at 128.88	B-1, B-3			
BUY Nov. 21, 1961 at 134.25	B-4, B-9			
BUY Dec. 1, 1961 at 133.13	B-1			
BUY Dec. 5, 1961 at 134.75	B-7			
BUY Dec. 11, 1961 at 138.25	B-7			

Date and Action	Signal	Profit	Loss	Cumulative
BUY Dec. 19, 1961 at 135.75	B-3			
BUY Dec. 21, 1961 at 135.63	B-1			
SELL Jan. 2, 1962 at 133.63	S-7	4.75		15.38
BUY Jan. 9, 1962 at 131.75	B-3			
BUY Jan. 10, 1962 at 131.88	B-8			
BUY Jan. 19, 1962 at 131.50	B-4			
SELL Jan. 30, 1962 at 127.25	S-7		4.50	10.88
SELL Jan. 31, 1962 at 128.00	S-4	(These cancel.		
BUY Jan. 31, 1962 at 128.00	B-8	NO action.)		
SELL Feb. 6, 1962 at 131.00	S-1			
BUY Feb. 16, 1962 at 132.75	B-7			
SELL Feb. 21, 1962 at 133.50	S-8	.75		11.63
SELL Mar. 7, 1962 at 131.50	S-7			
SELL Mar. 14, 1962 at 132.37	S-7			
SELL Mar. 21, 1962 at 130.75	S-7			
BUY Apr. 2, 1962 at 129.37	B-8			
SELL Apr. 11, 1962 at 128.63	S-8		.75	10.88
SELL Apr. 13, 1962 at 127.25	S-4	(These cancel.		
BUY Apr. 13, 1962 at 127.25	B-3, B-8	NO action.)		
BUY Apr. 26, 1962 at 127.13	B-2			
BUY Apr. 30, 1962 at 124.00	B-3			
SELL May 1, 1962 at 124.00	S-3		3.13	7.75
SELL May 3, 1962 at 125.13	S-3	(These cancel.		
BUY May 3, 1962 at 125.13	B-7	NO action.)		
SELL May 4, 1962 at 124.75	S-8			
BUY May 10, 1962 at 117.50	B-3			
BUY May 11, 1962 at 116.00	B-3	(These cancel.		
SELL May 11, 1962 at 116.00	S-4	NO action.)		
SELL May 15, 1962 at 120.50	S-3	3.00		10.75
SELL May 16, 1962 at 120.50	S-3			
BUY May 24, 1962 at 115.13	B-3			
BUY May 28, 1962 at 100.63	B-3	(These cancel.		
SELL May 28, 1962 at 100.63	S-9	NO action.)		
SELL May 31, 1962 at 113.25	S-2, S-3		1.88	8.88
SELL June 1, 1962 at 111.75	S-3			
BUY June 4, 1962 at 106.88	B-3			
BUY June 5, 1962 at 109.37	B-3			
SELL June 6, 1962 at 108.75	S-3	1.88		10.75
BUY June 7, 1962 at 109.25	B-3			
BUY June 13, 1962 at 102.25	B-3			
BUY June 14, 1962 at 101.50	B-3			
BUY June 15, 1962 at 105.88	B-3			
SELL June 18, 1962 at 103.50	S-2, S-3		5.75	5.00
BUY June 19, 1962 at 104.25	B-3			
SELL June 21, 1962 at 101.00	S-7	(These cancel.		
BUY June 21, 1962 at 101.00	B-3	NO action.)		

Date and Action	Signal	Profit	Loss	Cumulative
BUY June 22, 1962 at 100.37	B-3			
BUY June 25, 1962 at 101.25	B-3, B-8			
SELL June 26, 1962 at 100.37	S-3		3.88	1.13
BUY June 27, 1962 at 102.00	B-3			
SELL June 28, 1962 at 104.63	S-3	2.63		3.75
SELL June 29, 1962 at 103.75	S-3			
BUY July 2, 1962 at 106.00	B-3			
BUY July 5, 1962 at 108.37	B-7	(These cancel.		
SELL July 5, 1962 at 108 37	S-3	NO action.)		
SELL July 11, 1962 at 113.25	S-3	7.25		11.00
SELL July 12, 1962 at 113.00	S-2, S-3, S-8			
BUY July 13, 1962 at 112.75	B-3			
BUY July 19, 1962 at 109.13	B-3			
SELL Aug. 1. 1962 at 111.13	S-8		1.63	9.38

American Telephone fell from 139.00 to 100.37 between December 1961 and June 1962. The price action toward the end of that period was very erratic. The trader would have been only on the long side and did not do too well. Yet the trading record using OBV buy and sell signals ended up with a gain (not counting the commissions to be deducted). The point made here is that with a stock not normally traded on a day-to-day basis and under very adverse circumstances a theoretical trading gain was still possible.

The Summing up

Here was illustrated the importance of OBV as an aid in determining important bottoms. The favorable combination of circumstances occurs when the stock records a new low price, followed by an advance which is then followed by another low price approximately equal to the first. *If on-balance volume is higher on this second low and the field has also improved an important price advance usually follows.*

You have also seen the important exception to the long-term selling rule, a *too rapid advance* to new lows. At both extremes things are moving too rapidly. When the stock was topping out at 139 in December 1961 the stock went through the typical motions of a stock peaking out, these typical motions being rapid acceleration of OBV accompanied by price gaps. On the other end of the line the stock bottomed out by rapid acceleration of OBV on the downside accompanied by downside price gaps. Incidentally, note that those price gaps recorded between 100.63 and 113.25 (May 28-31, 1961) were all filled in between May 31st and July 20th.

Chapter Nine

Further Applications of
the Field Theory

*How the field theory relates to percentage changes, the
short interest and the 200-day moving average price line.*

What You Are about to Learn

Here the field theory is summed up briefly together with a discussion of the significance of net volume changes between each field as well as the percentage changes
between each field. The reader will then get a better feel of when the trend in a stock
is beginning to show a significant change. The trader will soon more readily recognize
when a stock is acting out of character by the application of these additional techniques of recording changing volume characteristics.

After reviewing the field theory with these additional techniques, it will be
shown how important short interest figures can be when related to on-balance volume
figures. This will be followed by a discussion of how valuable OBV can be when related to the 200-day moving average price line.

Reviewing the Field Theory

The theory of rising and falling fields (alternating clusters of buying and selling
pressures) is the logical resolution of an obvious earlier difficulty in the interpretation
of on-balance volume breakouts. This earlier difficulty stemmed from assigning a

bullish or bearish connotation to each OBV breakout regardless of what "key" it was in. The field theory resolves this by pointing up bullish breakouts within the framework of a bearish volume pattern and bearish breakouts within the framework of a bullish volume pattern. Such breakouts can also be in harmony with their field.

In determining the interpretation of each field an important observation comes to light: *No single upleg or downleg makes a trend.* The application of this observation helps eliminate any misinterpretations which might otherwise be a common occurrence when sharp thrusts to new peaks or new lows are recorded by on-balance volume figures. This helps combat the earlier difficulty which might have developed from a false assumption that each new on-balance volume peak for a stock was necessarily bullish. A good example of this is the top OBV of 96,300 on Allied Chemical reached on February 8, 1962. That did not occur in a way to create a rising field trend, the field still doubtful on account of the previous field recording a lower low.

The field theory is built around a series of upward and downward zig-zags in on-balance volume figures. A rising field requires four OBV readings of maximum pressure (the last reading in a cluster of ups or downs), a low, a high, a higher low and a higher high. Any deviation from this creates a doubtful field. A falling field is of course the opposite, a high, a low, a lower high and a lower low.

Going through the previous tables and charts, several other significant things are noted. For instance, a single OBV breakout is not nearly as important as a *cluster*. Between December 1961 and August 1962 Woolworth recorded many series or clusters of DOWNS but very few UPS. The UPS were spaced far apart and seldom occurred in groups of more than two at a time. Just a glance of the eye on the heavy concentration of DOWNS denotes the trend of pressure a stock is under.

You will also note how the old law of action and reaction tends to come into play in the alternating on-balance volume up and down pressures. American Telephone serves as an excellent example of how all *extremes* call for strong action in the *opposite* direction. Turn back to the American Telephone fields recorded between June and December 1961. Between July and November of that year the on-balance volume fluctuated between a low of 22,800 and a high of 299,700. Suddenly this pattern was *shattered* with a sharp rise in OBV to 518,600 on December 12, 1961. *This was out of character with the previous range of OBV fluctuation.* It tended to create a *final gap.* The next maximum pressure point was sharply lower at 244,800, *a drop greater than the entire previous average range of OBV fluctuation.* That is an example of action and reaction.

That action and reaction example was later dwarfed in 1962 by the same stock. Note the extremely sharp drop in OBV from 352,900 to a minus 265,800 between May 3rd and 28th, 1962. That was a total net OBV swing of 618,700, *totally out of character with anything in the previous pattern.* It created a downside gap which suggested a selling climax. Speaking of extremes, however, note the reaction in the on-balance volume which followed that selling climax. Within two days the figure rose from minus 265,800 to a plus 490,900, a total net OBV swing of 756,700. This more than compensated for the downswing and this immediately became a *buying climax*. Despite the fact that 490,900 was the highest OBV figure in the table (an OBV upside breakout) *it did not put the stock into a rising field trend*. This is another effective example of the fact that *one leg does not create a trend*. There was no upward zig-zag in the OBV extremes and thus the stock was still looked at as being in a *doubtful* trend at that time.

The field theory can be explained as a *plotting of maximum buying and selling pressure points* instead of prices. The trader then attempts to move in the opposite direction of what human nature dictates. The trader tries to buy into maximum weakness and sell into maximum strength, the field theory suggesting when peak pressure points of strength and weakness occur. Bullishness begets bullishness and bearishness begets bearishness. When a stock keeps moving up on expanding volume the temptation to buy it waxes strong and when a stock declines on expanding volume the temptation to sell it becomes almost irresistible. The trader attempts to capitalize on these temptations. When a down field signals long-term selling the trader sells the stock on the next rally, knowing that such maximum downside pressures will result in a probable pullback of sorts to the upside. The trader would hardly ever sell into what might be measured in terms of OBV as maximum weakness. He would be more likely to buy at that point. When a stock is in an up field and the trader happens to be short of it, he should be more inclined to cover his short sale on the next reaction, *not on the rally*. Human nature dictates the opposite in both instances and thus the successful trader must steel himself to *go counter to human nature*. The field theory would help him to do this because here the trader could more easily and mechanically sell on the last UP designation and buy on the last DOWN designation, these decisions determined by on-balance volume support and resistance levels.

The interpretive factor enters into the picture when determining these maximum volume pressure points on the upside and downside. The orthodox technical measurements of support and resistance are usefully employed. This takes into account the filling of gaps, ascending or descending highs and lows and all the other usual technical measurements which most analysts have heretofore applied to stock prices. In an oversimplified sense the trader is always looking for something *out of character*. This tends to activate the law of action and reaction. The greater the action the greater the reaction. That is the theory.

Let us review a few examples of this idea of "out of character" moves and how the trader could capitalize on such moves:

Aluminum Company of America.   Look again at the early 1962 figures. In the minus column the on-balance volume pressure extremes fluctuated as follows: 59, 72, 51, 85, 68 and then suddenly 100. The 100 is *out of character* with the previous readings. It creates a maximum selling pressure and thus the trader *buys*. In this instance he would have been rewarded with a 10-point gain right in the face of a *falling* field, the field trend pointing to the ultimate direction of the stock, the trader only being interested in the direction of the next *short-term* price swing.

American Tobacco.   Field maximum on-balance volume figures from August to November 1961 showed alternate readings of (in thousands) 43, 29, 61, 29, 72, 56, 76, 67 and then 114. The latter reading, being out of character with the previous pattern of smaller OBV readings, conveys an important technical message to the trader. The 114 indicates a stronger buying pressure than was seen previously and so the trader would sell short on this evidence. Now go back and look at the chart on American Tobacco at that point.

Chrysler.   A study of the fields on this stock in the June to December 1961 period showed a *sudden change of character* when the on-balance volume figure moved from 268,700 on November 6, 1961 to a minus 48,800 on November 30, 1961. That was a total change of 317,500 on the downside, totally out of character with what had happened previously. That maximum sell pressure flashed a technical BUY signal to the trader, the price at that time being 45½. The field trend became a rising one in early January 1962 and Chrysler subsequently moved to 62.13 by February 20, 1962, this taking place *after* the Dow-Jones Industrial Average had recorded a major top in December 1961. This points up the technical reliability of the on-balance volume signals *regardless of the trend of the market.*

Some New Techniques

It is essential then to immediately detect sudden and exaggerated changes in the maximum buying and selling pressure points. Such exaggerations are more easily noted by re-expressing the field theory tables in terms of *differentials between each maximum on-balance volume level.* This would be an expression of the total on-balance volume force on each leg in a field trend. Here are a few examples:

AMERICAN TELEPHONE

Field Theory with Net OBV Change

Interpretation of Field	Net OBV Change	Type of Field°	Price	Date
	73,400	UP	117.50	June 28, 1961
	−30,000	DOWN	116.88	June 30, 1961
Rising	66,500	UP	120.00	July 7, 1961
Rising	−44,800	DOWN	118.50	July 17, 1961
Rising	50,900	UP	120.13	July 19, 1961
Doubtful	−51,000	DOWN	119.50	July 24, 1961

Interpretation of Field	Net OBV Change	Type of Field*	Price	Date
Doubtful	168,400	UP	123.75	Aug. 22, 1961
Doubtful	−210,600	DOWN	117.25	Sept. 26, 1961
Doubtful	79,100	UP	121.75	Oct. 13, 1961
Doubtful	−33,700	DOWN	120.38	Oct. 23, 1961
Rising	231,500	UP	129.00	Nov. 8, 1961
Rising	−77,800	DOWN	127.88	Nov. 15, 1961
Rising	296,700	UP	139.00	Dec. 12, 1961

* It must be kept in mind that stocks are sold on maximum UP readings and bought on maximum DOWN readings.

The two salient points in this table show up right away. The *maximum OBV differential on the downside* was the minus 210,600 change completed on September 26, 1961. *Here was a technical signal to buy the stock at 117.25.* The maximum OBV differential on the upside stands out as being the net change of 296,700 recorded on December 12, 1961. *Here was a technical signal to sell the stock at 139.00.*

Now let us continue on into 1962 on the American Telephone OBV differentials between each field:

Interpretation of Field	Net OBV Change	Type of Field	Price	Date
Rising	−273,800	DOWN	131.75	Jan. 9, 1962
Doubtful	85,400	UP	131.50	Jan. 19, 1962
Falling	−94,700	DOWN	127.25	Jan. 30, 1962
Doubtful	150,400	UP	134.00	Feb. 20, 1962
Doubtful	−127,400	DOWN	129.00	Mar. 30, 1962
Doubtful	44,800	UP	129.63	Apr. 10, 1962
Falling	−115,400	DOWN	126.88	Apr. 16, 1962
Doubtful	166,000	UP	125.13	May 3, 1962
Falling	−618,700	DOWN	100.63	May 28, 1962
Doubtful	756,700	UP	113.25	May 31, 1962
Doubtful	−580,400	DOWN	100.37	June 22, 1962
Doubtful	497,400	UP	113.25	July 11, 1962
Doubtful	−192,500	DOWN	108.37	July 18, 1962

In terms of OBV differentials between each field, the wider swings stand out in *bold relief*. The most outstanding initial change in the above table is the minus 618,700 recorded on May 28th. It was *totally out of character* with the other net changes in OBV. This was maximum selling pressure and attractive to the trader who saw it as an immediate buying opportunity. Such a radical change in OBV called for an equally radical OBV change on the plus side. In line with action and reaction, such was the case. The next move was an incredible OBV change of 756,700 on the plus side. Since this was also a *radical change,* the trader would see it as an immediate selling opportunity. The next buying opportunity on the minus

580,400 was significant for two reasons. The stock scored a *double bottom* with the second bottom showing an *abatement of selling pressure*.

These changes in the OBV swings between each field can also be expressed in terms of percentages. In this manner not only do the radical swings show up, but also the relationship between action and reaction.

Here is the entire combined table of American Telephone from June 1961 to August 1962 with field changes expressed in terms of percentages:

AMERICAN TELEPHONE

Field Changes in Percentages

Interpretation of Field	On-Balance Volume Percentage Change	Type of Field	Price	Date
	−40.8%	DOWN	116.88	June 30, 1961
Rising	221.6%	UP	120.00	July 7, 1961
Rising	−67.3%	DOWN	118.50	July 17, 1961
Rising	113.6%	UP	120.13	July 19, 1961
Doubtful	−100.1%	DOWN	119.50	July 24, 1961
Doubtful	330.1%	UP	123.75	Aug. 22, 1961
Doubtful	−125.0%	DOWN	117.25	Sept. 26, 1961
Doubtful	37.5%	UP	121.75	Oct. 13, 1961
Doubtful	−42.6%	DOWN	120.38	Oct. 23, 1961
Rising	686.9%	UP	129.00	Nov. 8, 1961
Rising	−33.6%	DOWN	127.88	Nov. 15, 1961
Rising	381.3%	UP	139.00	Dec. 12, 1961
Rising	−92.2%	DOWN	131.75	Jan. 9, 1962
Doubtful	31.1%	UP	131.50	Jan. 19, 1962
Falling	−110.8%	DOWN	127.25	Jan. 30, 1962
Doubtful	158.7%	UP	134.00	Feb. 20, 1962
Doubtful	−84.6%	DOWN	129.00	Mar. 30, 1962
Doubtful	35.1%	UP	129.63	Apr. 10, 1962
Falling	−257.5%	DOWN	126.88	Apr. 16, 1962
Doubtful	143.8%	UP	125.13	May 3, 1962
Falling	−372.4%	DOWN	100.63	May 28, 1962
Doubtful	122.3%	UP	113.25	May 31, 1962
Doubtful	−76.7%	DOWN	100.37	June 22, 1962
Doubtful	85.6%	UP	113.25	July 11, 1962
Doubtful	−38.7%	DOWN	108.37	July 18, 1962

The percentage method of expressing net volume changes between each field brings into *bold relief* climactic changes which might be more lightly passed over when expressed otherwise. Look at the percentage table again as it refers to American Telephone. *The 686.9% figure catches the eye immediately.* It was a technically climactic figure even if the price of the stock did go a bit higher for awhile. Now look at the other high percentage changes on the upside, the 381.3%, the 158.7% and the other lesser figures. *This pictured the loss of upside energy.* Relating these percentage figures back into the net volume change figures from the preceding table they become 231,500, 296,700 and 150,400. Those were the net volume measurements on the buying pressure points of November 8, 1961, December 12, 1961 and February 20, 1962. Going back now to the original American Telephone table of on-balance volume readings, the figures were 299,700 on November 8, 1961, 518,600 on December 12, 1961 an 385,900 on February 20, 1962. While these latter figures show December 12, 1961 to be the climax movement in American Telephone, the percentage figures, which are based on the change in the size of the field over the previous field, show the ADVANCE TECHNICAL WARNING of climax on November 8, 1961. It is advisable then to add the percentage method to the other volume studies on a stock so as to provide still better technical evidence as to when a stock is in a climactic area.

Let us now run through this analytical process once again, using Chrysler as an example.

To start with, go back to the field tables on Chrysler and convert this into a *net volume change* table, measuring the volume change between each field. The table would then look like this:

(The following table is extended beyond the August 1962 date in order to show the subsequent market action of this stock as it advanced rapidly on heavy OBV)

CHRYSLER

Field Theory with Net Volume Change

Interpretation of Field	Net OBV Change	Type of Field	Price	Date
Doubtful	−22,800	DOWN	44.63	June 29, 1961
Doubtful	24,000	UP	45.25	July 7, 1961
Doubtful	−35,300	DOWN	43.00	July 25, 1961
Doubtful	304,800	UP	52.75	Aug. 7, 1961
Doubtful	−87,500	DOWN	50.38	Aug. 15, 1961
Rising	115,200	UP	54.50	Sept. 6, 1961
Rising	−78,300	DOWN	53.00	Sept. 11, 1961
Rising	131,300	UP	57.25	Sept. 15, 1961
Doubtful	−138,800	DOWN	53.13	Sept. 26, 1961
Doubtful	30,500	UP	56.50	Oct. 4, 1961
Falling	−119,700	DOWN	50.75	Oct. 20, 1961
Doubtful	143,700	UP	55.13	Nov. 6, 1961
Falling	−317,500	DOWN	45.50	Nov. 30, 1961
Falling	121,600	UP	50.63	Dec. 13, 1961
Doubtful	−67,200	DOWN	47.88	Dec. 22, 1961
Rising	175,500	UP	53.13	Jan. 8, 1962
Rising	−107,700	DOWN	51.37	Jan. 17, 1962
Rising	204,600	UP	56.88	Feb. 8, 1962

Interpretation of Field	Net OBV Change	Type of Field	Price	Date
Rising	−31,700	DOWN	56.75	Feb. 9, 1962
Rising	243,500	UP	62.13	Feb. 20, 1962
Rising	−165,200	DOWN	55.75	Mar. 19, 1962
Doubtful	17,600	UP	56.50	Mar. 23, 1962
Falling	−94,900	DOWN	51.88	Apr. 9, 1962
Falling	37,300	UP	54.50	Apr. 19, 1962
Falling	−104,600	DOWN	46.37	May 23, 1962
Falling	37,500	UP	46.88	May 25, 1962
Falling	−118,300	DOWN	38.88	June 14, 1962
Falling	63,400	UP	41.13	June 25, 1962
Doubtful	−39,100	DOWN	42.25	July 6, 1962
Rising	301,600	UP	57.63	Aug. 22, 1962
Rising	−61,700	DOWN	54.88	Aug. 29, 1962
Rising	100,400	UP	59.63	Sept. 6, 1962
Doubtful	−353,200	DOWN	52.00	Oct. 1, 1962
Doubtful	90,100	UP	57.00	Oct. 9, 1962
Falling	−285,600	DOWN	55.00	Oct. 26, 1962
Doubtful	814,000	UP	70.75	Nov. 21, 1962
Doubtful	−152,100	DOWN	69.75	Nov. 29, 1962
Doubtful	117,800	UP	73.37	Dec. 4, 1962
Falling	−240,700	DOWN	69.88	Dec. 10, 1962
Falling	187,400	UP	74.37	Dec. 19, 1962
Doubtful	−140,400	DOWN	72.25	Jan. 2, 1963
Rising	717,100	UP	85.88	Feb. 4, 1963
Rising	−220,200	DOWN	82.88	Feb. 6, 1963
Rising	749,000	UP	94.75	Feb. 13, 1963
Rising	−564,200	DOWN	87.63	Mar 1, 1963
Doubtful	199,100	UP	92.00	Mar. 13, 1963

These net OBV change figures are then converted into percentage changes.

CHRYSLER

Field Changes in Percentages

Interpretation of Field	On-Balance Volume Percentage Change	Type of Field	Price	Date
Doubtful	− − −	DOWN	44.63	June 29, 1961
Doubtful	105.2%	UP	45.25	July 7, 1961
Doubtful	−147.0%	DOWN	43.00	July 25. 1961
Doubtful	863.4%	UP	52.75	Aug. 7, 1961
Doubtful	−28.6%	DOWN	50.38	Aug. 15. 1961
Rising	131.6%	UP	54.50	Sept. 6, 1961
Rising	−67.9%	DOWN	53.00	Sept. 11, 1961
Rising	167.6%	UP	57.25	Sept. 15, 1961
Doubtful	−105.7%	DOWN	53.13	Sept. 26, 1961

Interpretation of Field	On-Balance Volume Percentage Change	Type of Field	Price	Date
Doubtful	21.9%	UP	56.50	Oct. 4, 1961
Falling	−392.4%	DOWN	50.75	Oct. 20, 1961
Doubtful	120.0%	UP	55.13	Nov. 6, 1961
Falling	−220.9%	DOWN	45.50	Nov. 30, 1961
Falling	38.2%	UP	50.63	Dec. 13, 1961
Doubtful	−55.2%	DOWN	47.88	Dec. 22, 1961
Rising	261.1%	UP	53.13	Jan. 8, 1962
Rising	−61.3%	DOWN	51.37	Jan. 17, 1962
Rising	189.9%	UP	56.88	Feb. 8, 1962
Rising	−15.4%	DOWN	56.75	Feb. 9, 1962
Rising	768.1%	UP	62.13	Feb. 20, 1962
Rising	−67.8%	DOWN	55.75	Mar. 19, 1962
Doubtful	10.6%	UP	56.50	Mar. 23, 1962
Falling	−539.2%	DOWN	51.88	Apr. 9, 1962
Falling	39.3%	UP	54.50	Apr. 19, 1962
Falling	−280.4%	DOWN	46.37	May 23, 1962
Falling	35.8%	UP	46.88	May 25, 1962
Falling	−315.4%	DOWN	38.88	June 14, 1962
Falling	53.5%	UP	41.13	June 25. 1962
Doubtful	−61.6%	DOWN	42.25	July 6, 1962
Rising	771.3%	UP	57.63	Aug. 22, 1962
Rising	−20.4%	DOWN	54.88	Aug. 29, 1962
Rising	162.7%	UP	59.63	Sept. 6, 1962
Doubtful	−351.7%	DOWN	52.00	Oct. 1, 1962
Doubtful	25.5%	UP	57.00	Oct. 9, 1962
Falling	−316.9%	DOWN	55.00	Oct. 26, 1962
Doubtful	285.0%	UP	70.75	Nov. 21, 1962
Doubtful	−18.6%	DOWN	69.75	Nov. 29, 1962
Doubtful	77.4%	UP	73.37	Dec. 4, 1962
Falling	−204.3%	DOWN	69.88	Dec. 10, 1962
Falling	77.8%	UP	74.37	Dec. 19, 1962
Doubtful	−74.9%	DOWN	72.25	Jan. 2, 1963
Rising	510.7%	UP	85.88	Feb. 4, 1963
Rising	−30.7%	DOWN	82.88	Feb. 6, 1963
Rising	340.1%	UP	94.75	Feb. 13, 1963
Rising	−75.3%	DOWN	87.63	Mar. 1, 1963
Doubtful	35.2%	UP	92.00	Mar. 13, 1963

Chrysler rose 20 points right through a series of doubtful and falling fields (the period from October 1 to Jan. 2- 1962-63). The power of this move and its persistence may very well have owed much to the short interest trend. The table below shows the Chrysler fields extended from August 1962 to March 1963 together with the recorded monthly short interest:

CHRYSLER

August 1962 through March 1963 Field Trend With Short Interest

Interpretation of Field	Field Maximum On-Balance Volume	Monthly Short Interest	Price	Date
Doubtful	123,500	23,255	42.25	July 6, 1962
Rising	425,100	50,212	57.63	Aug. 22, 1962
Rising	363,400	50,212	54.88	Aug. 29, 1962
Rising	463,800	50,212	59.63	Sept. 6, 1962
Doubtful	110,600	82,359	52.00	Oct. 1, 1962
Doubtful	200,700	82,359	57.00	Oct. 9, 1962
Falling	−84,700	100,078	55.00	Oct. 26, 1962
Doubtful	729,100	189,706	70.75	Nov. 21, 1962
Doubtful	577,000	189,706	69.75	Nov. 29, 1962
Doubtful	694,800	189,706	73.37	Dec. 4, 1962
Falling	454,100	189,706	69.88	Dec. 10, 1962
Falling	641,500	186,466	74.37	Dec. 19, 1962
Doubtful	501,100	186,466	72.25	Jan. 2, 1963
Rising	1,218,200	169,405	85.88	Feb. 4, 1963
Rising	998,000	169,405	82.88	Feb. 6, 1963
Rising	1,747,000	169,405	94.75	Feb. 13, 1963
Rising	1,182,800	167,416	87.63	Mar. 1, 1963
Doubtful	1,381,900	167,416	92.00	Mar. 13, 1963

Here is an example of powerful on-balance volume, so strong that it overrides the minor falling field trends. When the fields became falling ones they were never extended more than one downward zig-zag. Each falling field was higher than the last. The falling fields were an example of the *simple* downside field zig-zag. As noted earlier in the book, the simple field zig-zag is capable of being easily reversed. They do not constitute a real trend. As can be seen in the table above, the major sweep of OBV figures was dramatically upward. Such an upward sweep of OBV when combined with a definite rising trend of short interest made for a steep price advance and Chrysler left nothing to be desired in that respect. It would have been easy to misinterpret the minus 84,900 OBV reading of October 26, 1962 as being bearish but that did not take into consideration the lack of price confirmation, the price at that time being 9½ points *above* the critical level.

On-Balance Volume and the 200-Day Moving Average Price Line

Upside and downside penetrations of the 200-day moving average price line have proven to be significant. Below is a chart of International Paper showing the bullish turn in late 1962 and early 1963, the price making an upside penetration of the 200-

day line at a depressed level. In order that such turns be additionally tested for their reliability, it is useful to record a field trend on the stock covering those critical periods when a significant change is suspected to be taking place.

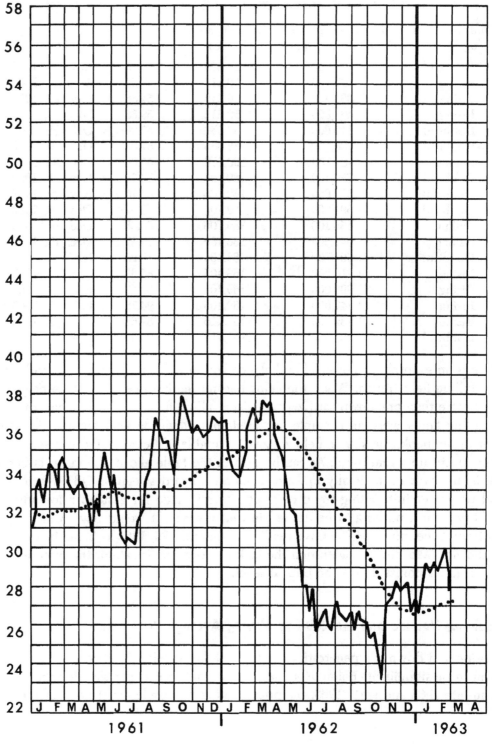

INTERNATIONAL PAPER

Chart 49

INTERNATIONAL PAPER

June 1962 to March 1963 The Field Trend

Interpretation of Field	Field Maximum On-Balance Volume	Type of Field	Price	Date
Falling	53,600	DOWN	25.25	June 27, 1962
Falling	165,700	UP	26.75	July 5, 1962
Falling	49,500	DOWN	25.63	July 26, 1962
Falling	96,800	UP	27.00	Aug. 3, 1962
Falling	27,800	DOWN	26.13	Aug. 17, 1962
Falling	88,500	UP	27.38	Aug. 24, 1962
Doubtful	35,200	DOWN	25.88	Sept. 6, 1962
Rising	93,200	UP	26.88	Sept. 14, 1962
Doubtful	−8,400	DOWN	25.25	Oct. 1. 1962
Doubtful	30,400	UP	25 63	Oct. 10, 1962
Falling	−113,200	DOWN	23.25	Oct. 23, 1962
Doubtful	50,400	UP	28.50	Nov. 23, 1962
Doubtful	14,100	DOWN	27.50	Dec. 3, 1962
Rising	65,000	UP	28.50	Dec. 7, 1962
Doubtful	−36,200	DOWN	26.63	Dec. 18, 1962
Doubtful	90,600	UP	29.25	Jan. 28, 1963
Doubtful	35,600	DOWN	28.37	Feb. 7, 1963
Rising	131,100	UP	29.88	Feb. 19, 1963
Doubtful	27,200	DOWN	27.63	Mar. 6, 1963

The OBV figures back up the chart using the 200-day moving average price line. Note the price pullback in late December which held well above the October low followed by the subsequent upside breakthrough in January 1963, the 200-day line then turning upward. All this was confirmed in the OBV figures. First the climactic low of minus 113,200 in October 1962 followed by a brief rise. Then the pullback occurred, OBV coming back down to minus 36,200 in the middle of December corresponding with the price pullback. This was then followed by a January OBV breakout on the upside in January 1963. Another pullback occurred in early March, OBV this time stopping well above the previous pullback level of December. The ascending pullback levels were bullish. OBV helps to confirm what is happening in the 200-day moving average price line charts.

The Summing up

Here the field theory was reviewed. You have now seen clarified "minor key" breakouts and "major key" breakouts, an application and interpretation of the simple, compound and trend field zig-zags. It has been emphasized that no single leg makes a trend. You have also learned that "clusters" of UPS and DOWNS are more important than single designations. By re-expressing the on-balance volume in terms of total OBV on each swing and percentage changes between each field the law of action and reaction is better seen as it tends to play on each field. You should now better understand why it is important for traders to move counter to the dictates of human nature, knowing that maximum pressure always calls for some kind of price reversal useful for traders to act upon. The trader will always be on the lookout for a move which is "out of character" with the previous normal pattern of price or OBV fluctuation. These "out of character" changes denote significant changes which can be profitably acted upon.

Two additional field theory applications were discussed here: (1) linking OBV with the short interest trend and (2) testing 200-day moving average price line chart turns with an OBV confirmation. You learned that OBV trends turn down before the 200-day line turns down and up before the 200-day line turns up and that a rising short interest together with a rising OBV line is a powerful bullish combination.

Chapter Ten

The Balance of the

Dow-Jones Stocks

A visual review of 25 additional Dow-Jones issues showing the salient points of change in the 1961-62 market in terms of their OBV signals.

What You Are about to Learn

As the Chinese say, a picture is worth a thousand words. Now that you are more keenly aware of the importance of on-balance volume, a quick glance at the following charts will show the dramatic change which took place as the charts weakened in late 1961 and early 1962, culminating in the sharp break of May 1962. A few outstanding features about each chart are listed below the pictorial presentation, features such as (a) line formations which were broken, (b) long-term support level, (c) date when long-term support level was broken, (d) important confirmations and non-confirmations between OBV and price and other key points. Also included are the dates when high and low OBV readings occurred together with comparative dates of salient changes in the 200-day moving average price lines, things such as the first downside penetration and the month when the 200-day lines turned down.

American Can

Vital Statistics

Long-term support level (OBV)	249,100 Nov. 6, 1961 at 44.88
Date when long-term support broken	Long-term support NOT broken
First falling field recorded	April 9, 1962
High OBV before May 1962 break	381,300 on April 19, 1962
Low OBV after April 1962	329,900 on May 28, 1962
Short interest trend	Started to rise May 1962
Downside penetration of 200-day line	January 1962
200-day Line Turned Down	May 1962

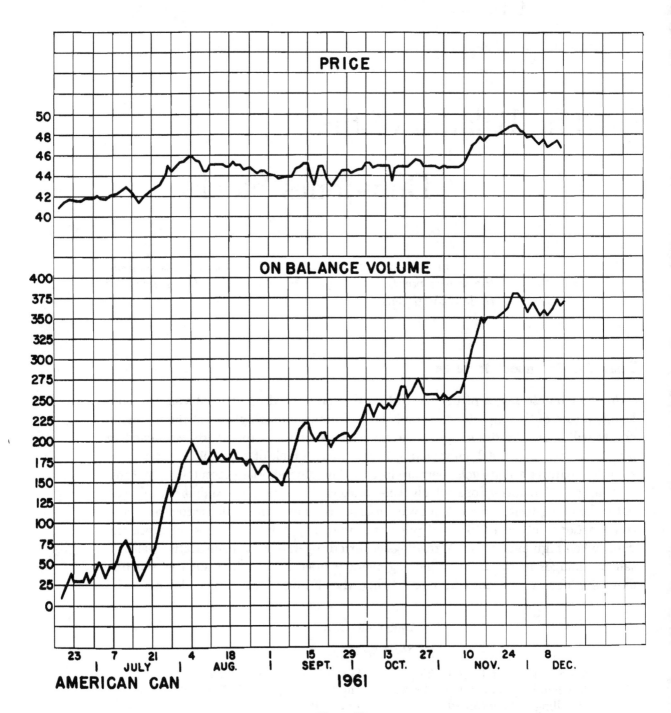

PRICE

ON BALANCE VOLUME

AMERICAN CAN   1961

Chart 50

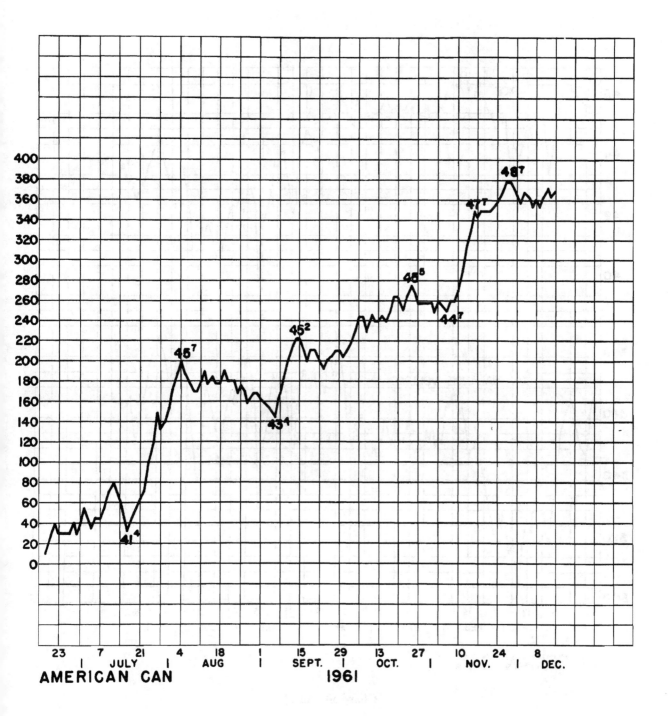

AMERICAN CAN 1961

Chart 50 (cont.)

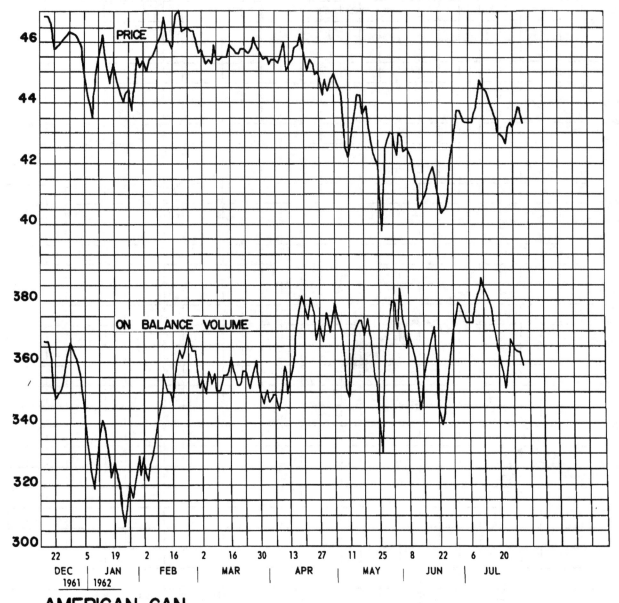

AMERICAN CAN

Chart 50 (cont.)

Summary of American Can. This stock showed amazing stability throughout the 1962 market break. The long-term support of 249,100 OBV was not broken and thus the move in price down to a low of 39.75 on May 28, 1962 with OBV at 329,900 marked a *major non-confirmation*, the price at a new low with OBV standing at 80,800 *above* the major support level. With the stock an indicated BUY on May 28, 1962 it is interesting to note that the short interest trend began to rise that month. It is also interesting to note that the 200-day moving average price line started to turn down *on the month the bottom was reached*. It seemed too late to sell the stock when the short interest started moving higher. It also seemed too late to sell the stock when the 200-day moving average price line started to turn down.

ANACONDA

Vital Statistics

Long-term support level (OBV)	Minus 100,000 Oct. 30, 1961 at 47.63
Date when long-term support broken	May 25, 1962 at minus 106,100
First falling field recorded	August 25, 1961
High OBV before May 1962 break	Nov. 22, 1961 at 15,600
Low OBV after April 1962	Minus 118,900 on May 28, 1962
Short interest trend	No trend
Downside penetration of 200-day moving average price line	July 1961
200-day line turned down	October 1961

Summary of Anaconda. This stock showed definite topping out by key dates recorded on July, August, October and November 1961.

BETHLEHEM STEEL

Vital Statistics

Long-term support level (OBV)	Minus 359,500 Oct. 24, 1961 at 40.00
Date when long-term support broken	April 23, 1962 at minus 380,400
First falling field recorded	July 20, 1961
High OBV before May 1962 break	December 6, 1961 at minus 153,900
Low OBV after April 1962	June 26, 1962 at minus 814,300
Short interest trend	No trend
Downside penetration of 200-day moving average price line	June 1961
200-day line turned down	August 1961

Summary of Bethlehem Steel. June, July and August 1961 statistics showed the first major weakness. When long-term OBV support was broken the short interest lack of trend provided no technical support.

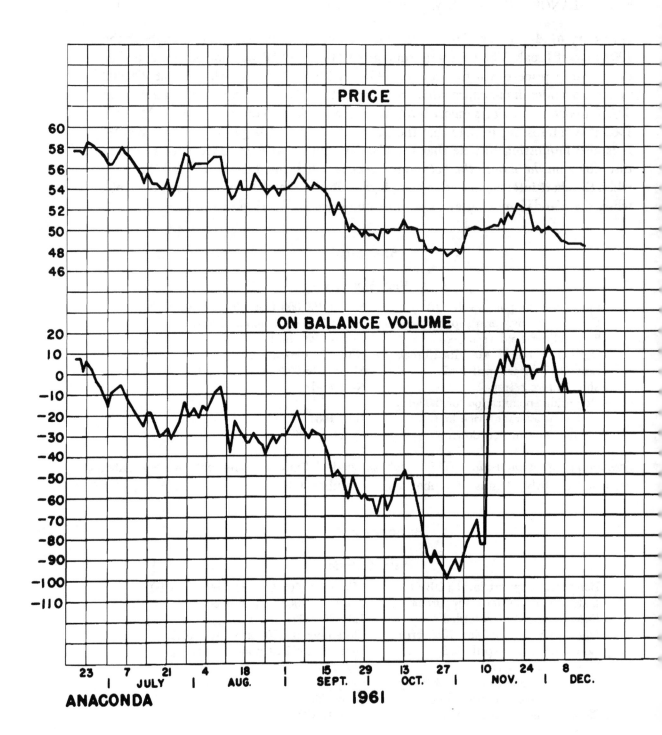

ANACONDA   1961

Chart 51

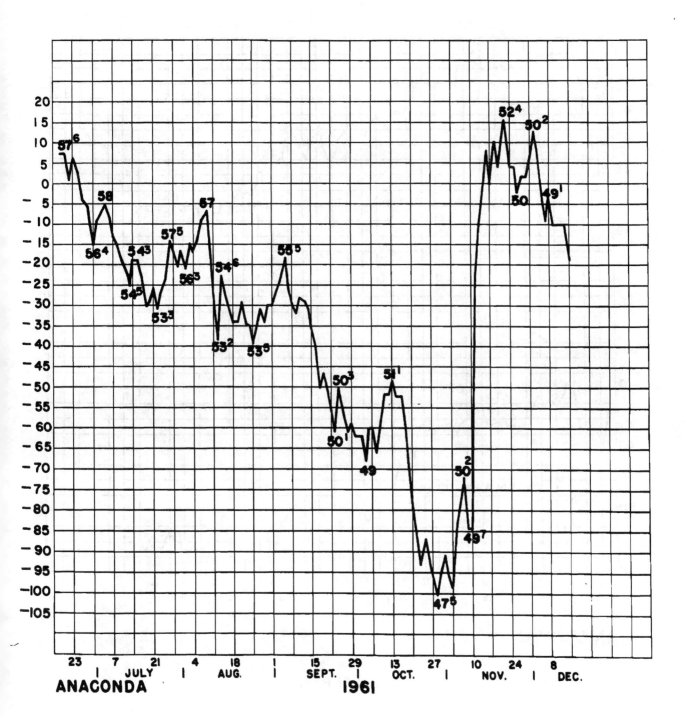

ANACONDA 1961

Chart 51 (cont.)

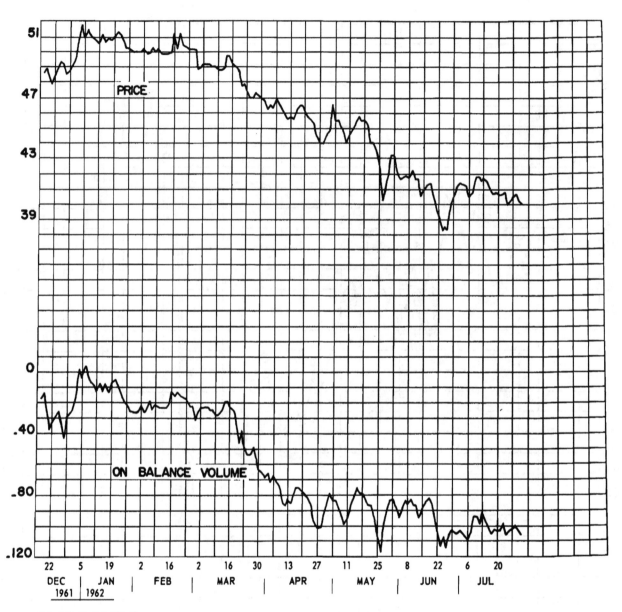

PRICE

ON BALANCE VOLUME

22	5	19	2	16	2	16	30	13	27	11	25	8	22	6	20
DEC	JAN	FEB	MAR	APR	MAY	JUN	JUL
1961	1962

ANACONDA

Chart 51 (cont.)

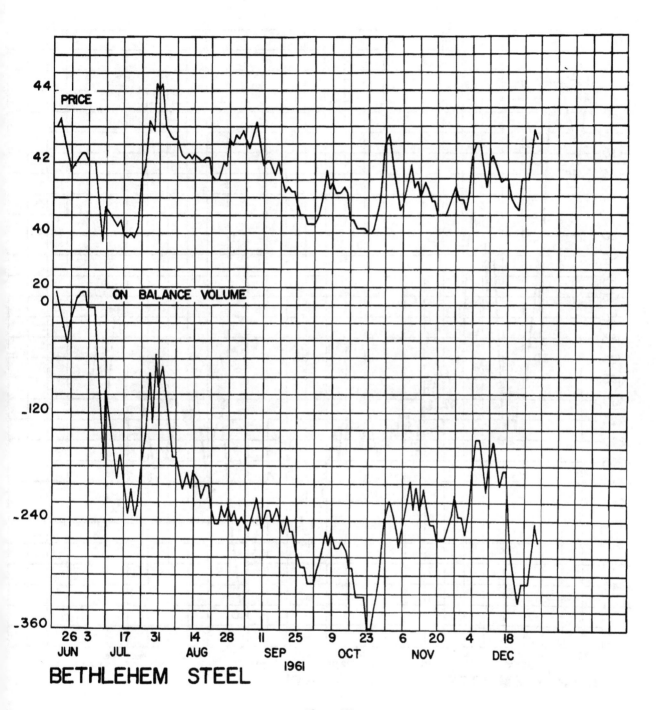

44 PRICE

42

40

20
0 ON BALANCE VOLUME

-120

-240

-360

26 3   17   31   14   28   11   25   9   23   6   20   4   18
JUN   JUL   AUG   SEP   OCT   NOV   DEC
1961

BETHLEHEM STEEL

Chart 52

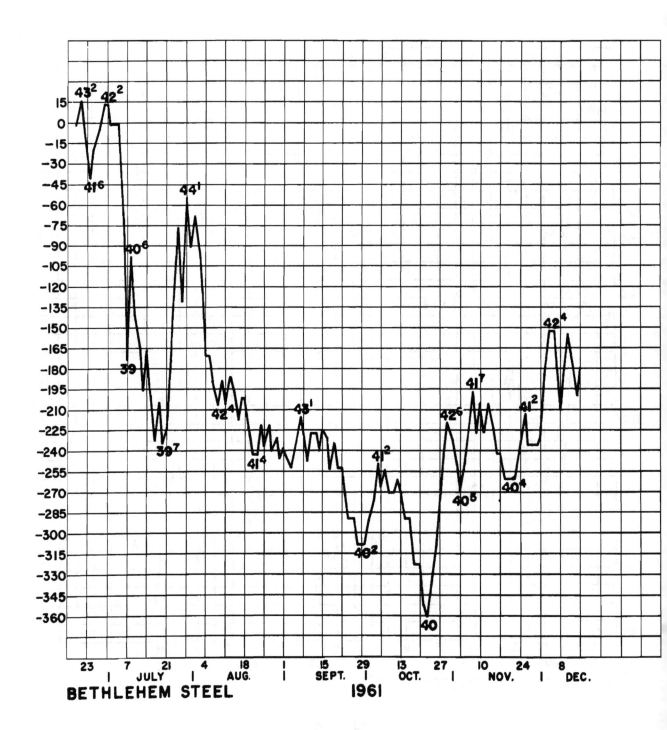

BETHLEHEM STEEL   1961

Chart 52 (cont.)

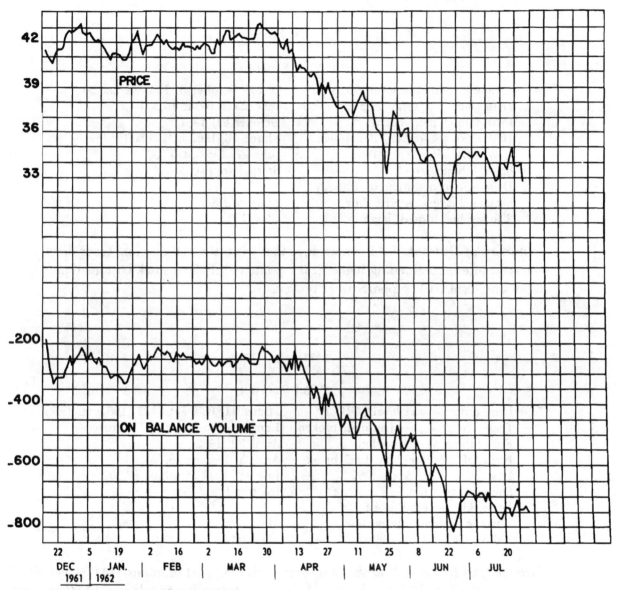

42

39 PRICE

36

33

-200

ON BALANCE VOLUME

-400

-600

-800

22	5	19	2	16	2	16	30	13	27	11	25	8	22	6	20
DEC	JAN.		FEB		MAR			APR		MAY		JUN		JUL	
1961	1962														

BETHLEHEM STEEL

Chart 52 (cont.)

Du Pont

Vital Statistics

Long-term support level (OBV)	20,400 October 3, 1961 at 220.50
Date when long-term support broken	June 25, 1962 at 19,300
First falling field recorded	October 31, 1961
High OBV before May 1962 break	March 16, 1962 at 104,500
Low OBV after April 1962	June 27, 1962 at 6,100
Short interest trend	Started to rise May 1962
Downside penetration of 200-day moving average price line	January 1962
200-day line turned down	May 1962

Summary of DuPont.   It is shown here that when the 200-day line turns down and the short interest is trending higher it is too late to sell. The stock bottomed out right after long-term OBV supports were broken.

Eastman Kodak

Vital Statistics

Long-term support level (OBV)	Minus 114,600 Sept. 25, 1961 at 98.50
Date when long-term support broken	Long-term support NOT broken
First falling field recorded	April 30, 1962
High OBV before May 1962 break	April 5, 1962 at 48,700
Low OBV after April 1962	July 18, 1962 at minus 96,200
Short interest trend	No trend
Downside penetration of 200-day moving average price line	May 1962
200-day line turned down	May 1962

Summary of Eastman Kodak.   Long-term OBV support of minus 114,600 was NOT broken in the May 1962 break and yet the price descended to a low of 85.50 on June 22, 1962, OBV at that time standing at minus 74,600. Here the price was 13 points under the September 25, 1961 level *and yet OBV was 40,000* higher, this constituting a major non-confirmation between OBV and price, a major buying signal on this wide discrepancy. It is these major non-confirmations between on-balance volume and price which constitute the important long-term buy and sell signals.

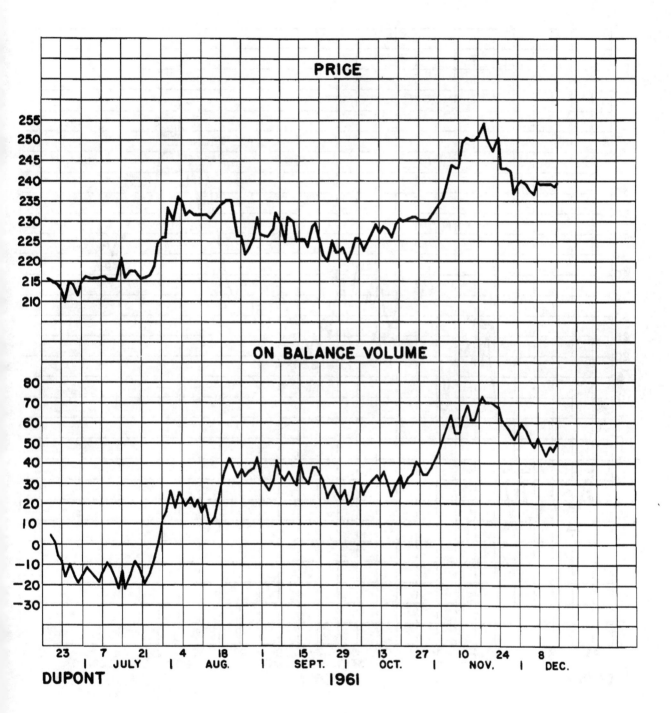

Chart 53

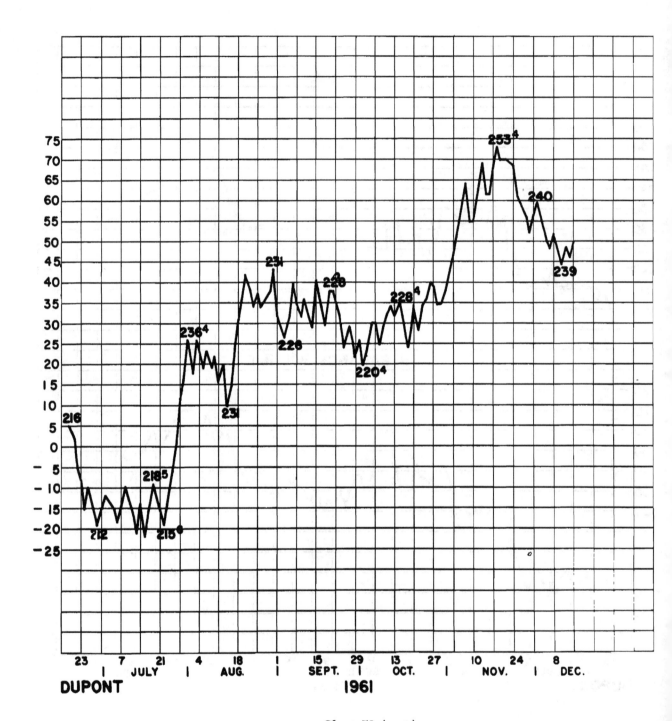

DUPONT   1961

Chart 53 (cont.)

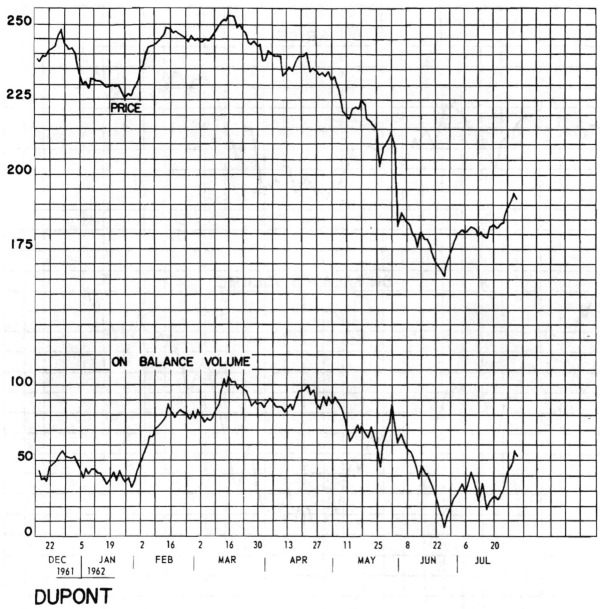

DUPONT

Chart 53 (cont.)

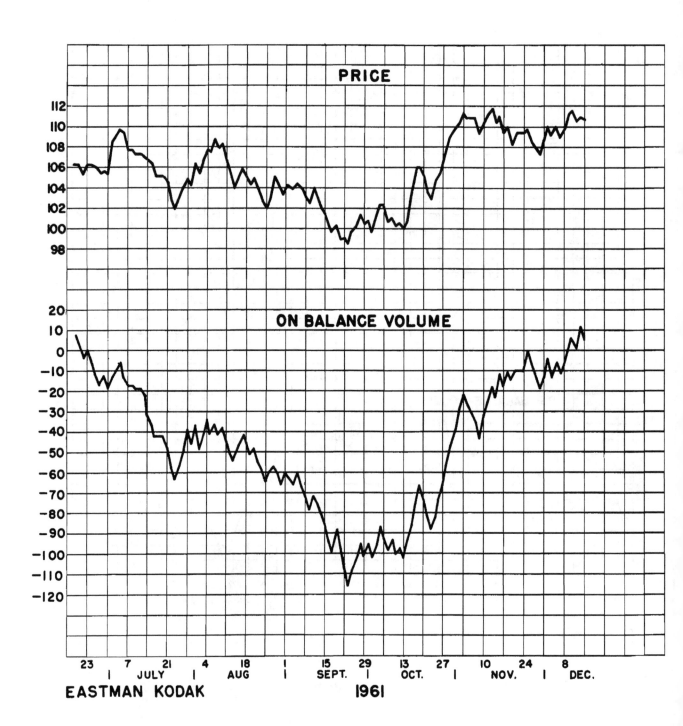

PRICE

ON BALANCE VOLUME

EASTMAN KODAK   1961

Chart 54

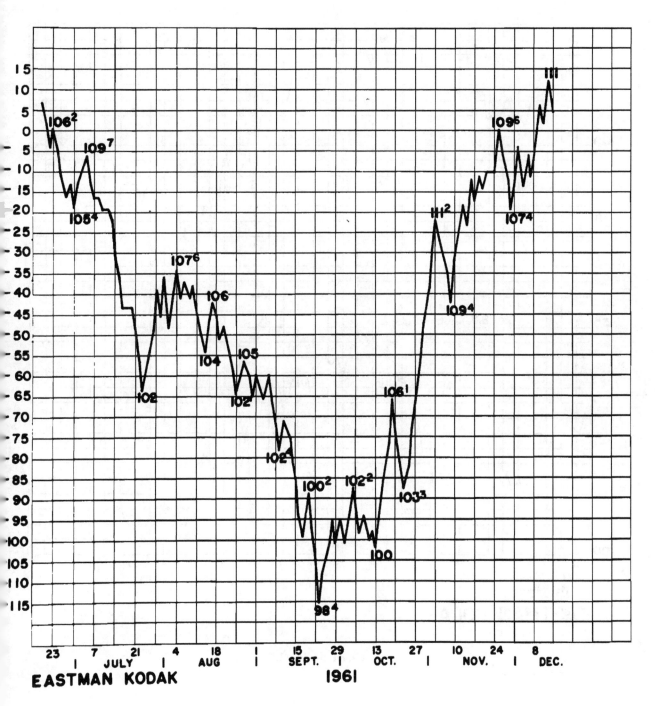

EASTMAN KODAK   1961

Chart 54 (cont.)

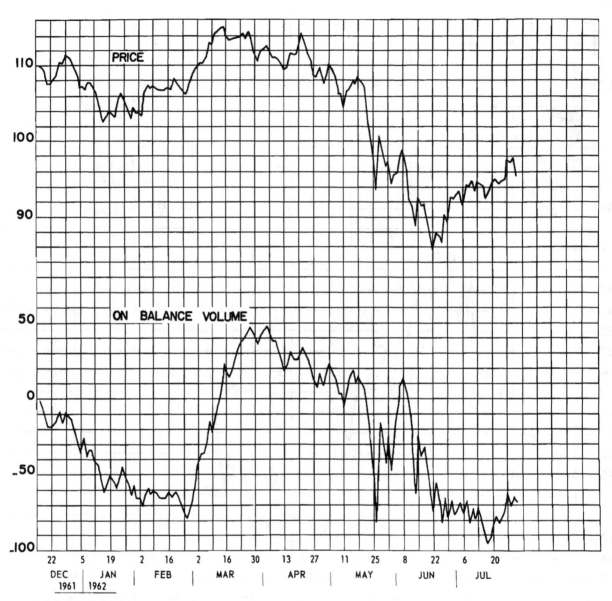

PRICE

ON BALANCE VOLUME

110

100

90

50

0

-50

-100

22 5 19 2 16 2 16 30 13 27 11 25 8 22 6 20

DEC JAN FEB MAR APR MAY JUN JUL
1961 1962

EASTMAN KODAK

Chart 54 (cont.)

GENERAL ELECTRIC

Vital Statistics

Long-term support level (OBV)	90,800 August 24, 1961 at 68.00
Date when long-term support broken	Long-term support NOT broken
First falling field recorded	April 2, 1962
High OBV before May 1962 break	December 1, 1961 at 521,800
Low OBV after April 1962	May 28, 1962 at 153,400
Short interest trend	Rising February 1962
Downside penetration of 200-day moving average price line	January 1962
200-day line turned down	May 1962

Summary of General Electric. On-balance volume ran all the way from 90,800 on August 24, 1961 up to a high of 521,800 on December 1, 1961 with no DOWN designations inbetween. This unbroken string covered a period of almost *three and a half months,* an unusually long time for a single field. When an up field lasts long it has *climactic* characteristics. You will recall that Chrysler recorded excessive OBV swings on the upside but, checking these, you will find that the fields were of only a few weeks duration. Here is another example of long-term OBV support remaining unbroken in the face of the May 1962 break. The stock moved down to a low of 55.50 on June 22, 1962 with OBV standing at 199,600, above that of 153,400 recorded on May 28th when the price of the stock was higher. This constituted another of those conspicuously outstanding *non-confirmations* which tend to precede major turns.

GENERAL FOODS

Vital Statistics

Long-term support level (OBV)	87,300 November 1, 1961 at 96.63
Date when long-term support broken	Nov. 27, 1961 at 85,200. Price 101.50
First falling field recorded	February 21, 1962
High OBV before May 1962 break	November 14, 1961 at 119,500
Low OBV after April 1962	June 27, 1962 at minus 87,200
Short interest trend	Started to rise in May 1962
Downside penetration of 200-day moving average price line	January 1962
200-day line turned down	March 1962

Summary of General Foods. First weakness in this issue was shown by volume figures in November 1961. Short interest began to rise as stock became oversold.

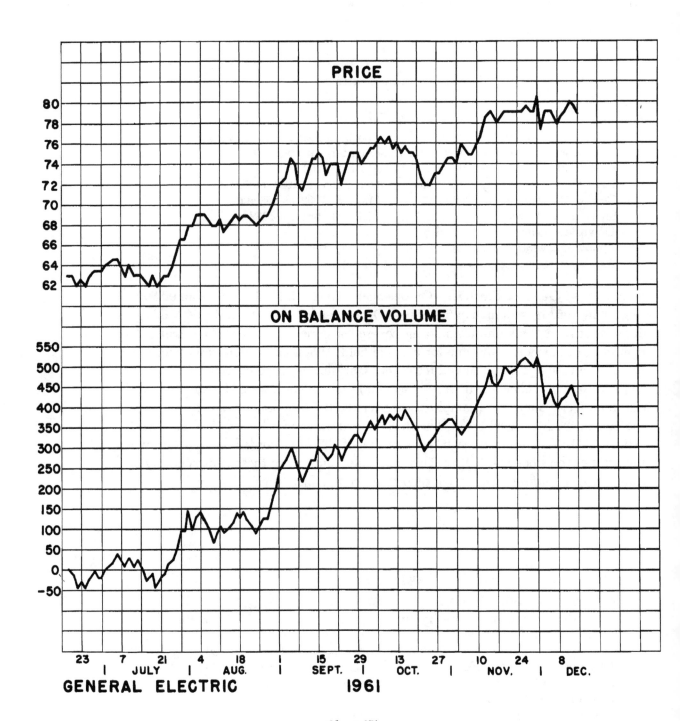

Chart 55

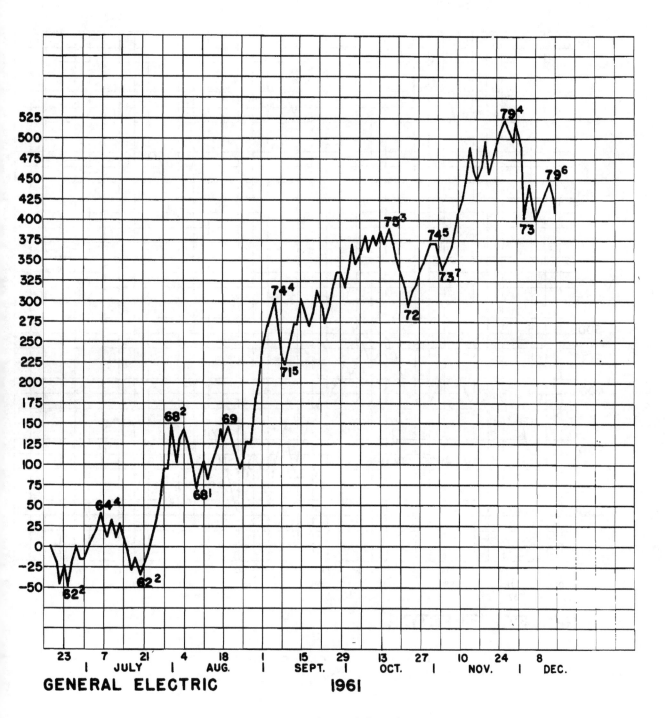

GENERAL ELECTRIC   1961

Chart 55 (cont.)

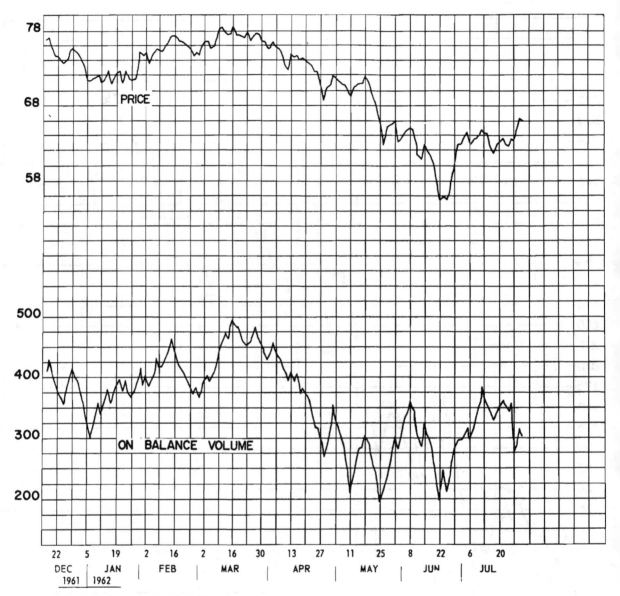

GENERAL ELECTRIC

Chart 55 (cont.)

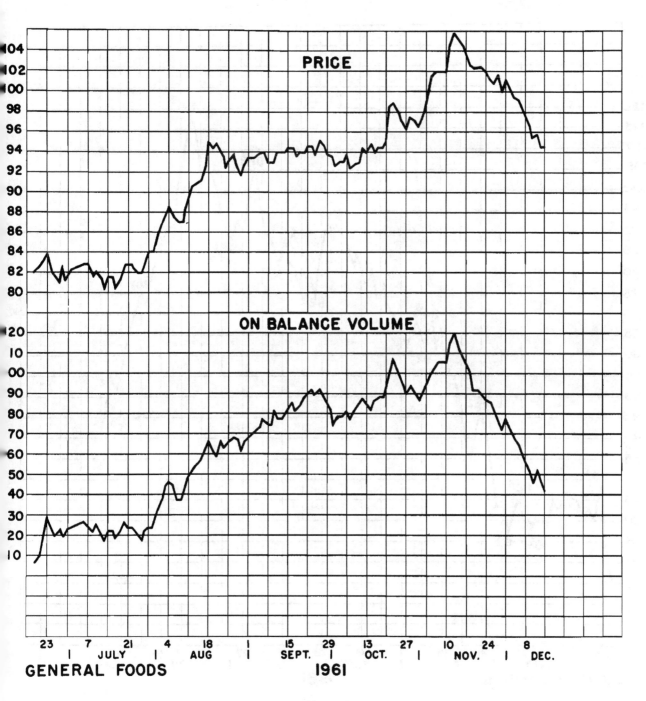

PRICE

ON BALANCE VOLUME

GENERAL FOODS   1961

Chart 56

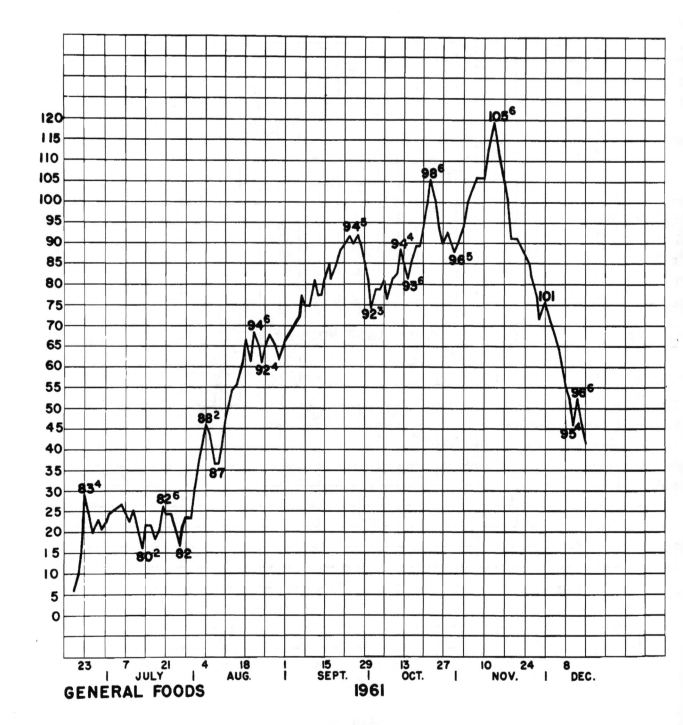

GENERAL FOODS   1961

Chart 56 (cont.)

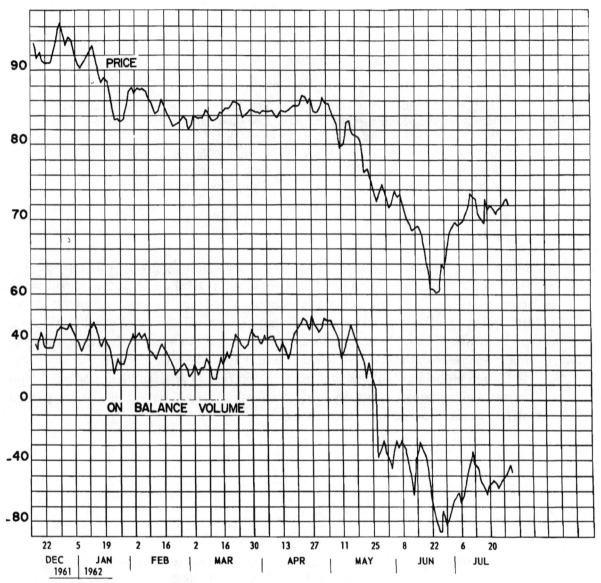

GENERAL FOODS

Chart 56 (cont.)

General Motors

Vital Statistics

Long-term Support level (OBV)	271,200 November 16, 1961 at 52.75
Date when long-term support broken	Long-term support NOT broken
First falling field recorded	April 4, 1962
High OBV before May 1962 break	February 15, 1962 at 828,500
Low OBV after April 1962	June 25, 1962 at 462,900
Short interest trend	Rising from January 1962
Downside peneration of 200-day moving average price line	May 1962
200-day line turned down	June 1962

Summary of General Motors. This stock was apparently giving a long-range forecast that the May 1962 market break was not a bear market and that the market would recover once again. Long-range OBV support was not broken, the stock merely attempting to fill the on-balance volume gap between 271,200 and 688,300. With the stock down to 45.75 on June 25, 1962 and OBV standing at 462,900 the stock was many times stronger than the last time it was selling at around 46.00, that being in September 1961 when on-balance volume was a minus 156,700. That is another example of important non-confirmation between price and volume, such non-confirmations preceding important trend-making price swings.

Goodyear

Vital Statistics

Long-term support level (OBV)	127,800 September 25, 1961. Price 42.13
Date when long-term support broken	January 19, 1962
First falling field recorded	January 18, 1962
High OBV before May 1962 break	November 15, 1961 at 211,600
Low OBV after April 1962	June 27, 1962 at minus 106,900
Short interest trend	Rising from June 1962
Downside penetration of 200-day moving average price line	November 1961
200-day line turned down	March 1962

Summary of Goodyear. This was one of the weaker looking Dow-Jones issues, weakness in evidence in late 1961 with OBV confirmations in January 1962.

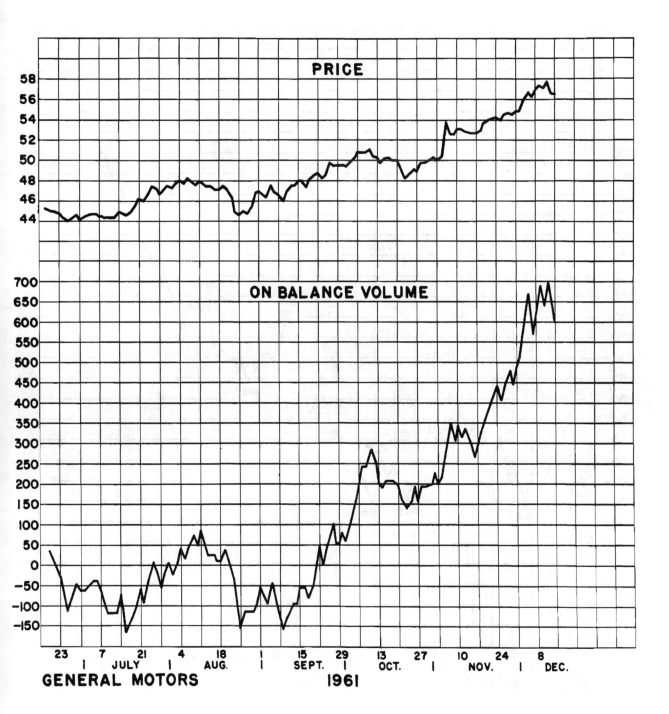

PRICE

ON BALANCE VOLUME

GENERAL MOTORS 1961

Chart 57

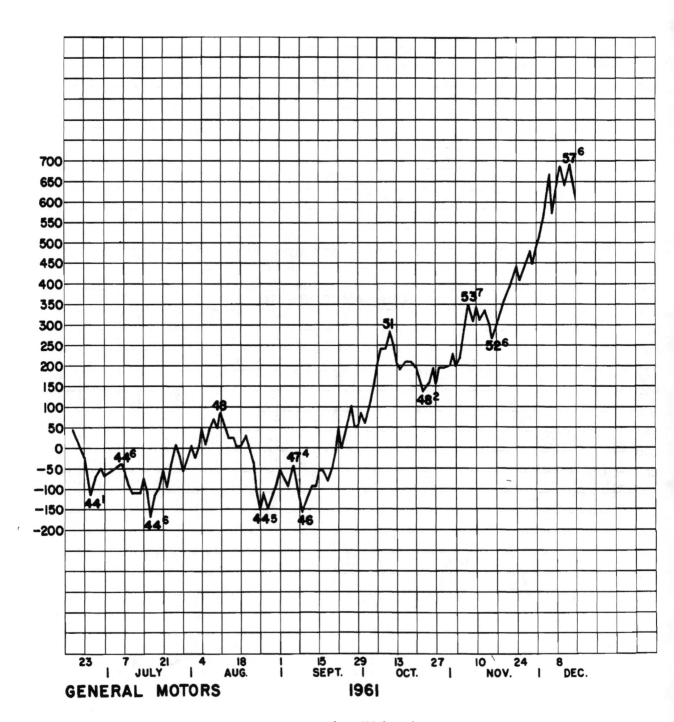

GENERAL MOTORS   1961

Chart 57 (cont.)

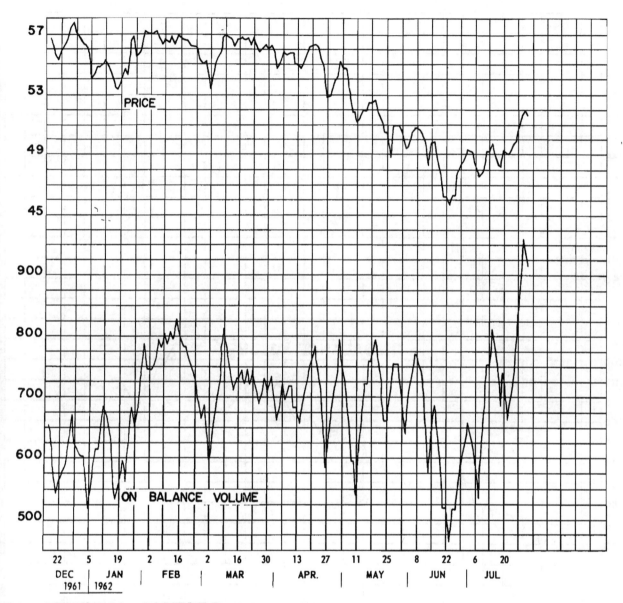

GENERAL MOTORS

Chart 57 (cont.)

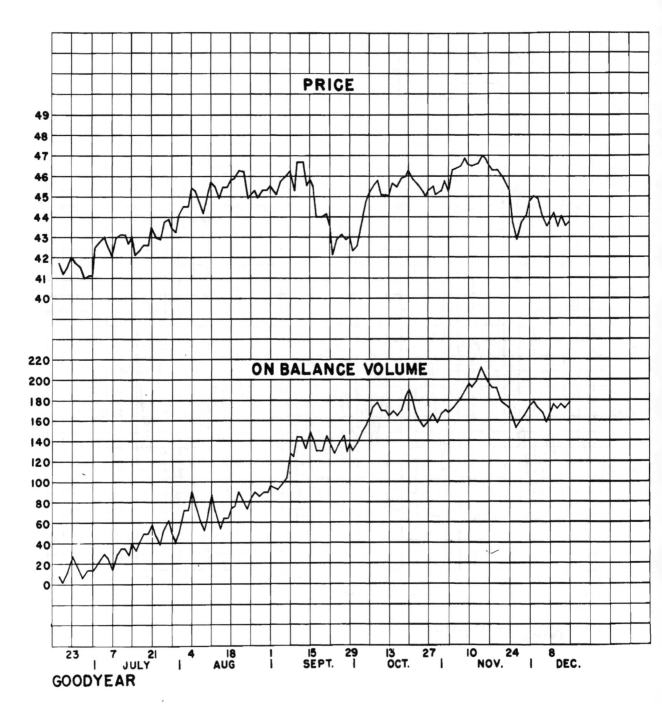

PRICE

ON BALANCE VOLUME

GOODYEAR

Chart 58

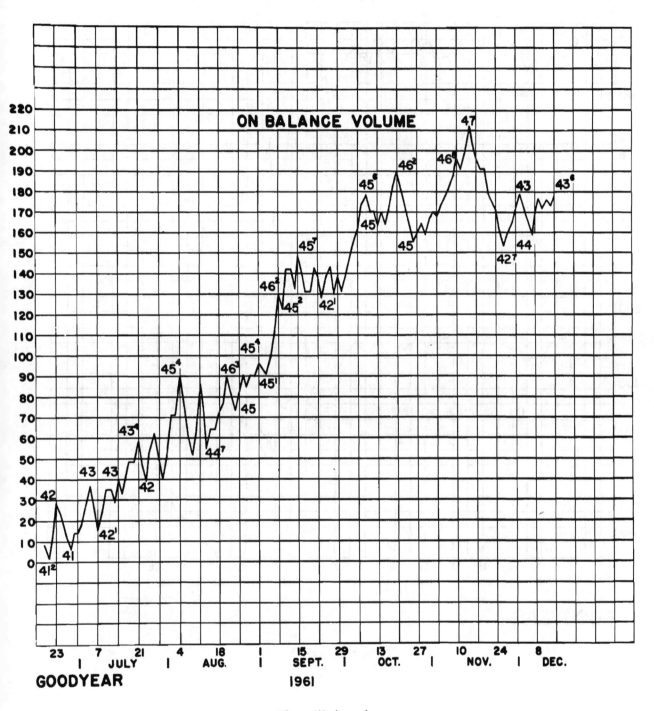

Chart 58 (cont.)

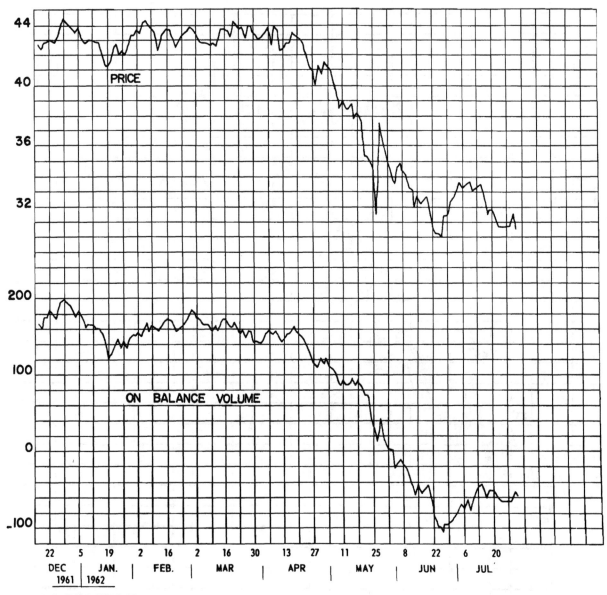

GOODYEAR

Chart 58 (cont.)

INTERNATIONAL HARVESTER

Vital Statistics

Long-term support level (OBV)	Minus 66,800 Oct. 26, 1961 at 48.00
Date when long-term support broken	Long-term support NOT broken
First falling field recorded	April 11, 1962
High OBV before May 1962 break	March 1, 1962 at 56,600
Low OBV after April 1962	June 27, 1962 at minus 5,200
Short interest trend	No trend
Downside penetration of 200-day moving average price line	May 1962
200-day line turned down	June 1962

Summary of International Harvester. Here is another example of a Dow-Jones stock which did not go under the late 1961 OBV support level in the 1962 break. The fact that the stock moved down to a low of 44.63 on June 27, 1962 with OBV holding up at minus 5,200 proved to be an important turning point.

INTERNATIONAL NICKEL

Vital Statistics

Long-term support level (OBV)	175,000 February 5, 1962 at 77.50
Date when long-term support broken	May 25, 1962
First falling field recorded	May 10, 1962
High OBV before May 1962 break	255,100 on April 23, 1962
Low OBV after April 1962	102,100 on June 25, 1962
Short interest trend	No trend
Downside penetration of 200-day moving average price line	November 1961
200-day line turned down	February 1962

Summary on International Nickel. Here was a case of high on-balance volume taking place long after the stock had topped out, an example of *non-confirmation on the upside*.

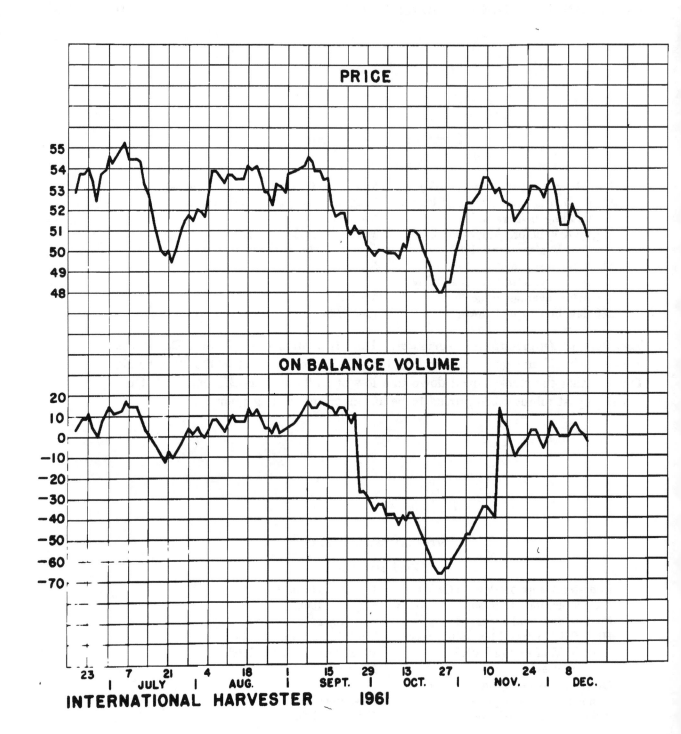

PRICE

ON BALANCE VOLUME

INTERNATIONAL HARVESTER   1961

Chart 59

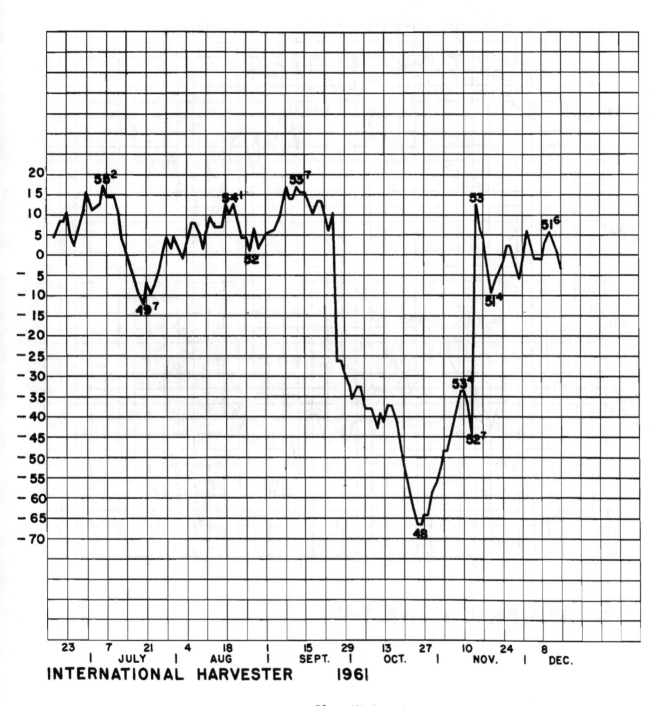

INTERNATIONAL HARVESTER   1961

Chart 59 (cont.)

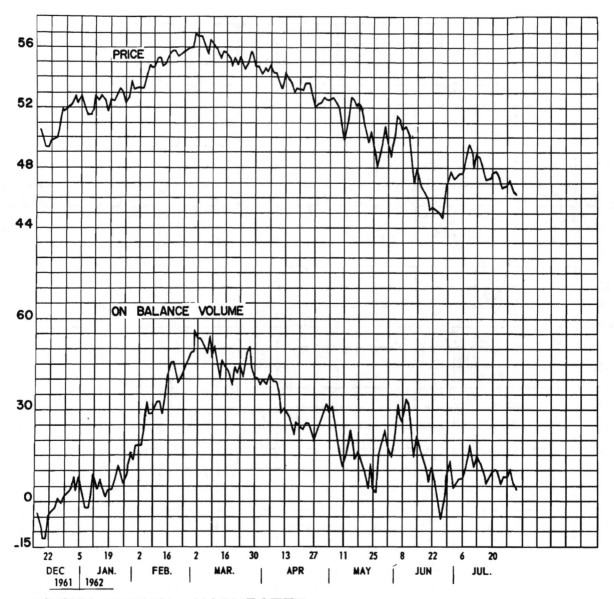

PRICE

ON BALANCE VOLUME

56

52

48

44

60

30

0

-15

22   5   19   2   16   2   16   30   13   27   11   25   8   22   6   20
DEC | JAN. | FEB. | MAR. | APR | MAY | JUN | JUL.
1961 | 1962 |

INTERNATIONAL HARVESTER

Chart 59 (cont.)

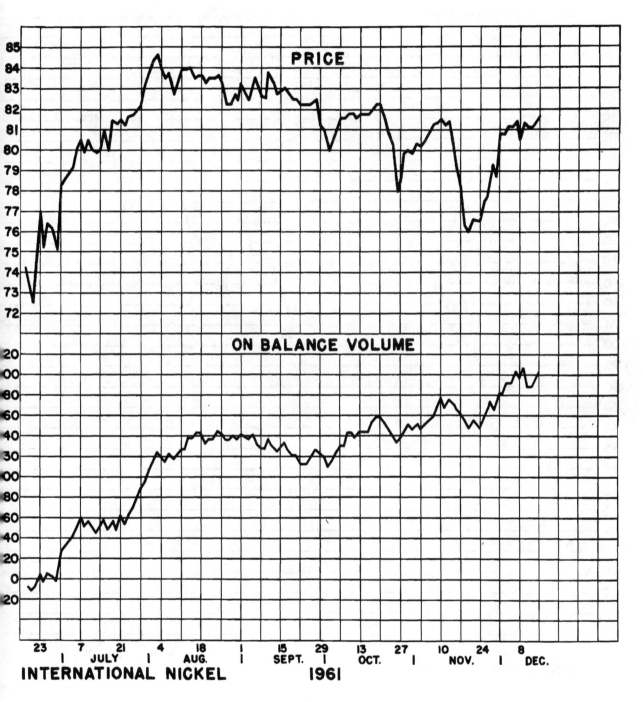

PRICE

ON BALANCE VOLUME

INTERNATIONAL NICKEL   1961

Chart 60

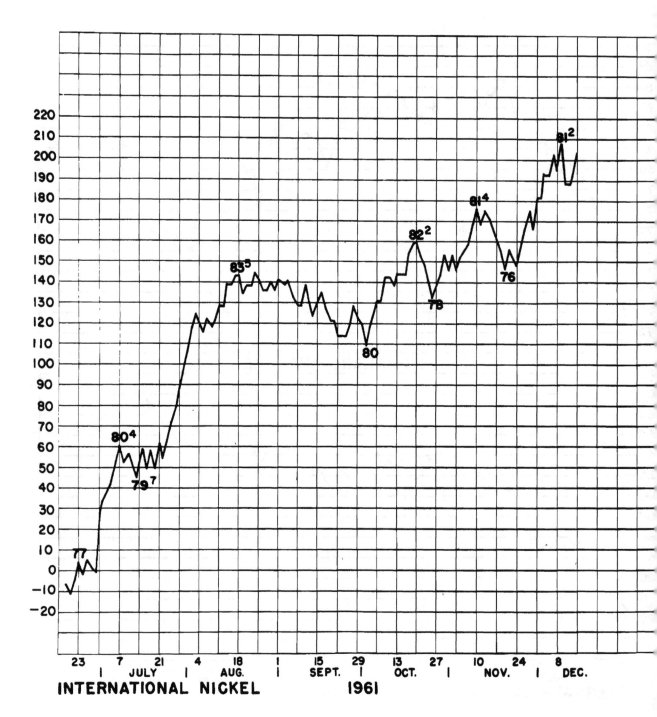

INTERNATIONAL NICKEL   1961

Chart 60 (cont.)

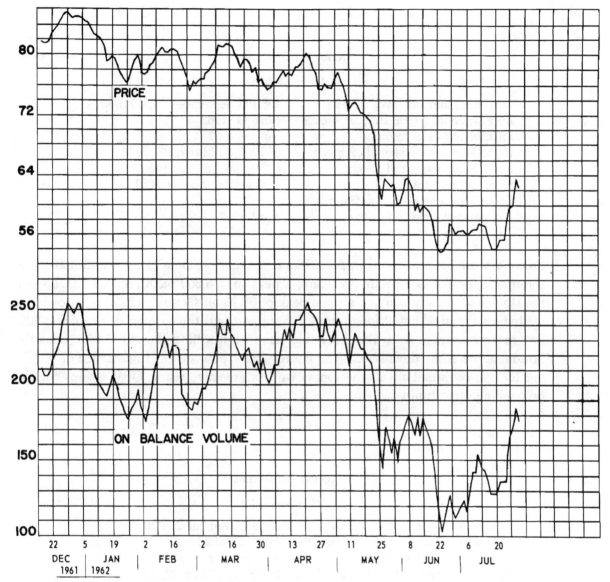

INTERNATIONAL NICKEL

Chart 60 (cont.)

INTERNATIONAL PAPER

Vital Statistics

Long-term support level (OBV)	108,100 September 25, 1961 at 33.50
Date when long-term support broken	June 14, 1962
First falling field recorded	Nov. 9, 1961
High OBV before May 1962 break	373,200 on March 28, 1962
Low OBV after April 1962	49,500 on July 26, 1962
Short interest trend	Rising after August 1962
Downside penetration of 200-day moving average price line	April 1962
200-day line turned down	May 1962

Summary on International Paper. Here is another example of non-confirmation on the upside, on-balance volume reaching a peak of 373,200 on March 28, 1962 when the stock had already reached a price peak of 38.13 on October 11, 1961. If one had waited for the breaking of long-term OBV support and the turning down of the 200-day moving average price line he would have been selling the stock very near the bottom of the entire downswing. The figures above point to the importance of watching for non-confirmations at the top as well as excessive rising OBV figures for the best selling opportunities.

JOHNS MANVILLE

Vital Statistics

Long-term support level (OBV)	1,700 November 2, 1961
Date when long-term support broken	April 25, 1962
First falling field recorded	November 2, 1961
High OBV before May 1962 break	48,800 on March 19, 1962
Low OBV after April 1962	Minus 92,600 on July 25, 1962 at 40.63
Short interest trend	Rising after July 1962
Downside penetration of 200-day moving average price line	July 1961
200-day line turned down	October 1961

Summary on Johns Manville. Wide non-confirmation on the upside occurred on March 19, 1962 when Johns Manville showed high OBV of 48,800 with the stock 11 points under the August 22, 1961 price high of 69. All the early weakness showed up in 1961.

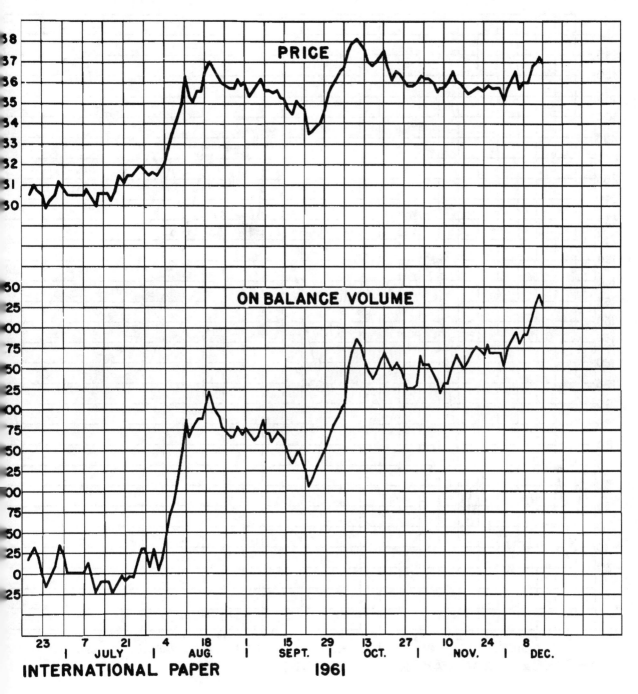

PRICE

ON BALANCE VOLUME

23   7   21   4   18   1   15   29   13   27   10   24   8
    JULY   AUG.   SEPT.   OCT.   NOV.   DEC.

INTERNATIONAL PAPER   1961

Chart 61

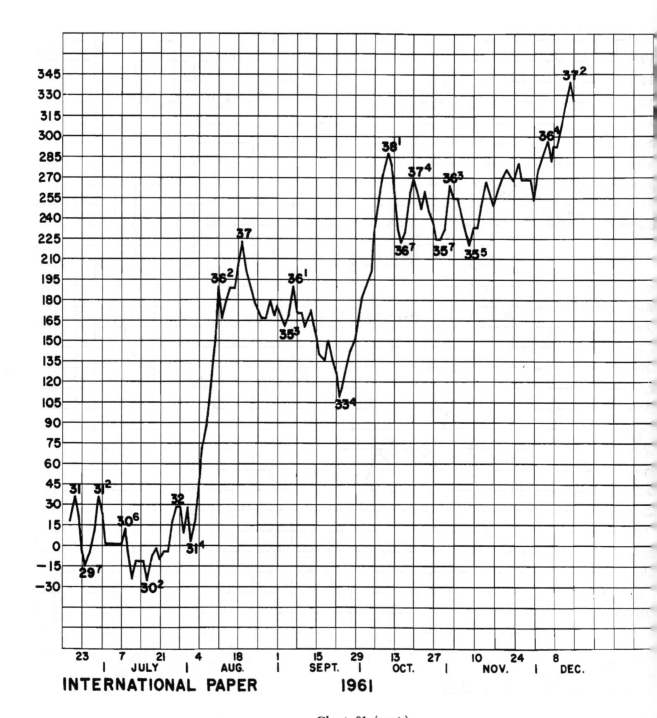

INTERNATIONAL PAPER   **1961**

Chart 61 (cont.)

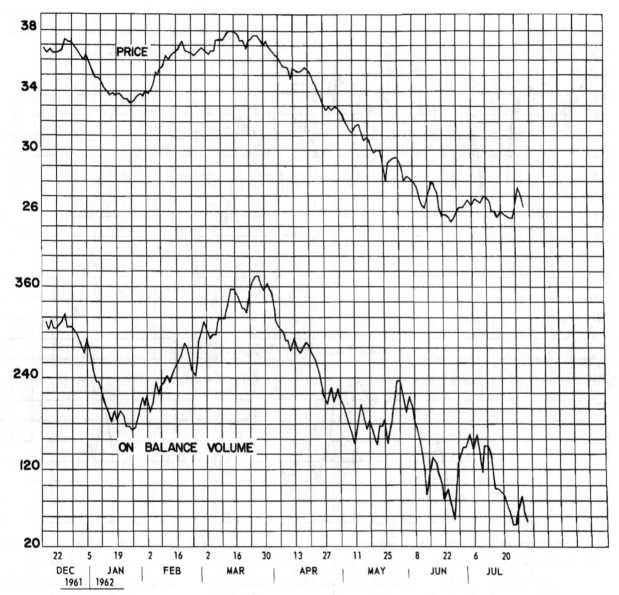

PRICE

ON BALANCE VOLUME

22 5 19 2 16 2 16 30 13 27 11 25 8 22 6 20

DEC | JAN | FEB | MAR | APR | MAY | JUN | JUL
1961 | 1962

INTERNATIONAL PAPER

Chart 61 (cont.)

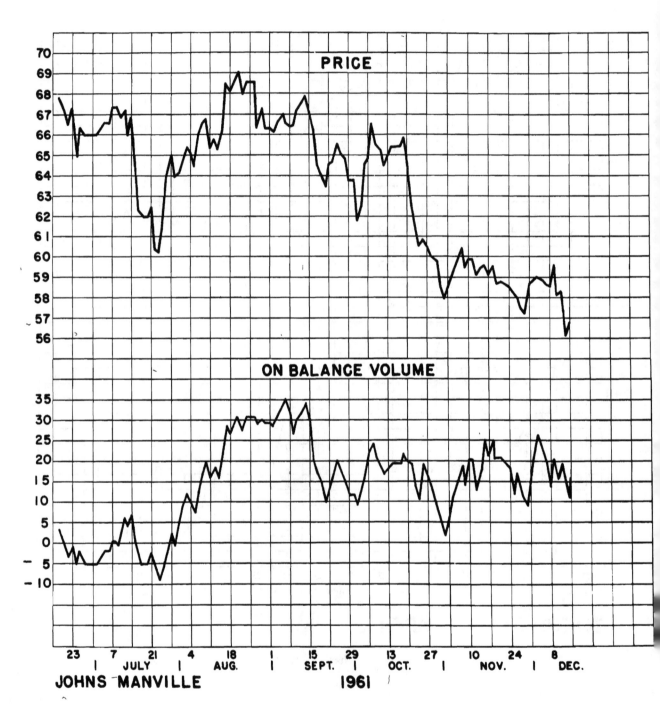

PRICE

ON BALANCE VOLUME

JOHNS MANVILLE   1961

Chart 62

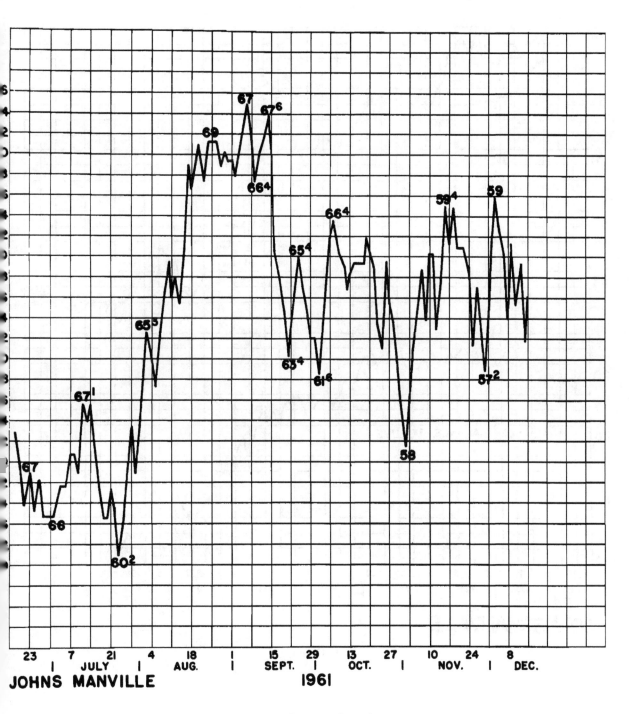

JOHNS MANVILLE   1961

Chart 62 (cont.)

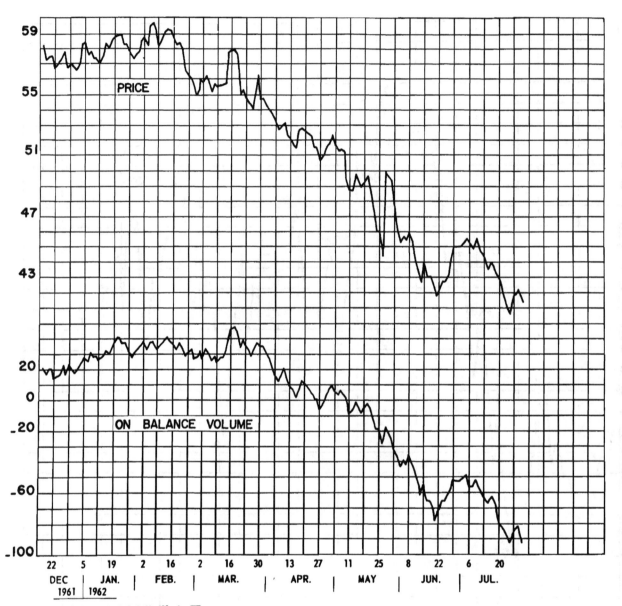

PRICE

ON BALANCE VOLUME

59
55
51
47
43

20
0
-20

-60

-100

22 | 5 | 19 | 2 | 16 | 2 | 16 | 30 | 13 | 27 | 11 | 25 | 8 | 22 | 6 | 20
DEC | JAN. | FEB. | MAR. | APR. | MAY | JUN. | JUL.
1961 | 1962

JOHNS MANVILLE

Chart 62 (cont.)

Owens Illinois Glass

Vital Statistics

Long-term support level (OBV)	Minus 21,400 October 24, 1961
Date when long-term support broken	April 4, 1962
First falling field recorded	January 29, 1962
High OBV before May 1962 break	25,100 on December 26, 1961
Low OBV after April 1962	Minus 67,400 June 25, 1962 at 67.00
Short interest trend	No trend
Downside penetration of 200-day moving average price line	January 1962
200-day line turned down	May 1962

Summary of Owens-Illinois Glass. December 1961 and January 1962 statistics gave sufficient reason to sell the stock.

Procter & Gamble

Vital Statistics

Long-term support level (OBV)	65,600 October 30, 1961
Date when long-term support broken	January 8, 1962
First falling field recorded	October 27, 1961
High OBV before May 1962 break	159,700 on December 11, 1961
Low OBV after April 1962	Minus 125,100 June 27, 1962 at a price of 58.37
Short interest trend	Rising after February 1962
Downside penetration of 200-day moving average price line	January 1962
200-day line turned down	January 1962

Summary of Procter and Gamble. The high price on this stock was reached on November 16, 1961 at 101.50, on-balance volume being 140,700 at that time. On the high OBV of 159,700 reached on December 11, 1961 the price fell short of the old high, being at 98.25. This non-confirmation was followed by the gradual decline to a low of 58.37 in late June 1962.

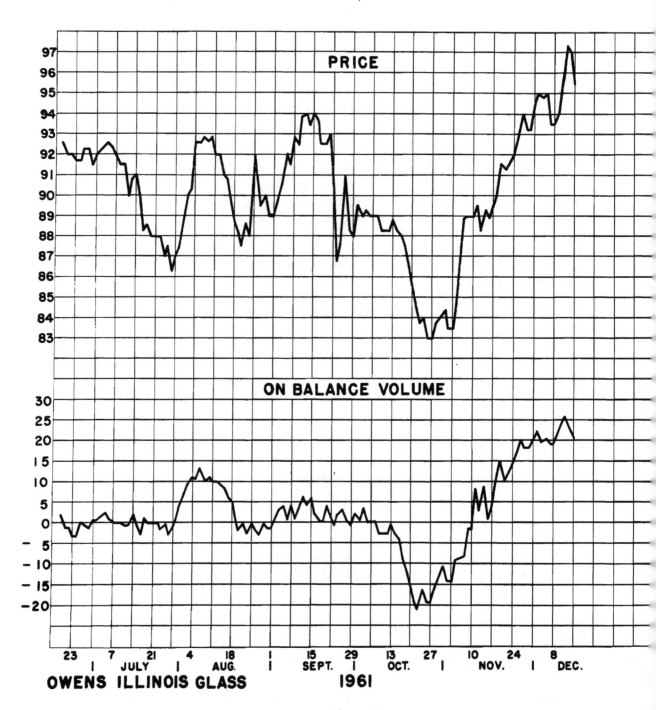

PRICE

ON BALANCE VOLUME

OWENS ILLINOIS GLASS   1961

Chart 63

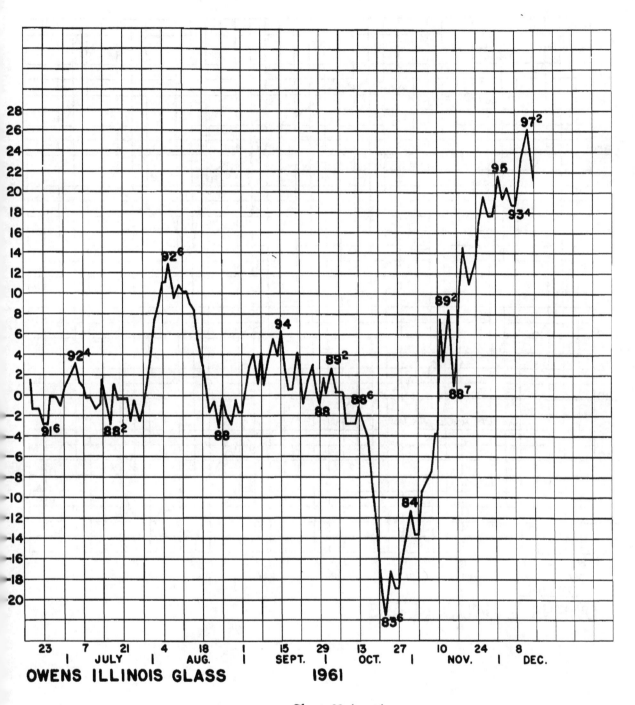

OWENS ILLINOIS GLASS   **1961**

Chart 63 (cont.)

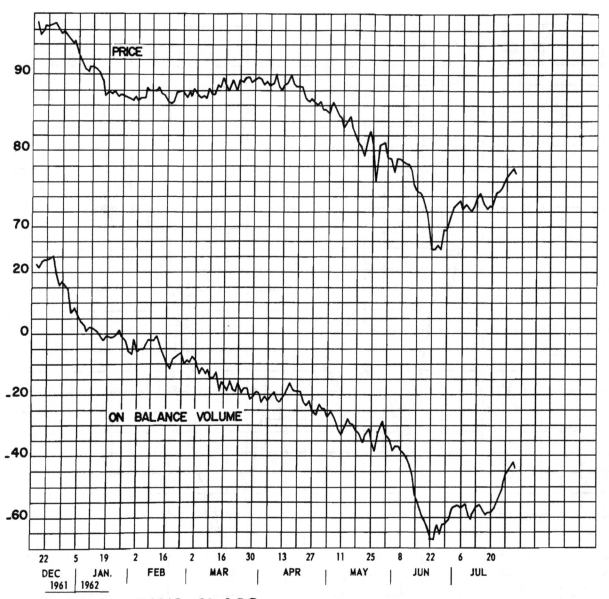

OWENS ILLINOIS GLASS

Chart 63 (cont.)

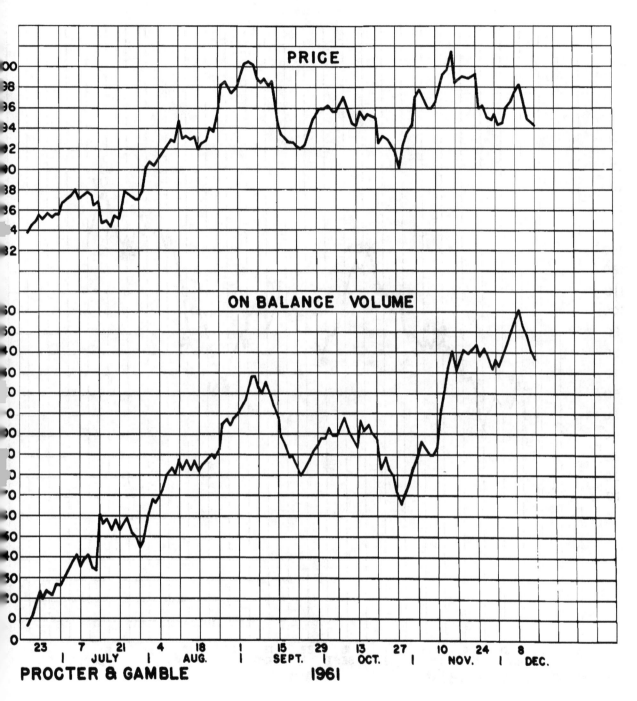

PRICE

ON BALANCE VOLUME

23   7   21   4   18   1   15   29   13   27   10   24   8
      JULY   AUG.   SEPT.   OCT.   NOV.   DEC.

PROCTER & GAMBLE   **1961**

Chart 64

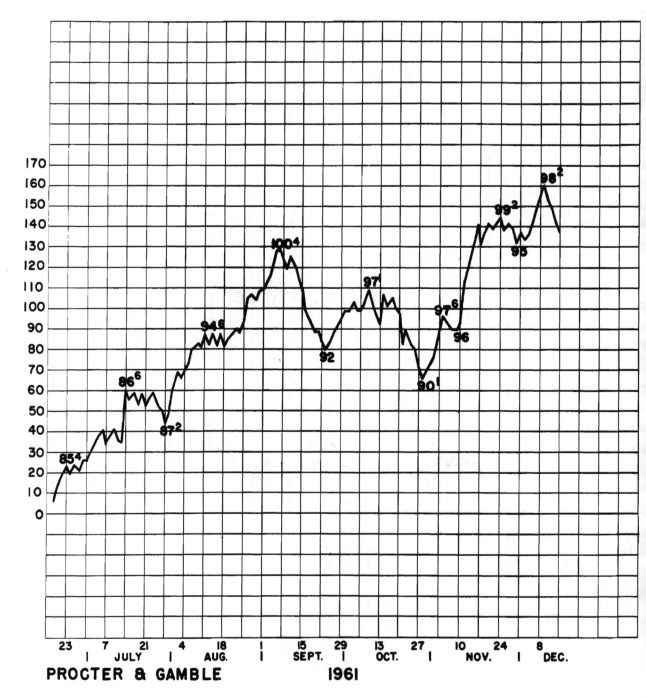

PROCTER & GAMBLE   1961

Chart 64 (cont.)

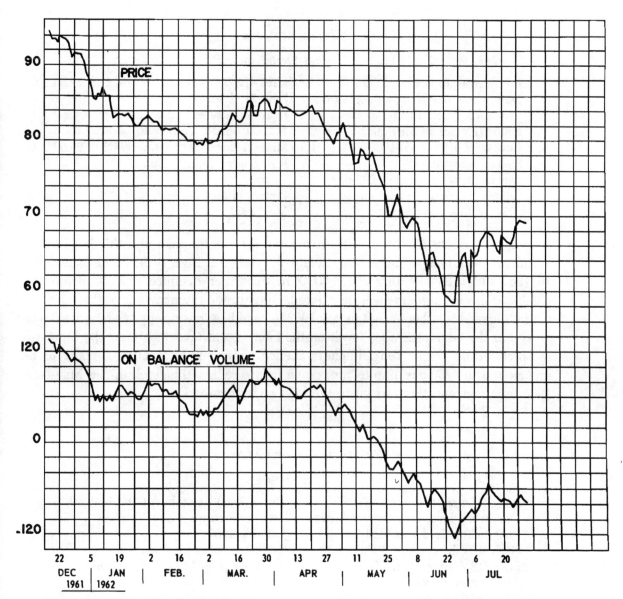

PROCTER & GAMBLE

Chart 64 (cont.)

SEARS ROEBUCK

Vital Statistics

Long-term support level (OBV)	Minus 28,500 January 29, 1962 at 72.50
Date when long-term support broken	June 21, 1962
First falling field recorded	January 4, 1962
High OBV before May 1962 break	132,400 on November 16, 1961
Low OBV after April 1962	Minus 113,600 on June 27, 1962 at 60.00
Short interest trend	Rising after March 1962
Downside penetration of 200-day moving average price line	January 1962
200-day line turned down	May 1962

Summary of Sears Roebuck. No two cases are exactly alike and this is why it is useful to check many things. Sears Roebuck reached a high of 93.00 on November 16, 1961 with OBV standing at 132,400. The stock then declined to 77.00 before the rising 200-day average line was penetrated. Only upside disparity above that line and the falling field trend of early January 1962 gave indications of approaching weakness as well as the OBV resistance levels on the intermittent upswings after the high was recorded in November 1961. If one waited for the long-term OBV support to be broken and the 200-day line to turn down before selling the stock in the May-June 1962 time segment, this was when the lows were recorded.

STANDARD OIL OF CALIFORNIA

Vital Statistics

Long-term support level (OBV)	Minus 75,600 October 9, 1961 at 48.25
Date when long-term support broken	Long-term support NOT broken
First falling field recorded	June 13, 1962
High OBV before May 1962 break	153,900 on May 21, 1962
Low OBV after April 1962	39,100 on June 14, 1962 at 51.38
Short interest trend	No trend
Downside penetration of 200-day moving average price line	May 1962
200-day line turned down	Did NOT turn down

Summary of Standard Oil of California. The above statistics show that this was one of the strongest of all the Dow-Jones issues throughout the 1962 break. Long-term supports held, the 200-day line stayed up and the stock literally went against the market right up to a week before the plunge of May 28, 1962. This action was forecasting a long-range further upswing, another Dow-Jones issue refusing to recognize the 1962 market action as long range bearish.

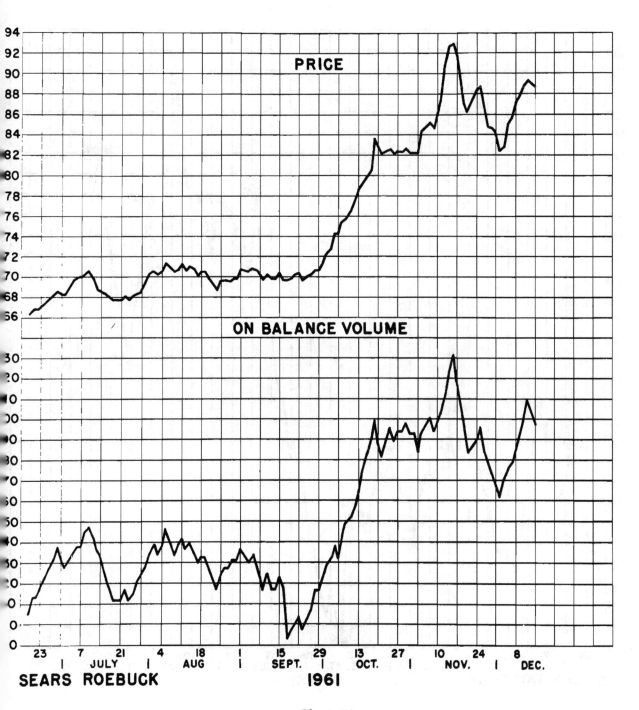

Chart 65

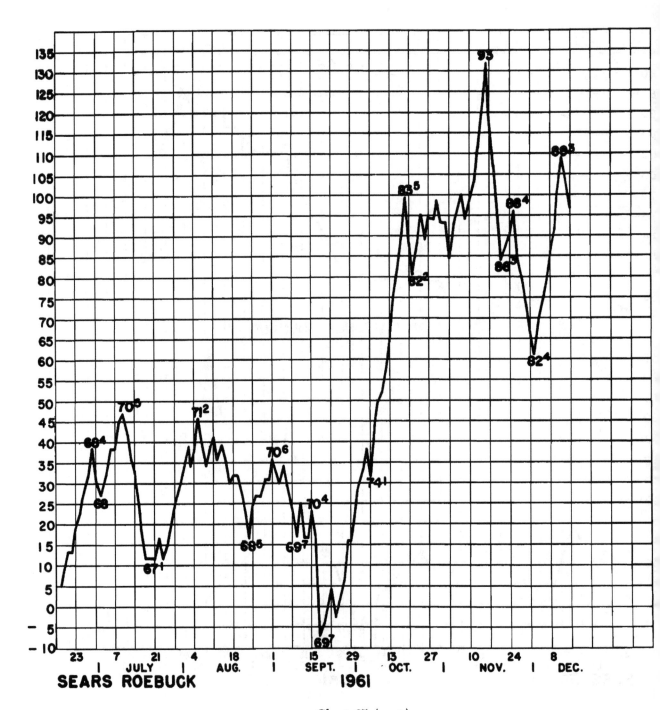

SEARS ROEBUCK 1961

Chart 65 (cont.)

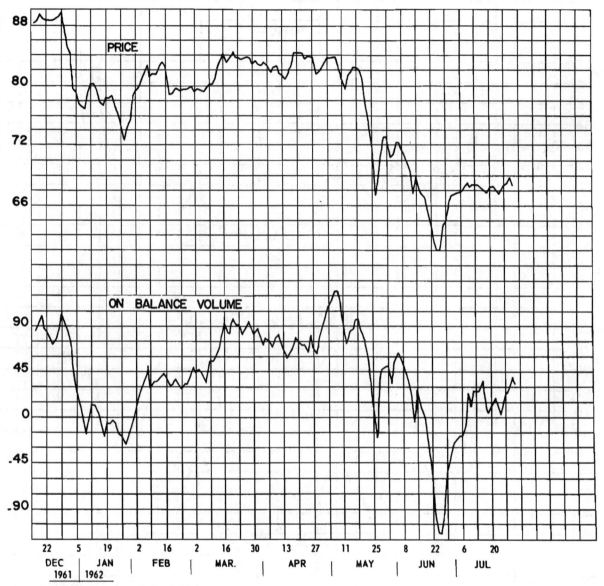

SEARS ROEBUCK

Chart 65 (cont.)

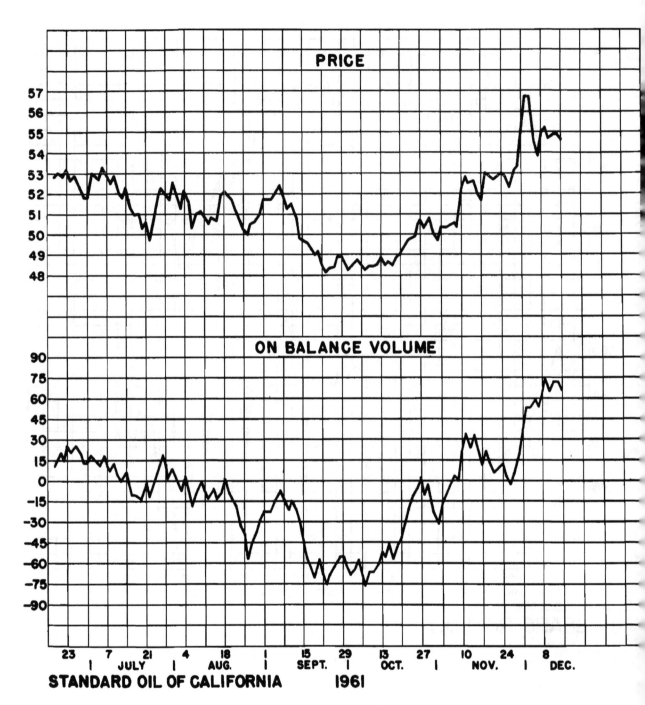

PRICE

ON BALANCE VOLUME

STANDARD OIL OF CALIFORNIA   1961

Chart 66

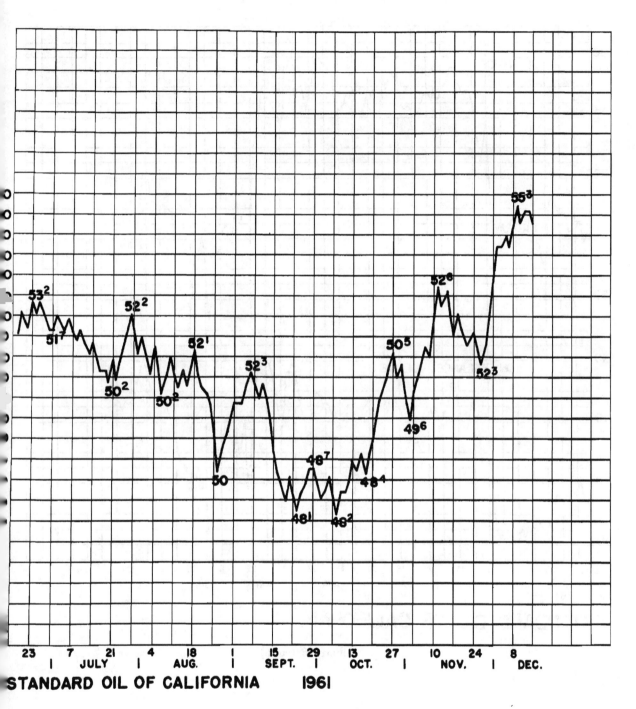

STANDARD OIL OF CALIFORNIA   1961

Chart 66 (cont.)

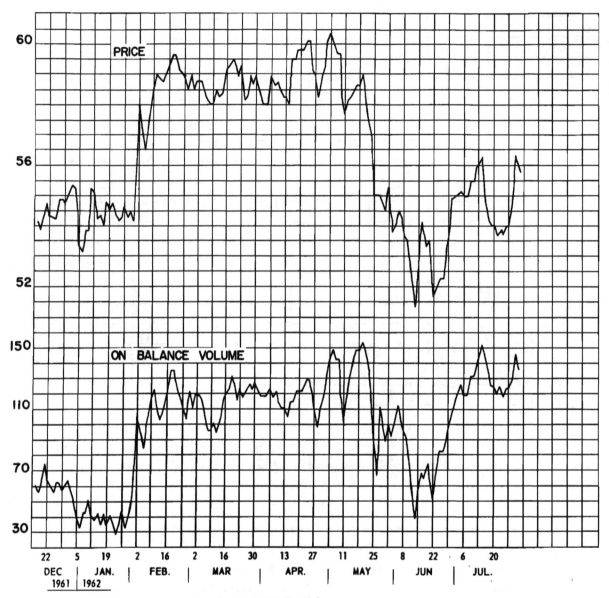

STANDARD OIL OF CALIFORNIA

Chart 66 (cont.)

STANDARD OIL (NEW JERSEY)

Vital Statistics

Long-term support level (OBV)	Minus 303,300 Oct. 4, 1961 at 43.00
Date when long-term support broken	Long-term support NOT broken
First falling field recorded	April 4, 1962
High OBV before May 1962 break	1,396,000 on March 1, 1962
Low OBV after April 1962	927,100 on June 26, 1962 at 48.25
Short interest trend	Rising after November 1961
Downside penetration of 200-day moving average price line	May 1962
200-day line turned down	Did NOT turn down

Summary of Standard Oil (New Jersey). Like Standard Oil of California, this issue never gave a long-term sell signal. It was one of the few stocks which bottomed out in late 1961 and went against the general market in the 1962 downswing.

SWIFT

Vital Statistics

Long-term support level (OBV)	4,800 November 1, 1961 at 39.13
Date when long-term support broken	Long-term support NOT broken
First falling field recorded	April 16, 1962
High OBV before May 1962 break	82,800 on February 20, 1962
Low OBV after April 1962	22,000 June 26, 1962 at 33.13
Short interest trend	No trend
Downside penetration of 200-day moving average price line	April 1962
200-day line turned down	June 1962

Summary of Swift. The long-term OBV support was not broken here despite the fact that the stock declined to a low of 33.13 on June 26, 1962. Here a bullish non-confirmation occurred, OBV remaining well above the 4,800 level of November 1, 1961 while the price went 6 points under that old price.

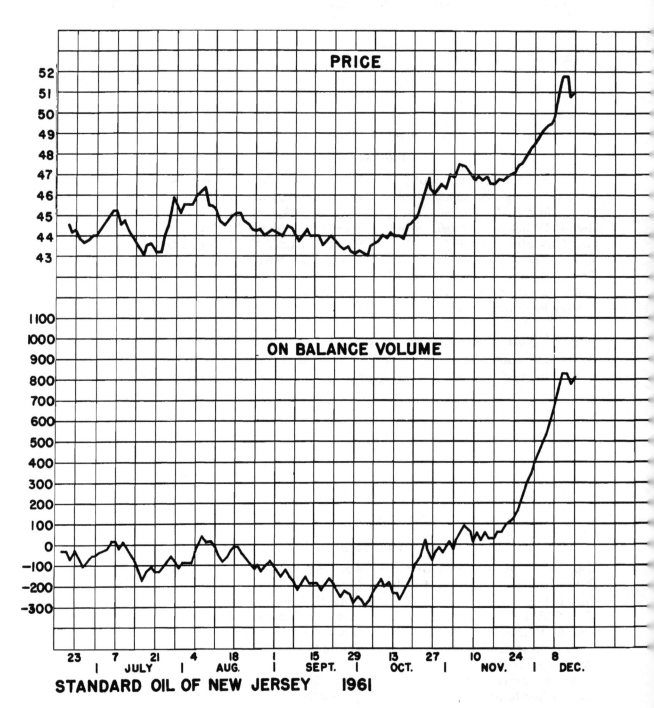

PRICE

ON BALANCE VOLUME

STANDARD OIL OF NEW JERSEY   1961

Chart 67

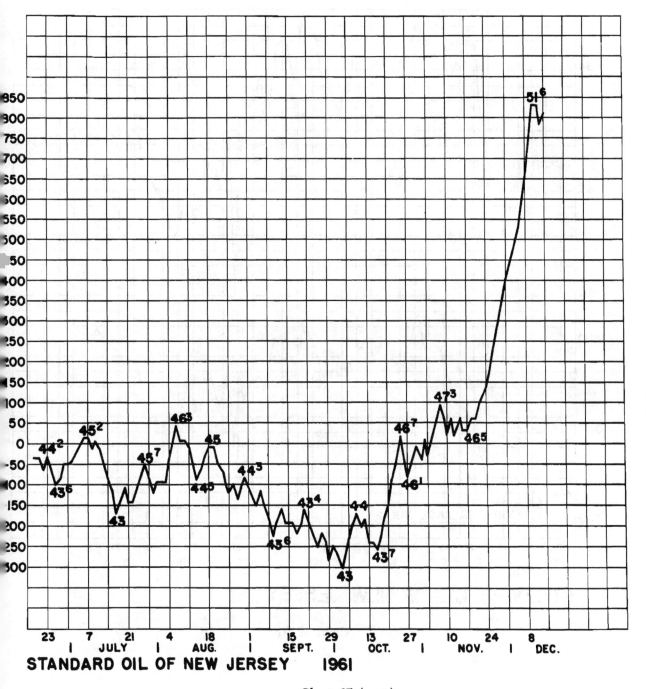

STANDARD OIL OF NEW JERSEY   1961

Chart 67 (cont.)

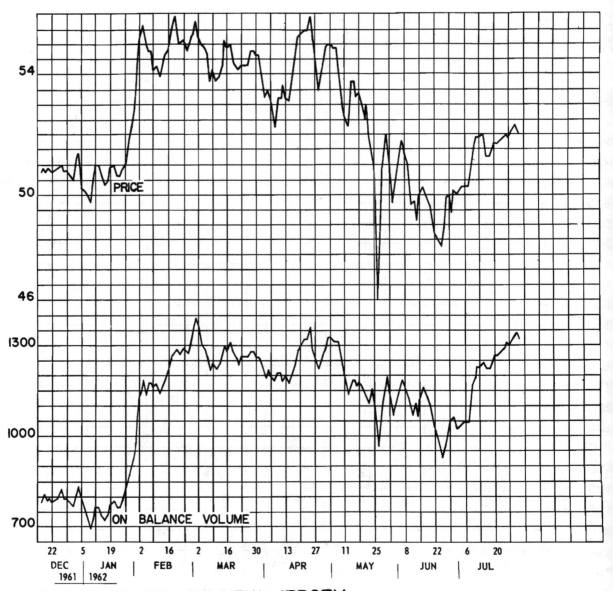

54

50 PRICE

46

1300

1000

700 ON BALANCE VOLUME

22	5	19	2	16	2	16	30	13	27	11	25	8	22	6	20
DEC	JAN		FEB		MAR			APR		MAY		JUN		JUL	
1961	1962														

STANDARD OIL OF NEW JERSEY

Chart 67 (cont.)

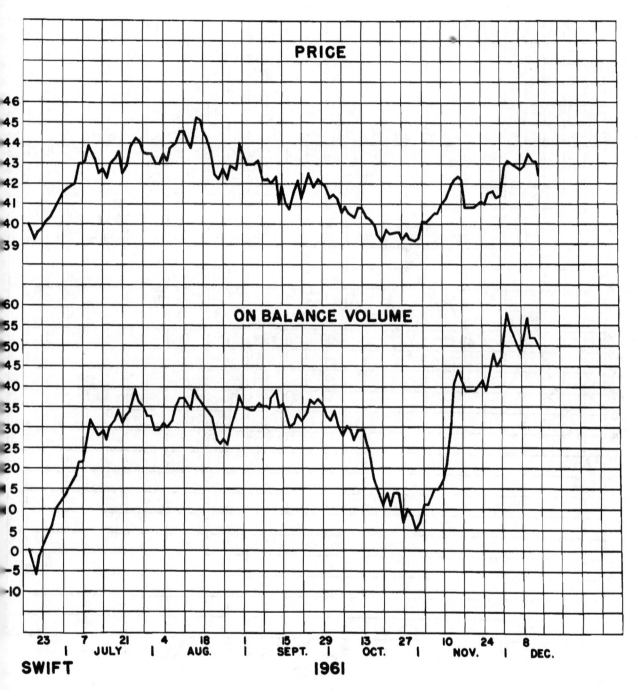

PRICE

ON BALANCE VOLUME

SWIFT   1961

Chart 68

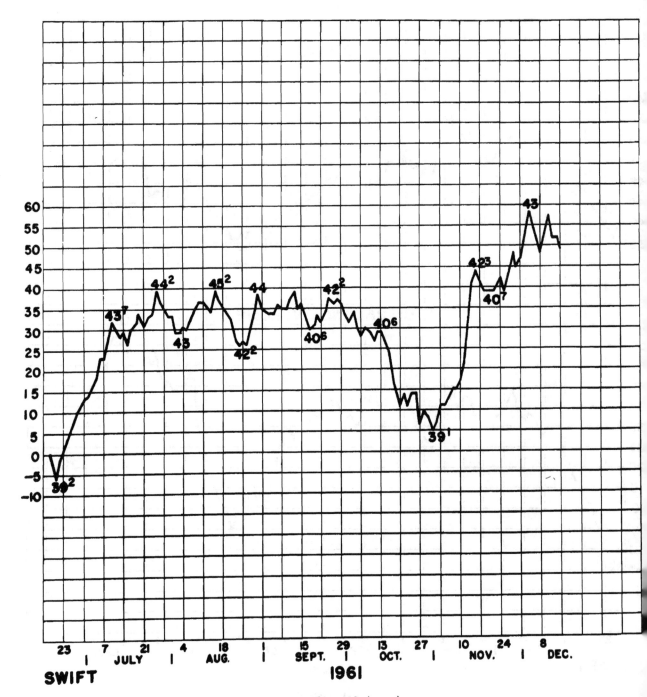

SWIFT

1961

Chart 68 (cont.)

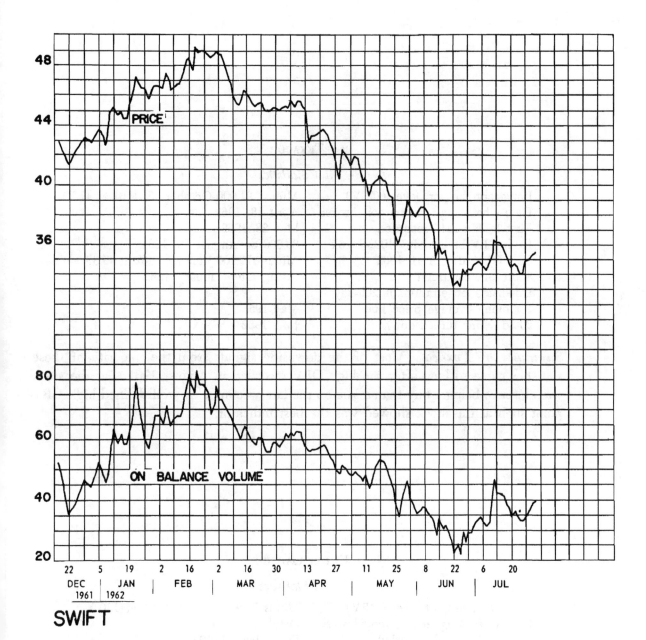

SWIFT

Chart 68 (cont.)

TEXACO

Vital Statistics

Long-term support level (OBV)	Minus 191,900 October 13, 1961 at 47.50
Date when long-term support broken	April 18, 1962
First falling field recorded	May 28, 1962
High OBV before May 1962 break	32,600 on August 18, 1961
Low OBV after April 1962	Minus 377,100 June 25, 1962 at 45.37
Short interest trend	Rising after January 1962
Downside penetration of 200-day moving average price line	May 1962
200-day line turned down	June 1962

Summary of Texaco. Most of the downside signals from the majority of these statistics came so long after the high OBV recorded in August 1961 that the stock was closer to being a buy than a sale on the late weakness. A well defined high OBV point such as this stock showed was the best indicator.

UNION CARBIDE

Vital Statistics

Long-term support level (OBV)	Minus 7,100 July 19, 1961 at 130.00
Date when long-term support broken	October 16, 1961
First falling field recorded	December 12, 1961
High OBV before May 1962 break	36,300 September 7, 1961
Low OBV after April 1962	Minus 272,600 June 26, 1962 at 84.00
Short interest trend	No trend
Downside penetration of 200-day moving average price line	September 1961
200-day line turned down	November 1961

Summary of Union Carbide. This stock showed all the weakness signals in 1961.

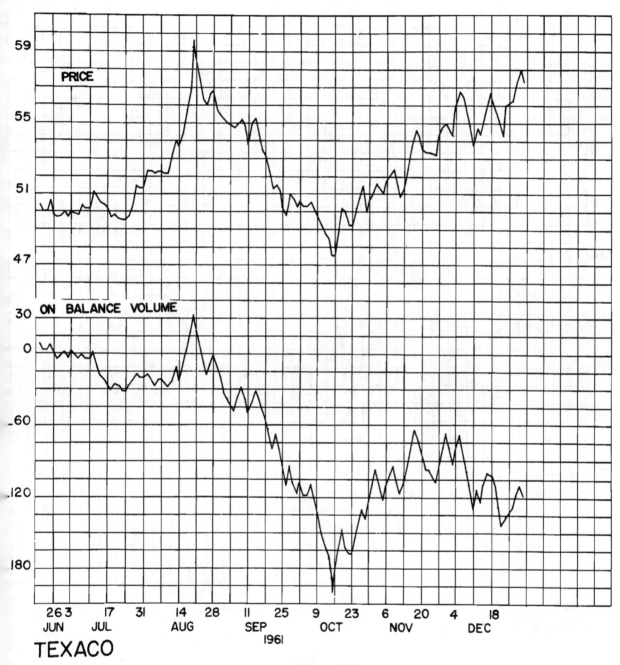

PRICE

ON BALANCE VOLUME

TEXACO

Chart 69

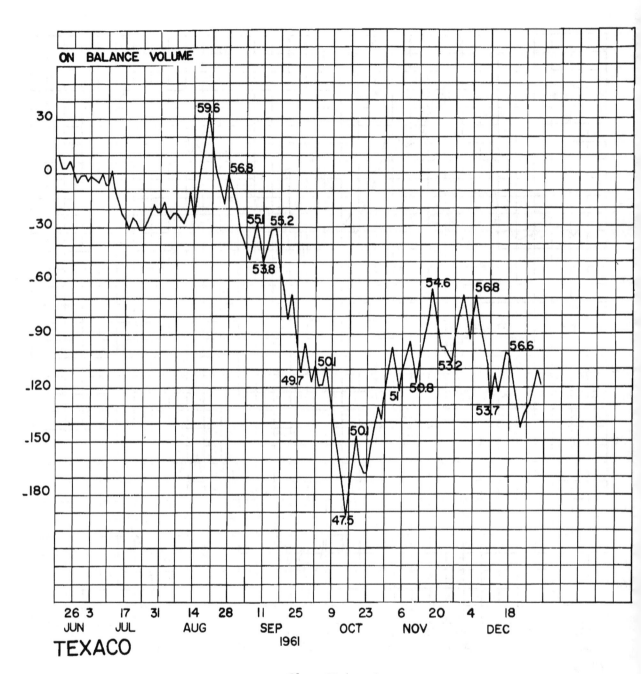

ON BALANCE VOLUME

TEXACO

Chart 69 (cont.)

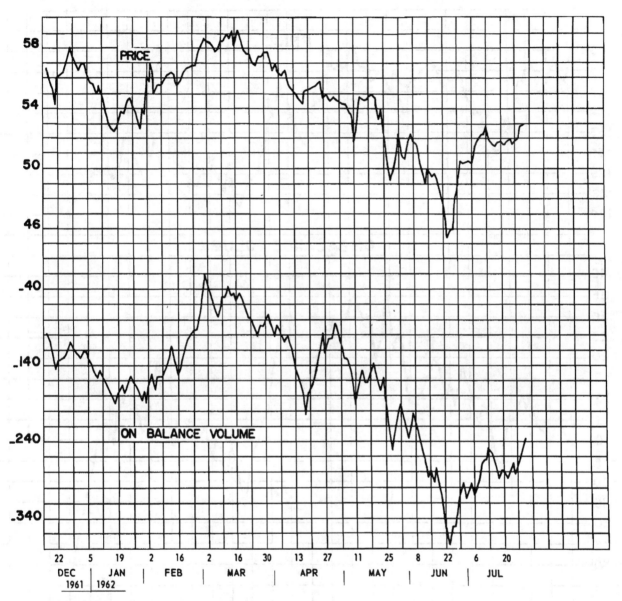

PRICE

ON BALANCE VOLUME

58

54

50

46

-.40

-.140

-.240

-.340

22   5   19   2   16   2   16   30   13   27   11   25   8   22   6   20

DEC   JAN   FEB   MAR   APR   MAY   JUN   JUL
1961 1962

TEXACO

Chart 69 (cont.)

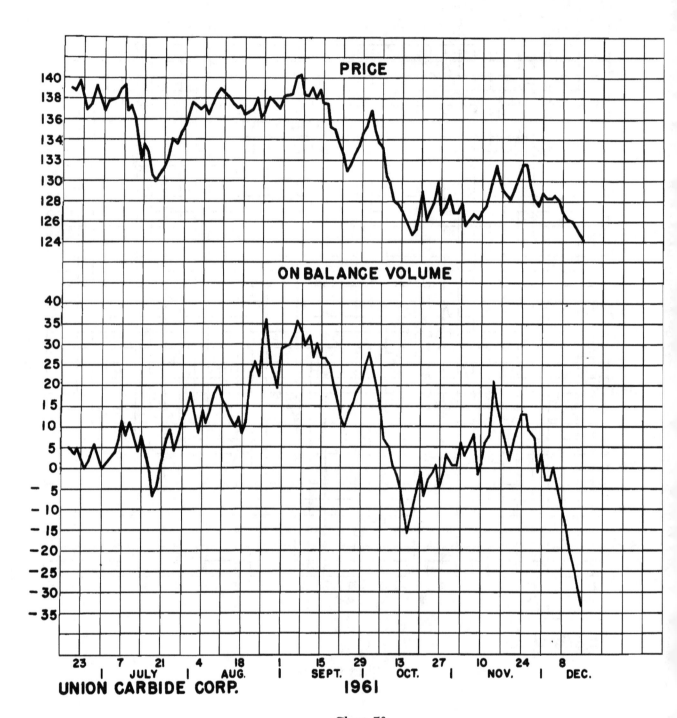

PRICE

140
138
136
134
133
130
128
126
124

ON BALANCE VOLUME

40
35
30
25
20
15
10
5
0
- 5
- 10
- 15
- 20
- 25
- 30
- 35

23   7   21   4   18   1   15   29   13   27   10   24   8
   | JULY | AUG. | SEPT. | OCT. | NOV. | DEC.

UNION CARBIDE CORP.   1961

Chart 70

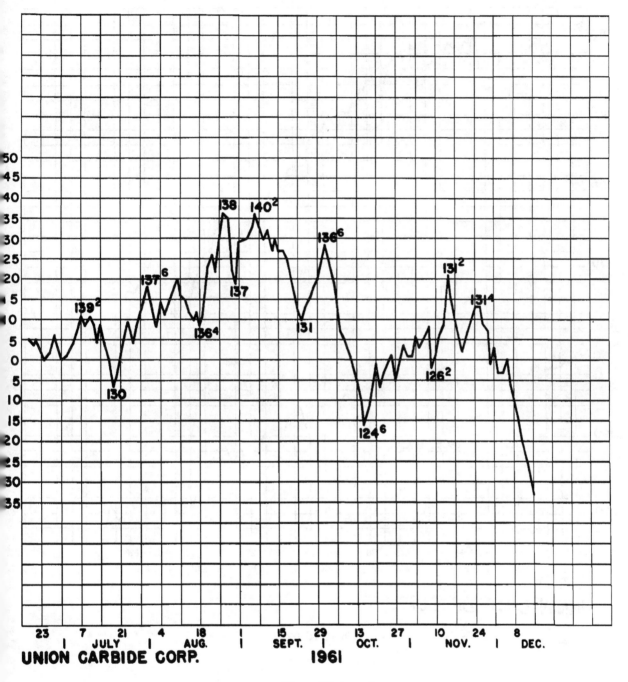

UNION CARBIDE CORP.   1961

Chart 70 (cont.)

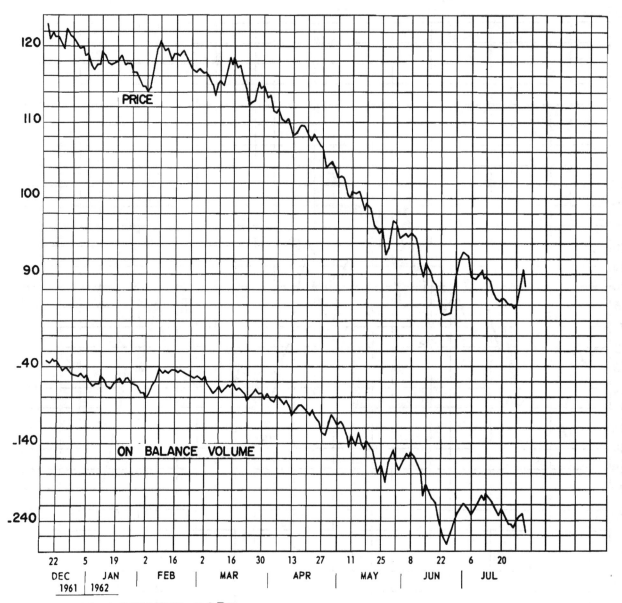

UNION CARBIDE CORP.

Chart 70 (cont.)

UNITED AIRCRAFT

Vital Statistics

Long-term support level (OBV)	67,600 August 2, 1961 at 49.50
Date when long-term support broken	October 2, 1961
First falling field recorded	November 14, 1961
High OBV before May 1962 break	119,000 September 6, 1961
Low OBV after April 1962	Low OBV recorded on Jan. 9, 1962 at 5,500
Short interest trend	No trend
Downside penetration of 200-day moving average price line	October 1961
200-day line turned down	November 1961

Summary of United Aircraft. September, October and November signals were quite definitive in late 1961 for this issue. On-balance volume was a useful aid in determining extent and timing of the weakness.

UNITED STATES STEEL

Vital Statistics

Long-term support level (OBV)	Minus 160,800 November 20, 1961 at 76.50
Date when long-term support broken	January 31, 1962
First falling field recorded	January 2, 1962
High OBV before May 1962 break	75,900 August 31, 1961
Low OBV after April 1962	Minus 1,270,900 June 26, 1962 at 41.63
Short interest trend	Rising after March 1962
Downside penetration of 200-day moving average price line	June 1961
200-day line turned down	September 1961

Summary of U.S. Steel. Most of the signs of weakness were recorded here in 1961, confirmed in January 1962.

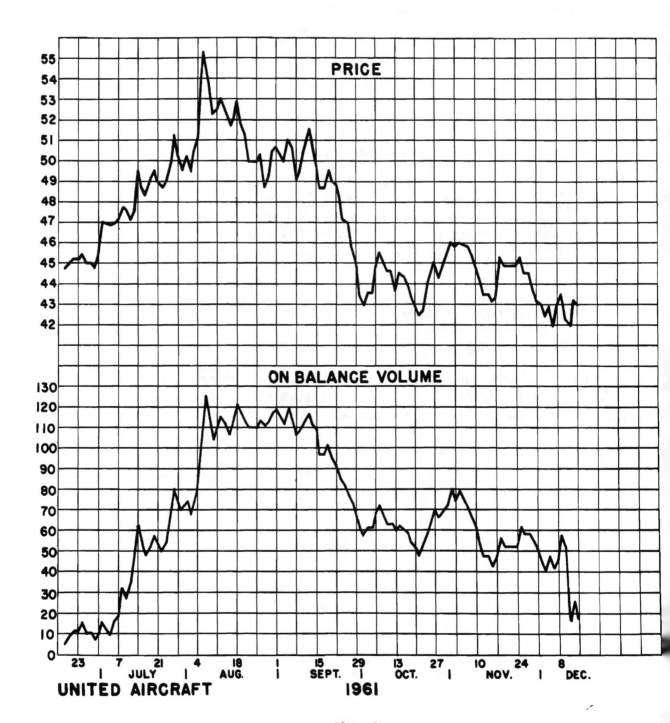

PRICE

ON BALANCE VOLUME

UNITED AIRCRAFT   1961

Chart 71

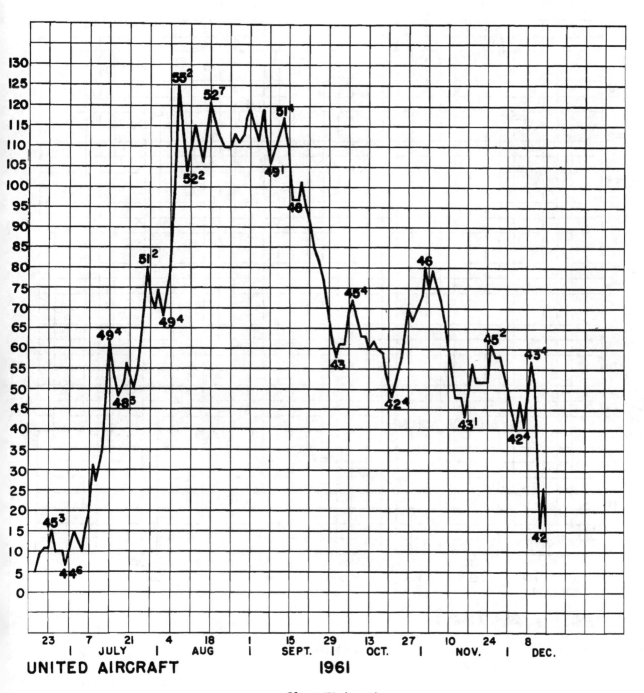

UNITED AIRCRAFT   1961

Chart 71 (cont.)

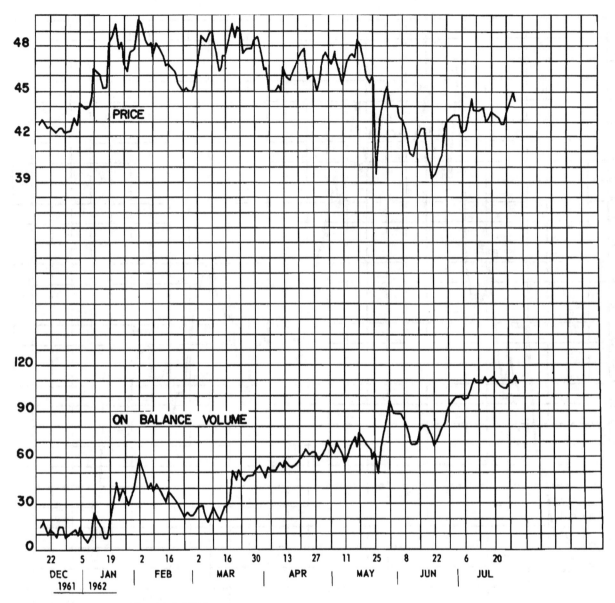

PRICE

ON BALANCE VOLUME

| 22 | 5 | 19 | 2 | 16 | 2 | 16 | 30 | 13 | 27 | 11 | 25 | 8 | 22 | 6 | 20 |
| DEC | JAN | FEB | MAR | APR | MAY | JUN | JUL |

1961 | 1962

UNITED AIRCRAFT

Chart 71 (cont.)

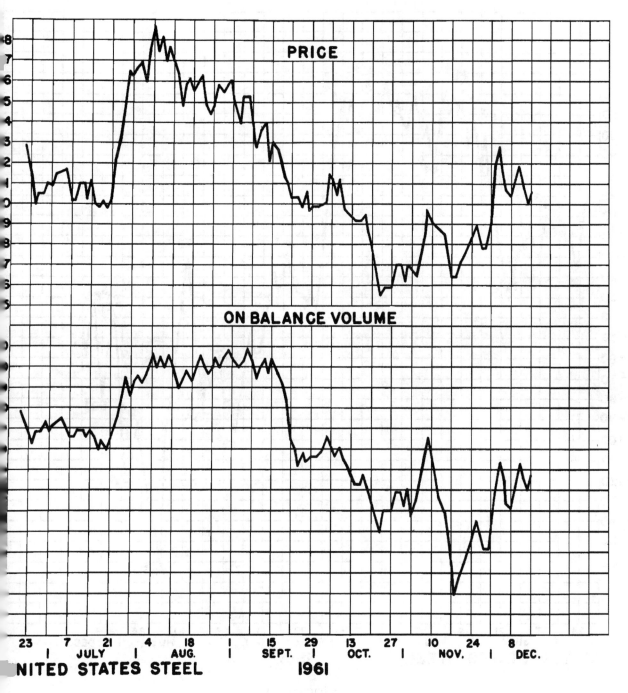

PRICE

ON BALANCE VOLUME

23 7 21 4 18 1 15 29 13 27 10 24 8
   JULY   AUG.   SEPT.   OCT.   NOV.   DEC.

UNITED STATES STEEL   1961

Chart 72

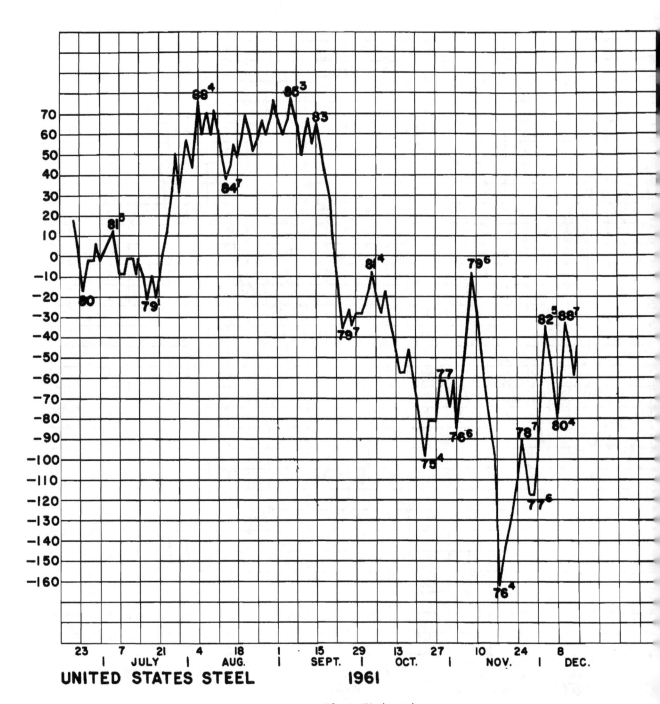

UNITED STATES STEEL   1961

Chart 72 (cont.)

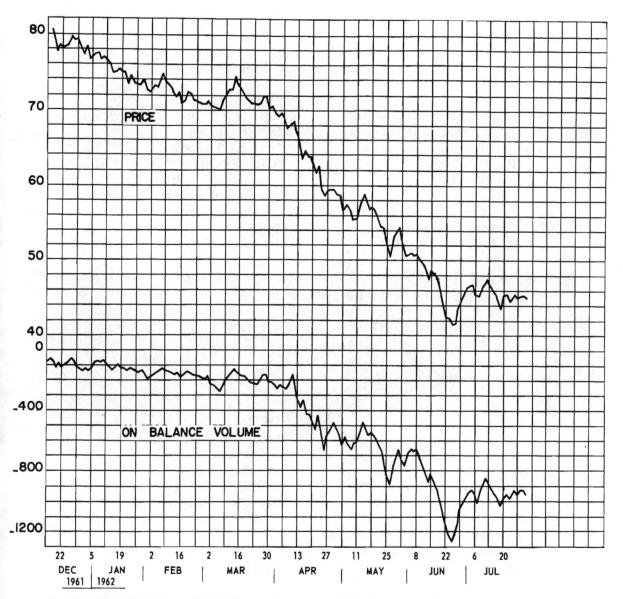

80

70

PRICE

60

50

40
0

-400

ON BALANCE VOLUME

-800

-1200

22 | 5 | 19 | 2 | 16 | 2 | 16 | 30 | 13 | 27 | 11 | 25 | 8 | 22 | 6 | 20
DEC | JAN | FEB | MAR | APR | MAY | JUN | JUL
1961 | 1962

UNITED STATES STEEL

Chart 72 (cont.)

WESTINGHOUSE ELECTRIC

Vital Statistics

Long-term support level (OBV)	Minus 64,500 July 21, 1961 at 40.63
Date long-term support broken	October 19, 1961
First falling field recorded	November 17, 1961
High OBV before May 1962 break	100,700 September 7, 1961 at 45.88
Low OBV after April 1962	Minus 654,600 July 24, 1962 at 26.00
Short interest trend	Declining after November 1961
Downside penetration of 200-day moving average price line	October 1961
200-day line turned down	, Line had been constantly moving down

Summary of Westinghouse Electric. All the signs here were showing continued weakness in 1961 long before the 1962 decline.

WOOLWORTH

Vital Statistics

Long-term support level (OBV)	11,400 August 10, 1961 at 73.13
Date when long-term support broken	June 21, 1962
First falling field recorded	December 22, 1961
High OBV before May 1962 break	85,700 December 12, 1961
Low OBV after April 1962	Minus 7,400 July 24, 1962 at 65.00
Short interest trend	No Trend
Downside penetration of 200-day moving average price line	April 1962
200-day line turned down	May 1962

Summary of Woolworth. December volume signals were sufficient for selling.

Summation of All These Signals

It is informative to now look at this group of stocks *grouped under each signal heading.* This provides a general view of how the Dow-Jones Industrial Average was shaping up in forecasting the 1962 weakness which followed the 1961 performance. The comparative value of each of the signals can also be seen in one glance down the list.

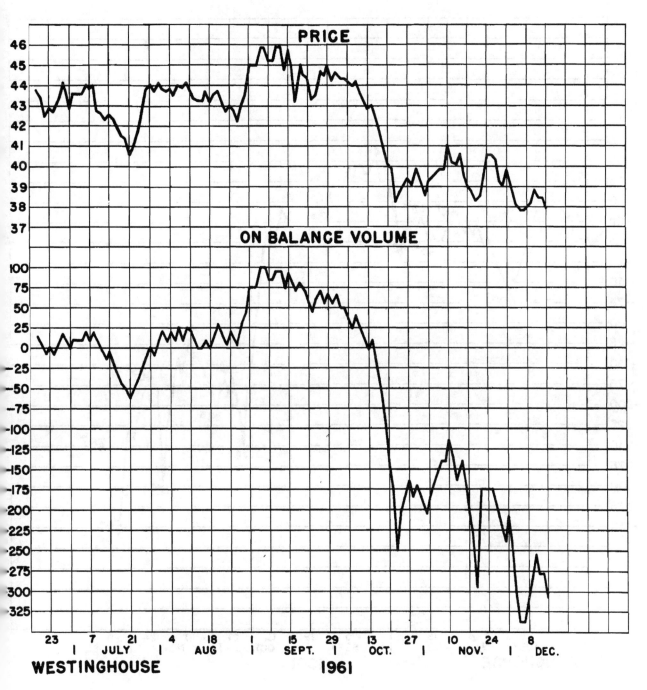

WESTINGHOUSE   **1961**

Chart 73

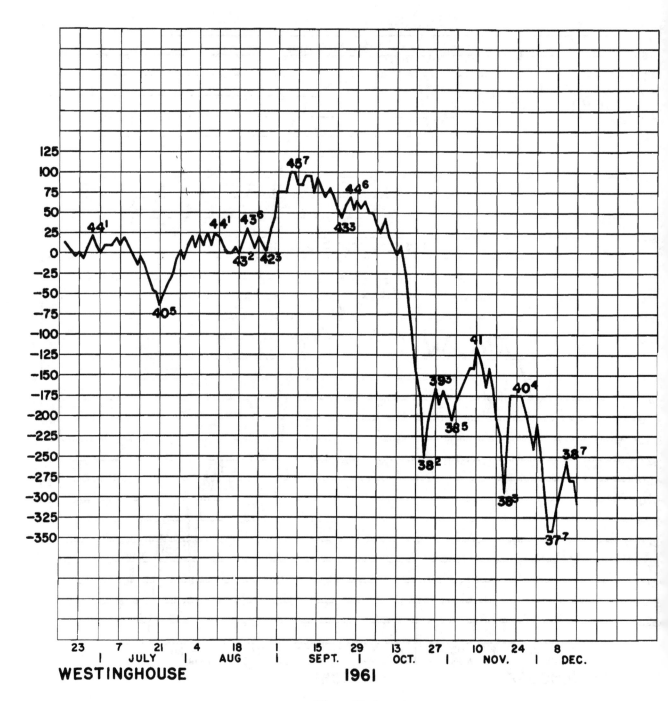

WESTINGHOUSE 1961

Chart 73 (cont.)

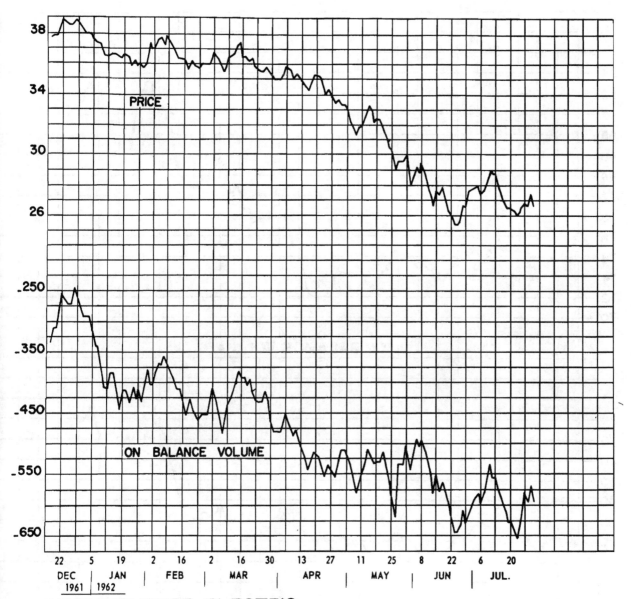

WESTINGHOUSE ELECTRIC

Chart 73 (cont.)

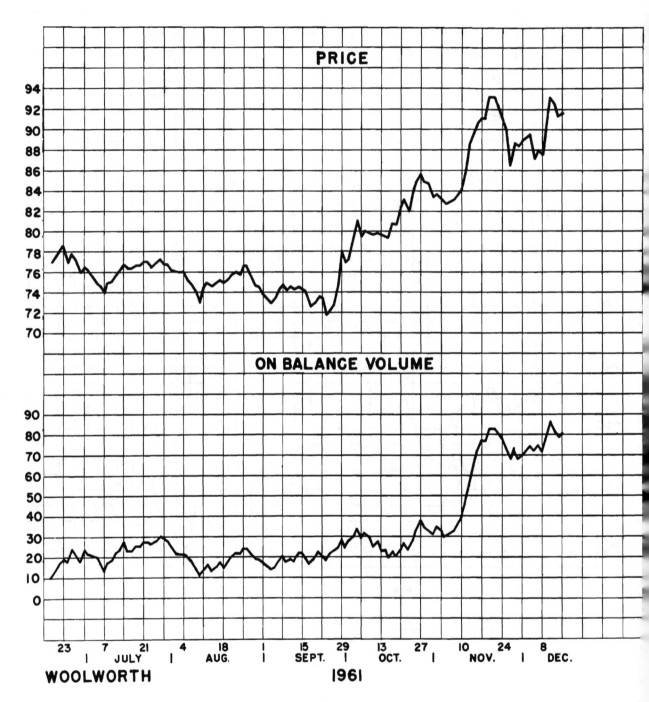

Chart 74

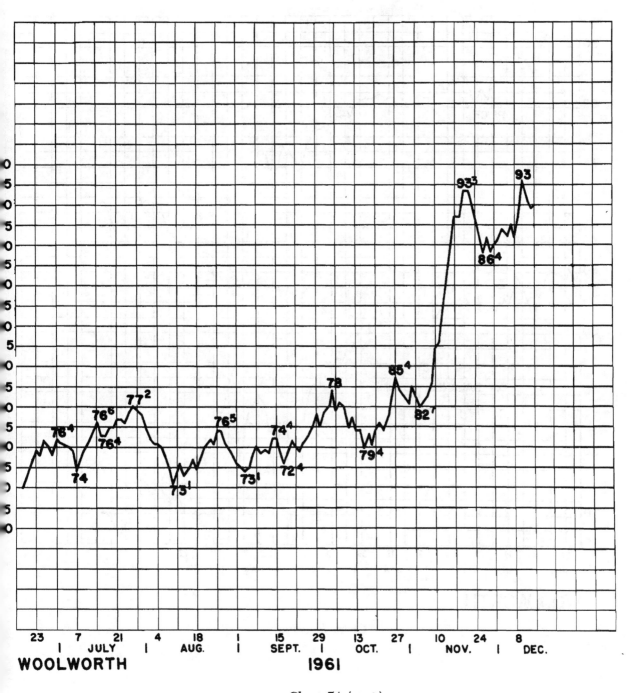

WOOLWORTH   1961

Chart 74 (cont.)

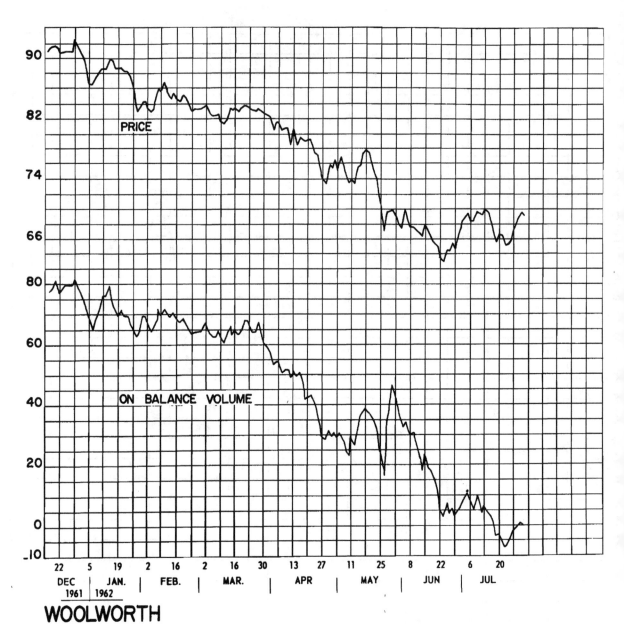

WOOLWORTH

Chart 74 (cont.)

Date When Long-Term OBV Support Broken

American Can	Long-Term support NOT broken
Anaconda	May 25, 1962
Bethlehem Steel	April 23, 1962
DuPont	June 25, 1962
Eastman Kodak	Long-Term support NOT broken
General Electric	Long-Term support NOT broken
General Foods	November 27, 1961
General Motors	Long-Term support NOT broken
Goodyear	January 19, 1962
International Harvester	Long-Term support NOT broken
International Nickel	May 25, 1962
International Paper	June 14, 1962
Johns Manville	April 25, 1962
Owens Illinois Glass	April 4, 1962
Procter & Gamble	January 8, 1962
Sears Roebuck	June 21, 1962
Standard Oil of California	Long-Term support NOT broken
Standard Oil of New Jersey	Long-Term support NOT broken
Swift	Long-Term support NOT broken
Texaco	April 18, 1962
Union Carbide	October 16, 1961
United Aircraft	October 2, 1961
U.S. Steel	January 31, 1962
Westinghouse	October 19, 1961
Woolworth	June 21, 1962

Summary of this Signal

	Stocks Under Long-Term Support (Cumulative)
September 1961	None
October 1961	3
November 1961	4
December 1961	4
January 1962	7
February 1962	7
March 1962	7
April 1962	11
May 1962	13
June 1962	17

With 8 Dow-Jones issues NOT breaking long-term OBV support in the face of a 209-point drop in the Dow-Jones Industrial Average between December 1961 and June 1962 the major bear market thesis was invalidated. Advance warnings of trouble

can be derived by the breaking of long range OBV supports. First there were none in September 1961, 3 in October, one more in November and three more in January etc. *By the time the majority of these 25 stocks had cracked the long-term OBV supports it was generally too late to sell stocks.*

First Falling Field Recorded

American Can	April 9, 1962
Anaconda	August 25, 1961
Bethlehem Steel	July 20, 1961
DuPont	October 31, 1961
Eastman Kodak	April 30, 1962
General Electric	April 2, 1962
General Foods	February 21, 1962
General Motors	April 4, 1962
Goodyear	January 18, 1962
International Harvester	April 11, 1962
International Nickel	May 10, 1962
International Paper	November 9, 1961
Johns Manville	November 2, 1961
Owens Illinois Glass	January 29, 1962
Procter & Gamble	October 27, 1961
Sears Roebuck	January 4, 1962
Standard Oil of California	June 13, 1962
Standard Oil of New Jersey	April 4, 1962
Swift	April 16, 1962
Texaco	May 28, 1962
Union Carbide	December 12, 1961
United Aircraft	November 14, 1961
U.S. Steel	January 2, 1962
Westinghouse	November 17, 1961
Woolworth	December 22, 1961

Summary of this Signal

	Cumulative Number of Stocks Recording First Falling Field
June 1961	None
July 1961	1
August 1961	2
September 1961	2
October 1961	4
November 1961	8
December 1961	10
January 1962	14

	Cumulative Number of Stocks Recording First Falling Field
February 1962	15
March 1962	15
April 1962	22
May 1962	24
June 1962	25

By the time all these 25 stocks had recorded their first falling field the market had reached bottom. The very earliest start in the rise in this number is advance warning of trouble ahead.

High OBV Before May 1962 Break

American Can	April 19, 1962
Anaconda	November 22, 1961
Bethlehem Steel	December 6, 1961
DuPont	March 16, 1962
Eastman Kodak	April 5, 1962
General Electric	December 1, 1961
General Foods	November 14, 1961
General Motors	February 15, 1962
Goodyear	November 15, 1961
International Harvester	March 1, 1962
International Nickel	April 23, 1962
International Paper	March 28, 1962
Johns Manville	March 19, 1962
Owens Illinois Glass	December 26, 1961
Procter & Gamble	December 11, 1961
Sears Roebuck	November 16, 1961
Standard Oil of California	May 21, 1962
Standard Oil of New Jersey	March 1, 1962
Swift	February 20, 1962
Texaco	August 18, 1961
Union Carbide	September 7, 1961
United Aircraft	September 6, 1961
U.S. Steel	August 31, 1961
Westinghouse	September 7, 1961
Woolworth	December 12, 1961

Summary of this Signal

	Number of Stocks Through Recording High OBV (Cumulative)
July 1961	None
August 1961	2
September 1961	5
October 1961	5
November 1961	9

	Number of Stocks Through Recording High OBV (Cumulative)
December 1961	14
January 1962	14
February 1962	16
March 1962	21
April 1962	24
May 1962	25

This signal precedes the others. By December 1961 14 stocks out of these 25 had already shown peak OBV whereas the other signals had only affected 4 and 10 stocks respectively by the same month.

Short Interest Trend

	Started to Rise
American Can	May 1962
Anaconda	No trend
Bethlehem Steel	No trend
DuPont	May 1962
Eastman Kodak	No trend
General Electric	February 1962
General Foods	May 1962
General Motors	January 1962
Goodyear	June 1962
International Harvester	No trend
International Nickel	No trend
International Paper	August 1962
Johns Manville	July 1962
Owens Illinois Glass	No trend
Procter & Gamble	February 1962
Sears Roebuck	March 1962
Standard Oil of California	No trend
Standard Oil of New Jersey	November 1961
Swift	No trend
Texaco	January 1962
Union Carbide	No trend
United Aircraft	No trend
U.S. Steel	March 1962
Westinghouse	Declining November 1961
Woolworth	No trend

Summary of this Signal

	Cumulative Number of Stocks Showing Rising Short Interest
October 1961	None
November 1961	1
December 1961	1

	Cumulative Number of Stocks *Showing Rising Short Interest*
January 1962	3
February 1962	5
March 1962	7
April 1962	7
May 1962	10
June 1962	11
July 1962	12
August 1962	13

When over half of the 25 issues showed rising short interest indications *the market had already bottomed out.* Here is an illustration of the "bread line" principle. Those first in line are more likely to get some bread than those who bring up the rear when the line is long. Short selling is shown to be more profitable when the short interest is low than when it is high.

Downside Penetration of the 200-day Line

	Date When 200-day Line Penetrated *On the Downside*
American Can	January 1962
Anaconda	July 1961
Bethlehem Steel	June 1961
DuPont	January 1962
Eastman Kodak	May 1962
General Electric	January 1962
General Foods	January 1962
General Motors	May 1962
Goodyear	November 1961
International Harvester	May 1962
International Nickel	November 1961
International Paper	April 1962
Johns Manville	July 1961
Owens Illinois Glass	January 1962
Procter & Gamble	January 1962
Sears Roebuck	January 1962
Standard Oil of California	May 1962
Standard Oil of New Jersey	May 1962
Swift	April 1962
Texaco	May 1962
Union Carbide	September 1961
United Aircraft	October 1961
U.S. Steel	June 1961
Westinghouse	October 1961
Woolworth	April 1962

Summary of this Signal

	Cumulative Number of Stocks Having Made Downside Penetration of the 200-day Moving Average Price Line
May 1961	None
June 1961	2
July 1961	4
August 1961	4
September 1961	5
October 1961	7
November 1961	9
December 1961	9
January 1962	16
February 1962	16
March 1962	16
April 1962	19
May 1962	25

By the time all the 25 stocks were under their 200-day moving average price lines the market was *close to the bottom*.

200-Day Line Turned Down

	Date When 200-day Moving Average Price Line Turned Down
American Can	May 1962
Anaconda	October 1961
Bethlehem Steel	August 1961
DuPont	May 1962
Eastman Kodak	May 1962
General Electric	May 1962
General Foods	March 1962
General Motors	June 1962
Goodyear	March 1962
International Harvester	June 1962
International Nickel	February 1962
International Paper	May 1962
Johns Manville	October 1961
Owens Illinois Glass	May 1962
Procter & Gamble	January 1962
Sears Roebuck	May 1962
Standard Oil of California	Did NOT turn down
Standard Oil of New Jersey	Did NOT turn down
Swift	June 1962
Texaco	June 1962

	Date When 200-day Moving Average Price Line Turned Down
Union Carbide	November 1961
United Aircraft	November 1961
U.S. Steel	September 1961
Westinghouse	Line had been down all through this period
Woolworth	May 1962

Summary of this Signal

	Cumulative Number of Stocks Showing Declining 200-day Lines
July 1961	None
August 1961	1
September 1961	2
October 1961	4
November 1961	6
December 1961	6
January 1962	7
February 1962	8
March 1962	10
April 1962	10
May 1962	18
June 1962	22

Once again, when the majority of these stocks had downturn trend lines the market was just about at the bottom.

Which Signal is the Most Effective?

Putting these signals side by side for comparison a better idea of their comparative effectiveness can be noted.

	Long-Term OBV Support Broken	*First Falling Field*	*High OBV*	*Short Interest Rising*	*Downside Penetration of 200-day*	*200-day Line Down*
May 1961	0	0	0	0	0	0
June 1961	0	0	0	0	2	0
July 1961	0	1	0	0	4	0
Aug. 1961	0	2	2	0	4	1
Sept. 1961	0	2	5	0	5	2
Oct. 1961	3	4	5	0	7	4
Nov. 1961	4	8	9	1	9	6
Dec. 1961	4	10	14	1	9	6

		Long-Term OBV Support Broken	First Falling Field	High OBV	Short Interest Rising	Downside Penetration of 200-day	200-day Line Down
Jan.	1962	7	14	14	3	16	7
Feb.	1962	7	15	16	5	16	8
Mar.	1962	7	15	21	7	16	10
Apr.	1962	11	22	24	7	19	10
May	1962	13	24	25	10	25	18
June	1962	17	25		11		22
July	1962				12		
Aug.	1962				13		

The Dow-Jones Industrial Average reached a peak level on December 13, 1961 at 734.91 and yet the table just shown indicates that on that key date four Dow-Jones stocks had already broken long-term on-balance volume support, ten of the issues had shown their first falling fields, fourteen of the stocks had already recorded top OBV readings, nine had scored downside penetrations of their 200-day moving average price lines and six actually showed declining 200-day lines. The most decisive figure of this group of signals was the number of stocks having passed their high OBV points, another way of saying that almost half the entire Dow-Jones Industrial Average had passed the peak of upside energy. This indication and the number of falling fields recorded constituted as decisive a set of signals as the movements of the 200-day lines. On-balance volume signals qualified as good "early warnings".

The Summing up

Here you learned that once a stock has recorded a high point of on-balance volume that from that point on it is losing upside energy. You also learned that this is one of the most decisive of the "early warning" signals and when a good number of Dow-Jones issues record this signal then the market as a whole is signalling an important decline ahead. Inasmuch as the price of a stock normally reaches a peak in a strong market well above its 200-day moving average price line, then weakness *prior to a downside penetration of that line* can better be measured in terms of volume changes as an early warning of that weakness. By definition in this respect OBV would have to lead the downside penetration of that average line.

Chapter Eleven

The Dow-Jones Industrial Average

How volume trading in the 30 industrials is related to subsequent price moves, again using the on-balance volume indicators—plus a supplemental measure called the Climax Indicator.

What You Are about to Learn

You have thus far seen how to analyze a single Dow-Jones issue in terms of the on-balance volume indicators. In this chapter you will be shown how to put those thirty stocks together so as to derive an indication in terms of on-balance volume as to what the *average* is likely to do. You will see that there are two important ways to look at the average in terms of on-balance volume and that each method is a useful check on the other. The first thing to be demonstrated here is how to use total on-balance volume for the average as an indicator and the second thing will be the construction and use of the Climax Indicator, the latter being a most revealing index as to the true state of the Dow-Jones Industrial Average and where it is probably headed. These things will be demonstrated by way of a master time table.

The Master Time Table

Once you have recorded the individual OBV figures each day for the separate Dow-Jones stocks together with their UP and DOWN designations on their breakout days you have the raw material for the construction of a master time table for the Dow-Jones Industrial Average, a table showing broad implications for the market as a whole.

The first step in the construction of this table is to compute the total on-balance volume for the *combined* thirty Dow-Jones Industrial stocks. This is done by a *net* addition of the thirty individual OBV totals. A different total will be reached and recorded each day. As this total rises and falls each day it will occasionally record an upside or downside penetration (breakout) of a previous high or low and these breakouts will again be marked by UP for an upside breakout and DOWN for a downside breakout, the same thing which was done for the Dow-Jones stocks separately. We now have the on-balance volume line for the Dow-Jones Industrial Average. It is the *first* column after the date in the master table and is labeled *Dow-Jones OBV.*

The Climax Indicator

Now we are ready to complete the construction of the master table by recording a *net addition* of the on-balance volume breakouts recorded by the Dow-Jones stocks each day, this being a *net* daily count of the individual UP and DOWN designations. This net figure serves as an exceedingly revealing *index number* having strong implications as to where the Dow-Jones Industrial Average is headed. It will be demonstrated that this index number is a *leading indicator,* tending to score highs and lows *before* the Dow-Jones Industrial Average does. This index number will be called the Climax Indicator from here on out.

In order to find out the level of the Climax Indicator each day, it is necessary to first count up all the upside OBV breakouts among the 30 Dow-Jones issues. This total is recorded in the UP COLUMN each day. In the next column all the DOWN designations recorded for the day for the individual Dow-Jones issues are totalled and placed in the DOWN COLUMN. For instance, suppose five Dow-Jones stocks recorded UP designations (upside OBV breakouts) and eight other Dow-Jones issues recorded DOWN designations (downside OBV breakouts). The net figure would then be MINUS THREE and that would be *the Climax Indicator reading for that particular day.* Those daily indicator readings occur in the next column headed *Climax Indicator.*

In the last column is the daily closing of the Dow-Jones Industrial Average and from this it will become clear that the Climax Indicator has a useful tendency *to move ahead of the Dow Jones Industrial Average.*

This master time table is now shown covering the period from June 20 to December 15, 1961:

Date	On-Balance Volume	Upside Breakouts	Downside Breakouts	Climax Indicator	Dow-Jones Ind. Average
June 20	248,700	0	0	0	687.87
June 21	215,800	0	0	0	686.09
June 22	73,700	3	1	2	685.62
June 23	153,700	5	4	1	688.66
June 26	−74,800 DOWN	1	11	−10	681.16
June 27	−82,300 DOWN	6	7	−1	683.88

Date	On-Balance Volume		Upside Breakouts	Downside Breakouts	Climax Indicator	Dow-Jones Ind. Average
June 28	58,300		6	7	−1	684.59
June 29	88,400		4	7	−3	681.95
June 30	72,800		6	5	1	683.96
July 3	178,900	UP	10	1	9	689.81
July 5	317,500	UP	11	2	9	692.77
July 6	334,800	UP	14	2	12	694.27
July 7	193,700		10	4	6	692.73
July 10	242,200		8	4	4	693.16
July 11	234,300		5	4	1	694.47
July 12	70,400	DOWN	2	13	−11	690.79
July 13	−67,100	DOWN	2	16	−14	685.90
July 14	63,300		5	6	−1	690.95
July 17	−177,800	DOWN	2	15	−13	684.59
July 18	−424,700	DOWN	1	17	−16	679.30
July 19	−245,900		6	9	−3	682.74
July 20	−266,800		4	8	−4	682.97
July 21	−218,700	UP	3	4	−1	682.81
July 24	−203,400	UP	4	5	−1	682.14
July 25	9,400	UP	9	3	6	686.37
July 26	392,400	UP	16	2	14	694.19
July 27	597,900	UP	20	2	18	702.80
July 28	722,500	UP	13	1	12	705.13
July 31	749,300	UP	8	0	8	705.37
Aug. 1	1,069,000	UP	19	1	18	713.94
Aug. 2	869,100		10	7	3	710.46
Aug. 3	1,006,100		8	5	3	715.71
Aug. 4	1,237,900	UP	14	2	12	720.69
Aug. 7	1,288,700	UP	10	3	7	719.58
Aug. 8	1,286,900		10	5	5	720.22
Aug. 9	1,199,700		8	8	0	717.57
Aug. 10	1,353,000	UP	8	1	7	720.49
Aug. 11	1,446,600	UP	9	3	6	722.61
Aug. 14	1,264,900		5	4	1	718.93
Aug. 15	1,167,600	DOWN	5	9	−4	716.18
Aug. 16	1,220,900		7	6	1	718.20
Aug. 17	1,376,200		9	3	6	721.84
Aug. 18	1,418,900		9	4	5	723.54
Aug. 21	1,471,200	UP	8	3	5	724.75
Aug. 22	1,442,400		12	7	5	725.76
Aug. 23	1,267,200		5	9	−4	720.46
Aug. 24	1,067,800	DOWN	2	13	−11	714.03
Aug. 25	1,046,000	DOWN	5	7	−2	716.70
Aug. 28	1,117,000		6	5	1	716.01
Aug. 29	1,009,800	DOWN	3	5	−2	714.15
Aug. 30	1,204,400	UP	8	2	6	716.90

Date	On-Balance Volume		Upside Breakouts	Downside Breakouts	Climax Indicator	Dow-Jones Ind. Average
Aug. 31	1,310,700	UP	10	7	3	719.94
Sept. 1	1,418,200	UP	9	4	5	721.19
Sept. 5	1,273,900		7	12	−5	718.72
Sept. 6	1,547,000	UP	13	1	12	726.01
Sept. 7	1,455,400		10	8	2	726.53
Sept. 8	1,244,700	DOWN	4	9	−5	720.91
Sept. 11	1,034,200	DOWN	0	13	−13	714.36
Sept. 12	1,290,000		3	2	1	722.61
Sept. 13	1,408,000		5	5	0	722.20
Sept. 14	1,289,800		3	10	−7	715.00
Sept. 15	1,436,500	UP	7	7	0	716.30
Sept. 18	1,198,400	DOWN	1	16	−15	711.24
Sept. 19	932,600	DOWN	0	22	−22	702.54
Sept. 20	1,093,200		1	10	−9	707.32
Sept. 21	1,130,200		5	13	−8	706.31
Sept. 22	953,000		2	16	−14	701.57
Sept. 25	661,600	DOWN	2	20	−18	691.86
Sept. 26	671,600		1	10	−9	693.20
Sept. 27	886,900		4	3	1	701.13
Sept. 28	803,200		5	5	0	700.28
Sept. 29	816,000		6	9	−3	701.21
Oct. 2	821,600		3	7	−4	699.83
Oct. 3	940,300	UP	7	10	−3	698.66
Oct. 4	953,600	UP	12	5	7	703.31
Oct. 5	1,131,500	UP	11	4	7	708.49
Oct. 6	1,189,300	UP	9	6	3	708.25
Oct. 9	1,246,100	UP	9	8	1	705 42
Oct. 10	1,300,400	UP	9	7	2	706.67
Oct. 11	1,295,100		11	13	−2	705.62
Oct. 12	1,272,100		5	8	−3	705.50
Oct. 13	1,096,700		6	13	−7	703.31
Oct. 16	1,037,100		5	7	−2	703.15
Oct. 17	1,000,800		6	12	−6	701.98
Oct. 18	1,013,600		6	9	−3	704.20
Oct. 19	975,200	DOWN	7	12	−5	704.85
Oct. 20	913,800	DOWN	7	11	−4	705.62
Oct. 23	760,600	DOWN	4	11	−7	698.98
Oct. 24	694,400	DOWN	4	9	−5	697.24
Oct. 25	939,000		10	4	6	700.72
Oct. 26	972,100		8	6	2	700.68
Oct. 27	966,500		4	4	0	698.74
Oct. 30	1,102,600	UP	5	4	1	701.09
Oct. 31	1,241,400	UP	7	3	4	703.92
Nov. 1	1,249,700	UP	7	5	2	703.84
Nov. 2	1,378,300	UP	8	3	5	706.83

Date	On-balance Volume		Upside Breakouts	Downside Breakouts	Climax Indicator	Dow-Jones Ind. Average
Nov. 3	1,372,400		8	3	5	709.26
Nov. 6	1,632,800	UP	13	2	11	714.60
Nov. 8	2,102,200	UP	21	1	20	723.74
Nov. 9	1,929,100		13	2	11	722.28
Nov. 10	2,080,100		13	2	11	724.83
Nov. 13	2,045,400		12	2	10	728.43
Nov. 14	2,225,800	UP	14	4	10	732.56
Nov. 15	2,341,200	UP	14	4	10	734.34
Nov. 16	2,180,800		10	8	2	733.33
Nov. 17	2,019,900		2	5	−3	729.53
Nov. 20	2,124,800		9	4	5	730.09
Nov. 21	2,110,400		10	4	6	729.32
Nov. 22	2,252,200	UP	9	4	5	730.42
Nov. 24	2,393,700	UP	7	4	3	732.60
Nov. 27	2,524,000	UP	10	7	3	731.99
Nov. 28	2,548,700	UP	9	6	3	728.07
Nov. 29	2,556,000	UP	6	4	2	727.18
Nov. 30	2,431,800		2	9	−7	721.60
Dec. 1	2,708,300	UP	6	1	5	728.80
Dec. 4	2,873,200	UP	11	4	7	731.22
Dec. 5	2,917,200	UP	10	6	4	731.31
Dec. 6	2,961,700	UP	7	5	2	730.09
Dec. 7	2,858,600		4	9	−5	726.45
Dec. 8	2,955,900		5	7	−2	728.23
Dec. 11	3,313,600	UP	10	5	5	732.56
Dec. 12	3,610,700	UP	10	5	5	734.02
Dec. 13	3,641,400	UP	7	4	3	734.91
Dec. 14	3,480,600		4	3	1	730.94
Dec. 15	3,402,400		3	6	−3	729.40

The above figures are now charted against the Dow-Jones Industrial Average:

Climax Indicator Rules

If a downside move in the market is shaping up the Climax Indicator should decisively show an *overbought* condition. Conversely, if the market is readying to go up the Climax Indicator should decisively show an *oversold* condition. This indicator by definition is free from the distortions which can arise when one or two stocks within the industrial average are overly strong or weak. The Master Time Table shows that the Climax Indicator in terms of its forecasting value has greater accuracy than Dow-Jones Industrial Average on-balance volume taken alone.

You have already seen the principle expressed in terms of on-balance volume, the 200-day moving average price line penetrations, the short interest and other measurements *that when too many things are going in one direction the market is about to*

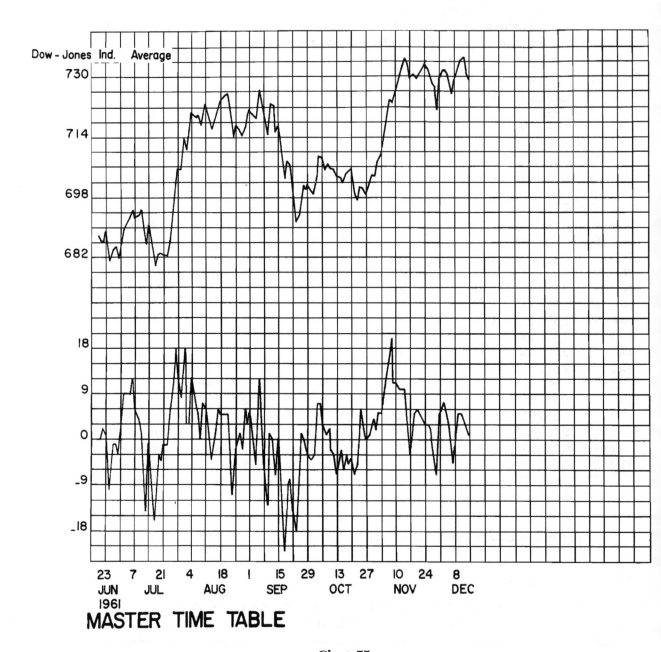

MASTER TIME TABLE

Chart 75

THE DOW-JONES INDUSTRIAL AVERAGE

go in the other direction. The Climax Indicator is a measurement of excesses. If there are too many simultaneous upside breakouts in terms of on-balance volume the market is overbought. An excess of downside OBV breakouts indicates that the market is over-sold. Since there are 30 Dow-Jones stocks, the highest possible Climax Indicator reading would be a plus 30. This has never occurred simply because experience has shown that Climax Indicator readings of plus 18, 19, 20, 21 and 22 have resulted in selling opportunities. Conversely, a minus 30 reading is mathematically possible but has never occurred. Experience has shown that a series of minus readings as low as minus 28 have occurred and these have resulted in almost immediate buying opportunities. Most of the important market lows have occurred when minus readings have been around the −21 to −24 area.

Here then are some workable rules regarding the Climax Indicator:

(1) *A cluster of MINUS readings in the magnitude of 16 or greater denotes an approaching bottom, in the D.J.I.A.*

(2) *A cluster of PLUS readings in the magnitude of 18 or greater denotes an approaching top in the D.J.I.A.*

(3) *The greater the magnitude, the greater the importance of the ultimate top or bottom in the industrial average.*

(4) *The lead time between the Climax Indicator and the Dow-Jones Industrial Average tends to be shorter on approaching bottoms rather than on approaching tops.* (market has shown a tendency to bottom out a few days after a negative climactic reading or right on the day while tops have a tendency to show up one to five weeks after a positive climactic reading).

Review of June-December 1961 Period

After the initial rise from the June 19th low of 672.66 in the Dow-Jones Industrial Average, a second downside test occurred in July. For the stock market this was par for the course. Practically all advances of importance are tested with a subsequent approach to the initial low. If the test is successful, then the next upswing is usually a powerful one. This always reminds the writer of the novel "Return To Peyton Place", or the saying that the criminal always returns to the scene of the crime.

The Master Time Table is set up starting the day after the June 19th low. The Climax Indicator (on-balance number of Dow-Jones stock OBV breakouts) is then studied as the *key to coming change* in the Dow-Jones Industrial Average. The decline in the Indicator to minus 10 on June 26th coincided with a dip in the Dow-Jones Industrial Average to 681.16, holding just above the June 19th closing low of 680.68. The next day saw the Dow-Jones Industrial Average rise to 683.88 but the Climax Indicator improved *sharply* to a minus 1. The day after that, June 28th, the Dow-Jones Industrial Average rose again to 684.59 but on the same day the Climax Indicator *remained the same at minus 1*. This meant that the average made no real technical improvement that day and another little downside test was in store.

Following through on those indications, the Climax Indicator fell back to a minus 3 while the Dow-Jones Industrial Average declined to 681.95. This occurred on June 29th. It was actually mildly bullish because a minus 3 reading with the Dow average at 681.95 compared most favorably with the previous closest comparable reading of 681.16 on June 26th when the Indicator showed a minus 10.

Anything better than a minus 1 for the Indicator would constitute an upside breakout on a day-to-day basis and bring in a few days of higher prices. The next day (June 30th) saw the Indicator rise to a plus 1 with the Dow-Jones Industrial Average back up to 683.96. *Note that the Dow-Jones Industrial Average was technically stronger at 683.96 on June 30th with an Indicator reading of plus 1 than it was two days before at 684.59 when the Indicator reading was minus 1.* THE CLIMAX INDICATOR REVEALS WHETHER THE DOW-JONES INDUSTRIAL AVERAGE READING IS MEANINGFUL IN A BULLISH OR BEARISH SENSE. The Indicator LEADS and does not follow the Dow-Jones Industrial Average.

Following the implications of the Climax Indicator upside breakout, the Dow-Jones Industrial Average jumped quickly in three days to 694.27 (July 6th) and the Climax Indicator rose to a plus 12. The next signal to occur was one of technical weakness. The next day saw both the Climax Indicator and the Dow-Jones Industrial Average decline but on July 10th and 11th the average turned around and went up through the July 6th high of 694.27, closing at 694.47. While this might have had the surface appearance of a technical confirmation of strength to those who follow just the industrial average, *IT WAS A SIGN OF TECHNICAL WEAKNESS ON TWO IMPORTANT COUNTS.* Note that the Climax Indicator had fallen from a plus 12 to a plus 1 between July 6th and 11th and note that the Dow-Jones on-balance volume failed to break through the 334,800 recovery high reading of July 6th. While the Dow-Jones Industrial Average was a little higher, this figure had fallen down to 234,300.

Here then were a pair of day-to-day signs that the market would make another test of the June 19th lows (Peyton Place Revisited). At this juncture it is interesting to note what some of the other indicators were pointing to. The Barron's Confidence Index called for a new high in the Dow-Jones Industrial Average sometime between June and August. The Climax Indicator could show the turn to the upside but by July 11th, 1961 was pointing to another test of the June lows dead ahead. At this point the *quarterly indicator* came into play. This is a tendency for the market to reverse the previous directional swing on or about January 17th, April 17th, July 17th and October 17th*. It is usually a valid indicator during normal markets. This indicator strongly suggested that the turn to the upside predicted by the Confidence Index would probably occur around July 17th with some downside climax and a successful test of the June 19th low.

The Dow-Jones Industrial Average then dropped over 15 points between July

---

* See Page 139 in *"A Strategy of Daily Stock Market Timing For Maximum Profit"*

11th and July 18th in downside climactic action with a successful holding above the June 19th low. The July 18th low was under the June 19th closing low but stayed above the intra-day June 19th lows.

This was a successful test and *there was another key indication that the decline at that point had come to an end.* A look as the Climax Indicator shows it dropping into the minus area which coincides with market lows (minus 16 or greater). The readings were minus 11, minus 14, minus 1, minus 13 and minus 16 in that order. The minus 16 reading occurred on July 18th, almost coinciding exactly with the July 17th quarterly indicator turning date.

THE CLIMAX INDICATOR FOLLOWED RULES 1 AND 4. A negative magnitude of 16 indicated a bottom and the lead time on bottoms is the shortest, in this case simultaneous.

The next four days, July 19th through the 24th, were particularly interesting because the Dow-Jones Industrial Average itself remained practically unchanged at the 682 level and anybody looking at that average alone would have been totally unaware that the market turn had just taken place on July 18th and that the average was about to shoot up to new all-time record highs. While the average was at the 682 level, note what the Climax Indicator was doing and also note the changes in the net differential (Dow-Jones OBV). *These indicators immediately confirmed the July 18th reading as definitely the low and the base point for the rally to new highs.*

While the Dow-Jones Industrial Average was temporarily paralyzed at 682 for four days, the Climax Indicator (following the minus 16 reading) traced out a minus 3, minus 4, minus 1, minus 1 order of readings. The first minus 1 reading on July 21st constituted an *upside breakout* (upward zig-zag). Note also that on July 21st the on-balance volume figure for the Dow-Jones Industrial Average recorded an UP designation which symbolizes an upside breakout. Note also that on the fourth day at 682 in the Dow-Jones Industrial Average (July 24th) the on-balance volume figure scored another upside breakout. *Now the market was fully set to rally.*

The market then rallied forcefully from July 25th on and the Climax Indicator moved up to a plus 18. The first plus 18 was recorded on July 27th when the Dow-Jones Industrial Average stood at 702.80 and the second plus 18 was recorded when the Dow-Jones Industrial Average stood at 713.94 on August 1st. *The Dow-Jones Industrial Average started out the month of August at an all-time new high as previously indicated by the Confidence Index.*

With the Dow-Jones Industrial Average at another new all-time high the market outlook brightened considerably but at the same time *the Climax Indicator had posted a technical warning by topping out on August 1st with a plus 18 reading.* Inasmuch as the Climax Indicator leads the Dow-Jones Industrial Average, the caution signal occurred while the average was still going up. Look at the Master Time Table and note how the Climax Indicator was falling in August 1961 as the Dow-Jones Industrial Average advanced, energy rapidly being dissipated on the upside.

The Dow-Jones Industrial Average peaked out at 726.53 on September 7, 1961 for this interim top and then declined rapidly to a low of 691.86 on September 25th.

THE CLIMAX INDICATOR FOLLOWED RULES 2 AND 4. A positive magnitude of 18 indicated an approaching top and the top took place on September 7th, *roughly five weeks after the August 1st signal.*

While the Dow-Jones Industrial Average was recording that top the Climax Indicator had been falling and by September 19th had recorded a negative magnitude of 22, a good signal that the next low point in the Dow-Jones Industrial Average was at best just a few days away. Check the Master Time Table and you will see that the bottom occurred on September 25th, six days after the Climax Indicator signal.

THE CLIMAX INDICATOR FOLLOWED RULES 1 AND 4. The negative magnitude of 22 indicated the approaching bottom and the bottom took place on September 25th, six days after the Climax Indicator signal.

The Climax Indicator was already on the way up as the market bottomed out once again and by November 8, 1961 was recording a major positive magnitude of 20. This was a warning that a still more important top in the Dow-Jones Industrial Average lay ahead and that this top could be expected about one to five weeks later.

On December 13, 1961 the Dow-Jones Industrial Average topped out at 734.91. Note that on that day the Climax Indicator had fallen to a plus 3 reading, technical energy within the Dow-Jones Industrial Average running out again.

THE CLIMAX INDICATOR FOLLOWED RULES 2, 3 and 4. The positive magnitude of 20 indicated the approaching top, the next rule stated that it would be an important one (great magnitude), and the last rule indicated that the top would probably occur around one to five weeks after the signal, which it did.

This review will be continued by covering the period from late December 1961 up to August 1962 together with notes covering late 1962 market action. The Master Time Table is first shown and then reviewed.

MASTER TIME TABLE

(December 1961 to August 1962)

Date	On-balance Volume	Upside Breakouts	Downside Breakouts	Climax Indicator	Dow-Jones Ind. Average
Dec. 18	3,223,700	3	12	−9	727.71
Dec. 19	3,056,600	0	10	−10	722.41
Dec. 20	2,954,700	2	9	−7	722.57
Dec. 21	2,830,000 DOWN	2	14	−12	720.10
Dec. 22	2,832,600	6	9	−3	720.87
Dec. 26	2,867,300	3	5	−2	723.09
Dec. 27	3,169,500	9	2	7	731.43
Dec. 28	3,190,300	6	4	2	731.51
Dec. 29	3,103,800	7	3	4	731.14

Date	On-balance Volume		Upside Breakouts	Downside Breakouts	Climax Indicator	Dow-Jones Ind. Average
Jan. 2	2,916,700		5	8	−3	724.71
Jan. 3	3,030,400		6	8	−2	726.01
Jan. 4	2,949,300		8	10	−2	722.53
Jan. 5	2,935,700		4	14	−10	714.84
Jan. 8	2,647,700	DOWN	4	18	−14	708.98
Jan. 9	2,495,900	DOWN	2	17	−15	707.64
Jan. 10	2,387,400	DOWN	0	12	−12	706.02
Jan. 11	2,513,700		2	7	−5	710.67
Jan. 12	2,610,500		4	8	−4	711.73
Jan. 15	2,494,100		2	9	−7	709.50
Jan. 16	2,326,000	DOWN	2	12	−10	705.29
Jan. 17	2,076,400	DOWN	0	16	−16	697.41
Jan. 18	2,095,400		3	11	−8	696.03
Jan. 19	2,105,100		6	1	5	700.72
Jan. 22	2,384,300		9	2	7	701.98
Jan. 23	2,210,400		4	9	−5	698.54
Jan. 24	2,294,400		6	10	−4	698.17
Jan. 25	2,363,700		5	5	0	696.52
Jan. 26	2,307,600		3	8	−5	692.19
Jan. 29	2,320,400		3	14	−11	689.92
Jan. 30	2,569,100	UP	8	6	2	694.09
Jan. 31	2,833,800	UP	12	5	7	700.00
Feb. 1	2,838,400	UP	12	6	6	702.54
Feb. 2	3,128,300	UP	12	3	9	706.55
Feb. 5	3,220,400	UP	8	5	3	706.14
Feb. 6	3,319,900	UP	9	0	9	710.39
Feb. 7	3,563,600	UP	14	0	14	715.73
Feb. 8	3,642,100	UP	14	3	11	716.82
Feb. 9	3,642,400	UP	6	4	2	714.27
Feb. 12	3,538,200		6	3	3	714.92
Feb. 13	3,624,300		7	6	1	714.32
Feb. 14	3,606,000		6	6	0	713.67
Feb. 15	3,807,300	UP	11	6	5	717.27
Feb. 16	3,820,700	UP	8	6	2	716.46
Feb. 19	3,885,600	UP	7	5	2	714.36
Feb. 20	4,057,700	UP	10	4	6	717.55
Feb. 21	3,785,600		3	8	−5	713.02
Feb. 23	3,629,400		4	13	−9	709.54
Feb. 26	3,465,300	DOWN	3	12	−9	706.22
Feb. 27	3,607,900		6	6	0	709.22
Feb. 28	3,735,500		6	7	−1	708.05
Mar. 1	3,899,300		12	4	8	711.81
Mar. 2	3,764,800		7	4	3	711.00
Mar. 5	3,629,000		7	7	0	709.99
Mar. 6	3,529,000		5	9	−4	708.17

Date	On-balance Volume		Upside Breakouts	Downside Breakouts	Climax Indicator	Dow-Jones Ind. Average
Mar. 7	3,433,800	DOWN	5	12	−7	706.63
Mar. 8	3,747,500		8	3	5	713.75
Mar. 9	3,843,500		8	7	1	714.44
Mar. 12	3,859,000		9	5	4	714.68
Mar. 13	3,954,900	UP	11	6	5	716.58
Mar. 14	4,088,900	UP	15	3	12	720.95
Mar. 15	4,209,600	UP	13	1	12	723.54
Mar. 16	4,237,700	UP	10	1	9	722.27
Mar. 19	4,146,700		6	3	3	720.38
Mar. 20	4,040,500		4	6	−2	719.66
Mar. 21	3,967,400		5	7	−2	716.62
Mar. 22	3,894,600		6	9	−3	716.70
Mar. 23	3,912,000		4	9	−5	716.46
Mar. 26	3,758,700	DOWN	2	13	−11	710.67
Mar. 27	3,726,800	DOWN	4	11	−7	707.28
Mar. 28	3,951,200	UP	7	5	2	712.25
Mar. 29	3,905,300		2	5	−3	711.28
Mar. 30	3,661,200	DOWN	4	11	−7	706.95
Apr. 2	3,625,100	DOWN	3	11	−8	705.42
Apr. 3	3,423,900	DOWN	1	16	−15	700.60
Apr. 4	3,234,600	DOWN	1	15	−14	696.88
Apr. 5	3,422,000		3	6	−3	700.88
Apr. 6	3,378,700		2	3	−1	699.63
Apr. 9	3,170,600	DOWN	1	14	−13	692.96
Apr. 10	3,285,300		5	8	−3	695.46
Apr. 11	3,382,000		8	11	−3	694.90
Apr. 12	3,071,500	DOWN	0	19	−19	685.67
Apr. 13	2,994,100	DOWN	3	12	−9	687.90
Apr. 16	2,680,600	DOWN	2	15	−13	684.06
Apr. 17	2,892,100		6	8	−2	688.43
Apr. 18	2,854,000		7	7	0	691.01
Apr. 19	3,015,100	UP	9	4	5	694.25
Apr. 23	2,917,700		8	5	3	694.61
Apr. 24	2,972,700		7	4	3	693.00
Apr. 25	2,677,600	DOWN	3	14	−11	683.69
Apr. 26	2,297,500	DOWN	2	17	−15	678.68
Apr. 27	2,113,700	DOWN	1	17	−16	672.20
Apr. 30	2,091,700	DOWN	0	18	−18	665.33
May 1	2,480,900		4	4	0	671.24
May 2	2,602,700		6	2	4	669.96
May 3	2,767,900		9	2	7	675.49
May 4	2,524,700		5	5	0	671.20
May 7	2,440,500		4	6	−2	670.99
May 8	2,204,600		1	9	−8	663.90
May 9	1,767,600	DOWN	1	18	−17	654.70

Date	On-Balance Volume		Upside Breakouts	Downside Breakouts	Climax Indicator	Dow-Jones Ind. Average
May 10	1,445,100	DOWN	0	21	−21	647.23
May 11	1,170,600	DOWN	0	19	−19	640.63
May 14	1,600,800		1	6	−5	646.20
May 15	2,125,700		5	1	4	655.36
May 16	2,083,200		6	2	4	654.04
May 17	1,909,100		3	5	−2	649.79
May 18	1,939,800		4	4	0	650.78
May 21	1,822,200	DOWN	3	6	−3	648.59
May 22	1,549,500	DOWN	0	13	−13	636.34
May 23	1,140,800	DOWN	0	18	−18	626.52
May 24	893,800	DOWN	0	14	−14	622.56
May 25	318,600	DOWN	1	21	−20	611.88
May 28	−1,062,900	DOWN	0	26	−26	576.93
May 29	451,800		3	4	−1	603.96
May 31	1,393,400		11	0	11	613.36
June 1	1,079,600		5	3	2	611.05
June 4	431,700		0	7	−7	593.68
June 5	906,200		4	3	1	594.96
June 6	1,233,200		10	0	10	603.91
June 7	1,215,500		5	2	3	602.20
June 8	1,191,500		9	4	5	601.61
June 11	802,000		1	14	−13	595.17
June 12	281,000	DOWN	0	24	−24	580.94
June 13	−197,700	DOWN	0	23	−23	574.04
June 14	−644,000	DOWN	0	28	−28	563.00
June 15	−149,800		2	0	2	578.18
June 18	−196,800		1	2	−1	574.21
June 19	−303,900		0	6	−6	571.61
June 20	−681,700	DOWN	3	15	−12	563 08
June 21	−1,195,300	DOWN	0	18	−18	550.49
June 22	−1,742,700	DOWN	0	24	−24	539.19
June 25	−2,018,700	DOWN	1	21	−20	536.27
June 26	−2,220,800	DOWN	1	14	−13	535.76
June 27	−2,092,200		3	11	−8	536.98
June 28	−1,508,000		8	0	8	557.35
June 29	−1,224,000		9	1	8	561.28
July 2	−897,800		10	0	10	573.75
July 3	−685,400		12	0	12	579.48
July 5	−539,800		14	2	12	583.87
July 6	−714,700		0	2	−2	576.17
July 9	−707,500		9	1	8	580.82
July 10	−83,300	UP	18	3	15	586.01
July 11	167,500	UP	17	3	14	589.06
July 12	287,600	UP	14	2	12	590.27
July 13	200,100		10	3	7	590.19

Date	On-Balance Volume		Upside Breakouts	Downside Breakouts	Climax Indicator	Dow-Jones Ind. Average
July 16	165,200		5	4	1	588.10
July 17	−366,900		2	12	−10	577.85
July 18	−504,500		0	12	−12	571.24
July 19	−550,900		0	10	−10	573.16
July 20	−371,700		1	5	−4	577.18
July 23	−456,600		1	12	−11	577.47
July 24	−499,000		4	10	−6	574.12
July 25	−422,800		8	12	−4	574.67
July 26	−195,600	UP	9	6	3	579.61
July 27	−133,500	UP	10	2	8	585.00
July 30	92,500	UP	17	1	16	591.44
July 31	328,100	UP	18	1	17	597.93
Aug. 1	56,200		3	5	−2	591.36

Review of December 1961 Through to August 1962

The opening decline which started in December 1961 had been well signalled by the Climax Indicator peaking out at plus 20 on November 8, 1961. The next move was for the indicator to signal some kind of bottom. This was done when a negative magnitude of 16 was recorded on January 17, 1962. The Dow-Jones Industrial Average scored the next low on January 29, 1962 at 689.92, twelve days after the Climax Indicator signal.

THE CLIMAX INDICATOR FOLLOWED RULES 1 AND 4. The negative magnitude of 16 preceded the low in the averages by twelve days. Note that the minus-16 is not as powerful a bottom as a minus 21 or 22. This will grow in significance as more is reviewed.

As the interim low in the average was being recorded on January 29th, the Climax Indicator had already begun to improve and by February 7th had reached a positive magnitude of 14. The inability of the Indicator to rise above that magnitude suggested a pattern of declining tops, the *indicated secondary peak* in the Dow-Jones Industrial Average slated to occur one to five weeks later. Five weeks later was March 15, 1962 and on that day the Dow-Jones Industrial Average had recovered to 723.54 but the minor positive magnitude of 14 recorded by the Climax Indicator on February 7th eliminated the chance for a new high in the Dow-Jones Industrial Average. By March 15, 1962 the Climax Indicator could only show a top magnitude of 12 and that confirmed the pattern of declining tops in the Indicator since November 1961. By May 3rd the Climax Indicator could only record a positive magnitude of 7 on a rally and on the declines the Indicator did not hit a maximum negative magnitude until May 28, 1962 when the Climax Indicator declined to a negative 26.

The negative magnitude of 26 was greater than the minimum requirement of minus-16 and greater than the previous high negative magnitude of minus-21 recorded on May 10th. Anything greater than a minus-21 on the Climax Indicator

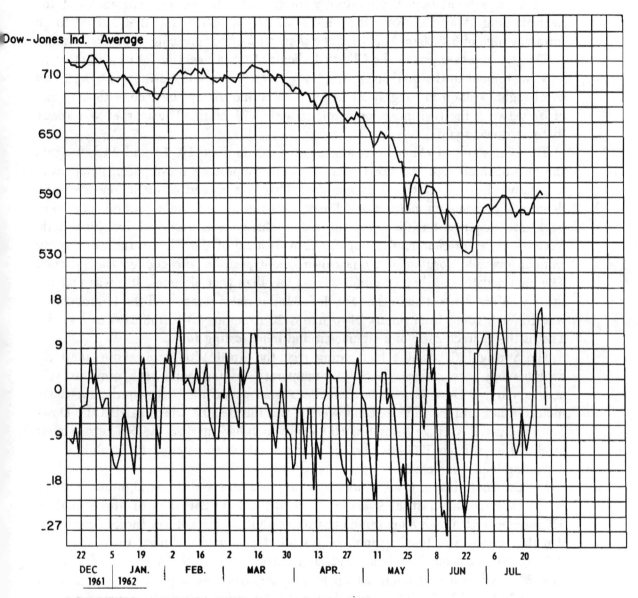

Dow - Jones Ind.   Average

710

650

590

530

18

9

0

-9

-18

-27

22 | 5 | 19 | 2 | 16 | 2 | 16 | 30 | 13 | 27 | 11 | 25 | 8 | 22 | 6 | 20

DEC | JAN. | FEB. | MAR | APR. | MAY | JUN | JUL
1961 | 1962

MASTER TIME TABLE

Chart 76

offers a magnificent buying opportunity for traders. The market bottomed out the next morning (May 29, 1962) at an intra-day low of 553.75 and then rallied to an intra-day high of 625.00 on May 31st, *the sharpest 24-hour upswing in market history*.

The fast improvement in the Climax Indicator from a negative 26 to a positive 11 was tantamount to the market moving from a vastly oversold position to a seriously overbought position in roughly 24 hours. This would always be true with a spread of 37 between the two indicator readings within 24 hours. The market was ready to come down again.

The next series of climactic readings occurred on June 12, 13 and 14 but again the turn on June 15th saw the Climax Indicator improving *too rapidly*, going from a negative 28 to a positive 2 in one day. That is a spread of 30 in one day and denotes a *one-day upswing*. The Climax Indicator turned right around and went back into negative territory and the major change was reserved for June 25th. *Note the different characteristic of this turn.* Instead of the Climax Indicator going from an oversold position to a quick overbought position, *the change was gradual.* The high negative reading of minus-24 was less than that of June 14th, was reached the day before the bottom in the Dow-Jones Industrial Average and the improvement was gradual, going from minus 24 to minus 20 to minus 13 to minus 8 and so on. That is the characteristic of a significant and *more lasting turn.*

The Spring 1962 decline had swung past the April 17th date, those quarterly dates having been rather effective as temporary turning points the previous July and January, a Dow Theory bear market signal occurring between the quarterly indicator date and the slide that followed. It was this decline which carried the Dow-Jones Industrial Average below the 650 level which had marked the 50% retracement level of the previous 1960-61 advance, a signal which threatened to invalidate any remaining bullish indicators.

The Climax Indicator is an important *swing indicator* and the straightline descent of the Dow-Jones Industrial Average down to the June 25th low of approximately 525 coupled with a high magnitude negative reading on the Climax Indicator showed that the average was heading into some kind of powerful technical reversal.

The next swing on the Climax Indicator carried it from the oversold position of June 22nd when it was minus-24 up to a minor overbought position of a plus 15 on July 10th, 1962. The Dow-Jones Industrial Average backed off as was expected and the Climax Indicator then moved down to a minor oversold position of a negative 12 reading on July 18th. The average turned up once again and this time the Climax Indicator moved above the July 10th reading pointing to a further rise in the Dow-Jones Industrial Average.

For the benefit of the reader, additional Climax Indicator readings beyond August 1, 1962 are given here in order that it can be seen how well the Indicator pointed to the August 1962 rally high, the October 1962 low at the time of the Cuban Crisis and the great rise which took place after that low.

CLIMAX INDICATOR FROM AUGUST TO NOVEMBER 1962

Date	Climax Indicator (Net)	DJIA	Date	Climax Indicator (Net)	DJIA
Aug. 2	6	593.83	Oct. 2	9	578.73
Aug. 3	12	596.38	Oct. 3	6	578.52
Aug. 6	−2	593.24	Oct. 4	11	582.41
Aug. 7	−5	588.35	Oct. 5	13	586.59
Aug. 8	−2	590.94	Oct. 8	6	586.09
Aug. 9	2	591.19	Oct. 9	7	587.18
Aug. 10	6	592.32	Oct. 10	6	588.14
Aug. 13	8	595.29	Oct. 11	−2	586.47
Aug. 14	15	601.90	Oct. 12	−1	586.47
Aug. 15	19	606.76	Oct. 15	3	589.69
Aug. 16	11	606.71	Oct. 16	4	589.35
Aug. 17	10	610.02	Oct. 17	−1	587.68
Aug. 20	16	612.86	Oct. 18	−15	581.15
Aug. 21	2	608.64	Oct. 19	−23	573.29
Aug. 22	16	615.54	Oct. 22	−25	568.60
Aug. 23	4	616.00	Oct. 23	−22	558.06
Aug. 24	−3	613.74	Oct. 24	1	576.68
Aug. 27	−6	612.57	Oct. 25	−1	570.86
Aug. 28	−12	605.25	Oct. 26	−1	569.02
Aug. 29	−12	603.24	Oct. 29	8	579.35
Aug. 30	−7	602.32	Oct. 30	20	588.98
Aug. 31	5	609.18	Oct. 31	14	589.77
Sept. 4	−9	602.45	Nov. 1	20	597.13
Sept. 5	−16	599.14	Nov. 2	22	604.58
Sept. 6	−9	600.81	Nov. 5	18	610.48
Sept. 7	−3	600.86	Nov. 7	21	615.75
Sept. 10	−4	602.03	Nov. 8	4	609.14
Sept. 11	1	603.99	Nov. 9	10	616.13
Sept. 12	6	606.34	Nov. 12	20	624.41
Sept. 13	2	603.99	Nov. 13	6	623.11
Sept. 14	7	605.84	Nov. 14	17	630.48
Sept. 17	0	607.63	Nov. 15	11	629.14
Sept. 18	2	607.09	Nov. 16	3	630.98
Sept. 19	−2	607.09	Nov. 19	−2	626.21
Sept. 20	−15	601.65	Nov. 20	11	632.94
Sept. 21	−22	591.78	Nov. 21	11	637.25
Sept. 24	−22	582.91	Nov. 23	20	644.87
Sept. 25	−7	588.22	Nov. 26	9	642.06
Sept. 26	−13	578.48	Nov. 27	12	648.05
Sept. 27	−19	574.12	Nov. 28	17	651.85
Sept. 28	−5	578.98	Nov. 29	10	652.61
Oct. 1	−19	571.95	Nov. 30	3	649.30

Date	Climax Indicator (Net)	DJIA	Date	Climax Indicator (Net)	DJIA
Dec. 3	1	646.41	Dec. 13	−5	645.20
Dec. 4	6	651.48	Dec. 14	3	648.09
Dec. 5	8	653.99	Dec. 17	−6	645.49
Dec. 6	0	651.73	Dec. 18	−13	640.14
Dec. 7	4	652.10	Dec. 19	4	647.00
Dec. 10	−7	645.08	Dec. 20	1	648.55
Dec. 11	−5	645.16	Dec. 21	1	646.41
Dec. 12	0	647.33	Dec. 24	−2	647.71

The market did not become technically weak again until the Climax Indicator began to come down from the positive reading of 19 recorded on August 15, 1962. A top was reached 8 days later on August 23rd. The first oversold condition was reached on September 21st and 24th with a negative C.I. reading of 22. The ability of the C.I. to come up to only a *minor* positive climax of 13 on October 5th indicated that another downswing lay ahead. This materialized and was accentuated by the Cuban Crisis but the Climax Indicator negative reading of 25 reached on October 22nd nevertheless gave a *true indication of rally ahead.* The rally started two days later and turned out to be one of the sharpest on record.

Additional Notes on the Climax Indicator

There are three important areas of discussion to be covered on the Climax Indicator, these being (a) lead time, (b) spread and (c) velocity.

Lead time. In review, the Climax Indicator lead time tends to be almost *coincidental* following major negative magnitudes. The lead time is *greater* following major positive magnitudes. This implies that short sales should be covered when the Climax Indicator comes down to a minus-20, 21, 22 and higher. On the other hand, the Dow-Jones Industrial Average may not record a top until one to five weeks after a major positive reading of 19 or higher. The great climaxes have always followed such negative magnitudes of 25 and higher and very important tops have always followed great positive magnitudes of 22 and higher. Readings around the 16 area denote minor climax indications.

Putting these conclusions into tabular form, the important climax readings in the 1961-62 period are recorded together with their lead times:

THE ABILITY OF THE CLIMAX INDICATOR TO LEAD
THE DOW-JONES INDUSTRIAL AVERAGE

(A Quick Review)

Date of Index Low	Date of Low In D.J.I.A.	Date of Index High	Date of High In D.J.I.A.
July 18, 1961(−16)	July 18, 1961	Aug. 1, 1961(18)	Sept. 7, 1961
Sept. 19, 1961(−22)	Sept. 25, 1961	Nov. 8, 1961(20)	Dec. 13, 1961
Jan. 17, 1962(−16)	Jan. 29, 1962	Feb. 7, 1962(14)	Mar. 15, 1962
May 28, 1962(−26)	May 28, 1962	July 10, 1962(15)	July 12, 1962
June 14, 1962(−28)	June 14, 1962	July 31, 1962(17)	July 31, 1962
June 22, 1962(−24)	June 25, 1962	Aug. 15, 1962(19)	Aug. 23, 1962
Sept. 24, 1962(−22)	Oct. 1, 1962	Nov. 2, 1962(22)	Dec. 5, 1962
Oct. 22, 1962(−25)	Oct. 23, 1962		

Spread. The word "spread" denotes how far the Climax Indicator moves between various readings. For instance, if the Indicator moved from a negative magnitude of 26 to a positive magnitude of 11 as it did between May 28, 1962 and May 31, 1962 that is a "spread" of 37 on the upside which would indicate a quick buying climax and an opportunity for traders to go short. On June 14, 1962 there was a negative magnitude of 28 and in one day the Climax Indicator moved up to a positive magnitude of 2. That was a "spread" of 30 on the upside, another example of a "one day" rally. The improvement was too sharp to be sustained. The movement following the June 22nd, 1962 negative magnitude of 24 showed "spreads" of 4, 7, 5, 16, 0, 2, 2 etc, normal spreads which indicated the furtherance of the rally at that time.

In the following table a record of the wider spreads is presented:

CLIMAX INDICATOR SPREADS

Spreads of From 10-19

Date	Spread	What Happened Next
June 26, 1961	1 to −10 (−11)	Average rose for next two days. Very moderate gain.
July 12, 1961	1 to −11 (−12)	Average fell generally 10 points over next 4 sessions
July 14, 1961	−14 to −1 (13)	Average fell 10 points and then rallied.
July 17, 1961	−1 to −13 (−12)	Average fell for one day, consolidated and then rallied.
July 19, 1961	−16 to −3 (13)	Average consolidated and then rallied.
Aug. 1, 1961	8 to 18 (10)	One day setback followed by rally.
Aug. 2, 1961	18 to 3 (−15)	Immediate rally.

Spreads of From 10-19

Date	Spread	What Happened Next
Sept. 5, 1961	5 to −5 (−10)	One-day sharp upswing.
Sept. 6, 1961	−5 to 12 (17)	Consolidated for one day followed by sharp drop.
Sept. 7, 1961	12 to 2 (−10)	Immediate decline.
Sept. 12, 1961	−13 to 1 (14)	One day consolidation followed by decline.
Sept. 18, 1961	0 to −15 (−15)	Sharp one-day drop followed by brief rise and then another decline.
Sept. 20, 1961	−22 to −9 (13)	Three-day sharp decline.
Sept. 27, 1961	−9 to 1 (10)	Brief mild decline followed by very mild rise.
Oct. 4, 1961	−3 to 7 (10)	One day rise followed by very mild decline.
Oct. 25, 1961	−5 to 6 (11)	Brief consolidation followed by sharp rally.
Dec. 1, 1961	−7 to 5 (12)	3-point gain followed by consolidation.
Jan. 19, 1962	−8 to 5 (13)	One day very small advance followed by further decline.
Jan. 23, 1962	7 to −5 (−12)	Brief holding action and then further decline.
Jan. 30, 1962	−11 to 2 (13)	Immediate strong rally.
Feb. 21, 1962	6 to −5 (−11)	7-point decline in two sessions followed by moderate rally.
Mar. 8, 1962	−7 to 5 (12)	Immediate 10-point rally in next 5 sessions.
Apr. 5, 1962	−14 to −3 (11)	Rather steady decline over next few sessions.
Apr. 9, 1962	−1 to −13 (−12)	One-day rise followed by further decline.
Apr. 10, 1962	−13 to −3 (10)	Steady near-term decline.
Apr. 12, 1962	−3 to −19 (−16)	9-point rally over next 5 sessions.
Apr. 13, 1962	−19 to −9 (10)	7-point rally over next 4 sessions.
Apr. 17, 1962	−13 to −2 (11)	Two day rise of 6 points followed by sharp decline.
Apr. 25, 1962	3 to −11 (−14)	Sharp continuing decline.
May 1, 1962	−18 to 0 (18)	One day decline, further rise and then sharp drop.
May 14, 1962	−19 to −5 (14)	Brief one-day 10-point gain followed by further decline.
May 22, 1962	−3 to −13 (−10)	Start of four-day selling climax.
May 31, 1962	−1 to 11 (12)	Immediate sharp decline.

Spreads of From 10-19

	Spread	What Happened Next
June 11, 1962	5 to −13 (−18)	Immediate sharp decline.
June 28, 1962	−8 to 8 (16)	Sharp rally.
July 6, 1962	12 to −2 (−14)	Further sharp rally.
July 9, 1962	−2 to 8 (10)	Further sharp rally.
July 17, 1962	1 to −10 (−11)	Sharp brief decline followed by rally.
Aug. 1, 1962	17 to −2 (−19)	5-point rise in 2 sessions followed by brief consolidation.
Aug. 6, 1962	12 to −2 (−14)	One-day decline followed by good rally.
Aug. 21, 1962	16 to 2 (−14)	Two-day rise followed by sharp decline.
Aug. 22, 1962	2 to 16 (14)	One-day holding action followed by declining trend.
Aug. 23, 1962	16 to 4 (−12)	Immediate declining trend.
Aug. 31, 1962	−7 to 5 (12)	Two-day decline.
Sept. 4, 1962	5 to −9 (−14)	One-day decline followed by rally.
Sept. 20, 1962	−2 to −15 (−13)	Immediate sharp decline.
Sept. 25, 1962	−22 to −7 (15)	Immediate 14-point decline.
Sept. 28, 1962	−19 to −5 (14)	One-day decline followed by good rally.
Oct. 1, 1962	−5 to −19 (−14)	Immediate rally.
Oct. 18, 1962	−1 to −15 (−14)	Three day very sharp decline.
Oct. 30, 1962	8 to 20 (12)	Further rally.
Nov. 8, 1962	21 to 4 (−17)	Further sharp rally.
Nov. 12, 1962	10 to 20 (10)	Slight irregularity followed by further sharp rally.
Nov. 13, 1962	20 to 6 (−14)	Further rally.
Nov. 14, 1962	6 to 17 (11)	Slight irregularity followed by further rally.
Nov. 20, 1962	−2 to 11 (13)	Two-day sharp rally.

Spreads Above 19

Date	Spread	What Happened Next
May 29, 1962	−26 to −1 (25)	Very sharp rally of one day followed by continuing decline
June 15, 1962	−28 to 2 (30)	Sharpest upside spread recorded. It resulted in immediate decline.
Oct. 2, 1962	−19 to 9 (28)	1-day holding action followed by rally.
Oct. 24, 1962	−22 to 1 (23)	2-day minor decline then sharp rally.

Velocity. This is the speed of change in the Climax Indicator going from one extreme to another in X number of days. There apparently is a relationship to the type of market swing which follows. The formula would be:

$$\text{C.I. Velocity} = \frac{\text{Total Spread}}{\text{No. of Days}}$$

In the table below total spreads are given, time of swing, velocity of C.I. and market results on next swing in the averages:

CLIMAX INDICATOR VELOCITY

Total Spread	Number of Days	Velocity	Next Swing in the Dow-Jones Industrial Av.
July 18 to August 1, 1961 (−16 to 18 making spread of 34)	10	3.4	34.67 point decline between Sept. 7th and Sept. 25th, 1961
August 1 to Sept. 19, 1961 (18 to −22 making spread of −40)	34	−1.1	43.05 point advance between Sept. 25th and Dec. 13, 1961
Sept. 19 to Nov. 8, 1961 (−22 to 20 making spread of 42)	35	1.2	44.99 point decline between Dec. 13th, 1961 and Jan. 29, 1962
Nov. 8, 1961 to Jan. 17, 1962 (20 to −16 making spread of −36)	47	−0.7	33.62 point advance between Jan. 29th and March 15, 1962
Jan. 17 to Feb. 7, 1962 (−16 to 14 making spread of 30)	15	2.0	146.61 point decline between March 15th and May 28th, 1962
Feb. 7 to June 14, 1962 (14 to −28 making spread of −42)	88	−0.4	79.73 point advance between June 25th and Aug. 23, 1962
June 14th to Aug. 15, 1962 (−28 to 19 making spread of 47)	43	1.0	57.94 point decline between Aug. 23rd and Oct. 23, 1962
Aug. 15th to Oct. 22nd, 1962 (19 to −25 making spread of −44)	47	−0.9	95.93 point advance between Oct. 23rd and December 5, 1962

Theory behind the Climax Indicator

As can be seen now, the Climax Indicator measures the buying and selling pressures within the Dow-Jones Industrial Average utilizing the principle of the on-balance volume line technique. Each on-balance volume breakout is counted and the net figure of breakouts constitutes the Indicator. Think in terms now of each individual Dow-

Jones stock. A steady cluster of DOWN designations is readying the stock for a rally and a steady cluster of UP designations is readying the stock for a decline. In order for the Climax Indicator to reach an overbought position of a positive magnitude of 22 and higher it would follow that many Dow-Jones issues had been rallying for some time with a string of UPS. On the other hand, if the Indicator jumped rapidly to a plus 22 with big gaps (2, 8, 15 and 22 for instance in that order) it would follow that the average might only have a one-day setback followed by more rally simply because the fast move to 22 did not allow for much length in the number of consecutive UPS among the 30 stocks. The same follows for a rapid move to a negative magnitude of 22 or greater leaving many wide gaps. This would imply that a steady line of DOWN designations had not excessively built up among the 30 stocks and, following perhaps a one-day rally, the market would continue to decline.

The true overbought situation is shown when the Climax Indicator moves up past a positive magnitude of 20 and stays in the 10 to 20 area eight to ten days or more. That means that 10 to 20 Dow-Jones issues have developed long clusters of UPS. It's the same theory when the indicator shows a negative magnitude of 22, 23, 24 and higher. That implies that there was a sustained selling pressure, enough to create clusters of DOWN designations on a majority of Dow-Jones issues. As the reader will recall, the *single* DOWN designations or the *single* UPS on Dow-Jones issues were seldom important. It was the *clusters* which designated *real* buying pressure and selling pressure and *it takes clusters to drive the Climax Indicator to overbought and oversold magnitudes.*

Be Careful When Interpreting the High Climax Indicator Readings

The Climax Indicator is presented as a market "swing" indicator. It is primarily useful to market traders and only has an occasional message for the long-term investor. The plus 20 reading of November 8, 1961 had a selling message for both traders and investors inasmuch as it has been shown that on that date four Dow-Jones stocks had already broken long-term OBV support, eight had already registered their first falling field trends, nine had already passed their points of high OBV, the short interest trend was in the very earliest phase of rise, nine stocks had gone under their 200-day moving average price lines and six had shown falling 200-day lines. The plus 22 reading of November 2, 1962 required a *different interpretation.* True, the signal was valid for a short-term market peak roughly five weeks later (December 5, 1962) but the message was *only directed to day-to-day traders* inasmuch as the major measurements such as rising fields, high OBV, short interest, 200-day moving average price line measurements and other things were showing the market to be in a healthy forward advance status.

When there is any question as to the validity of a high Climax Indicator reading then the individual OBV breakouts can be looked at, determining whether they are major breakouts or merely *secondary upside breakouts in falling field trends*, what this writer calls "lower key" breakouts.

The Bread Line Concept

One must always be on guard to watch for *over-popularity*. Everything that is done in the market tends to become overdone and when one is alert to signs of excess he must quickly prepare to move in the opposite direction. We have already seen how excess price acceleration (vertical price advance) can lead into a sharp price decline. We have seen how major bottoms show a climactic *excess* of new lows over new highs and how the major tops are identified with an excessive number of new highs. We have seen how too rapid a build-up of net upside volume can lead into reaction and vice versa. We have seen how an excess of optimism demands caution and how excessive pessimism demands bullishness. We have seen some of the best opportunities spring from bankruptcy and some of the sharpest declines spring from solid high-priced blue chip equities which might have been loudly proclaimed as the best and safest buys. The theory of excess gives us the odd lot transactions indicator. Now, it is the same with the short interest.

Picture a bread line. All those standing in the front of the line are going to get some bread. The longer the line grows the less likely it will be that there will be any bread left to go around. Those who sell short when there is a very small short interest are the first to get in line. Their chances of getting bread are excellent. The idea of standing in the bread line is not popular. If it was popular the line would be a long one. When the line is the shortest stock prices are generally still going up and there is great optimism about. Usually the bread line only becomes popular as stock prices start to go down and an air of pessimism develops. As stock prices continue to drop the idea of going short gets more popular and more people then get into the bread line. All this time the bread (short sale profits) is being passed out to those who were first in line (those who shorted nearer the top) and this means that there is less bread (profits) left for the rest of the people standing in line.

Now the line is growing rapidly as everybody can see that stocks are really declining now. However, the bread runs out and all those who shorted stocks late in the decline are now caught in a sharp rally. Joining a long bread line (large short interest) is the popular thing to do but the most unprofitable. Joining a short bread line (small short interest) is the unpopular thing to do but the most profitable for shortsellers. In *buying* stocks then it is better to fight the big bread line (large short interest) because pessimism is *excessive* and in selling stocks or going short it is better to join the small breadline of shortsellers because optimism is *excessive* and pessimism unpopular. In short, there is an additional technical attraction in stocks with a growing short interest (the more excessive the better) and there is technical weakness in stocks with a declining short interest (the more rapidly it is declining the better). Or to put it another way—don't short a stock when so many other people before you had the same idea, you won't get any bread. Don't buy a stock if the short interest is dwindling rapidly because in that case the shortsellers will get some bread since the breadline is small. You would be buying because the stock is over-popular but again too many people had the buying idea before you did and thus again you are too late and you should have been looking for the bread (short sale profits).

Rothschild was so right when he said that you buy them when nobody else wants them. A quickly rising short interest would tell you that not many people wanted the stock.

Popularity also Measured in Terms of Volume and Price Acceleration

Note the speed-up of selling near bottoms and the speed-up of buying near tops. Astute traders are quick to accept profits when they see excessive volume on the upside build up in a stock which up until then has not entered the most active list but has shown persistent price advance for some time. The entry into the most active list *early in the rise* is bullish. However, if the stock makes the most active list *after* a good price advance then it is usually a pretty good time to consider taking some profits. Conversely, traders of long experience quickly recognize the buying opportunities when stocks are being sold because they know that the best rallies are born from excess pessimism. *Any signs of excess should be capitalized upon by a move in the opposite direction.* It is the *gradual* movements in terms of both price and volume which are the most capable of being continued. Deviations from the gradual are the signs which precede price reversals.

The Summing up

Here it has been pointed out how to put the 30 Dow-Jones Industrial stocks together in a single on-balance volume figure which can prove to be helpful in determining where the Dow-Jones Industrial Average might be headed. In addition to this, you are now better acquainted with the Climax Indicator, a supplemental index which *tends to rise and fall ahead of the Dow-Jones Industrial Average.* You have a workable set of rules to help you determine what this indicator is saying, knowing the probable lead time involved on tops and bottoms in the industrial average. You also have seen that the interpretation of the Climax Indicator has slightly different meanings in bull and bear markets but you now know that the Indicator always has a message for the short-term trader. When there is any doubt as to what the Climax Indicator is saying you now know that the problem can be resolved by checking out the major background indications such as rising and falling fields, short interest and 200-day moving average price line measurements. You would know that a Climax Indicator reading of plus 20 in a weak market background would be a major selling opportunity for both traders and long-term investors and that the same reading in a healthy market would only have short-term selling implications for day-to-day traders.

There are still many unanswered questions. You can recognize accumulation now when it is taking place but you do not yet know how to recognize the *three phases* of accumulation a stock often goes through before it tops out. You have not yet learned how to handle velocity figures as an important addition to weighing the importance of the existing accumulation. If the stock undergoes a sharp price break in the middle of the upswing you have yet to learn how to determine whether the reaction is final or is offering a key buying opportunity with fresh price peaks to follow. You have yet to learn more about the theory of gaps, the overhead supply concept and other important extensions of the writer's on-balance volume concept. Before you can seriously start prospecting on your own for the great stock moves of the future, you must first recognize the symptoms of profitability from the examples of the past.

You are now ready to move on and apply the new volume theory to some other stocks.

Chapter Twelve

American Motors

Application of the entire theory to a specific stock

What You Are about to Learn

All the foregoing knowledge means nothing unless it can be successfully applied to specific stocks. The writer's purpose in this chapter is to demonstrate how these technical things have applied to certain stocks in the past. In this chapter you will be taken through various demonstrations of accumulation and distribution, overhead supply, gaps, velocity (the new "spring" principle) and many other things which showed up in the past performance of such stocks as American Motors, NAFI and Avnet. Familiarity with the past examples should help you to recognize new trading opportunity when the stocks you begin to trade in begin to trace out certain familiar formations.

In time to come you should be better able to recognize which stocks are most likely to be important before they rise very much pricewise. Anybody can recognize a price advance in retrospect but on-balance volume is a new tool and its use may considerably advance your knowledge about which stocks are importantly on the move, knowledge which is usually forthcoming before it is generally known by chartists following orthodox price charts.

American Motors—One of the Better Examples of Theory in Action

American Motors common stock during the period of 1958 and 1959 represents a good demonstration of every technical concept covered in this book. In the pages ahead, this past performance will be used to demonstrate each of these concepts in action.

This table of past performance is set up as follows:

Column 1 —   The date
Column 2 —   On-Balance Volume
Column 3 —   On-Balance Volume as a percentage of capitalization (explained below)
Column 4 —   Cumulative total volume
Column 5 —   Cumulative total volume expressed as a percentage of capitalization (velocity). This is explained below.
Column 6 —   Daily closing price

On-Balance Volume as a Percentage of Capitalization

There are two reasons for the inclusion of this column: (1) The first reason is the more obvious of the two. Inasmuch as the on-balance volume figures in a long period of accumulation tend to grow quite large, it is difficult for the eye to follow the gradual changes. As long as the on-balance volume is a percentage of a *fixed* figure (the capitalization) it is easier for the eye to see the upside and downside penetrations since only two or three figures in a percentage are necessary. (2) The second reason is less obvious *but actually more important. Once the on-balance volume can exceed 20% of the capitalization it will usually run to 50% and more before the stock reaches the final price peak.* In the case of American Motors this figure rose to 81.5%. NAFI peaked out when this percentage was at 104.2%. Avnet peaked out at 58.2%.

Most of the sensational type stock price advances came about once the on-balance volume exceeded 20% of the capitalization.

Cumulative Total Volume Expressed as a Percentage of Capitalization

This column records the measurement of VELOCITY. The word velocity here simply expresses in percentages how many times the entire capitalization of the stock turns over. Some of the more important stock price advances have seen the capitalization turning over at least once. One complete turn would be expressed as 100%. It must be kept in mind, however, that velocity alone means little unless it is *accompanied by accumulation.* All stocks in time turn their capitalizations over and over but the prices may do little simply because the stocks were not under consistent accumulation. A rising on-balance volume line is indicative of accumulation. It is the *combination* of high velocity AND accumulation which is an important technical characteristic accompanying most of the major stock price advances.

Initial Phase Shows Accumulation with Little or No Price Movement

The American Motors table is presented with the first thought in mind to demonstrate what meaningful accumulation looks like. Remember these points: (1) A stock is more likely to rise importantly *following* accumulation and (2) accumulation is more easily detected by way of a rising on-balance volume line on the theory that volume has a tendency to precede price.

AMERICAN MOTORS

First Phase

(The Base Line—Accumulation)

Date	On-Balance Volume		On-Balance Volume as % of Capitalization	Cumulative Total Volume	Velocity	Price
Jan. 2, 1958	31,600		0.5%	31,600	0.5%	8.63
Jan. 3, 1958	31,600		0.5	52,600	0.8%	8.63
Jan. 6, 1958	48,500		0.8	69,500	1.1	8.75
Jan. 7, 1958	33,200		0.5	84,800	1.4	8.50
Jan. 8, 1958	33,200		0.5	93,600	1.5	8.50
Jan. 9, 1958	33,200		0.5	96,400	1.6	8.50
Jan. 10, 1958	26,200		0.4	103,400	1.7	8.38
Jan. 13, 1958	32,600		0.5	109,800	1.8	8.50
Jan. 14, 1958	32,600		0.5	119,100	1.9	8.50
Jan. 15, 1958	36,500		0.6	123,000	2.0	8.63
Jan. 16, 1958	48,500		0.8	135,000	2.2	8.75
Jan. 17, 1958	39,200		0.6	144,300	2.4	8.63
Jan. 20, 1958	124,300	UP	2.0	229,400	3.8	9.50*
Jan. 21, 1958	90,700		1.5	263,000	4.3	9.38
Jan. 22, 1958	76,500		1.2	277,200	4.6	9.25
Jan. 23, 1958	76,500		1.2	291,700	4.8	9.25
Jan. 24, 1958	156,400	UP	2.6	371,600	6.1	9.63*
Jan. 27, 1958	156,400	UP	2.6	398,400	6.6	9.63*
Jan. 28, 1958	156,400	UP	2.6	406,400	6.7	9.63*
Jan. 29, 1958	139,100		2.3	423,700	7.0	9.50
Jan. 30, 1958	139,100		2.3	433,800	7.2	9.50
Jan. 31, 1958	122,400		2.0	450,500	7.5	9.38
Feb. 3, 1958	100,400		1.6	472,500	7.8	9.25
Feb. 4, 1958	100,400		1.6	484,600	8.0	9.25
Feb. 5, 1958	100,400		1.6	496,200	8.2	9.25
Feb. 6, 1958	79,800		1.3	516,800	8.6	9.00
Feb. 7, 1958	79,800		1.3	538,400	8.9	9.00
Feb. 10, 1958	85,700		1.4	545,300	9.0	9.13

* Price breakouts on the upside.

Date	On-Balance Volume		On-Balance Volume as % of Capitalization	Cumulative Total Volume	Velocity	Price
Feb. 11, 1958	85,700		1.4	551,400	9.1	9.13
Feb. 12, 1958	77,600	DOWN	1.2	559,500	9.3	9.00
Feb. 13, 1958	77,600	DOWN	1.2	565,600	9.4	9.00
Feb. 14, 1958	77,600	DOWN	1.2	570,300	9.5	9.00
Feb. 17, 1958	77,600	DOWN	1.2	575,700	9.5	9.00
Feb. 18, 1958	77,600	DOWN	1.2	593,600	9.8	9.00
Feb. 19, 1958	77,600	DOWN	1.2	604,400	10.0	9.00
Feb. 20, 1958	77,600	DOWN	1.2	613,300	10.2	9.00
Feb. 21, 1958	77,600	DOWN	1.2	635,300	10.5	9.00
Feb. 24, 1958	65,600	DOWN	1.0	647,300	10.7	8.88
Feb. 25, 1958	59,700	DOWN	0.9	653,200	10.8	8.63
Feb. 26, 1958	69,900		1.1	663,400	11.0	8.75
Feb. 27, 1958	53,300	DOWN	0.8	680,000	11.3	8.50
Feb. 28, 1958	53,300	DOWN	0.8	687,600	11.4	8.50
Mar. 3, 1958	45,100	DOWN	0.7	695,800	11.5	8.25
Mar. 4, 1958	55,400		0.9	706,100	11.7	8.38
Mar. 5, 1958	69,500		1.1	720,200	12.0	8.50
Mar. 6, 1958	69,500		1.1	726,600	12.1	8.50
Mar. 7, 1958	69,500		1.1	732,300	12.2	8.50
Mar. 10, 1958	59,500		0.9	742,300	12.3	8.38
Mar. 11, 1958	48,400		0.8	753,400	12.5	8.25
Mar. 12, 1958	54,800		0.9	759,800	12.6	8.38
Mar. 13, 1958	59,400		0.9	764,400	12.7	8.50
Mar. 14, 1958	55,700		0.9	768,100	12.8	8.38
Mar. 15, 1958	52,300		0.8	771,500	12.8	8.25
Mar. 18, 1958	52,300		0.8	779,500	12.9	8.25
Mar. 19, 1958	58,000		0.9	785,200	13.0	8.50
Mar. 20, 1958	53,900		0.8	789,300	13.1	8.38
Mar. 21, 1958	53,900		0.8	794,400	13.2	8.38
Mar. 24, 1958	63,200	UP	1.0	803,700	13.3	8.50
Mar. 25, 1958	63,200	UP	1.0	813,500	13.5	8.50
Mar. 26, 1958	90,800	UP	1.5	841,100	14.0	8.63
Mar. 27, 1958	116,100	UP	1.9	866,400	14.4	8.88
Mar. 28, 1958	95,500		1.5	887,000	14.7	8.75
Mar. 31, 1958	95,500		1.5	901,200	15.0	8.75
Apr. 1, 1958	89,100		1.4	907,600	15.1	8.63
Apr. 2, 1958	89,100		1.4	913,300	15.2	8.63
Apr. 3, 1958	83,100		1.3	919,300	15.3	8.50
Apr. 7, 1958	107,200		1.7	943,400	15.7	8.63
Apr. 8, 1958	107,200		1.7	958,200	15.9	8.63
Apr. 9, 1958	107,200		1.7	971,100	16.1	8.63
Apr. 10, 1958	170,800	UP	2.8	1,034,700	17.2	9.13

Date	On-Balance Volume		On-Balance Volume as % of Capitalization	Cumulative Total Volume	Velocity	Price
Apr. 11, 1958	170,800	UP	2.8	1,160,500	19.2	9.13
Apr. 14, 1958	204,700	UP	3.4	1,194,400	19.9	9.50
Apr. 15, 1958	252,800	UP	4.2	1,242,500	20.7	9.63
Apr. 16. 1958	231,600		3.8	1,263,700	21.0	9.50
Apr 17, 1958	254,900	UP	4.2	1,287,000	21.4	9.63
Apr. 18, 1958	271,900	UP	4.5	1,304,000	21.7	9.75*

The Base Line

The *first* phase of a stock price movement is the backing and filling in a very narrow range called the 'base line. The price movement attracts very little attention on the base line because the price is going nowhere. Since most poeple only look at price the stock will only attract attention at higher prices. An ordinary price chart of the stock while it is on the base line tells the trader and investor very little. Such a chart will not answer the most important of all questions: (1) is the stock under accumulation or distribution? and (2) when will the breakout occur?

Without the answer to these two questions one might buy a stock because it is moving sideways on a long base line and he may be sitting with the stock six months later or a year later with no price gain. Or one might buy a stock which appears to be making a base and then discover (to his dismay) that the stock breaks out on the *downside*. You will recall the earlier example of S. H. Kress. This difficulty in detecting evidence of accumulation' or distribution in an ordinary price chart accompanied by a volume bar chart can possibly be eliminated by now using on-balance volume instead of volume bar charts. On-balance volume seems to offer an improved technical device in helping to detect either accumulation, distribution, or a state of neutrality. These are the new technical tools which may be added to others to aid you in working toward higher stock market profits.

Let's Apply these New Technical Tools to American Motors

Turn back now to the first phase performance of American Motors. This is called the first phase because the price of the stock was still forming a base and had not yet made the major upside breakout.

In the January to early April period of 1958 we see that the price of the stock fluctuated in the very narrow range of 8¼ on the downside and 9⅝ on the upside. That is a very narrow range for a stock over a longer than three month period. Looking at the

* Price breakouts on the upside

stock purely from a price viewpoint, one might say that nothing technically important took place until April 18, 1958 when the price broke out from the narrow trading range and moved up to 9¾. Those traders who follow prices only would not have been strongly attracted to the stock until this price breakout on the upside. If price was the only consideration there would have been a risk in buying the stock at 9⅝ because it was at that level before during January and it was followed by a decline to 8¼. Therefore, the follower of price waits until the upside breakout in price and then buys the stock. However, the volume signals derived from the on-balance volume indicated earlier buying opportunities long before the price moved up to the breakout level of 9¾.

Now being aware that volume has a tendency to precede price, we look to on-balance volume and here we find a line of *accumulation*. When the technical evidence is strongly suggesting accumulation by way of a clearly marked rising trend of OBV, there is an opportunity to buy BEFORE THE MAJORITY DOES since it is still a safe assumption that the majority looks at price first and volume second. Between January and April 1958 American Motors fluctuated in the narrow price range of 8¼ and 9⅝ but the on-balance volume rose from 26,200 to 254,900 BEFORE THE PRICE BREAKOUT. The stock was technically saying that an upside price breakout was becoming increasingly likely. This constitutes an example of *accumulation on the base line.*

Look at the price again. Check out each price against the corresponding reading of the on-balance volume line. *In every instance there was the proof of expanding technical power.* Rearranging the figures, let's record the on-balance volume figures chronologically at each one-eighth level from 8¼ up to 9⅝:

The below figures indicate with few exceptions that each time the stock returned

	Chronological Order of On-Balance Volume Line
Price	Readings
8¼	45,100
	48,400
	52,300
8⅜	26,200
	55,400
	59,500
	54,800
	55,700
	53,900
8½	33,200
	32,600
	53,300
	69,500
	59,400

Price	*Chronological Order of On-Balance Volume Line Readings*
	58,000
	63,200
	83,100
8⅝	31,600
	36,500
	39,200
	59,700
	90,800
	89,100
	107,200
8¾	48,500
	69,900
	95,500
8⅞	65,600
	116,100
9	79,800
	77,600
9⅛	85,700
	170,800
9¼	76,500
	100,400
9⅜	90,700
	122,400
9½	124,300
	139,100
	204,700
	231,600
9⅝	156,400
	252,800
	254,900

to a previous *similar* price level it became technically *stronger* (higher on-balance volume) than the last time it sold at that price. In other words, the stock indicated expanding technical strength at each closing price level. By the time the stock reached the 9⅝ level on April 15th (the previous high) the on-balance volume showed a higher reading of 252,800 against 156,400. *This indicated that the stock was 61%* stronger on April 15, 1958 at 9⅝ than it was on January 24, 1958 when it also closed at 9%. *This strongly suggested the upside price breakout which followed three days later.*

So here was a situation where the price was practically *unchanged* for over three months and yet the on-balance volume rose from 26,200 to 254,900, an increase in technical power (energy) of over 872%. This was a build-up of great potential.

By adhering to such volume signals rather than price signals alone, a strong advantage is achieved. Suppose, for example, that an investor was aware of these things and decided that he wished to accumulate 30,000 shares of American Motors. It would have meant that he could have done this during the January-April period of 1958 at an average price of $9 a share with little serious competition. If he had waited for the *price* breakout on April 18, 1958 then he would have ended up paying a good deal more because the *average* price of American Motors stock the month following the price breakout was $12 a share. This investor would have been able to save himself considerable money by following the *volume* indications.

Accumulation Must Be Smooth and Persistent

Remember what we saw in the music of Bach, Beethoven and Kosma earlier. There was a tendency to fill spaces, voids and gaps. In stock price charts gaps tend to occur because of bursts of enthusiasm or depression. These create spaces or *vacuums* and, remembering the natural law of vacuums, these vacuums tend to be filled. Most excesses are corrected. Once all the spaces are filled then the movement generally is free to advance further.

Look at the on-balance volume line between January 2, 1958 and January 20, 1958. The first volume upside breakout occurred on January 20, 1958 with a jump from 39,200 to 124,300. This created a gap (an excess of enthusiasm) and it indicated that it would probably be filled with volume readings in the 50, 60, 70, 80, 90, 100 and 110 thousand levels. The second gap occurred when the volume line jumped from 76,500 to 156,400 on January 24, 1958. This again indicated that the line would probably return to the 80, 90, 100, 110, 120, 130 and 140 thousand share levels. Between January 28, 1958 and April 10, 1958 the on-balance volume line filled these gaps by hitting each of those in-between volume readings. Once this was done *the period of base line accumulation was just about completed and the stock was technically ready for the upside price breakout and the commencement of the SECOND PHASE.*

The important price upside breakout was strongly suggested *eight days earlier* on April 10, 1958 when the volume line broke out to a new high of 170,800. This was an example of the tendency of volume to precede price.

AMERICAN MOTORS

Second Phase

*(Breakout from phase one through
to the first price shakeout)*

Date	On-Balance Volume		On-Balance Volume as a % of Capitalization	Cumulative Total Volume	Velocity	Price
Apr. 21, 1958	333,100	UP	5.5	1,365,200	22.7	10.13°
Apr. 22, 1958	491,800	UP	8.1	1,523,900	25.3	11.25°
Apr. 23, 1958	690,100	UP	11.5	1,722,200	28.7	11.50°
Apr. 24, 1958	602,500		10.0	1,810,800	30.1	11.38
Apr. 25, 1958	602,500		10.0	1,889,800	31.4	11.38
Apr. 28, 1958	579,100		9.6	1,913,200	31.8	11.25
Apr. 29, 1958	542,200		9.0	1,949,100	32.4	11.00
Apr. 30, 1958	567,200		9.4	1,974,100	32.9	11.13
May 1, 1958	589,100		9.8	1,996,000	33.2	11.25
May 2, 1958	595,200		9.9	2,002,100	33.3	11.38
May 5, 1958	664,000		11.0	2,070,900	34.5	12.00°
May 6, 1958	664,000		11.0	2,117,100	35.2	12.00°
May 7, 1958	726,500	UP	12.1	2,179,600	36.3	12.38°
May 8, 1958	781,200	UP	13.0	2,234,300	37.2	12.75°
May 9, 1958	924,000	UP	15.4	2,377,100	39.6	13.50°
May 12, 1958	1,102,800	UP	18.3	2,555,900	42.5	14.25°
May 13, 1958	1,102,800	UP	18.3	2,633,100	43.8	14.25°
May 14, 1958	984,000		16.4	2,751,900	45.8	12.88
May 15, 1958	1,044,400		17.4	2,812,300	46.8	13.38
May 16, 1958	1,012,800		16.8	2,843,900	47.3	13.25
May 19, 1958	1,030,400		17.1	2,861,500	47.6	13.50
May 20, 1958	1,062,900	UP	17.7	2,894,000	48.2	14.00
May 21, 1958	1,013,300		16.8	2,943,600	49.0	13.50
May 22, 1958	1,031,100		17.1	2,961,400	49.2	13.63
May 23, 1958	1,009,500	DOWN	16.8	2,983,000	49.7	13.25
May 26, 1958	978,900	DOWN	16.3	3,013,600	50.2	12.88
May 27, 1958	1,006,900		16.7	3,041,600	50.6	13.25
May 28, 1958	989,800		16.4	3,058,700	50.9	13.00
May 29, 1958	979,700		16.3	3,068,800	51.1	12.88
June 2, 1958	963,600	DOWN	16.0	3,084,900	51.4	12.75
June 3, 1958	992,200		16.5	3,113,500	51.8	13.13
June 4, 1958	1,006,200		16.7	3,127,500	52.1	13.25
June 5, 1958	1,006,200		16.7	3,142,600	52.3	13.25
June 6, 1958	1,033,700	UP	17.2	3,170,100	52.8	13.38
June 9, 1958	1,024,000		17.0	3,179,800	52.9	13.25
June 10, 1958	1,024,000		17.0	3,190,800	53.1	13.25

° Price breakouts on the upside.

Date	On-Balance Volume		On-Balance Volume as a % of Capitalization	Cumulative Total Volume	Velocity	Price
June 11, 1958	1,013,000		16.8	3,201,800	53.3	13.00
June 12, 1958	1,029,500		17.1	3,218,300	53.6	13.13
June 13, 1958	1,029,500		17.1	3,227,800	53.7	13.13
June 16, 1958	1,004,500	DOWN	16.7	3,252,800	54.2	12.75
June 17, 1958	1,030,000	UP	17.1	3,278,300	54.6	13.00
June 18, 1958	1,030,000	UP	17.1	3,302,600	55.0	13.00
June 19, 1958	1,009,600		16.8	3,322,000	55.3	12.75
June 20, 1958	917,600	DOWN	15.2	3,414,000	56.9	12.25
June 23, 1958	804,200	DOWN	13.4	3,527,400	58.7	11.63
June 24, 1958	882,900		14.7	3,606,100	60.1	12.50
June 25, 1958	851,800		14.1	3,637,200	60.6	12.13
June 26, 1958	836,700		13.9	3,652,300	60.8	11.63
June 27, 1958	856,900		14.2	3,672,500	61.2	12.00
June 30, 1958	912,100	UP	15.2	3,727,700	62.1	12.88
July 1, 1958	886,700		14.7	3,753,100	62.5	12.75
July 2, 1958	873,900		14.5	3,765,900	62.7	12.38
July 3, 1958	873,900		14.5	3,773,500	62.8	12.38
July 7, 1958	883,300		14.7	3,782,900	63.0	12.50
July 8, 1958	877,200		14.6	3,789,000	63.1	12.25
July 9, 1958	857,700	DOWN	14.2	3,808,500	63.4	11.75
July 10, 1958	871,800		14.5	3,822,600	63.7	12.25
July 11, 1958	866,700		14.4	3,827,700	63.7	12.00
July 14, 1958	860,900		14.3	3,833,500	63.8	11.88
July 15, 1958	850,600	DOWN	14.1	3,843,800	64.0	11.75
July 16, 1958	850,600	DOWN	14.1	3,854,400	64.2	11.75
July 17, 1958	862,500		14.3	3,866,300	64.4	12.13
July 18, 1958	882,300		14.7	3,884,100	64.7	12.25
July 21, 1958	904,000	UP	15.0	3,905,800	65.0	12.75
July 22, 1958	894,700		14.9	3,915,100	65.2	12.50
July 23, 1958	886,000		14.7	3,923,800	65.3	12.38
July 24, 1958	1,076,700	UP	17.8	4,113,500	68.5	14.25
July 25, 1958	1,252,700	UP	20.8	4,292,500	71.5	14.63*
July 28, 1958	1,192,700		19.8	4,352,500	72.5	14.38
July 29, 1958	1,192,700		19.8	4,377,000	72.9	14.38
July 30, 1958	1,174,400		19.5	4,395,300	73.2	14.25
July 31, 1958	1,141,700		19.0	4,428,000	73.8	14.00
Aug. 1, 1958	1,167,900		19.4	4,454,200	74.2	14.25
Aug. 2, 1958	1,167,900		19.4	4,478,200	74.6	14.25
Aug. 5, 1958	1,148,200		19.1	4,497,900	74.9	14.00
Aug. 6, 1958	1,203,800	UP	20.0	4,553,500	75.8	14.50
Aug. 7, 1958	1,293,300	UP	21.5	4,643,000	77.3	15.00*
Aug. 8, 1958	1,293,300	UP	21.5	4,713,400	78.5	15.00*
Aug. 11, 1958	1,364,300	UP	22.7	4,784,400	79.7	15.63*
Aug. 12, 1958	1,468,700	UP	24.4	4,888,800	81.4	15.88*
Aug. 13, 1958	1,475,500	UP	24.5	4,895,600	81.5	16.25*

* Price breakouts on the upside.

Date	On-Balance Volume		On-Balance Volume as a % of Capitalization	Volume Total Cumulative	Velocity	Price
Aug. 14, 1958	1,626,200	UP	27.1	5,046,300	84.1	17.50°
Aug. 15, 1958	1,612,700		26.8	5,059,800	84.3	16.50
Aug. 18, 1958	1,612,700		26.8	5,120,200	85.3	16.50
Aug. 19, 1958	1,656,600	UP	27.6	5,164,100	86.0	17.00
Aug. 20, 1958	1,630,700		27.1	5,190,000	86.5	16.88
Aug. 21, 1958	1,630,700		27.1	5,191,900	86.5	16.88
Aug. 22, 1958	1,613,300		26.8	5,209,300	86.8	16.75
Aug. 25, 1958	1,587,300	DOWN	26.4	5,235,300	87.2	16.38
Aug. 26, 1958	1,547,700	DOWN	25.7	5,284,900	88.0	16.13
Aug. 27, 1958	1,547,700	DOWN	25.7	5,303,100	88.3	16.13
Aug. 28, 1958	1,529,900		25.4	5,320,900	88.6	15.88
Aug. 29, 1958	1,548,700		25.8	5,339,700	88.9	16.38
Sept. 2, 1958	1,589,000		26.4	5,380,000	89.6	17.25
Sept. 3, 1958	1,589,000		26.4	5,433,600	90.5	17.25
Sept. 4, 1968	1,568,600		26.1	5,454,000	90.9	16.88
Sept. 5, 1958	1,557,800		25.9	5,464,800	91.0	16.75
Sept. 8, 1958	1,575,100		26.2	5,482,100	91.3	17.13
Sept. 9, 1958	1,562,000		26.0	5,495,200	91.5	16.63
Sept. 10, 1958	1,562,000		26.0	5,507,900	91.7	16.63
Sept. 12, 1958	1,592,700	UP	26.5	5,538,600	92.3	17.25
Sept. 13, 1958	1,647,900	UP	27.4	5,593,800	93.2	18.00°
Sept. 16, 1958	1,647,900	UP	27.4	5,661,500	94.3	18.00°
Sept. 17, 1958	1,647,900	UP	27.4	5,701,000	95.0	18.00°
Sept. 18, 1958	1,728,700	UP	28.8	5,781,800	96.3	18.88°
Sept. 19, 1958	1,856,000	UP	30.9	5,909,100	98.4	20.38°
Sept. 22, 1958	1,973,000	UP	32.8	6,027,000	100.4	20.50°
Sept. 23, 1958	1,904,400		31.7	6,096,500	101.6	20.25
Sept. 24, 1958	1,876,600		31.2	6,124,300	102.0	19.88
Sept. 25, 1958	1,820,600		30.3	6,180,300	103.0	19.25
Sept. 26, 1958	1,844,300		30.7	6,204,000	103.4	19.38
Sept. 29, 1958	1,877,600		31.2	6,237,300	103.9	20.13
Sept. 30, 1958	1,941,600		32.3	6,301,300	105.0	20.50
Oct. 1, 1958	1,909,600		31.8	6,333,300	105.5	20.13
Oct. 2, 1958	1,889,200		31.4	6,353,700	105.8	20.00
Oct. 3, 1958	1,889,200		31.4	6,406,600	106.7	20.00
Oct. 6, 1958	1,935,400		32.2	6,452,800	107.5	20.63°
Oct. 7, 1958	2,053,400	UP	34.2	6,570,800	109.5	21.75°
Oct. 8, 1958	2,158,400	UP	35.9	6,675,800	111.2	22.50°
Oct. 9, 1958	2,158,400	UP	35.9	6,733,300	112.2	22.50°
Oct. 10, 1958	2,204,400	UP	36.7	6,779,300	112.9	23.00°
Oct. 13, 1958	2,290,700	UP	38.1	6,865,600	114.4	24.13°
Oct. 14, 1958	2,170,000		36.1	6,986,300	116.4	23.25
Oct. 15, 1958	2,079,900		34.6	7,076,400	117.9	23.00
Oct. 16, 1958	2,228,500		37.1	7,235,000	120.5	25.50°
Oct. 17, 1958	2,247,300		37.4	7,253,800	120.8	27.25°

° Price breakouts on the upside.

Date	On-Balance Volume		On-Balance Volume as a % of Capitalization	Volume Total Cumulative	Velocity	Price
Oct. 20, 1958	2,428,600	UP	40.4	7,435,100	123.9	29.50°
Oct. 21, 1958	2,314,400		38.5	7,549,300	125.8	28.37
Oct. 22, 1958	2,263,400		37.7	7,600,300	126.6	28.13
Oct. 23, 1958	2,315,900		38.5	7,652,800	127.5	28.87
Oct. 24, 1958	2,478,400	UP	41.3	7,815,300	130.2	31.88°
Oct. 27, 1958	2,687,900	UP	44.7	8,024,800	133.7	33.63°
Oct. 28, 1958	2,828,200	UP	47.1	8,165,100	136.0	34.25°
Oct. 29, 1958	2,945,800	UP	49.0	8,282,700	138.0	35.63°
Oct. 30, 1958	2,858,300		47.6	8,370,200	139.5	34.37
Oct. 31, 1958	2,683,500		44.7	8,545,000	142.4	32.13
Nov. 3, 1958	2,761,900		46.0	8,623,400	143.7	33.63
Nov. 5, 1958	2,823,200		47.0	8,684,700	144.7	34.37
Nov. 6, 1958	2,767,300		46.1	8,740,600	145.6	33.13
Nov. 7, 1958	2,736,500		45.6	8,771,400	146.1	33.00
Nov. 10, 1958	2,762,200		46.0	8,797,100	146.6	33.37
Nov. 11, 1958	2,739,900		45.6	8,819,400	146.9	32.75
Nov. 12, 1958	2,618,000	DOWN	43.6	8,941,300	149.0	31.13
Nov. 13, 1958	2,842,100	UP	47.3	9,165,400	152.7	33.00
Nov. 14, 1958	2,751,100		45.8	9,256,400	154.2	31.87
Nov. 17, 1958	2,712,500		45.2	9,295,000	154.9	31.75
Nov. 18, 1958	2,737,900		45.6	9,320,400	155.3	31.88
Nov. 19, 1958	2,737,900		45.6	9,344,900	155.7	31.88
Nov. 20, 1958	2,854,500	UP	47.5	9,461,500	157.6	34.13
Nov. 21, 1958	2,806,600		46.7	9,509,400	158.4	33.50
Nov. 24, 1958	2,969,400	UP	49.4	9,672,200	161.2	34.50
Nov. 25, 1958	3,091,900	UP	51.5	9,794,700	163.2	35.25
Nov. 26, 1958	3,181,600	UP	53.0	9,884,400	164.7	36.13°
Nov. 28, 1958	3,130,500		52.1	9,935,500	165.5	35.00
Dec. 1, 1958	3,087,400		51.4	9,978,600	166.3	34.25
Dec. 2, 1958	3,051,900		50.8	10,014,100	166.9	33.50
Dec. 3, 1958	3,098,400		51.6	10,060,600	167.6	34.50
Dec. 4, 1958	3,151,500		52.5	10,113,700	168.5	34.75
Dec. 5, 1958	3,184,400	UP	53.0	10,146,600	169.1	34 88
Dec. 8, 1958	3,161,500		52.6	10,169,500	169.4	33.63
Dec. 9, 1958	3,191,200	UP	53.1	10,199,200	169.9	33.75
Dec. 10, 1958	3,245,300	UP	54.0	10,253,300	170.8	34 75
Dec. 11, 1958	3,213,100		53.5	10,285,500	171.4	34.63
Dec. 12, 1958	3,295,800	UP	54.9	10,368,200	172.8	36.13
Dec. 15, 1958	3,471,500	UP	57.8	10,543,900	175.7	39.75°
Dec. 16, 1958	3,316,100		55.2	10,699,300	178.3	39.50
Dec. 17, 1958	3,316,100		55.2	10,741,500	179.0	39.50
Dec. 18, 1958	3,278,400		54.6	10,779,200	179.6	39.38
Dec. 19, 1958	3,228,400		53.8	10,829,200	180.4	38.13
Dec. 22, 1958	3,197,500	DOWN	53.2	10,860,100	181.0	37.75
Dec. 23, 1958	3,237,600		53.9	10,900,200	181.6	38.00

° Price breakouts on the upside.

Date	On-Balance Volume		On-Balance Volume as a % of Capitalization	Volume Total Cumulative	Velocity	Price
Dec. 24, 1958	3,285,200		54.7	10,947,800	182.4	39.88°
Dec. 29, 1958	3,322,700		55.3	10,985,300	183.0	40.25°
Dec. 30, 1958	3,279,400		54.6	11,028,600	183.8	39.38
Dec. 31, 1958	3,279,400		54.6	11,061,200	184.3	39.38
Jan. 2, 1959	3,318,500		55.3	11,100,300	185.0	39.63
Jan. 5, 1959	3,290,700		54.8	11,128,100	185.4	39.00
Jan. 6, 1959	3,265,400	DOWN	54.4	11,153,400	185.8	38.63
Jan. 7, 1959	3,310,900		55.1	11,198,900	186.6	38.75
Jan. 8, 1959	3,360,700	UP	56.0	11,248,700	187.4	40.25
Jan. 9, 1959	3,399,300	UP	56.6	11,287,300	188.1	40.38°
Jan. 12, 1959	3,382,600		56.3	11,304,000	188.4	39.88
Jan. 13, 1959	3,366,500		56.1	11,320,100	188.6	39.50
Jan. 14, 1959	3,478,400	UP	57.9	11,432,000	190.5	42.75°
Jan. 15, 1959	3,380,500		56.3	11,529,900	192.1	41.75
Jan. 16, 1959	3,346,400	DOWN	55.7	11,564,000	192.7	41.25
Jan. 19, 1959	3,409,000		56.8	11,626,600	193.7	43.00°

Second Phase Shows Sharp Velocity Gains

While the second phase of advance terminates with only an intermediate price peak, it is the phase which shows the sharpest percentage gains and the most rapid velocity build-up. Velocity of a stock is measured by keeping a running total of all the volume traded regardless of price movements and equating this running total as a percentage of the total capitalization of the stock. The first phase of the American Motors cycle ended with a velocity reading of 21.7%. This meant that between January 2, 1958 and April 18, 1958 21.7% of the total capitalization of 6,000,000 shares of American Motors stock turned over. The second phase ended with a velocity reading of 193.7%. The entire capitalization of American Motors had turned over almost twice by January 19, 1959. Another way of seeing the rapid build-up during the second phase is to compare the readings of the on-balance volume expressed as a percentage of total capitalization. This is the second column in the table. Note that at the end of the first phase the upside breakout to 9¾ occurred with the on-balance volume at 271,900. The latter figure was 4.5% of the total capitalization. By the end of the second phase that figure jumped from 4.5% to 56.8%, a tremendous degree of acceleration. This indicated that over half the entire capitalization of American Motors was committed to the buy side by the end of the second phase.

Characteristic of Smoothness Continues throughout Second Phase

The major characteristic of the second phase is a continuation of the smoothness and persistency evidenced in the first phase of accumulation on the base line but this

° Price breakouts on the upside.

302   AMERICAN MOTORS

time the price does not back and fill but *moves up steadily with the volume.* In the second phase the price of American Motors advanced from 9¾ to 43, a percentage gain of over 341%. The price movement was smooth with little or no deviation on the downside. On the way from 9¾ to 43 there were only two small price gaps, *one at 26 and the other at 30.* Keep those figures in mind. *The stock was able to later fill in those gaps.*

Now look at the on-balance volume figures and check for gaps. Checking this in terms of hundred thousands, the first column starting with April 21, 1958 would read as follows: 3, 4, 6, 6, 6, 5, 5, 5, 5, 5, 6, 6, 7, 7, 9, 11, 11, 9, 10, 10 and so on. Remember Bach's music? Here again is shown the tendency to fill in missing spaces. The first skip is 5. It was later filled in. The next skip is 8 and then 10. The 10 readings were filled in first and this left the 8 space to be satisfied. Note that the stock made no further progress until after the string of 8 readings was recorded between June 23, 1958 and July 23, 1958. When all these *volume gaps* were filled in the stock was *better qualified* from a technical standpoint to advance. The next volume breakout happened to occur *two days* after the string of missing 8's was terminated.

This is what is meant by smoothness. All the holes in the pattern (both price and volume) have a tendency to be filled. *This is not definitely required* and does not always happen. However, when it does take place it tends to solidify the technical degree of strength that much more. All the volume gaps in American Motors were filled up through July 25, 1959 and we will now continue looking at the stock from that point forward. Running through all the rest of the volume advance-decline readings up to the end of the second phase we find that there is only one missing volume level and that is a reading of 25 (or 2,500,000). Keep this figure in mind.

Stock Now Ready for Third Phase Shakeout

The stock has now gone through two phases, the first phase of base accumulation (little or no price movement) and the second phase of accumulation (with strong price movement). Actually a stock has a tendency to go through three phases with the third phase being the final vertical price movement (sharp price gains) ending in a blow-off. More often than not, the third phase of price movement is usually preceded by some type of decline (or shakeout) and for this reason that shakeout phase will be described here as the third phase with the final vertical price movement constituting the fourth and final phase.

Up until January 19, 1959 American Motors had experienced no price correction, the stock smoothly advancing from 9¾ to 43 throughout the second phase. What were some of the technical warning signs that the second phase was drawing to a close? Look back over the second phase volume and price figures and you will note that up until December 15, 1958 all price breakouts to new highs were either simultaneously accompanied by volume breakout confirmations or soon thereafter. As long as the volume was confirming the price strength the advance had a good chance of continuing. After December 15, 1958, however, there were several new highs in price WITHOUT VOLUME BREAKOUT CONFIRMATIONS. Look at the *unconfirmed* price highs of December 24, December 29 and January 9. On January 14, 1959 the volume line did come up and make a new high corresponding with the new price high of 42¾ but by this time the price of the stock had jumped three points since the last *confirmed* price high and the *net differential* between the two volume highs was only 6,900 shares. THIS WAS NOT ENOUGH NET VOLUME GAIN TO JUSTIFY A THREE POINT IMPROVEMENT IN THE STOCK PRICE. A further disparity then occurred on January 19, 1959 when the stock price recorded another high and in the meantime the volume line had moved lower and was unable to confirm the validity of that last advance. The stock was finally showing some technical weakness and the price reaction lay ahead. NOTE ONCE AGAIN THAT THE SIGNAL OF IMPENDING WEAKNESS WAS COMING FROM THE VOLUME COLUMN RATHER THAN FROM THE PRICE COLUMN (volume showing a tendency to precede price).

AMERICAN MOTORS

Third Phase

(Shakeout, lasting until previous gaps were filled)

Date	On-Balance Volume	On-Balance Volume as % of Capitalization	Cumulative Total Volume	Velocity	Price
Jan. 20, 1959	3,305,200 DOWN	55.0	11,730,400	195.5	41.25
Jan. 21, 1959	3,245,000 DOWN	54.0	11,790,600	196.5	40.00
Jan. 22, 1959	3,172.500 DOWN	52.8	11,863,100	197.7	39.00
Jan. 23, 1959	3,121,500 DOWN	52.0	11,914,100	198.5	38.63
Jan. 26, 1959	3,034,400 DOWN	50.5	12,001,200	200.0	36.63
Jan. 27, 1959	3,121,500	52.0	12,088,300	201.4	37.00
Jan. 28, 1959	3,163,400	52.7	12,130,200	202.1	37.25
Jan. 29, 1959	3,133,900	52.2	12,159,700	202.6	37.00
Jan. 30, 1959	3,150,700	52.5	12,176,500	202.9	37.13
Feb. 2, 1959	3,089,000 DOWN	51.4	12,238,200	203.9	35.38
Feb. 3, 1959	3,146,800	52.4	12,296,000	204.9	37.00
Feb. 4, 1959	3,085,400 DOWN	51.4	12,357,400	205.9	35.50
Feb. 5, 1959	2,956,700 DOWN	49.2	12,486,100	208.1	34.25
Feb. 6, 1959	2,883,500 DOWN	48.0	12,559,300	209.3	33.38
Feb. 9, 1959	2,803,700 DOWN	46.7	12,639,100	210.6	32.38
Feb. 10, 1959	2,855,500	47.5	12,690,900	211.5	34.13
Feb. 11, 1959	2,821,200	47.0	12,725,200	212.0	33.75
Feb. 12, 1959	2,799,100 DOWN	46.6	12,747,300	212.4	33.00
Feb. 13, 1959	2,816,600	46.9	12,764,800	212.7	33.75

Date	On-Balance Volume	On-Balance Volume as % of Capitalization	Cumulative Total Volume	Velocity	Price
Feb. 16, 1959	2,796,300 DOWN	46.6	12,785,100	213.0	33.63
Feb. 17, 1959	2,796,300 DOWN	46.6	12,808,200	213.4	33.63
Feb. 18, 1959	2,822,100 UP	47.0	12,834,000	213.9	34.00
Feb. 19, 1959	2,755,700 DOWN	45.9	12,900,400	215.0	32.50
Feb. 20, 1959	2,546,100 DOWN	42.4	13,110,000	218.5	30.13
Feb. 24, 1959	2.447,100 DOWN	40.7	13,209,000	220.1	29.00
Feb. 25, 1959	2,177,800 DOWN	36.2	13,478,300	224.6	26.13

Four Column Analysis Indicates Short-Term Sell Signal

American Motors showed a little technical weakness when several price highs during the time period after December 15, 1958 were *unconfirmed* by the on-balance volume. The first signs of weakness appeared in terms of volume and *not* price. The price confirmation of weakness occurred later *and at a lower price.* One such sell signal could be derived from using what the writer calls the *four column analysis.*

At the end of the day *four* prices are shown in the newspaper for each stock, the opening price, the high of the day, the low of the day and the closing price. If one kept a record of these prices in four columns each column could be treated *separately* in order to record upside price breakouts and downside price penetrations. The theory here is that if the stock is going to really be strong it will record upside breakouts in *all four columns* and serious weakness would be reflected by a downside penetration of previous lows in *all four columns.* Think of a four-legged chair. Take away a leg and it still stands but take away another leg and the chair topples over. A four-price confirmation provides final proof of near-term strength or weakness. It is like saying that four charts are better than one and in this way four price charts can be set up for any stock. Below, the four-column figures are given for American Motors starting on December 16, 1958. The support levels are given together with the subsequent price penetration points on the downside:

Date	#1 Open	#2 High	#3 Low	#4 Close
Dec. 16, 1958	40.00	41.50	39.00	39.50
Dec. 17, 1958	40.25	40.38	39.25	39.50
Dec. 18, 1958	39.88	40.25	39.13	39.38
Dec. 19, 1958	38.88	39.00	37.75	38.13
Dec. 22, 1958	38.50	38.50 *Supp.*	37.25 *Supp.*	37.75 *Supp.*
Dec. 23, 1958	37.50 *Supp.*	39.25	37.50	38.00
Dec. 24, 1958	37.88	.39.88	37.88	39.88
Dec. 29, 1958	40.88	40.88	40.13	40.25
Dec. 30, 1958	40.38	41.00	39.38	39.38
Dec. 31, 1958	39.50	39.75	39.00	39.38

Date	#1 Open	#2 High	#3 Low	#4 Close
Jan. 2, 1959	39.63	40.63	39.38	39.63
Jan. 5, 1959	40.00	40.00	39.00	39.00
Jan. 6, 1959	38.75	39.00	38.25	38.63
Jan. 7, 1959	38.38	39.38	38.38	38.75
Jan. 8, 1959	38.75	40.38	38.75	40.25
Jan. 9, 1959	40.88	41.00	40.13	40.38
Jan. 12, 1959	40.13	40.38	39.75	39.88
Jan. 13, 1959	39.75	40.25	39.50	39.50
Jan. 14, 1959	39.75	42.75	39.63	42.75
Jan. 15, 1959	42.50	43.38	41.50	41.75
Jan. 16, 1959	41.88	42.00	41.00	41.25
Jan. 19, 1959	42.25	43.25	41.63	43.00
Jan. 20, 1959	41.50	42.38	41.13	41.25
Jan. 21, 1959	41.25	41.25	40.00	40.00
Jan. 22, 1959	40.00	40.13	38.75	39.00
Jan. 23, 1959	38.75	39.13	38.50	38.63
Jan. 26, 1959	38.50	38.50	36.25 *Break*	36.63 *Break*
Jan. 27, 1959	36.38 *Break*	37.38 *Break*	35.75	37.00

Here there is four-column price confirmation on the downside by January 27, 1959, a price sell signal for the trader at 37 on the close. Two volume signals were *previously* given: (1) failure to confirm the price closing high of 43 and (2) decline in volume line to 3,172,500 on January 22, 1959, a downside volume penetration under the 3,197,500 on-balance volume level of December 22, 1958. The very latest the stock would have been sold on a *volume* signal would have been on January 22, 1959 at a price of 39, *two points above the price weakness signal of January 27, 1959.* Once again here is some evidence which suggests the volume precedence over price.

End Of Shakeout in American Motors Suggested by Gap Theory

The price shakeout in American Motors was rather rapid. One of the physical principles seemed to apply in this case: it takes more energy to go up than down or, to put it another way, it would take many minutes to climb several flights of stairs but the whole route could be retraced in seconds if one fell out the window at the top. It took American Motors 62 trading days to rise from 25½ to 43 but only *26 trading days* to decline from 43 to 26⅛.

The stock price began to decline so rapidly that it appeared to the technically uninitiated that there was no bottom in sight. Did the stock suggest in any way where the bottom of the move was? *According to the gap theory the stock did suggest where the decline would end.* On the way up the stock left a gap at 25 (or 2,500,000) in the on-balance volume line and two price gaps on a closing basis, one at 26 and the other at 30. The theory of gaps (filling of vacuums) suggested that these holes in the volume and price patterns might be filled. On February 20, 1959 the volume gap was filled with a reading of 2,546,100 and the first price gap on the way down was also filled on that day with a closing price of 30⅛. This left only one remaining price gap, the price gap at 26. This was filled two trading days later on February 25, 1959 with a closing price of 26⅛. The filling of these gaps technically suggested that American Motors had ended the shakeout phase. The gap theory had done well in pinpointing this. Following the thesis that volume has a tendency to precede price, note once again that here *the volume gap was filled before the price gaps.*

End Of American Motors Shakeout Also Suggested By Excessive Pessimism

Excess optimism is unfavorable and excess pessimism is favorable. American Motors indicated signs of excess pessimism between February 18th and February 25th, 1959 when the on-balance volume broke sharply from 2,822,100 to 2,177,800 in four trading days and the velocity of the stock rose sharply in the same period from 213.9 to 224.6. *Note that in that four-day period the price of the stock recorded almost half of the entire 26-day decline.* The climactic characteristics here were very strong. Any undue deviation from pattern strongly suggests a *reversal in the opposite direction.* Maximum pessimism coincided here with maximum technical attraction.

New Concept of Overhead Supply Suggests End of Shakeout .

On December 16, 1958 the price of American Motors stock crossed into the 40's for the first time and then topped out at 43 on January 19, 1959. On January 22nd, 1959 the stock moved out of the 40's on the downside. All the volume recorded in the 40's is now totalled. It amounted to 1,047,200 shares. This represents what is called the *overhead supply.* The overhead supply concept is simply this: *When the total volume recorded on the downside matches the overhead supply then the decline may be close to termination and the stock in a technical position to advance again.*

In the table which follows, the cumulative volume recorded on the decline under 40 is equated as a percentage of the overhead supply. At 100% the overhead supply has been matched on the downside and the decline is theoretically terminated. Let us see how well this concept worked out on the American Motors shakeout from a price of 43 to a low of 26:

Date	Price	Daily Volume	Cumulative Volume	Percentage of Overhead Supply
Jan. 23, 1959	38.63	51,000	51,000	4.8%
Jan. 26, 1959	36.63	87,100	138,100	13.1
Jan. 27, 1959	37.00	87,100	225,200	21.5
Jan. 28, 1959	37.25	41,900	267,100	25.5
Jan. 29, 1959	37.00	29,500	296,600	28.3
Jan. 30, 1959	37.13	16,800	313,400	29.9
Feb. 2, 1959	35.38	61,700	375,100	35.8
Feb. 3, 1959	37.00	57,800	432,900	41.3

Date	Price	Daily Volume	Cumulative Volume	Percentage of Overhead Supply
Feb. 4, 1959	35.50	61,400	494,300	47.2
Feb. 5, 1959	34.25	128,700	623,000	59.4
Feb. 6, 1959	33.38	73,200	696,200	66.4
Feb. 9, 1959	32.38	79,800	776,000	74.1
Feb. 10, 1959	34.13	51,800	827,800	79.0
Feb. 11, 1959	33.75	34,300	862,100	82.3
Feb. 12, 1959	33.00	22,100	884,200	84.4
Feb. 13, 1959	33 75	17,500	901,700	86.1
Feb. 16, 1959	33.63	20,300	922,000	88.0
Feb. 17, 1959	33.63	23,100	945,100	90.2
Feb. 18, 1959	34.00	25,800	970,900	92.7
Feb. 19, 1959	32.50	66,400	1,037,300	99.0
Feb. 20, 1959	30.13	209,600	1,246,900	119.5
Feb. 24, 1959	29.00	99,000	1,345,900	129.0
Feb. 25, 1959	26.13	269,300	1,615,200	154.9

From this table it can be seen that the stock was *two days away from the bottom when 100% of the overhead supply was cleaned up*. This provided an important additional technical confirmation of the shakeout terminal point. In review then, shakeout terminal points are determined by:

    (a) The filling of gaps (volume and price)
    (b) The velocity speed-up
    (c) Price acceleration on downside toward the end
    (d) Matching of overhead supply on the downside

Stock now Ready for Fourth Phase Leading to Price Maturity

Now that all gaps were filled the stock was once again "technically solid" and ready to advance. The next phase was about to start and this one showed the "vertical price movement" which denotes *maturity*. Study the on-balance figures carefully on this last phase. The steady evidence of technical strength continued until "the spring snapped" and this will become more evident in later discussion.

AMERICAN MOTORS

Fourth Phase

(Vertical price climb to full maturity)

Date	On-Balance Volume	On-Balance Volume as % of Capitalization	Cumulative Total Volume	Velocity	Price
Feb. 26, 1959	2,324,000	38.7%	13,624,500	227.0%	28.63
Feb. 27, 1959	2,423,000	40.3	13,723,500	228.7	29.63
Mar. 2, 1959	2,499,800	41.6	13,800,300	230.0	29.88

(Vertical price climb to full maturity)

Date	On-Balance Volume		On-Balance Volume as % of Capitalization	Cumulative Total Volume	Velocity	Price
Mar. 3, 1959	2,462,700		41.0	13,837,400	230.6	29.13
Mar. 4, 1959	2,432,700		40.5	13,867,400	231.1	28.50
Mar. 5, 1959	2,458,800		40.9	13,893,500	231.5	29.38
Mar. 6, 1959	2,429,400	DOWN	40.4	13,922,900	232.0	29.25
Mar. 9, 1959	2,414,700	DOWN	40.2	13,937,600	232.2	29.00
Mar. 10, 1959	2,460,100	UP	41.0	13,983,000	233.0	30.50
Mar. 11, 1959	2,497,600	UP	41.6	14,020,500	233.6	30.63
Mar. 12, 1959	2,456,300		40.9	14,061,800	234.3	29.50
Mar. 13, 1959	2,434,700		40.5	14,083,400	234.7	29.25
Mar. 16, 1959	2,398,900	DOWN	39.9	14,119,200	235.3	29.00
Mar. 17, 1959	2,439,000		40.6	14,159,300	235.9	31.75
Mar. 18, 1959	2,394,200	DOWN	39.9	14,204,100	236.7	30.88
Mar. 19, 1959	2,378,200	DOWN	39.6	14,220,100	237.0	30.75
Mar. 20, 1959	2,420,600		40.3	14,262,500	237.7	32.25
Mar. 23, 1959	2,377,200	DOWN	39.6	14,305,900	238.6	31.63
Mar. 24, 1959	2,405,300		40.0	14,334,000	238.9	32.50
Mar. 25, 1959	2,473,100	UP	41.2	14,401,800	240.0	34.13
Mar. 26, 1959	2,571,700	UP	42.8	14,500,400	241.6	35.00
Mar. 30, 1959	2,496,300		41.6	14,575,800	242.9	34.50
Mar. 31, 1959	2,537,000		42.2	14,616,500	243.6	34.75
Apr. 1, 1959	2,579,500	UP	42.9	14,659,000	244.3	35.25
Apr. 2, 1959	2,673,900	UP	44.5	14,753,400	245.8	37.63
Apr. 3, 1959	2,597,400		43.2	14,829,900	247.1	37.13
Apr. 6, 1959	2,528,800		42.1	14,888,500	248.1	36.13
Apr. 7, 1959	2,592,200		43.2	14,951,900	249.1	36.50
Apr. 8, 1959	2,592,200		43.2	14,973,900	249.5	36.50
Apr. 9, 1959	2,607,400		43.4	14,989,100	249.8	36.75
Apr. 10, 1959	2,593,200		43.2	15,003,300	250.0	36.63
Apr. 13, 1959	2,566,500		42.7	15,030,000	250.5	36.00
Apr. 14, 1959	2,554,700		42.5	15,041,800	250.6	35.63
Apr. 15, 1959	2,536,400		42.2	15,060,100	251.0	35.38
Apr. 16, 1959	2,574,500		42.9	15,098,200	251.6	37.75
Apr. 17, 1959	2,536,600		42.2	15,136,100	252.2	37.25
Apr. 20, 1959	2,481,700	DOWN	41.3	15,191,000	253.1	36.63
Apr. 21, 1959	2,513,700		41.8	15,223,000	253.7	36.88
Apr. 22, 1959	2,555,400		42.5	15,264,700	254.6	37.25
Apr. 23, 1959	2,808,000	UP	46.8	15,517,300	258.6	39.88
Apr. 24, 1959	2,686,500		44.7	15,638,800	260.6	39.25
Apr. 27, 1959	2,629,700		43.8	15,695,600	261.5	38.88
Apr. 28, 1959	2,597,600		43.2	15,727,700	262.1	38.25
Apr. 29, 1959	2,563,800		42.7	15,761,500	262.6	37.88
Apr. 30, 1959	2,541,300		42.3	15,784,000	263.0	37.50
May 1, 1959	2,610,900		43.5	15,853,600	264.2	38.50
May 4, 1959	2,589,700		43.1	15,874,800	264.5	37.75

* Price breakouts on the upside

(Vertical price climb to full maturity)

Date	On-Balance Volume		On-Balance Volume as % of Capitalization	Cumulative Total Volume	Velocity	Price
May 5, 1959	2,570,700		42.8	15,893,800	264.8	37.00
May 6, 1959	2,522,800	DOWN	42.0	15,941,700	265.6	36.00
May 7, 1959	2,579,300		42.9	15,998,200	266.6	37.25
May 8, 1959	2,676,100	UP	44.6	16,095,000	268.2	38.88
May 11, 1959	2,777,500	UP	46.2	16,196,400	269.9	39.50
May 12, 1959	2,739,700		45.6	16,234,200	270.5	39.13
May 13, 1959	2,770,500		46.1	16,265,000	271.0	39.63
May 14, 1959	2,727,000	DOWN	45.4	16,308,500	271.8	38.38
May 15, 1959	2,797,700	UP	46.6	16,379,200	272.9	39.25
May 18, 1959	2,783,100		46.3	16,393,800	273.2	38.50
May 19, 1959	2,767,700		46.1	16,409,200	273.4	37.88
May 20, 1959	2,804,100	UP	46.7	16,445,600	274.0	39.13
May 21, 1959	2,776,300		46.2	16,473,400	274.5	38.63
May 22, 1959	2,763,600	DOWN	46.0	16,486,100	274.7	38.38
May 25, 1959	2,791,600		46.5	16,514,100	275.2	38.50
May 26, 1959	2,763,400	DOWN	46.0	16,542,300	275.7	36.88
May 27, 1959	2,763,400	DOWN	46.0	16,557,000	275.9	36.88
May 28, 1959	2,779,700		46.3	16,573,300	276.2	37.50
May 29, 1959	2,834,400	UP	47.2	16,628,000	277.1	38.63
June 1, 1959	2,809,800		46.8	16,652,600	277.5	37.75
June 2, 1959	2,809,800		46.8	16,671,700	277.8	37.75
June 3, 1959	2,793,000		46.5	16,688,500	278.1	37.50
June 4, 1959	2,770,400		46.1	16,711,100	278.5	37.25
June 5, 1959	2,782,900		46.3	16,723,600	278.7	37.50
June 8, 1959	2,754,800	DOWN	45.9	16,751,700	279.1	35.88
June 9, 1959	2,789,900	UP	46.4	16,786,800	279.7	36.50
June 10, 1959	2,816,200	UP	46.9	16,813,100	280.2	37.63
June 11, 1959	2,794,500		46.5	16,834,800	280.5	36.63
June 12, 1959	2,794,500		46.5	16,849,600	280.8	36.63
June 15, 1959	2,819,400	UP	46.9	16,874,500	281.2	37.25
June 16, 1959	2,830,100	UP	47.1	16,885,200	281.4	37.50
June 17, 1959	2,890,100	UP	48.1	16,945,200	282.4	39.38
June 18, 1959	2,789,800	DOWN	46.4	17,045,500	284.0	38.88
June 19, 1959	2,774,900	DOWN	46.2	17,060,400	284.3	38.63
June 22, 1959	2,774,900	DOWN	46.2	17,075,100	284.5	38.63
June 23, 1959	2,883,400		48.0	17,183,600	286.3	40.50
June 24, 1959	3,018,200	UP	50.3	17,318,400	288.6	42.00
June 25, 1959	3,189,100	UP	53.1	17,489,300	291.4	44.13°
June 26, 1959	3,110,800		51.8	17,567,600	292.7	43.00
June 29, 1959	3,186,600		53.1	17,643,400	294.0	44.88°
June 30, 1959	3,118,000		51.9	17,712,000	295.2	44.75
July 1, 1959	3,083,000	DOWN	51.3	17,747,000	295.7	44.00
July 2, 1959	3,115,500		51.9	17,779,500	296.3	44.75
July 6, 1959	3,144,600		52.4	17,808,600	296.8	46.50°

° Price breakouts on the upside

(Vertical price climb to full maturity)

Date	On-Balance Volume		On-Balance Volume as % of Capitalization	Cumulative Total Volume	Velocity	Price
July 7, 1959	3,204,800	UP	53.4	17,868,800	297.8	47.38*
July 8, 1959	3,281,200	UP	54.6	17,945,200	299.0	47.75*
July 9, 1959	3,248,700		54.1	17,977,700	299.6	47.38
July 10, 1959	3,217,900		53.6	18,008,500	300.1	46.25
July 13, 1959	3,253,300		54.2	18,043,900	300.7	46.88
July 14, 1959	3,316,100	UP	55.2	18,106,700	301.7	48.88*
July 15, 1959	3,286,600		54.7	18,137,200	302.2	48.13
July 16, 1959	3,246,200		54.1	18,177,600	302.9	46.88
July 17, 1959	3,226,300		53.7	18,197,500	303.2	46.63
July 20, 1959	3,175,200	DOWN	52.9	18,248,600	304.1	45.50
July 21, 1959	3,201,200		53.3	18,274,600	304.5	47.50
July 22, 1959	3,229,800		53.8	18,303,200	305.0	47.88
July 23, 1959	3,134,700	DOWN	52.2	18,398,300	306.6	45.88
July 24, 1959	3,188,500		53.1	18,452,100	307.5	47.25
July 27, 1959	3,228,400		53.8	18,492,000	308.2	47.63
July 28, 1959	3,211,500		53.5	18,508,900	308.4	46.75
July 29, 1959	3,226,900		53.7	18,524,300	308.7	46.88
July 30, 1959	3,226,900		53.7	18,543,700	309.0	46.88
July 31, 1959	3,245,400	UP	54.0	18,562,200	309.3	47.00
Aug. 3, 1959	3,229,800		53.8	18,578,600	309.6	45.88
Aug. 4, 1959	3,210,800	DOWN	53.5	18,595,800	309.9	45.63
Aug. 5, 1959	3,239,600		53.9	18,624,600	310.4	46.50
Aug. 6, 1959	3,223,100		53.7	18,641,100	310.6	46.13
Aug. 7, 1959	3,206,600	DOWN	53.4	18,657,600	310.9	45.38
Aug. 10, 1959	3,134,400	DOWN	52.2	18,729,800	312.1	43.63
Aug 11, 1959	3,156,200		52.6	18,751,600	312.5	44.50
Aug. 12, 1959	3,137,100		52.2	18,770,700	312.8	43.25
Aug. 13, 1959	3,115,200	DOWN	51.9	18,792,600	313.2	42.75
Aug. 14, 1959	3,131,300		52.1	18,808,700	313.4	43.38
Aug. 17, 1959	3,141,200		52.3	18,818,600	313.6	43.50
Aug. 18, 1959	3,127,900		52.1	18,831,700	313.8	42.63
Aug. 19, 1959	3,068,600	DOWN	51.1	18,891,000	314.8	42.13
Aug. 20, 1959	3,091,300		51.5	18,913,700	315.2	44.25
Aug. 21, 1959	3,081,000		51.3	18,924,000	315.4	43.38
Aug. 24, 1959	3,081,000		51.3	18,933,500	315.5	43.38
Aug. 25, 1959	3,069,200		51.1	18,945,300	315.7	43.25
Aug. 26, 1959	3,099,200	UP	51.6	18,975,300	316.2	45.50
Aug. 27, 1959	3,157,400	UP	52.6	19,033,500	317.2	47.00
Aug. 28, 1959	3,133,400		52.2	19,057,500	317.6	46.50
Aug. 31, 1959	3,158,900	UP	52.6	19,083,000	318.0	47.50
Sept. 1, 1959	3,240,300	UP	54.0	19,164,400	319.4	48.50
Sept. 2, 1959	3,388,000	UP	56.4	19,312,100	321.8	49.13*

* Price breakouts on the upside

(Vertical price climb to full maturity)

Date	On-Balance Volume		On-Balance Volume as % of Capitalization	Cumulative Total Volume	Velocity	Price
Sept. 3, 1959	3,334,800		55.5	19,365,300	322.7	48.50
Sept. 4, 1959	3,439,000	UP	57.3	19,469,500	324.4	51.50°
Sept. 8, 1959	3,597,900	UP	59.9	19,628,400	327.1	52.88°
Sept. 9, 1959	3,711,900	UP	61.8	19,742,400	329.0	53.00°
Sept. 10, 1959	3,641,900		60.6	19,812,400	330.2	51.75
Sept. 11, 1959	3,684,600		61.4	19,855,100	330.9	52.50
Sept. 14, 1959	3,644,900		60.7	19,894,800	331.5	50.88
Sept. 15, 1959	3,535,400	DOWN	58.9	20,004,300	333.4	50.38
Sept. 16, 1959	3,582,900		59.7	20,051,800	334.1	52.00
Sept. 17, 1959	3,582,900		59.7	20,116,100	335.2	52.00
Sept. 18, 1959	3,640,200		60.6	20,173,400	336.2	53.13°
Sept. 21, 1959	3,750,100	UP	62.5	20,283,300	338.0	54.13°
Sept. 22, 1959	3,829,300	UP	63.8	20,362,500	339.3	55.50°
Sept. 23, 1959	3,956,200	UP	65.9	20,489,400	341.4	58.38°
Sept. 24, 1959	4,083,400	UP	68.0	20,616,600	343.6	60.75°
Sept. 25, 1959	4,121,700	UP	68.6	20,654,900	344.2	61.38°
Sept. 28, 1959	4,069,200		67.8	20,707,400	345.1	60.00
Sept. 29, 1959	3,975,500		66.2	20,801,100	346.6	57.63
Sept. 30, 1959	3,975,500		66.2	20,892,400	348.2	57.63
Oct. 1, 1959	4,039,600	DOWN	67.3	20,956,500	349.2	60.50
Oct. 2, 1959	4,112,600		68.5	21,029,500	350.4	60.63
Oct. 5, 1959	4,068,900		67.8	21,073,200	351.2	58.88
Oct. 6, 1959	4,107,700		68.4	21,112,000	351.8	59.00
Oct. 7, 1959	4,163,100	UP	69.3	21,167,400	352.7	62.00°
Oct. 8, 1959	4,275,200	UP	71.2	21,279,500	354.6	62.25°
Oct. 9, 1959	4,320,500	UP	72.0	21,324,800	355.4	62.50°
Oct. 12, 1959	4,300,000		71.6	21,345,300	355.7	61.88
Oct. 13, 1959	4,353,600	UP	72.5	21,398,900	356.6	64.25°
Oct. 14, 1959	4,433,900	UP	73.8	21,479,200	357.9	64.38°
Oct. 15, 1959	4,368,700		72.8	21,544,400	359.0	63.50
Oct. 16, 1959	4,412,000		73.5	21,587,700	359.7	65.25°
Oct. 19, 1959	4,457,000	UP	74.2	21,632,700	360.5	65.88°
Oct. 20, 1959	4,521,800	UP	75.3	21,697,500	361.6	67.25°
Oct. 21, 1959	4,580,300	UP	76.3	21,756,000	362.6	67.63°
Oct. 22, 1959	4,530,000		75.5	21,806,300	363.4	66.25
Oct. 23, 1959	4,578,400		76.3	21,854,700	364.2	67.75°
Oct. 26, 1959	4,672,900	UP	77.8	21,949,200	365.8	72.63°
Oct. 27, 1959	4,824,700	UP	80.4	22,101,000	368.3	78.88°
Oct. 28, 1959	4,639,100		77.3	22,286,600	372.4	78.75
Oct. 29, 1959	4,537,800		75.6	22,387,900	373.1	77.75
Oct. 30, 1959	4,600,300		76.6	22,450,400	374.1	80.00°
Nov. 2, 1959	4,724,200		78.7	22,574,300	376.2	88.25°
Nov. 4, 1959	4,892,400	UP	81.5	22,742,500	379.0	95.25°

° Price breakouts on the upside

The Well Defined Characteristics of the Top

The outstanding technical characteristic of the price peak in American Motors was the final price run-up with the *weak* volume confirmation. With a price history of almost two years shown here, *there was an almost 54% price advance in the final 16 sessions.* This tremendous price acceleration created gaps which had never occurred before in the entire advance. Note that on October 27, 1959 the on-balance volume line stood at 4,824,700 with the price of the stock at 78.88. On the day of the top the on-balance volume reading had only climbed an additional 67,700 but the price of the stock was up to 95.25. This indicated that almost 17 points gained in the final week was technically unsupportable. The stock had finally reached a price zenith.

Before this final price run-up all the prices had been technically backed up by volume confirmations. When price ran ahead and made new highs without volume confirmation as shown in the June-July 1959 period, notice how the price had to react until volume was able to confirm in September 1959.

The price jump from 61.88 to 95.25 showed a net volume rise of 592,400 shares. The previous addition of 592,400 shares to the on-balance volume only corresponded with a price jump from 53 to 61.88. This meant that price was moving up *almost four times faster* in the period from October 12, 1959 to November 4, 1959 than in the period from September 21, 1959 to October 12, 1959. The sign here which indicates the probable end of a major price advance is PRICE ACCELERATION WITHOUT VOLUME CONFIRMATION. The price structure of American Motors was already shaky on October 27, 1959 when the price had advanced to almost 79 leaving a series of price gaps. These gaps skipped over prices at 68, 69, 70, 71, 73, 74, 75, 76 and 77. However, note that as late as October 27th there was a *volume confirmation*. This suggested that the stock could go higher. The price did go higher but note that *the next 10-point gain had no volume confirmation.* By the time there was a volume confirmation on November 4th, the price structure was so full of gaps (air holes) that the possibility of their being ultimately filled injected serious technical weakness into the picture. A state of vulnerability had been reached and the price advance was looking fully mature.

Despite the indications that a price peak in American Motors looked technically imminent, enthusiasm concerning the stock happened to be at the greatest (see Preface).

The "Spring" Principle

The writer was intrigued by what was happening to the velocity figures as they pertained to the phase-by-phase price movement of American Motors. These velocity figures were suggesting a new theory based upon what happens to a spring when it is wound up too tightly.

Velocity of a stock is measured in terms of how many times the entire capitalization of the stock turns over. Think of winding up a spring until it is so tight that it finally tends to snap. This is what happened with American Motors. Velocity is measured by adding up the total number of shares traded and expressing these cumulative totals as a percentage of the entire capitalization. Every time the entire capitalization turns over it is like winding up a giant spring and the resulting price movement is almost predictable. One turn of the spring would be 100% velocity, two turns would be 200% velocity and so on. In the preceding tables the velocity figures on American Motors were included. In order to clearly see this "spring" principle in action, monthly velocity figures on American Motors are given below together with the cumulative percentage price gains starting with the January 1958 figures:

Date	Velocity	Stock Price Rise
Jan. 1958	7.5%	8.6%
Feb. 1958	11.4	−1.0
Mar. 1958	15.0	1.0
Apr. 1958	32.9	28.9
May 1958	51.1	49.2
June 1958	62.1	49.2
July 1958	73.8	62.2
Aug. 1958	88.9	89.8
Sept. 1958	105.0	137.5
Oct. 1958	142.4	272.2
Nov. 1958	165.5	305.5
Dec. 1958	184.3	356.3
Jan. 1959	202.9	330.2
Feb. 1959	228.7	243.3
Mar. 1959	243.6	302.6
Apr. 1959	263.0	334.5
May 1959	277.1	347.6
June 1959	295.2	418.5
July 1959	309.3	444.6
Aug. 1959	318.0	450.4
Sept. 1959	348.2	567.7
Oct. 1959	374.1	826.9
Nov. 1959	379.0	1003.7

Velocity Precedes Price

In the above table note that the velocity percentages were greater than the price percentage gains during the first seven months of 1958. In the eighth month the percentage price gain surpassed the velocity and from that point on consistently stayed ahead with a great upward acceleration in the final two months. The first turn of the spring coincided with an acceleration in the price advance. Every stock will turn over its entire capitalization in time and so velocity alone is meaningless. The velocity measurement becomes important *when the stock is under accumulation.* Accumulation is always denoted by the rising on-balance volume line and so it was important to watch the velocity figures on American Motors in those early months of 1958. They provided the signals as to when the greatest degree of price acceleration would take place.

It took nine months for American Motors to turn over the entire capitalization of 6,000,000 shares. That was the first turn of the spring. The second turnover took only four months. The third turnover took 6 months, slowed up by the price shakeout and recovery from those lows. The spring was very tight now. Note that velocity was unable to get to 400%. The spring was so tight that it snapped at 379%. Now look at what the price was doing during these turns of the spring. *When the spring was the tightest the price acceleration was the greatest.*

Velocity	Cumulative Price Advance
100%	137.5%
200%	324.4%
300%	435.9%
379%	1003.7%

This then is the "spring" principle. It can be summed up by saying that the first turn of the spring precedes price while the stock is under accumulation in the first phase. When 100% velocity is reached the price suddenly accelerates. Each subsequent turn of the spring sees the price of the stock staying ahead of velocity until there is a "climactic" relationship developing between price and velocity. This "climactic" relationship is inescapable in the above figures when velocity rose from 300% to 379% while the price percentage gain rose from 435.9% to a whopping 1003.7%. The spring could turn no further. It was as tight as it could get.

By comparing price advance to velocity in ratio form the climactic phase is seen even more clearly:

Velocity	Ratio of Price Advance to Velocity
100%	1.37
200%	1.62
300%	1.45
379%	2.64

The Second Key Measurement of Price Maturity

You will note that in all the American Motors tables the on-balance volume figures were also expressed as a percentage of the capitalization. It is here that a clear mental image might be formed picturing *stock being temporarily taken off the market.* For instance, a stock goes up a quarter point on a volume of 10,000 shares one day and down a quarter point the next day on a volume of 5,000 shares. Here we are left with an on-balance volume accumulation of 5,000 shares. The mental picture formed is that 5,000 shares have been "taken off the market" temporarily. The theoretical question here is what happens when the *entire capitalization* of the stock has been temporarily "taken off the market"? This is of course purely theoretical but in actual practice there is an approach toward this theoretical condition and it is in that approach that the THAT THE STOCK PROVIDES AN ADDITIONAL SIGNAL OF PRICE MATURITY. In other words, *as the on-balance volume approaches the capitalization figure the stock suggests a tendency to top out.*

The capitalization of American Motors in the 1958-59 period was 6,000,000 shares. On November 4, 1959 the on-balance volume figure had risen to 4,892,400 shares. That represented 81.5% of the entire capitalization as being theoretically closely held and temporarily off the market, a very high figure. It was not the highest known however. NAFI topped out June 17, 1960 with a figure of 104.22% and a velocity of 320.75% and AVNET topped out May 8, 1961 with a figure of 58.23% and a velocity of 109.92%. Price maturity tends to be best shown by the price acceleration at the end (the vertical price movement) which leaves a series of unfilled price gaps.

Series of Price Gaps Most Reliable Indication of the Top

The presence of uncorrected price gaps late in the cycle of advance shows a vulnerable deviation from the volume accumulation pattern and it is in this deviation (disparity) that the stock is finally seen to be under distribution. The figures below show the characteristics of the final price run-ups in both NAFI and AVNET.

NAFI Corporation

Capitalization
1,216,000
Shares

Date	On-Balance Volume		On-Balance Volume as % of Capitalization	Cumulative Total Volume	Velocity	Price
May 17, 1960	978,600		80.47%	3,207,000	263.73%	43.00
May 18, 1960	949,200		78.06	3,236,400	266.14	41.75
May 19, 1960	966,900		79.51	3,254,100	267.59	42.13
May 20, 1960	1,004,000	UP	82.56	3,291,200	270.64	44.88°
May 23, 1960	1,056,700	UP	86.89	3,343,900	274.97	47.38°
May 24, 1960	1,023,700		84.18	3,376,900	277.68	46.75
May 25, 1969	1,007,800		82.87	3,392,800	278.99	46.63
May 26, 1960	1,033,600		85.00	3,418,600	281.12	47.25
May 27, 1960	1,052,100		86 52	3,437,100	282.64	47.38
May 31, 1960	1,052,100		86.52	3,450,700	283.77	47.38
June 1, 1960	1,038,700		85.41	3,464,100	284.88	46.13
June 2, 1960	1,063,100	UP	87.42	3,488,500	286.89	47.50°
June 3, 1960	1,063,100	UP	87.42	3,512,000	288.81	47.50°
June 6, 1960	1,055,200		86.77	3,519,900	289.46	47.25
June 7, 1960	1,064,700	UP	87.55	3,529,400	290.24	48.00°
June 8, 1960	1,137,200	UP	93.51	3,601,900	296.20	52 63°
June 9, 1960	1,077,100		88.57	3,662,000	301.14	52.38
June 10, 1960	1,053,000		86.59	3,686,100	303.12	51.88
June 13, 1960	1,064,100		87.50	3,697,200	304.03	52.50
June 14, 1960	1,084,700		89.20	3,737,800	305.73	56.25°
June 15, 1960	1,115,400		91.72	3,768,500	308.25	56.38°
June 16, 1960	1,191,800	UP	98.00	3,844,900	314.53	62.25°
June 17, 1960	1,267,400	UP	104.22	3,920,500	320.75	64.50°

° Price breakouts on the upside

The key to the end of the rise in NAFI was seen in the action subsequent to June 8th, 1960. Although there was a volume confirmation on June 16th, 1960 at a price of 62¼, the stock had already moved up another 10 points with no volume confirmation and it was that *unconfirmed* 10-point rise which signalled the topping out which occurred on June 17th, 1960. The 12-point advance in the final four days was in itself enough to bring on the peaking out, the price gaps being the greatest created on the entire upswing.

Now examine the figures for the final month of trading in AVNET leading up to the top. Here again are the technical characteristics of finality, price maturity:

AVNET Corporation

Capitalization
2,100,000
Shares

Date	On-Balance Volume		On-Balance Volume as % of Capitalization	Cumulative Total Volume	Velocity	Price
Apr. 7, 1961	788,100	UP	37.52%°	1,556,100	74.11%	39.63°
Apr 10, 1961	840,800	UP	40.03	1,608,800	76.62	42.75°
Apr. 11, 1961	888,800	UP	42.32	1,656,800	78.91	44.13°
Apr. 12, 1961	845,200		40.24	1,700,400	80.99	42.00
Apr. 13, 1961	802,800		38.22	1,742,800	83.01	39.38
Apr. 14, 1961	857,700		40.84	1,797,700	85.63	39.50
Apr. 17, 1961	880,900		41.94	1,820,900	86.73	42.63
Apr. 18, 1961	864,400		41.16	1,837,400	87.51	42.13
Apr. 19, 1961	884,000		42.09	1,857,000	88.44	42.63
Apr. 20, 1961	876,100		41.71	1,864,900	88.82	41.13
Apr. 21, 1961	867,400		41.30	1,873,600	89.23	40.50
Apr. 24, 1961	851,800		40.56	1,889,200	89.97	38.13
Apr. 25, 1961	863,800		41.13	1,901 200	90.54	39.63
Apr. 26, 1961	880,800		41.93	1,918,200	91.34	42.50
Apr. 27, 1961	919,600	UP	43.79	1,957,000	93.20	43.63
Apr. 28, 1961	964,600	UP	45.93	2,002,000	95.34	46.63°
May 1, 1961	1,012,100	UP	48.19	2,049,500	97.60	49.00°
May 2, 1961	988,300		47.05	2,073,300	98.74	48.13
May 3, 1961	1,029,900	UP	49.04	2,114,900	100.73	53.38°
May 4, 1961	1,118,400	UP	53.25	2,203,400	104.94	56.25°
May 5, 1961	1,168,200	UP	55.62	2,253,200	107.31	60.75°
May 8, 1961	1,223,000	UP	58.23	2,308,000	109.92	65.75°

° Price breakouts on the upside

Here the stock went right up to the end with volume confirmation but the price gaps in the final days provided the technical telltale that the upswing was being terminated. Note that the price rise was "orderly" up through April 27th, 1961. Between that date and May 8th the stock had a rise of over 22 points leaving as many as 14 different price levels skipped, the pattern of serious price gaps denoting price maturity.

Tension—The "Snapback" Principle

something very interesting tends to follow. A *tension* builds up which often results in either a sharp advance or decline depending on the *direction* of the tension.

It will be noted that when on-balance volume and price get "out of gear" that

The physical principle which might be involved here could be expressed by describing the workings of a simple yo-yo. The price of the stock is likened to the yo-yo and the on-balance volume might be the hand that controls the yo-yo. The yo-yo and the hand work lower but before the yo-yo reaches the end of the string the hand moves up. At this point the two movements are "out of gear". Since the hand is moving up while the yo-yo is still dropping, the tension created is an *upward* one and the result is what is called the "snapback". The yo-yo (price) reverses and moves up following the direction of the hand (on-balance volume).

Suppose a stock had a smooth price advance (tending to fill in most of the gaps along the way) and rose from 10 to 20 with an on-balance volume build-up of 1,000,000 shares. Now suppose the price breaks suddenly and retreats to the 15 level while on-balance volume only comes down to 900,000 shares. This would tend to create an *upward tension* inasmuch as the stock declined 50% in price on only a 10% reduction in the on-balance volume. This kind of action might suggest the stock as being attractive at 15 because at that price the stock is *theoretically* indicated to be 80% stronger technically than it was the last time it was at 15 on the way up (assuming that on-balance volume was 500,000 shares when the stock was previously at 15).

This is the new theory of stock energy which reflects the tensions arising from disparities between price and on-balance volume. The law of action and reaction strongly suggests that a compensating *downward* tension results following a given period after the creation of the upward tension. The downward tension is simply created by the yo-yo rising while the hand starts downward for the next cycle. As in the example just given, the price rallies to 24 but instead of on-balance volume matching the technical energy of this upswing with a rise to 1,800,000 shares (equating with the initial upswing to 20), suppose OBV only comes up to 1,350,000 shares, or half the upside energy shown on the initial upswing. Here then price outdistanced volume on the upside and the compensating downward tension has been created. Here are compensating price and volume disparities which create interesting buy and sell opportunities.

The "yo-yo" principle is not an ironclad equation. It deals in tendencies, not exactitudes. If a stock is seen to be 80% stronger from a technical standpoint of price and OBV disparity, there is no equation involved which predicts that the stock will perform 80% better on the upside than it did the last time it was at that price level and on the way up. The *tendency* is for a better percentage upswing following the creation of upward tension and the advance may or may not achieve the mathematical optimum. One might think of it in terms of odds. Upward tension greatly increases the odds in favor of a better percentage gain.

The only technical factor which rules against optimum mathematical results being achieved following the build-up of upward tension is the fact that volume has a tendency to build up on the downside once the stock has moved under an important support level. If that takes place, then the OBV tends to equate somewhere along the line as the decline takes place and that would nullify the upward tension. If the price decline takes place on consistent light volume, however, then upward tension is maintained and good snap-back results might be expected.

This is but another application of what can be done with the on-balance volume (OBV) in measuring the *degree* of technical strength at each price level. Inasmuch as the majority of market observers are primarily influenced by what the *price* of a stock does, they can often miss the biggest portion of what the stock is actually saying technically, the story told by the advance-decline line of *volume*. This is especially true in the case of price declines which tend to create bearish sentiment when actually the volume characteristics might be signalling that the stock is a good buy.

The Summing up

Here you were introduced to the application of all that came before in terms of a specific stock, namely American Motors. You followed the on-balance volume line all the way through from the first phase of accumulation on the base line to the final phase of price maturity. You became acquainted with the fact that the great advances for a stock tend to run through three phases—the base line accumulation, the orderly 30 degree advance and the vertical climb to price maturity. Very often a shakeout phase precedes that final price run-up and this is why the American Motors move was described in terms of four phases.

Here you saw not only all gaps being filled in terms of price, but you had a clear demonstration that volume gaps (gaps in the on-balance volume) also had to be filled.

You now have new applications of such things as overhead supply (to determine points of decline) velocity (used in conjunction with rising OBV to determine points of upside climax), tension measurements to determine snap-back potential, but above all you now have the basic grasp of on-balance volume. You have learned how to construct it and how to generally interpret it. You know that if the line is in a rising trend then it is likely that higher prices may follow and that if the line is in a declining trend then it is likely that lower prices may follow.

These are the rudiments of the volume theory. Let us now see how they might be used in order that your trading in stocks might show improved profits.

Chapter Thirteen

How You Can Apply
this Theory Now

Seven specific steps recommended

What You Are about to Learn

Stock market theories are numerous and of little use unless they can be realistically applied in the hardest practical sense. Not only must the theory work, but it must have a rather unvarying degree of success in a clear majority of the applications, be relatively simple and yet escape the attention of the masses. The new theory puts most of the stress on volume in terms of interpreting on-balance volume and basing the buying and selling of stocks largely on what is worked out as OBV buying and selling signals. There is enough work involved to rule out the assumption that too many people are going to diligently overwork the theory. It is a simple and yet advanced concept. Once it is working, one can buy the stock it is applied to with greater confidence of profit possibilities. The first and foremost problem encountered is the selection of that particular stock.

This chapter is designed to help you overcome that problem. There are about 2,000 stocks listed on the New York Stock Exchange and the American Stock Exchange combined. At various times hundreds of stocks are under accumulation, hundreds more are neutral and the remaining hundreds may be under distribution.

Regardless of what the Dow-Jones Industrial Average is doing, there are almost always some stocks under accumulation and it is from these stocks which the selections for buying should be made.

In the pages ahead it will be pointed out how you may identify stocks which appear to be under accumulation and reduce the list to a dynamic handful without having to spend hours of research. By adopting the new volume approach your whole concept of the market can be changed. You can think differently. You can be greatly attracted to bad news when the volume figures are bullish and you may be taking profits in situations where the price action looks extremely bullish with unsupporting volume figures, you may interpret price declines as additional buying opportunities when you have determined that the stock is stronger technically on the second or third trip to the lows than it was in the first place. You are going to pay greater attention to static prices in situations which appear under accumulation. You may then more often find yourself invested in the right stocks before they move up importantly or break out from base formations. You should be in a better position to move into a capital gains time area at a time when many others are first being attracted to the stock because their attraction will be to price but yours was originally to volume. In short, you should be in a better position to think as an individual. The majority tends to act on price changes but you can now act first on volume changes. You are now going to have an opportunity to learn a degree of patience you never knew you had since impatience has been a factor preventing many investors from profiting more in the stock market.

The market could be compared to a big forest made up of many trees. The clear path to improving profit possibilities is not a brightly lit thoroughfare. In order to successfully cut through that maze of tangled underbrush, it is necessary to know where to start. Two thousand stocks make up the forest. A great deal of time and money can be saved by making sure that the first steps into that maze are on the ultimate path to improved profit possibilities and not toward the frustration of entangling losses.

A Possible New Path To Improved Profit Possibilities

In order to get a better start on the path to potential profits,. the writer suggests that the following seven steps be taken:

STEP 1   Selection of most promising chart patterns
STEP 2   Recording of on-balance volume (OBV) on the stocks selected.
STEP 3   Daily surveillance of the most active stocks
STEP 4   Purchase
STEP 5   Concentration
STEP 6   Patience
STEP 7   Sell

Selection Of Most Promising Chart Patterns (Step 1)

As pointed out in the *Strategy* book, all buying for maximum profit potentials should, in my opinion, be concentrated on stocks having the following types of chart patterns:

1. Long-term decline followed by a breakout.
2. Flat base breakout.
3. Coming off of a double or triple bottom
4. W Pattern
5. Growth
6. Cyclical at historical lows

1. *Long-term decline followed by a breakout.* This pattern is mentioned first because it is capable of producing the *greatest capital gains.* The pattern is exactly as described, a long-term decline (the longer the better) followed by an eventual bullish reversal above a previous declining peak. The stock gains an upside impetus *commensurate with the duration and extent of the previous decline.* The theory here is that the stock has been so utterly oversold that upon the first evidence of a turn for the better the stock will advance at a greater rate than it previously declined. More gains of 100% and better over a short period of time have sprung from this type of chart formation than from any other.

2. *Flat base breakout.* The longer the price of a stock remains in a very restricted range of fluctuation the greater is the potential rise upon a breakout above that price range. If the line of accumulation is at the bottom of a previous long-term decline so much the better. A stock coming off of a ten-year base is potentially ten times more bullish than a stock coming off of a one-year base. The base or plateau may be at a more advanced level but the same principle holds, a move above that restricted price line being quite bullish. The more advanced the plateau, the less bullish it is, the lower the base line the more bullish. Suppose a stock was once priced at $40 and then went into a severe long-term decline down to $5. Suppose it then fluctuated between $5 and $10 for ten years and then suddenly one day it managed to close at $11. The stock would be strongly signalling to be bought, having evidenced a degree of strength unseen in a decade. That would constitute a classic flat base breakout and possibilities of a 100% gain or better over the next few months by buying at $11 a share would be excellent.

3. *Coming off of a double or triple bottom.* When a stock has met support (demand) at a given level following a decline the stock must prove itself that it can hold at that level should the stock temporarily rise and then fall back again. If it is met by buying at the same bottom level then the stock is in a much better position to make a more sustained advance. The astute trader becomes interested in buying the stock *after* the double or triple bottom has been recorded and the stock has begun to rise.

Here are two observations to keep in mind:

    (a) The lower the bottoms the more bullish the implications.

    (b) The farther apart the bottoms are the more bullish the implications.

4. *W pattern.* By the very shape of the letter we can see that the double bottom formation traces out a letter W. The middle leg of the W is interpreted to represent a temporary level of supply (upside resistance) and when the right leg of the W exceeds the middle leg it indicates an important buy spot.

5. *Growth.* The growth pattern is characterized by a long-term continuing advance in the price of the stock with a tendency toward acceleration on the upside in the latter stages of its growth pattern. The astute trader aiming at maximum profits is only attracted to this type of pattern just prior to the most accelerated phase.

6. *Cyclical at historical lows.* This pattern is listed last because it contains the greatest degree of risk, a risk that can be only minimized by an expert judgment of timing factors. If the timing is right, the gains can be very great.

What You Can Do Now

Thumb through various chart books and make up a selection of the most bullish looking charts. Pick out about 15 or 20, paying particular attention to the long-term declines followed by a breakout and the long flat base charts.

Recording Of On-Balance Volume On The Stocks Selected (Step 2)

You now have the necessary raw material from which you can work, the charts. Not knowing which of these issues may be under accumulation, you will now embark on the second step, the recording of on-balance volume figures. If you have access to a back file of newspapers showing daily volume and closing prices you can start your on-balance volume tables at an earlier date in order to provide yourself with some immediate past performance. This will give you a headstart and may help enable you to decide whether the stock is a buy without waiting.

What You Can Do Now

You can start to regularly keep daily OBV records on the stocks you have selected.

Daily Surveillance Of The Most Active Stocks (Step 3)

You now have a number of stocks which can be followed by recording the on-balance volume daily. Some of these stocks may evidence good accumulation characteristics and some may not. They were chosen on a basis of *chart potential* but without accumulation they could be going nowhere. Since *volume* is the key indicator of accumulation, you can *expand* the list of stocks you are following by keeping a close eye on the *daily most active stock list* covering the New York Stock Exchange and the American Stock Exchange. Watch for *NEW FACES*, stocks which have not been seen on the list before. It does not take long to fill in the on-balance volume record going back a month or so and this can help confirm or deny whether the stock seems worth buying.

What You Can Do Now

Watch the lists of the most active stocks on the New York Stock Exchange and the American Stock Exchange. Every time a new face shows up immediately (1) check the chart pattern and (2) record OBV for the previous one or two months. Sometimes the most important thing you will see will be a low-priced stock making the most active list for the first time. The greatest percentage gainers often start off this way. *They seldom move up importantly without getting on that MOST ACTIVE LIST.*

Purchase (Step 4)

Up to this point you have been merely *recording* on-balance volume figures on the stocks which you have selected on the basis of chart potential and the probability of accumulation indicated by a new face in the most active list. You are now ready to consider buying. Here you apply all the rules. You do not buy on the first volume bulge but wait for a reaction to a level where you can verify that the OBV is importantly above a previous OBV level at the same price. Some of the stocks chosen on the basis of chart potential were not indicating accumulation yet and these were left alone until the OBV began to tell a story of accumulation.

What You Can Do Now

You are now ready to consider buying some stocks. You have already been keeping OBV and price records on a selection of stocks. Your purchases are centered on those issues where OBV is trending importantly higher. You try to catch the reactions after important price and OBV bulges. You can buy when you see the stock come down to a level where OBV is considerably higher than the last time the stock was at that particular level. You can sell when important OBV and price gaps occur. You can buy back when those gaps are showing a tendency to be filled.

Concentration (Step 5)

Maximum profit results can seldom be achieved until the element of concentration enters the picture. If you were holding ten stocks which were previously selected because of chart and OBV and three of them begin to act in an extraordinary technical manner exhibiting great strength, theoretically the other seven stocks could be sold and the proceeds *concentrated* in the three superlative issues.

What You Can Do Now

You can start by buying the *largest* number of shares in the *lowest* priced of the selected group you are following. If, after a series of purchases, OBV stands out particularly on three or four stocks and is becoming unimpressive on the others, you can sell the others and *concentrate* on the three or four most impressive OBV situations.

Patience (Step 6)

The biggest barrier to maximum profit achievement tends to be *lack of patience*. People, when in a situation clearly demonstrating important accumulation, generally *sell too soon*. With a knowledge of OBV and its great significance you are not so likely to be as impatient because if a stock is fluctuating around the 1¼ level for four months and the OBV is constantly rising then you have an indication that the stock is getting STRONGER while many others (who only watch prices) may tire of holding a stock with an unchanging price and sell just before it breaks out on the upside.

Familiarity with OBV indicates you can buy MORE of the stock when it dips since the knowledge of rising OBV suggests that your biggest ultimate profits often lie in *accumulating* one outstanding OBV situation. Many people scare easily and are out of a stock on first little reaction. That is no way to aim for the big money. The potentials for big money often lie in the recognition of accumulation, duplicating the process and patience. Many traders miss on all three points. They often buy into something that is not under accumulation, they only take one position at one price and then get scared out on the first reaction.

What You Can Do Now

You may now want to make a resolution that you will not sell a stock as long as it evidences accumulation. By following that resolution you should be better equipped to achieve the proper amount of patience to qualify for maximum profit potentials.

Sell (Step 7)

If you have successfully completed the first six steps then you should find the seventh the easiest of all, concentration on long-term profits where the tax rate is the least. Your concentration mostly on stocks breaking out from long-term declines, stocks breaking out from flat bases and cyclical stocks coming off of historical lows enhances your chances for capital gains rather than the less profitable short-term trades. Having a knowledge now of on-balance volume, you should not be as easily inclined to sell a stock on a reaction if the stock continues to evidence accumulation (evidence you probably did not have in the past to guide you).

What You Can Do Now

Make a real point of recording the date on each stock when you are eligible for capital gains. If the stock has advanced in price before that date of eligibility and then goes into a decline, it is easy to compute how much of a decline you can have on a *cost free* basis, providing you hold the stock until your capital gains eligibility date. For example, suppose you bought a stock at 10 and it moved up to 18 in four months. Suppose at this point the chart suggested a reaction but because of favorable OBV you did not wish to lose your position in it. How much of a decline would cost you *nothing* if you held the stock until your eligibility date? The answer would of course depend on your tax bracket. Here are a few sample answers: In the 43% bracket the 8-point short term gain would be equal to a 6-point long-term gain and thus 2-point decline in the stock would *cost nothing* providing it was held until the date of capital gains eligibility. The cost free decline in the 50% bracket would be 2⅝ points, in the 53% bracket 3 points and so on up to the top bracket of 91% where the holder could afford to hold the stock from 18 to as low as 11⅛ at *absolutely no cost,* no sacrifice. If OBV and other measurements showed technical support in the stock around 15 then the question as to whether to hold the stock or not in the fourth month at 18 in the face of an impending reaction is obvious.

When the market reacts sharply (as it did in the Spring of 1962) it is far too easy to get caught up in the emotional whirl of the stock ticker and stocks invariably get sold near the bottom of the swing without much thought at that point as to how much of a *cost free* decline one can take in a stock providing he holds it until his capital gains eligibility date. Obviously this is far more of a consideration for the high tax bracket trader and investor but it is something to keep in mind.

Remember to compute cost free declines and then match the theoretical decline against the OBV and price support points. If those support points are *above* the extent of the cost free decline then you can hold those stocks until your capital gains eligibility date because the decline will not be costing you a cent. You are less likely to lose a good position because of an emotional whim spontaneously but wrongly dictated by a sharp but perhaps temporary drop in the market.

The Summing up

The path to improving profit potentials was outlined in seven steps. You now have the *correct order of things.* You have been shown which chart patterns to select.

You follow up by recording on-balance volume. You can add to your list as new faces crop up in the most active list providing those stocks fall into the category of favorable chart patterns. You can start recording OBV on those additional stocks. You can then purchase the stocks within your select list which show the strongest OBV trends. Here you use the elements of concentration. You can buy many shares more of the lower priced stocks than the higher priced stocks. If OBV begins to look bad on any stock purchased, you can switch out and add those funds to the remaining strong ones, concentration enhancing your profit prospects. With the help of this new technical knowledge you can develop a new brand of patience, such patience helping you to carry stocks over into the far more profitable capital gains time area.

GLOSSARY

Accumulation. Any stock which evidences better volume on upside days than on downside days is said to be under accumulation. Important price advances are generally preceded by accumulation. Accumulation is best measured by on-balance volume.

Advance-decline line. The orthodox advance-decline line is a *net differential between the number of stocks advancing each day and the number of stocks declining each day kept on a cumulative basis.* The word orthodox is used here because most people are not yet aware of the *volume advance-decline line.* The orthodox advance-decline line is a measurement based on *price,* not volume. This is a technical indicator having broad implications concerning the trend of stock prices. A declining advance-decline line implies that one should be far more selective when purchasing stocks but it does not necessarily rule against new highs being recorded in the Dow-Jones Industrial Average. One, two or three new highs can be recorded by the Dow-Jones Industrial Average without a confirmation of strength by the advance-decline line, a third non-confirmation preceding every bear market since 1919. While the advance-decline line always has topped out ahead of the Dow-Jones Industrial Average, the Dow-Jones Industrial Average is capable of making a bottom *before* the advance-decline line but this is not necessarily so.

Bar chart. This term is used in the book to describe the orthodox presentation of volume when it is recorded with a stock price chart. As far as being able to detect accumulation and distribution, the bar chart on volume is entirely unsatisfactory.

Base. Practically all extensive upswings have begun from some kind of base or foundational formation. A base is formed by a series of backing and filling price movements within a comparatively narrow price range for a given period of time. The longer the base is the greater is the upswing potential but this potential is never realized until there is evidence of *accumulation* on the base line, evidence only forthcoming from *volume* considerations. The word *base* is used here to describe *first phase* price movements.

Bear market. True bear markets tend to start "out of the blue" with the majority at a loss to explain the first downswing. Bear market means a declining market but the term has come to be so loosely used that one must define the term in degrees of severity. In the 1929-1932 downswing the Dow-Jones Industrial Average scored a decline of 89 per cent. That was a bear market never to be forgotten. It was of major magnitude. The 1937 downswing lopped off 54 per cent of the Dow-Jones Industrial Average. That fully qualified as being an important bear market. In 1946 the Dow-Jones Industrial Average fell 24 per cent. That was a bear market but, while distressing to stockholders, it was not followed by a depression. Eversince 1937 all business downturns have been described as recessions. In 1957 the Dow-Jones Industrial Average made a 20 percent decline followed by a business recession. In 1960 the industrial average fell by 17 per cent accompanied by recession. In 1962 the industrial average fell a little over 28 per cent (between December 1961 and June 1962) and it was questionable whether a major bear market description could be fully justified (business still expanding all through that period). Late in a bull market all downturns are suspected as being bear markets. William Peter Hamilton (the great Dow Theory exponent), turned bearish in 1926 and had to reverse himself, the major bear market holding off until three years later.

This writer chooses to use the term bear "phase" when describing declines since a true bear market of major proportions (followed by business depression has not been an observable phenomenon for many years. Dow Theory provided bear market signals in 1949, 1953, 1957, 1960 and 1962 and yet the big picture shows the entire period to be a 13-year old bull market.

Bear phases. Bull and bear markets tend to run in three distinct phases. Generally speaking, the three bear phases constitute (1) disbelief (market declines and very few can explain why), (2) brief rally which fools the majority, and (3) final decline which creates maximum bearish sentiment as bottom is being formed. These three bearish phases can be squeezed into the format of a major bull market and this is why so many observers over the years have been shouting major bear market when actually the market was merely tracing out important secondary swings in a long-term major bull market. This of course will not always be so but, as of May and June 1962, sentiment was so bearish that another bull phase appeared to be an approaching reality.

Breakthrough (breakout). The term *breakthrough* and *breakout* are interchangeable. This implies that either a stock price or a price average have moved above a previous high resistance level or have moved below a previous low support level. Such breakthroughs imply that the movement will be enhanced in the direction of the breakout on the physical principle of bodies in motion. The same terms apply to on-balance volume movements through previous support or resistance levels.

Bull market. Any rising market may be called a bull market but that would be a very loose definition. A bull market actually implies a sweeping uptrend of many months duration, the long-term upward trend line continuously in evidence. Like bear markets, bull markets vary widely in scope and duration. It is like bubbles. One may say that there is one big all-encompassing bubble termed a long-term bull market. In side that bubble, however, there are many smaller bubbles or baby bull markets, all separated by baby bear markets of varying intensity, not intense enough to break the major bubble. Bull and bear markets are often a case of pure semantics. Some will speak about the 1957 bear market but others (keeping their eye on the major long-term bullish bubble) might look upon 1957 as merely a short-term interruption in the long-term bull market and be absolutely right. The same comparison showed up as well in 1953, 1960 and 1962. This writer uses the word *swings* when describing rising and falling markets and puts less stress on the terms bull and bear markets since semantics can always introduce some confusion as to ultimate indentification of such.

Bull phases. Bull markets can be broken up into phases, each phase having certain indentifiable characteristics. The phases constitute (1) disbelief (the market advances and very few can explain why), (2) the decline which fools the majority and (3) final advance which ends up in creating maximum bullish sentiment as top is being formed. It is even possible that these three bull phases can be squeezed into the format of a long-term bear market but this is less likely than in the opposite case.

Buying climax. A climax infers an ending. A buying climax is associated with such a sharp price run-up with everything so heavily one-sided on the rise a move in the opposite direction becomes inevitable. Such a climax may be of the one day variety ending a very short-term swing or it could be of intermediate or final significance ending months of advance or even years of advance. All climaxes involve *increased* volume.

Buy column. When a stock is up in price at the end of the day all the volume generated for the day is recorded on the upside and the figure is placed in the BUY column.

Capitalization. This is the number of shares of common stock which constitutes the total issue held by stockholders of a particular company. The capitalization becomes important when determining (1) thinness, (2) marketability and (3) velocity, as well as the effective application of the "Spring" principle.

Climactic. A term used to describe any movement which smacks of "excess", regardless of whether it is a price movement or a volume movement. Climactic moves are followed by moves in the *opposite* direction.

Climax indicator. The net differential of Dow-Jones Industrial stock on-balance volume breakouts makes up the climax indicator. When the reading approaches 22 an important top lies ahead and when the reading approaches minus 22 an important bottom is either reached or very close.

Confidence index. What is referred to here is the Barron's Confidence Index. This represents the ratio between the average yield on Barron's 10 highest-grade corporate bonds and that on Dow-Jones 40 Bonds (the ratio of primary to secondary bond yields). The ratio is high when investors demonstrate confidence by buying lower-grade liens, low when they take refuge in top-grade issues. Correlated with the movements of the stock market, the Index becomes a highly sensitive forecasting instrument, predicting the extent as well as the timing of general price advance and declines. Like any *single* indicator, it is not infallible.

Declining tops. A pattern of declining tops implies a loss of upside energy and an ultimate decline. Each peak is less than the previous one, showing increasing weakness. The pattern is significant both in terms of price and on-balance volume.

Defensive. Anything which tends to remain relatively stable in a declining market is a *defensive* situation. A defensive technique involves the purchase of bonds in a bear market or some stock capable of going against the market such as a gold stock. During a period when high-priced stocks are under attack it might be said that a move into very low-priced issues moving in a narrow range around their base lines would be a *defensive* measure. The best defense against a falling market is not to be in it.

Disparity. When two things are moving in the same direction at a different rate a *disparity* is created between them. This is a measurable differential which denotes the relative strength in one component and the relative weakness in the other. This writer's Disparity Index measures the changing differentials between the Dow-Jones Industrial Average and the comprehensive Standard & Poor 500 Stock Index. Bullish disparity is shown when the S & P is stronger than the Dow-Jones Industrial Average. Bearish disparity is when the Dow-Jones Industrial Average outperforms the S & P. Another disparity measurement is seen in the daily performance of the Dow-Jones Industrial Average and the Dow-Jones Rail Average. If Industrials go up and rails go down then the bullish implications of the industrial rise are considerably diluted. Conversely, if the industrials decline and rails post an advance the industrial decline tends to lose some bearish meaning.

Distribution. This covers the whole gamut of undercover signs of the stock market or, more specifically, individual stocks going from strong to weak hands. This takes the form of secondary stock offerings, stock splits, stock dividends but here in this book the term is used specifically to describe any *trend* of declining on-balance volume. Accumulation occurs at low prices and distribution takes place at high prices. Accumulation occurs under the cover of weak appearances while distribution occurs under the cover of strong appearances.

Dow-Jones industrials. These are the 30 stocks which go to make up the Dow-Jones Industrial Average. On-balance volume is computed on these stocks in order to determine the daily readings of the Climax Indicator.

Dow theory. The oldest theory relating to stock market price movements. Signals are late by definition and are often deceptive since the theory is based on price and not volume.

Down column. When on-balance volume is being computed all the volume on downside days is placed in the DOWN column. This is a cumulative volume total. It is subtracted from the volume in the UP column and the result is the on-balance volume.

Double bottom. This is the phenomenon of two prices coming into alignment at similar low points, points of technical support. The resulting rise has greater upside impetus than if it stemmed from a single low point. The "double bottom" phenomenon can also be observed in terms of on-balance volume figures.

Energy. This term is used in the book interchangeably with rising on-balance volume. It implies upside momentum, expanding technical strength.

First phase movement. Stocks tend to move up in three major phases. The first phase is characterized by relatively static price movement but strong evidence of accumulation in the form of rising on-balance volume.

Flat base. Some of the greatest percentage gains have stemmed from stocks breaking out from flat base formations. A flat base is made up of a long period of price fluctuations in a very narrow range. When accumulation can be detected the flat base situation becomes very attractive from a technical standpoint.

Flat base breakout. This is the actual price move above the long range of narrow price fluctuations which have traced out the flat base formation. Such breakouts are always *preceded* by rising on-balance volume.

Floating supply. This is a term used to describe how much stock is around which is not closely held, stock which is in the trading pool of supply. The smaller the "float" is the more susceptible the stock is to day-to-day supply and demand. When the float becomes small enough and the price high enough then maximum vulnerability to price decline is reached. A new rule of thumb introduced in this book to determine floating supply is the following: Capitalization less OBV equals *floating supply*. An added squeeze on the price of a stock is when the short interest comes up to *equal or exceed the floating supply*.

Force. A term used synonimously with *energy* or rising OBV.

Four column analysis. This is a separation of stock price analysis into *four* charts, a chart of the opening prices, the high prices, the low prices and the closing prices. The theory here is that no price penetration is necessarily valid unless confirmed by the other three charts. The separate series can be shown in price *columns* and thus the term four *column* analysis.

Gaps. These are visible separations or skips in either prices, on-balance volume or both. Gaps set up targets for retracement and it is not wise to ignore them. Gaps occurring early in a price upswing are not as bearish as those showing up in the third phase of price movement, a definite technical characteristic suggesting the end of the line on the upside.

Gravity. This word in technical analysis has the same meaning as it would in physics, that what goes up must come down. The effects of such gravity forces become irresistable late in the third phase of price upswing.

Group rotation. There is just enough periodicity in stock group movements to suggest that there is an *order of strength,* an order of rotation. This is far from being a perfect concept, a very rough approximation at best. More research is required, especially on the minor groups. Enough is known, however, to suggest where the "live" areas are.

Leading indicator. Any statistic which periodically turns down ahead of the market or turns up ahead of the market qualifies as a leading indicator, an indicator which "leads the way".

Live groups. These are the stock groups slated to come into the limelight in accord with their order in the pattern of group rotation.

Market leadership. These are the most active stocks for the day, week, month or year determined by the volume generated. The quality of such leadership can vary widely.

Master index. This term is interchangeable with the Climax Indicator.

Maturity. A term associated with price movements in the third phase, any movement smacking of a vertical ascent.

Momentum. This is the *rate* of acceleration in price or volume expansion, best noted by developing gaps in velocity figures or gaps in an on-balance volume series. Upside *mometum* is the greatest just short of price maturity and downside *momentum* tends to reach a peak at or near an important bottom.

Net differential. This is the difference between volume assigned to the *up* column and volume assigned to the *down* column. Obviously, *net differential* is the same as on-balance volume.

OBV. This is the abbreviation for *on-balance volume.*

Odd lot. Stock purchased or sold in lots of less than a round lot (100 shares) is called an odd lot.

Odd lot short sales. This is the amount of stock sold short in odd lot amounts in expectation that the market is going lower. In a major bull market rising odd lot short sales tend to have strong bullish implications but late in a major bear market they tend to lose bullish significance because *technical* shorting has developed into *fundamental* shorting (shorting with the true or primary trend of the market).

On-Balance. This is the difference between the plusses and the minuses in any situation. Here in the book the term is used in describing strengths and weaknesses in prices and volume.

On-balance volume. This is OBV, the result reached after subtracting all the volume on the downside from the volume on the upside. Readings can either be positive or negative.

Overbought. Price maturity and the term *overbought* are interchangeable descriptions. An overbought condition is detected when upside gaps show up in velocity, price and OBV. All vertical movements imply that a stock is overbought.

Overhead supply. This is the total amount of shares traded in a stock at higher price levels through which the stock (after a decline) is trying to cut through on the recovery movement. Some chartists call it the *high volume zone.* High volume at higher prices presents a formidable resistance on recovery movements. To put it another way: too many people are waiting to move out of the stock the minute it returns to the higher levels at which they originally made their purchase. If a stock can cut back through overhead supply it is a strongly bullish endorsement for a further upswing. Overhead supply can be measured and when a decline has generated an equal number of shares with the overhead supply then the decline is either over or just about to be terminated (overhead supply concept).

Oversold. This term is associated with *first phase* price movements. An oversold condition is detected by the presence of downside gaps in price and on-balance volume, or price returning to a key support level or OBV reaching down to fill some gap overlooked on the way up.

Price maturity. This description fits all third phase price movements. The term maturity can refer to price or volume movements, the term here referring specifically to vertical price movements.

Pullback. Practically all advances of importance are tested with a subsequent "pullback" to or near the starting point of the advance. The price is easily seen as merely a pullback when the OBV reading is higher on the return trip price than it was the first time it was at that price.

Quarterly indicator. This is the 17th of January, April, July and October, quarterly dates which have shown a tendency to coincide with price swings going opposite to the direction the market was previously going in.

Resistance. Any barrier to progress is resistance. Once a price support level is broken, that support level becomes the *resistance* point on the recovery movement. The theory of resistance also holds true in OBV movements.

Retracement. Any retrograde price movement or volume movement can be called a retracement. The long history of price movements shows that 50% retracements should not be violated in a long upward trend but, like all rules, there are exceptions. In late 1957 Parmelee Transportation was selling for $14 a share, an important low. It rallied in almost a straight line to $65 a share in early 1959. The 50% concept would rule that any decline below the halfway mark between 14 and 65 would dictate an inability to rally again to a new high. The halfway mark was 25½ or a price of 39½. By late 1960 the stock violated the 50% retracement level by falling to $33 a share. Instead of collapsing, the stock turned around and advanced to a new all-time high of 73¾ in 1962, a distinct exception to the important 50% retracement rule.

Rising bottoms. The ability of a stock to turn up above each preceding important low point traces out a pattern of *rising bottoms,* a bullish formation. This is only half the formation, however. To be complete there should also be an accompanying series of rising tops. Rising bottoms (by definition) precede rising tops and are thus the first technical requirement which must be met if a situation is to be termed a bullish one. The same formation should be looked for in OBV.

Rising tops. This is the typical pattern best seen in the second and third phase price movements. It must be seen in the first phase OBV movements otherwise the later bullish unfoldment will not be seen. Rising tops beget rising tops until the gravity rule of the third phase movement takes over.

Second phase movement. This describes the orderly 30-degree angle price ascent which follows the price breakout from the first phase of accumulation. At the peak of this movement one of the commonest errors is to interpret the second phase price peak as the *final* peak of the three-phase movement. For awhile (in retrospect) the second phase price peak will have all the appearances of a final peak since final peaks are often preceded by sharp shake-outs and, during that shake-out, the second phase pinnacle will look beyond attainment on a recovery move. When American Motors retreated from 43 to 26⅛ in early 1959 most market observers considered the major advance to be over. On the contrary, the stock turned around and rallied all the way to 96. The chief characteristic of the second phase movement is *smoothness,* very few gaps (if any) between prices and rising OBV.

Sell column. When a stock is down in price at the end of the day all the volume generated for the day is recorded on the downside and the figure is placed in the SELL column.

Selling climax. This is a situation which occurs when a clear majority of all stocks reach an oversold condition simultaneously. Selling climaxes have the following characteristics: (1) Heavy volume, (2) Decided plurality of declines over advances, (3) a very late tape, (4) a price reversal occurring before the session is over, (5) accompaniment of heavy odd-lot short sales.

Shake-out. A healthy technical correction of an overbought situation. The decline is sharp but comparatively short in duration. Shake-outs often terminate the second phase of price movement and this is why the American Motors shake-out was numbered as the third phase with the climactic swing to new highs labeled as the fourth phase. If one counts the shake-out as a full phase then it can be said that the bull cycle follows four phases. Shake-outs in the general market have been falsely labeled as major bear markets many times, the surface appearances often being deceptively alike.

Short interest ratio. This is the ratio of monthly short interest to the average daily trading volume for the month. When the ratio is under 1 for a long period of time it is construed as being bearish. A ratio above 1 is normal. If the ratio climbs above 1.5 then it is construed as being quite bullish.

Short selling. This is the process of selling a stock which is not owned with the expectation of buying it back (covering) at a lower price. The broker has to borrow the stock in order to make delivery. In a weak market short selling becomes increasingly popular. When it becomes excessive then the market embarks upon a strong technical rally (the shorts taking their profits by buying in or covering).

Snapback. A bullish technical property imparted to a stock if the price declines at a faster rate than the OBV. It implies that the stock has reached a true oversold position long before it would have under different circumstances. The price, being out of line with the OBV on the downside, therefore "snaps back".

Spring principle. Each turnover of capitalization accompanied by accumulation creates 100% of bullish velocity but at the same time winds up a spring which must by its own tightness eventually snap. The Spring principle states that the price advance will accelerate percentagewise with each turn of the spring (each turnover of capitalization) and that *in the later stages the percentage price rise will advance geometrically*. Velocity must be accompanied by rising OBV in order for the principle to be valid.

Support. Any barrier to decline is called support. Once a resistance level is successfully penetrated by a stock advance, the retreat from that level is expected to meet support at the old resistance level. The theory of support also holds true in OBV movements.

Tension. Any kind of disparity between price and OBV creates tension. If the price is outrunning OBV on the upside then the tension is distinctly bearish. If the price is declining faster then OBV then the tension is distinctly bullish. Bullish tension is the same as snapback.

Third phase movement. The third phase movement of stock prices denotes maturity, finality, a vertical rise which cannot last at that rate of climb. Accompanying characteristics of third phase movements are both price and OBV gaps.

Third phase shake-out. This is simply assigning the shake-out (which so often precedes the third phase price run-up) to the third phase instead of numbering it as the third phase.

Three phase movement. This is the whole price movement moving from first phase (base with accumulation), second phase (breakout from base through to the beginning of shake-out) and third phase (final price run-up preceded by brief but sharp shakeout). It is interesting to note that the three phase movement fits the Elliott Wave Theory (UP-DOWN-UP-DOWN-UP, the first four waves matching the first and second phase price movement and the fifth wave corresponding to the third phase which denotes maturity. The five waves could be fitted to the following things previously described: 1st wave—breakout from base, 2nd wave—normal pullback showing either double bottoms or rising bottoms but always higher OBV on the pullback, 3rd wave—pinnacle reached prior to shakeout, 4th wave—sharp shakeout, 5th wave—final run-up to last peak.).

Topping out. A term employed to denote loss of upside energy at the top after a long price run-up. Such a loss of energy would also show up in a pattern of declining tops or declining OBV.

Triple bottom. The more often a stock or the market has met support in a given area the more reliable that area becomes as an important bottom on which an advance can be built. The most effective triple bottoms are those where it can be demonstrated that OBV is higher at each of the bottoms.

Up column. When on-balance volume is being computed all the volume on upside days is placed in the UP column. This is a *cumulative* volume total. The figures in the down column are subtracted and the net volume derived is the on-balance volume.

Vacuum. This is another term having the same meaning as gap. It can either be a vacuum or gap in OBV or in price. Such vacuums or gaps are always potential targets for filling in.

Velocity. This is total cumulative volume expressed as a percentage of capitalization. Velocity only takes on meaning when it is accompanied by accumulation (rising OBV). It is an integral part of the "Spring" principle.

Vertical price movement. A price run-up is a vertical movement, at high levels always being the chief characteristic of a third phase movement of maturity or, at the very least, the topping out of the second phase just prior to a sharp shake-out.

Volume advance-decline line. The essence of this book is based on the volume advance-decline line, *a cumulative total of on-balance volume.*

Volume breakout. A new high in a series of on-balance volume figures. Such breakouts tend to *precede* price breakouts.

Volume differential. The difference between one OBV reading at one price and another at another price.

Volume explosion. This is a sharp rise in OBV which creates a volume gap. It immediately creates upside resistance, not diluted until the gap in OBV is filled.

W pattern. This is a double bottom followed by a breakout on the upside, a bullish price formation.

Index

Bullishness *(cont.)*
    time spent at base as measure of, 322
Bull market *(see also* Bullishness*), defined,* 328-29
Bull phases *(see also* Advances, Bearishness*),*
    defined, 329
Business trends, stock market behavior and, 20
Buy opportunities *(see also* Buy signals*):*
    accumulation as evidence of, 294
    characteristics of, 307
    detected with Climax Indicator, 269
    double bottom formation indicative of, 151
    lack of demand as a, 287
    "W-formation" indicative of, 323
Buy points in on-balance volume readings, 84-85
Buy pressure, as measured by Climax Indicator,
    284-85
Buy signals *(see* Signals, buy*)*
Buying:
    correlated with tops, 287
    Rothschild's philosophy of, 287
Buying climax *(see* Climax, buying*)*
Buy column, *defined,* 329

C

Cannon Mills, 22
Capital gains:
    enhancing early, 55-56
    greatest opportunity for, 322
Capitalization:
    defined, 329
    effect on of issue withdrawn from market, 315
    implication of on-balance volume equalling, 315
    marketability and, 329
    on-balance volume as a percentage of, 290
    and tension, 329
    "thinness" and, 329
    turnover of, 290
        as measure of stock velocity, 313
    velocity and, 329
Capitol Airlines, 23
Chart patterns:
    bearish, 45-49
    bullish, 45-49
Chart potential, concept of, 323
Charting techniques, innovations in, 63-72
Charts:
    bar chart, *defined,* 327
    implications of curve angles, 91
    long-term base line, 35
    patterns in:
        flatbase breakout, 322
        interpretation of, 26
        selecting promising, 322-23
        significance of the "W-formation" in, 26,
            322, 323, 336
    price, 293
        resistance area, the 32-33
        support area, the, 32-33
    and table of past performance, 289-90
Chrysler, 74, 126-39, 157, 160-63
Climactic price move, *defined,* 36-38
Climactic situation, *defined,* 330

Climax Indicator, the:
    buy pressure measured with, 284-85
    check on validity of, 285-86
    construction of, 264-67
    defined, 329
    detecting buy opportunities with, 269
    lead time determined with, 280-81
    rules for use of, *listed,* 269
    sell pressure measured with, 284-85
    signals given by:
        interpretation of, 285-86
        short position cover, 280
    spread determined with, 281-83
    theory of the, 284-85
Climaxes:
    buying, 38-40
    defined, 329
    increased volume as a function of, 329
    selling, 38-40
Clusters:
    as buy signals, 95
    defined, 88, 95
    indicative of up and down designations, 285
    as sell signal, 96
Concentration, technique of, 325-26
Confidence index *defined,* 329-30
    Barron's Confidence Index, 270
Confirmations:
    breakout, 303
    "in trend," *defined,* 133
    lack of as price advance determinant, 312
    "out of trend," *defined,* 133
    simultaneous, of price and on-balance
        volume, 132
Corporate developments, relevance of information
    on, 20
Corporate earnings, market behavior and, 20
Coverage of short position, 40
Credulity, popular:
    as ingredient of bearishness, 328
    as ingredient of bullishness, 329

D

Day-to-day stock price swings, 24
Day-to-day trader, signals for the:
    buy, *listed,* 95
    and position maintenance, 110
    sell, *listed,* 95-96
Declines *(see also* Bearishness; Shakeout phase*):*
    controlling costs of entrapment in, 326
    ephemeral:
        as ingredient of bearishness, 328
        as ingredient of bullishness, 329
    interpreting rates of, 150
    long-term, implications of breakouts
        following, 322
    peak ("declining tops,") *defined,* 330
    price:
        detection of forthcoming, 85-86
        preceded by acceleration, 286
        as sign of weakening stock position, 85-86

CPSIA information can be obtained
at www.ICGtesting.com
Printed in the USA
LVHW020854010720
659193LV00007B/288